INTO UEA/CITY London

SIMULTANEOUS INTERPRETATION
A COGNITIVE-PRAGMATIC ANALYSIS

BENJAMINS TRANSLATION LIBRARY

The Benjamins Translation Library aims to stimulate academic research and training in translation studies, lexicography and terminology. The Library provides a forum for a variety of approaches (which may sometimes be conflicting) in a historical, theoretical, applied and pedagogical context. The Library includes scholarly works, reference books, post-graduate text books and readers in the English language.

Volume 28

Robin Setton

Simultaneous Interpretation
A cognitive-pragmatic analysis

SIMULTANEOUS INTERPRETATION

A COGNITIVE-PRAGMATIC ANALYSIS

ROBIN SETTON

JOHN BENJAMINS PUBLISHING COMPANY
AMSTERDAM/PHILADELPHIA

The paper used in this publication meets the minimum requirements of
the American National Standard for Information Sciences – Permanence
of Paper for Printed Library Materials, ANSI z39.48-1984.

Library of Congress Cataloging-in-Publication Data

Setton, Robin.
    Simultaneous Interpretation : A cognitive-pragmatic analysis / Robin Setton.
    p.   cm. (Benjamins Translation Library, ISSN 0929-7316 ; v. 28)
    Includes bibliographical references and index.
    1. Translating and interpreting --Psychological aspects. 2. Pragmatics. I. Title. II. series.
    P306.2 .S48 1999   1999
    418/.02/019--dc21   99021419
    ISBN 978 90 272 1631 1 (EUR) / 978 1 55619 712 3 (US)   (Hb ; alk. paper)
    ISBN 978 90 272 8547 8   (Eb)

John Benjamins Publishing Co. · P.O. Box 36224 · 1020 ME Amsterdam · The Netherlands
John Benjamins North America · P.O. Box 27519 · Philadelphia PA 19118-0519 · USA

Contents

Abbreviations and Symbols

CP   Complementiser Phrase (GB theory)
DRT   Discourse Representation Theory
EVS   ear-voice span
GB   Government and Binding (Theory)
IF   illocutionary force
IP   information processing (theory)
IP   Inflection Phrase (GB theory)
IT   interpretive theory (*théorie du sens*)
LF   logical form
LTM   long-term memory
MH   Modularity Hypothesis
MM   mental model
MMT   mental models theory
PA   propositional attitude
PF   propositional form
PR   propositional representation
RT   Relevance theory
SI   simultaneous (conference) interpretation
SL   source language[1]
SR   semantic representation
spm   syllables per minute
STM   short-term memory
T & I translation and interpretation
TL   target language
wpm   words per minute

---

[1] Many writers in translation studies now distinguish text features from language features by the use of the terms 'source-language text' (SLT) and 'target-language text' (TLT). We use the abbreviations SL and TL for convenience, and trust that it will be clear when what is referred to is a feature of the source or output *discourse* (an extended utterance by a given Speaker in a given situation) rather than the language.

Syntactic, semantic and pragmatic features:

N	noun	*pro*	pro-form
PN	proper noun	p	particle
V	verb	pfv	perfective
A	adjective	dm	discourse marker/connective
d	determiner	T	Topic
D	demonstrative	C	Comment
Q	quantifier	cl	classifier
sm	subordination marker	>Obj	object marker
M, F ; N, G ,D ; S, P	gender, case and number inflections	>F	focus marker
		sui2	tone (Chinese)

P_0	current proposition	>>	infer
P_{-1}	previous proposition	([	unpredictable constituent structure
P_1	'next' proposition	?	moot syntactic attachment, sem-
i,j,k	arguments		antic scope or pragmatic domain
Italics	unresolved element	SMALL CAPS	modal, intentionality
:	resolved	CAPS	(intonational) stress
r	relation	SA	speech act
{}	scope	→	access (extratextual knowledge)
φ	predicate	SK	situation knowledge
⇐	results from	DK	discourse knowledge
⇒	results in	FK	frame knowledge
>	expect	⊃	is included in
⊂	includes	∨	disjunction
∧	conjunction		

Thematic roles: THeme, AGent, PATient, EXPeriencer, INSTrument, BENeficiary, PATH, TIME, SOUrce, GOAL, etc.

☺, ☹   indices of affect

Prosodic features:

-	pause	@, fp	filled pause ('er')
+	long pause	#	solecism, speech error
/ or '	rising pitch	\	falling pitch

the- (attached dash) or _ :   syllable lengthening, drawl
. (full stop following word): semi-pause, clipped ending

Preface

The ambition of this book is twofold: firstly, to update the state of the art in research on simultaneous interpretation with contributions from modern linguistic and cognitive theory, and in so doing, to make a critical examination of the 'primitives' of translation studies; and secondly, to demonstrate the value of T & I data to the study of language and the mind. It attempts a frontal attack on a problem which has blocked interpretation research—how to represent the knowledge and context available to the communicators, especially the interpreter—by placing the translation process within a theory of communication which suggests how these are constrained.

This is an exploratory study, for which no apology is made: there remains a lot to explore in translation from a linguistic viewpoint. But interpreting research has reached a point where we seem to be circling repetitively over the potential components of a theory: language, knowledge, the situation, the interpreter as an individual. The cognitive and pragmatic turns in translation studies have led to ever wider forays into related disciplines, from sociology, action and interaction theory (the German school) to the neurological substrate for interpreter's mental operations (Trieste) and the ultimate *fuite en avant* which leapfrogs all these questions directly into machine implementation. The present study is motivated by the belief that we have a lot to learn from the linguistics side of the cognitive sciences, where an important movement is underway to associate cognitive and pragmatic approaches into a broader framework theory of speech communication which can be plausibly applied to speech phenomena. This will be the basis for the present analysis. As to modelling implementation in the human brain (or on some other hardware), we will stop at a functional outline that seems justified by contemporary beliefs, with only passing attention to the implications of competing modular-symbolic and connectionist approaches.

As a psycholinguistic model, this is not an attempt to press for a more top-down account of discourse comprehension; in a sense, it is the opposite. After the disaffection with early versions of TG, psycholinguistics is taking linguistic description seriously again—partly since it has become clear, with the increasing sophistication of computational models of vision and speech, that 'there is more information in the bottom-up signal than was originally assumed' (Tanenhaus 1988: 18). The pragmatic revolution has shown that much of this information is given by linguistic pragmatics, as distinct from (and complementary to) the top-down 'sociopragmatic' information, such as knowledge about the situation, participants and purpose of the communication which are stressed in schools of translation studies such as the *skopos* paradigm. Confusion over this distinction partly explains the ambivalent use in translation studies of 'context' (the distinct term 'co-text' has not really stuck) to denote a linguistic concept ('the interpreter is waiting for more context') or a cognitive one (meaning extratextual knowledge).

On the theoretical linguistics side, the debate continues over the interface between semantics and pragmatics. But recent work on discourse components neglected in classical description, like connectives, adverbials or parentheticals, also illuminates the pragmatic functions of syntax (word-order choices) and phonology (prosody). 'Functional' grammars like Halliday's (1985) capture this insight and are accordingly popular in discourse analysis and translation studies; but without a link to some basic principles of communication or cognition, they ultimately only leave us with another complex descriptive nomenclature.

Relevance Theory, the main theoretical framework for the present study, has gained in popularity since the work was conceived. Relevantists are now engaged in the systematic re-interpretation of phenomena hitherto described in Gricean, speech-act theoretical, semiotic, functionalist, discourse-analytic and text-linguistic terms. RT has been well received in Japan, for example, by those who hope for a more satisfying account of pragmatic features in what they see as a 'modality-oriented' as opposed to an 'information content-oriented' language and culture (Takahara 1998). Recent work in RT has opened up new perspectives with the proposed distinction between procedural and conceptual encoding; these proposals, which have not been fully worked out, are not yet integrated into the present work: the informed pragmaticist is asked to bear with the intermediate mix of RT, Gricean and speech-act elements in the analysis, which we nevertheless trust are coherent with each other and not fundamentally incompatible with the more unified account currently being developed. Relevance also offers an approach to the problem of quantifying effort, which has exercised interpretation researchers in connection with estimating difficulty and criteria for evaluating quality.

This study addresses cross-cultural behaviour, and raises the question of underlying assumptions about universals and differences between groups of minds organised along linguistic and cultural lines. The general inspiration for our approach owes more to Evolutionary Psychology, which postulates cognitive universals (Brown 1991; Tooby and Cosmides 1992) than to what these authors call the Standard Social Science Model, which tends to emphasise anthropological diversity (see also Pinker 1994: 409). The study is, however, pitched at the middle or psychological level of inquiry into 'human science', venturing neither (or hardly) into philosophy and theories of consciousness, nor into the neural or 'subsymbolic' level of brain function. We assume modularity of the cognitive system in the sense of a mosaic of interdependent functions. Models based on massive (connectionist) interactivity above the 'sub-symbolic' or implementation level, i.e. competing with this modular assumption, have not been explored. On the other hand, we cannot yet accept unflinchingly the notion that modular organisation applies only to domain-specific faculties, or evolved instincts, to the exclusion of functions like memory or attention (Pinker 1994).

One avowed aim of this work is to encourage mainstream linguists and translation (interpretation) researchers to take a greater interest in each others' work. As a makeshift ropebridge across this misty divide, its structure may seem somewhat unorthodox (though not, one hopes, shaky) to readers from both these disciplines. Firstly, a good deal of theory, including a model (Chapter 3), is laid out before we approach the transcripts. This is justified by the need for a two-pronged approach: 'top-down' from cognitive science and linguistic theory, and 'bottom-up' from the data. The attempt to address two different and barely overlapping readerships (translation researchers and linguists) has forced some compromises. Interpreting researchers less familiar with the fads and torments of contemporary linguistics and cognitive science may be more comfortable reading the research review (Chapter 2) before approaching the second half of Chapter 1. Some technicality has been inevitable, notably for brief typological descriptions of the three corpus languages (Chapter 4) and the blow-by-blow microanalysis of synchronised SI samples; on the other hand, some topics, such as speech processing/parsing research, may have been dealt with too cursorily for some tastes. The glossary, inevitably, is partly subjective, and does not attempt to reflect the variety in existing definitions for terms like *proposition, discourse, cognitive* or *pragmatics*. The shape and details of the Language of Thought which is hypothesised to mediate translation are frankly speculative, as is the attempt to reconstruct and insert it between the input and output discourses in the form of a (admittedly rather indigestible) notation. For this and other impositions in a cognitively overloaded world we ask the reader's indulgence.

Acknowledgments

What readable and useful material has survived in this book is largely to the credit of the friends, colleagues and institutions who have advised and supported me in this work. My thanks go first to the faculty of the Department of English at the Chinese University of Hong Kong, in particular its Linguistics Programme, in accepting an application for a thesis outside the Department's traditional areas of specialisation, and for providing a stimulating, bicultural atmosphere in which to study language. My supervisors—Drs. Thomas Lee in the Department of English and David Pollard of the Department of Translation and the Institute of Chinese Studies—guided and supported me with their mutually complementary styles of encouragement. Thomas gave unstintingly of his time and expertise, directing me to valuable sources in every area of relevance to this necessarily interdisciplinary project, and frequently working late into the night to provide detailed comments on my drafts, particularly in the crucial final stages. Without him I could scarcely have hoped to bring together disparate strands of insight and understand SI issues in the wider context of the cognitive sciences: if this work can form a bridge between interpretation studies and mainstream linguistics, he deserves much of the credit. David, for his part, gave me the benefit of a lifetime of scholarship in Chinese studies, and the no less valuable gift of support to my flagging morale at times of crisis. His wisdom and intensely human approach to translation helped me to steer a sane course through the rigours and pitfalls of theory. I am also indebted to the other members of the Thesis Committee: to the External Examiner, Professor Ian Mason, and to Dr. Gu Yang and Professor Gladys Tang, for their forbearance in adapting to my sliding deadlines and agreeing to read drafts at very short notice; and to the Head of the Graduate Division of English, Professor Andrew Parkin, for his help in smoothing possible administrative obstacles.

My gratitude goes also to the colleagues who kindly agreed to the recording and use of their interpretation performances; to Sylvia Kalina, who recorded and generously supplied the 'live' Wurzburg sample[1]; and to the three institutions who provided premises and technical support for the recording of supplementary data, and colleagues there: at the Ecole Supérieure d'Interprètes et de Traducteurs (ESIT) of the Sorbonne (Paris III), Marianne Lederer and her staff; at the Graduate School of Translation and Interpretation Studies (GITIS) of Fujen Catholic University in Taipei, my successor Yang Chengshu and my colleague Liu Minhua, and GITIS students and staff; and at the Hong Kong Polytechnic University, John Minford and the Department of Chinese and Bilingual Studies.

My thanks go also to many colleagues in both professions for their support in various ways. Diane Blakemore and Thomas Lee are warmly thanked for their valuable comments on the Glossary. I am indebted also to Daniel Gile for repeated help with information and references; to Socorro Browning, for taking over some of my recruitment responsibilities during critical periods in Hong Kong; to Catherine

---

[1] This sample was recorded on site at the actual conference with the permission of the interpreters and event organisers. Permission to use the recordings for research was obtained through the University of Heidelberg. Copyright for the speeches themselves rests with the organizers of the symposium.

Stenzl, Jennifer Mackintosh, and the Research Committee of the International Association of Conference Interpreters (AIIC) for providing microfiche copies of existing theses; and in general, for their valuable comments, Clare Donovan, Daniel Gile, Anne Reboul, Danica Seleskovitch and many others, both fellow interpreters and fellow linguists, who contributed to this work consciously or unconsciously through conversations outside booths, email discussions, and other formal and informal consultations. Last but not least, I wish to thank Bertie Kaal, Ingrid Seebus and their colleagues at the Benjamins Translation Library for their friendly and efficient support as I prepared the manuscript for publication.

Hong Kong and Paris, 1997-8

Chapter 1 Introduction

1 Simultaneous conference interpretation

Simultaneous interpretation (SI), a service which allows participants at international meetings to speak and follow proceedings in their own languages, is widely viewed as a particularly impressive form of rapid, instant translation. In this book we will try to make sense of SI as a phenomenon of cognitive performance using the tools of contemporary 'communicative' linguistics and cognitive psychology. We shall be concerned here exclusively with *conference* SI as practised in professional conditions, in which interpreters in a sound-proof booth with headsets, control consoles and microphones, and a direct view on the meeting room, deliver versions of the discourse in different languages 'on line' with a lag of a few seconds, alternating every 20-30 minutes or as Speakers[1] take turns on the conference floor.

SI has been practised in this modern acoustically-assisted form for about fifty years, and has become the standard medium of multilingual communication in international organisations, both intergovernmental and private. At the United Nations, delegates communicate through SI in six languages, while the European Parliament routinely uses eleven, or 110 possible combinations in a single meeting.[2] Conference interpreters constitute a distinct profession, and are usually first trained in consecutive interpretation, in which discourse is rendered in five or ten-minute segments with the help of notes. (Consecutive interpretation was the standard medium of debate at the League of Nations, the UN's ancestor, and continues to be widely used at small, bilingual meetings and ceremonial occasions).

This book is motivated in part by the belief that the study of SI can make a unique contribution to the study of language in use. Traditionally, linguists study 'sovereign' oral and written monologue or dialogue (or sentences tested against native competence to discover language-internal rules). In psycholinguistics, experiments involve a variety of tasks which bias priorities and the use of cognitive resources in various ways, including default motivations assumed by subjects performing in 'neutral' conditions. SI is distinct from other forms of speech behaviour in combining several features which preclude direct extrapolation from experiment and observation in other disciplines, but at the same time make SI data a valuable source of inference in the study of language communication:

(i)   *Use of speech systems*: overlapping (simultaneous) listening and speaking.

(ii) *Goal orientation*: in translation, comprehension is oriented to production, not (as in everyday communication) to discursive-competitive exchange, learning, curiosity, entertainment or stimulation, nor (as in psycho-linguistic experiments) recalling words, or gist, or competing with other tasks.

(iii) *External pacing*: in SI (unlike written translation), the stimulus-processing-response cycle is externally paced. The relative immediacy of production following comprehension, as captured in SI recordings and transcripts, is a potentially valuable source for understanding the incremental course of comprehension and formulation.

(iv) *External sourcing*: translation (unlike 'sovereign' speech) expresses the product of someone else's thoughts, assumptions, reasoning, priorities, and objectives. Only formulation and articulation are the interpreter's. SI data thus provides a valuable source of inference about how we derive other people's intentions from their speech.

(v)   *Input and output in different languages*: translation can be seen as a 'mirror' process of sovereign conversation, where sovereign intentionalities alternate using the same code. Translation aims to maintain both the propositional content and intentionality (together, the 'Message') while changing the code. The variable in this case—the language code— is hardly more difficult to master for the researcher than the alternating motivations and intentions of conversation, which must be inferred.

The combination of these conditions makes SI a challenge to existing models of how language works, and at the same time a potentially valuable source of data for cognitive and communication studies. In speech-processing terms, immediacy, overlapping comprehension and production and the change of language (conditions (i), (iii) and (v)) require initial assumptions on two dimensions of the activity, justifying a cognitive-pragmatic approach:

1. the resources and limitations of the interpreter, with assumptions about competence and the flexibility of cognitive architecture;

2. the constraints and flexibilities inherent in languages, and their use in particular communicative situations (pragmatics).

Beyond the pure speech processing perspective, if psychology (intentions, motivation etc.) is deemed to influence speech at all, then conditions (ii) and (iv)—the external pacing and sourcing of the task—must also be significant.

Interpretation research has drawn broadly on concepts in cognitive science and linguistics (see review by Shlesinger 1995), but existing accounts have not managed to reconcile theories about language and theories about cognitive architecture. The few overall models which have so far been proposed draw chiefly on information-processing (IP) theory (Gerver 1976; Moser 1976; Massaro 1978; Gile 1995), but have presented little or no corpus analysis in support. The tendency in IP-inspired modelling is to divide the SI act into distinct component processes, adopting models of coordination from cognitive psychology but making simplifying assumptions about language in communication. The interpretive theory (IT), a more unified and holistic account (e.g. Seleskovitch 1968, Lederer 1981, Seleskovitch and Lederer 1989) places greater emphasis on the role of context in communication, and on the primacy of the Speaker's intent over linguistic structure, but glosses over possible limitations of the human language processing system. The IT account has been defended in detailed corpus analysis (Lederer 1981), but with little reference to contemporary pragmatic and cognitive theory. There is little or no dialogue between the two schools, which are sharply divided over training and theoretical issues such as the importance of language-specific factors. Neither paradigm has ventured to explore the intermediate representations or mental medium of translation.

Some recent writing has appealed to concepts in linguistic pragmatics like speech-acts and implicature (Chernov 1992; Jekat and Klein 1996 in addressing machine interpretation), but to our knowledge there has not yet been any attempt to apply them systematically to the analysis of an SI corpus.

What kind of theoretical framework is needed to do justice to SI, and why must it be 'cognitive-pragmatic'? The peculiar combination of conditions described above makes it difficult simply to extrapolate to SI from theories based on the study of other forms of speech behaviour, either as to how meaning is processed or how cognitive resources are coordinated. The task nature of SI, and observations of SI performance, suggest the need for a cognitive model which can accommodate a *goal-oriented* configuration of basic resources such as memory and peripheral processes. At the same time, to capture the linguistic phenomena, the situated nature of conference interpretation demands a pragmatic theory. In SI performance terms, we will claim that the improvements and changes which are observed with training and experience (Pinter 1969; Fabbro and Gran 1997) are more readily explained by a development in the skilled use of pragmatic and knowledge resources than by the improved coordination of limited processing capacity understood as the temporary storage, transformation and retrieval of linguistic forms.

In this book we explore the possibility of reconciling the dimensions of cognitive coordination and the transmission of meaning in SI through a better understanding of intermediate representation. We shall advance the hypothesis that a single contextualised model of the discourse is constructed for interpretation, allowing a more unitary account of coordination. In support of this claim we present a new cognitive model for SI combined with a pragmatic account based on a corpus in two language pairs, German-English and Chinese (Putonghua)-English.

2 The cognitive-pragmatic approach

Cognitive pragmatics lies at the boundary between two of the source disciplines of modern T & I theory: linguistics and cognitive psychology. As a research programme, it aims to develop an account of human language exchanges which models cognition *in* communication. Translation studies, after long being confined to philology or referred to contrastive linguistics, have been rejuvenated in the last few decades by two important movements: first, a revived emphasis on the communicative, situated nature of text and speech, which demands that translation process and products be studied in *contexts*—the time, the society, the purpose of the communication; and secondly, more recently, a growing interest in cognitive processes, both human, in cognitive psychology, neuroscience and philosophy of language, and simulated, in artificial intelligence (AI).

The application of generalised information-processing models to translation, perhaps because of its novelty, is fast becoming a dominant and almost exclusive paradigm, eclipsing the linguistic dimension. This book aims to restore the balance by re-injecting linguistics, updated with developments in pragmatics, into the new interdisciplinarity.

Pragmatics is the branch of linguistics which addresses its applied, communicative aspects: the role of context and inference, the relationship between the explicit and the implicit in linguistic communication, and those dimensions of meaning which are related to extralinguistic factors such as time, place and situation, and the knowledge available to the participants. All these factors are very much in evidence in translation, and particularly in conference interpretation.

Firstly, languages encode different aspects of meaning and leave different parts to inference from extralinguistic sources (Keenan 1978a). Translators and interpreters must encode meanings in the target language (TL) which are either logically implicit in the source discourse, or need to be inferred from other knowledge: an example is found in the Tense and Finiteness marking which is absent in Chinese but required in English. The implicit in the Speaker's message, whether deictic, logical or thematic[3], must therefore be included in any model of a translation process. Secondly, conference interpretation is intrinsically deictically anchored to a specific situation and audience, a condition reflected in the standard contract under which most professional interpreters work: 'the services of the interpreter shall be provided only for direct and immediate use by the listeners' (AIIC[4] General Conditions of Work, art. 4). Thirdly, the effectiveness of communication has been said to depend on the mutual knowledge, or assumptions, shared by Speakers and hearers. Interpreters and translators are usually external to the proceedings, and Speakers do not take their knowledge into account. Interpreters share neither the background nor the motivations of Speakers and Addressees, and therefore rely more strongly than other participants in the communicative event on inference from textual, situational and other (encyclopaedic) sources (Lederer 1981; Gile 1995: 96). Our hypothesis is that they construct a task-oriented mental model for this purpose.

The two dominant paradigms in SI research show a marked difference in their treatment of context. Information-processing accounts pay due lip-service to the notion, but seem reluctant to address what they cannot quantify; IT writing is pervaded by appeals to the importance of extralinguistic knowledge and context in general. But so far no attempt has been made at modelling context in relation to a corpus; rather, context and inference have been set aside as impenetrable subjective variables.

Pragmatic theory arises from the observation that the meaning encoded in language forms underdetermines the meaning intended by Speakers in producing utterances and derived by hearers in interpreting them. Any realistic theory of language communication must recognise that meaning is derived both from what is encoded in words and grammar and from the inferences drawn in processing these semantic representations in contexts. The scope of pragmatics is sometimes illustrated by the wide range of linguistic expressions which index or evoke contexts external to the sentence, or the types of context which may play a role in understanding, such as a shared culture or environment (Fillmore 1984). But while the potential contexts for interpreting utterances may indeed include any of the hearer's beliefs and perceptions, this insight remains trivial unless context and inference can be modelled in terms of a particular hearer receiving a particular utterance. Relevance theory (RT) considers this to be a central goal of pragmatics (Sperber and Wilson 1986/1995: 16), and suggests that inference in utterance interpretation can be modelled in a way that inference in independent thinking cannot, since firstly, Speakers actively guide hearers to intended meanings, or contexts for deriving them; and secondly, the immediacy of speech exchange places the previous utterance in the forefront of accessible contexts (ibid. 16; 49-54). The notion of the saliency or accessibility of contexts is therefore crucial to the modelling enterprise. Both RT and mental models theory treat context as a psychological construct of percepts and assumptions which are structured in terms of their strength or accessibility, independently of their truth or falsehood.

3 The theoretical framework

The model developed in this study draws on several bodies of theory: the primary sources are Relevance theory (Sperber and Wilson 1986/1995), cognitive or frame semantics (Fillmore 1982, 1984, 1985), mental models theory (Johnson-Laird 1983; Garnham 1987), and speech-act theory (Austin 1962; Searle 1969, 1983).

Relevance theory offers what is so far the most coherent articulation of pragmatics and cognitive psychology in an account linking cognition and communication. However, RT has focussed chiefly on conversation, so we will need to draw on other complementary sources, since SI concerns longer texts in a task perspective, where the interpreter is processing meaning not as an Addressee, but for Addressees.

Cognitive semantics relates the role of lexical meanings in comprehension to cognition, rather than to a language-internal code. Specifically, the frame semantics or 'U-semantics' pioneered by C. Fillmore (1982, 1984, 1985) provides an account of the organisation of concepts in long-term memory and the mechanisms by which conceptual structures are recovered, or evoked, by items in texts.

In the task perspective, mental models theory (Johnson-Laird 1983, Garnham 1987) provides a detailed hypothesis about the way in which text-based meaning and relevant contexts are integrated and organised in working memory, and hence a basis for modelling the economy and efficiency of complex mental representation under pressure.

Since an interpreter's task is to appropriate and recreate the extended speech act of another individual, an adequate psychological model must explain how she[5] retrieves and recreates the Speaker's intentionality through indications of illocution and propositional attitudes. Communicative intent, as we hope to demonstrate, is not simply an abstract quality which can be left to the words of a sincere and motivated translation to convey, but involves manifestations and representations which enter directly into the translation process, and can be traced in the language forms themselves. Intentionalities have more persistent scope through the discourse than sentence-level features, and once identified, can be appropriated and used by the interpreter in her own production.[6] To describe this elusive dimension in the transfer of the Message by an interpreter, we will draw both on the vocabulary of speech-act theory, and its development, notably by Searle (1983), into a theory of intentionality in language, and on recent RT work describing the 'procedural' dimension of communication.

These various theories are usually considered to be in competition with each other on some of the details of how language interacts with cognition. The following introduction aims to show how they can nevertheless be compatible within a general framework seen as a first approximation to describing processes in conference interpretation.

3.1 Relevance theory

Relevance theory (RT) develops the ideas of Grice (1967, 1989) on the cooperative basis of meaning derivation in speech exchanges, integrating Grice's inferential model with a parsing account of the primary decoding of language forms, from which meaning is then elaborated by inference in particular contexts. The cognitive model adopted is a strictly modular one: peripheral systems decode linguistic signals and yield semantic representations, which are logical forms (LF); these are developed to propositional form (PF) by three sub-tasks: disambiguation, reference assignment and enrichment. Propositional forms are further developed in the context of immediately activated encyclopaedic information into 'assumption schemas', which are placed in the context, first of the previous utterance, then of other expanded contexts (visual, encyclopaedic, etc.) until new cognitive effects—changes in assumptions—are exhaustively derived, or until further search is abandoned when the anticipated processing effort appears too high to be worthwhile. 'Meaning' on this account is not divided into what was 'said' and what was implied, but comprises a range of explicatures and implicatures at varying degrees of strength, and the resulting strengthening or weakening of assumptions in the hearer's mind. This theory allows for imperfect communication, vagueness, and 'interpretive' uses of language (see below) like metaphor or irony: there is no clear line between stronger and weaker implicatures, and there may be intentional vagueness (Sperber and Wilson 1986/1995: 56; Ch. 4.7).

In RT, communication is governed by a Principle of Relevance. In its technical, economic sense, rooted in a theory of evolutionary psychology, Relevance is a trade-off between the benefit of new information that can accrue to an Addressee and the cost of the processing effort required to derive it. Communication is 'ostensive-inferential': by manifesting an ostension or communicative intent, a Speaker guarantees that an Addressee can derive worthwhile contextual effects, through inference, at a reasonable cost in effort.

Ostensive acts form a continuum according to the strength of evidence of a communicative intent.

Although the connection is not made explicitly in RT, we may view the devices used by a speaker/writer to direct Addressees to relevance as realising and developing the act of ostension in the discourse itself. While Verbs, Nouns, Adjectives, etc. generally encode propositional content, features like sentence perspective, focus, connectives, prosody, optional word order and other non-conceptual elements in speech can be seen as 'procedural' devices directing hearers to relevant contexts in which to process the new information to infer the intended meanings (Wilson and Sperber 1993).

Pragmatics, and in particular Relevance theory, thus provides us with a principled basis for reconstructing the contexts used in understanding, but it basically addresses the case of sovereign communicators motivated by a desire to expand their cognitive environment or to influence others. Insofar as our motives for communicating condition our linguistic and cognitive behaviour, we need to specify the model for a translation task. Primary communication (as in conversation, the canonical case of situated and contextualised speech usually studied in pragmatics) involves sovereign Speakers and hearers: speech is driven by the communicative intents of Speakers and addressed to hearers who process it according to their own interests. Translation[7] differs from this scheme, and in general from other forms of communication studied in linguistics, in involving at least one participant who is neither the initiator nor the addressee of the message. The Speaker's ostension is not directed at the translator; the meanings or representations a translator derives are not destined for her own end-use (e.g. via selective long-term storage); she is not concerned to respond to an intentionality, but to reproduce it; nor can her production be modelled on a sovereign Speaker's, since it does not begin with her own thoughts.

Secondary communication through translation can be represented schematically as in Figure 1.1, in which each of the three horizontal lines indicates cognitive processes (memory, comprehension and/or formulation) in one of the 'cognitive devices' involved, while the thick vertical lines indicate communication, involving ostension, decoding and inference.

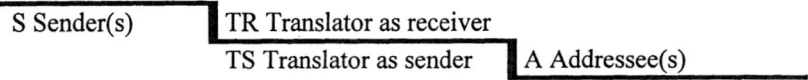

S Sender(s)   TR Translator as receiver
               TS Translator as sender   A Addressee(s)

Figure 1.1 Translation as secondary communication

In this model, each sender (S or TS) shapes his message according to the contexts (mental representations) he assumes are accessible to his Addressees, in particular those he himself has evoked and constructed. In secondary communication, such as translation, paraphrase or reporting (in contrast to merely shadowing the Sender's speech), the ostensive-inferential process is broken down into two stages. Firstly, the Message transits the intermediary's inferential activity; secondly (in translation), the target language offers different resources and constraints for the expression of both conceptual content, and for the ostensive and procedural devices which direct hearers to contexts and inferences: each ostensive-inferential bridge, in other words, is built from different materials.

Any theory of communication which does not view language as a self-contained code, and any compatible model of translation, must therefore take into account (a) possible differences in the contexts available to translators and Addressees; (b) the different encoding and indicating devices of different languages (and speakers), and (c) the translator's processing resources and constraints.

As already suggested, to manage these parameters in a model of simultaneous interpretation we shall need input from more than one sub-discipline of cognitive science. But first, a brief digression is necessary to illustrate the difference between *in situ* interpretation (particularly simultaneous), and deferred (written) translation, in terms of the first and third of these parameters: shifts in context, and processing constraints.

In deferred (written) translation, and certain forms of reporting, the 'horizontal' processes in the diagram (composing, recomposing and reading texts) may be stretched out in time; and more importantly, the 'vertical' processes— delivery of the message to primary and secondary audiences—are usually separated both in time and (cultural) space, sometimes by centuries and continents. The translation and transmission of sacred texts epitomises the challenge of conveying the 'same' message across widely diverging historic and societal contexts, and has accordingly generated much of the seminal writing on translation which explores the nature of the Message and the craft of negotiating its transmission. The practice of written translation typically allows more leisurely reflection on strategies to compensate for these contextual gaps, and a fairly open-ended reference base, usually comprising the whole text, plus sources like encyclopedias, dictionaries and other texts.

In interpretation, primary and secondary audiences are joined by the three dramatic unities of time, place and action, even though their individual and group assumptions may differ (as they do anyway in primary communication). The interpreter therefore has both more and less relevant context than the translator, and both more and fewer resources: for comprehension, she has perceptual access to the event, intonational clues, and sometimes, immediate feedback from Addressees; and for expression, the resource of intonation (not to mention the receivers' limited memory span!). Interpreters, like translators, must form intermediate representations. In consecutive interpretation, they may be supported externally by notes, and larger chunks of text are available for co-processing; but the simultaneous interpreter must rely on the short-term retention of propositional representations in addition to the mental model constructed for general understanding and contextualisation; and her receiver and sender roles overlap in time. These special constraints on timing and access to contexts, and the resources of live speech, make interpretation more interesting for the study of dynamic cognition and language use. One valuable potential contribution of SI data to linguistic theory lies in its demonstration of how approximations and decisions are made on units smaller than a proposition and, obviously, smaller than the text.

RT provides us with a working definition of the translator/interpreter's task in terms of linguistic pragmatics, through the distinction between the *descriptive* use of language, to express propositions as being true of certain state of affairs, and its *interpretive* uses, as in reported speech, paraphrase or tropes like irony or metaphor, in which thoughts (one's own or representations of someone else's as derived from his speech) are represented by forms which resemble them in some relevant way (Sperber and Wilson 1986/1995: 224 ff.). E.-A. Gutt (1991) has identified translation as an interpretive use of language which purports to achieve complete *interpretive resemblance* to the SL message-in-text by reproducing all its communicative clues, and thus providing access to all its cognitive effects at the same relative processing cost.

This means that at a first level of approximation, the translator would aim to state explicitly what is stated explicitly in the original, presuppose what is presupposed, and imply what is implied with the same strength of implication. Translation thus aims to make the same explicatures and implicatures available to its Addressees. This manifestly involves two problems: different languages and Speakers encode different aspects of the implicit and explicit; and different Addressees have different background contexts. It is therefore a fair assumption that (as the 'interpretive' theory of translation (IT) insists), in order to construct contexts and produce propositions in another language in such a way as to induce the same cognitive effects in her audience as those available to the primary addressees, the interpreter must form a representation of the Speaker's intended meaning at one remove from linguistic forms. But—*pace* IT theory—however competent, motivated and well-informed a translator may be, no credible model of translation can assume that she can 'identify with' the Speaker's communicative intent except through a process of decoding and inference (conscious and/or unconscious) from the available evidence.

A consequence of this secondary communication model is that not only the encoding of propositional substance, but also the ostensive and procedural dimension of discourse which directs hearers to relevance, are factored out into two steps. Both the unfolding of the semantic information, and the scope and distribution of devices like focus, vary across languages, so that in SI the balance is necessarily upset by both syntactic and pragmatic asymmetries: propositions appear sometimes before, sometimes after directions to their relevance. In trying to pre-empt or compensate for this condition, an interpreter must impose her own ostensive shaping of the discourse; conversely, as any Speaker, she can also rely for achieving fidelity, or the 'equivalent effect' of the communication, on a normal amount of inferencing by her Addressees.

Since the coding of implicit and explicit varies across languages, what is derived from code and what from inference would inevitably differ for receivers of the same message in different languages. In recreating the balance between content and ostension, a simultaneous interpreter (having no access to the Speaker's sentence plan) relies strongly on clues to the logical direction of the discourse, and specifically, on the relative weight or significance which the speaker intends to attach to the information he presents and evokes, and how he intends it to be processed. These clues are carried chiefly in a class of expressions which are not generally addressed in conventional sentence processing theory, but have been investigated and partly classified by Relevance theorists as 'constraints on relevance', and later, as 'procedural' elements in discourse.

Blakemore's (1987) study of the directive functions of connectives, modals and markers of coordination and subordination as indicators of 'dependent relevance' helps to track this dimension in SI source and output discourse. Blakemore analyses some discourse connectives, such as English *after all, moreover,* or *you see*, as a type of conventional implicature whose function is to guide the interpretation process by directing a hearer to a set of assumptions, or to establish an inferential connection between two segments (1987: 77), and shows how focus and stress interact with these expressions to point to which of the various possible entailments of an utterance is important. In the following example, one particular speech device, stress, directs the contrast in *however* to a different set of likely relevant assumptions, and thus predicts a different set of continuations—and, in translation, may license structurally very different responses by an interpreter sensitive to these different projections (my own hypothetical example):

'The NGO Forum has recommended a monitoring procedure.
However IF we adopt this text...

        Admettons que nous approuvions...
        (Assuming we adopt...)

However if we ADOPT this text...
                    Mais une fois ces mesures votées...
                            (But once these measures are passed/become law...)
However if WE adopt this text...
                    Mais l'aval de notre commission...
                    (But this Committee's approval...)

In a coherent discourse, two utterances may be connected by a relation of dependent relevance either in virtue of the fact that the first contains propositions used in establishing the relevance of the second, or that one is affected by the interpretation of the other (ibid: 122). This relationship is not necessarily encoded in an overt connective, as we can see from an utterance like *This proposal is not unsatisfactory, it's completely unacceptable.* Retroactive pointers to relevance may occur in utterance-final position, as in the case of some of the Japanese sentence endings discussed by Gile (1992), e.g. *...wake desu* 'this is the reason for...', or *...to iu kotoni narimasu* 'it becomes such that...'[8] These considerations are crucial if we are to integrate the course of availability of information about interclausal and inter-propositional relations into our model of timing and decision-making in SI, as well as the putative effects of intra-clausal word order which (perhaps in part because of the limited scope of traditional linguistic models) have hitherto been the main focus of controversy.

Relevance theory also recognises that the actual context for interpretation of an utterance is constrained by the organisation of the individual's encyclopaedic memory, and the mental activity in which he is engaged (Sperber and Wilson 1986/1995: 138). A fuller account of these two factors is provided by cognitive (frame) semantics and the theory of mental models respectively.

3.2 Cognitive semantics

Cognitive semantics provides an account of how conceptual structures may be organised in long-term memory and retrieved into immediate consciousness to support interpretation. C. Fillmore's frame semantics (Fillmore 1982, 1985) is in the empirical semantics tradition, in which words represent categorisations of experience. Fillmore observes that the selectional information which is assumed to become available with lexical items in grammar-based theories of comprehension is not enough to explain processes of interpretation, failing to capture many distinctions, as for instance between sentences like *Give this to John* and *Send this to Chicago*. Understanding in Fillmore's view requires larger cognitive structures, involving a set of participants' roles and a knowledge of underlying institutions. These 'frames' structure the word-meanings, and the word 'evokes' the frame. A frame is defined as 'any system of concepts related in such a way that to understand one of them you have to understand the whole structure into which it fits [...] when one of the things in such a structure is introduced into a text, or into a conversation, all of the others are automatically available' (1982: 111).

This approach draws on prototype theory, according to which words and other linguistic forms index (and hence, during speaking or listening, 'bootstrap') semantic or cognitive categories which themselves participate in larger conceptual structures associated with social and cultural institutions. 'Interactional' frames comprise 'roles, purposes, and natural or conventionalised sequences of event types' which set up an abstract structure of expectations (1982: 117). Some of these prototypes are scripts which are bootstrapped automatically by hearers to make routine bridging inferences (Clark and Clark 1977), thus allowing economy of expression by Speakers:

'He pushed against the door; [*it opened; he looked inside the room and saw that*] The room was empty.'

Understanding on this account ('U-semantics') involves retrieving frames and assembling them in some kind of envisionment of the world of the text. However—and importantly for SI where partial understanding must often be a basis for formulation—the envisionment does not have to be complete. U-semantics allows for some level of understanding even where some word meanings are not understood, through a 'top-down' compositionality whereby individual words evoke structured frames with slots for other expected events and states. This allows for the possibility of constructing propositions in SI which are only partially understood, but meaningful to Addressees given TL lexical items to fill the slots, a situation which may arise in technical conferences. Frame semantics also allows the existence of frames with single lexical representatives, a possibility ruled out in principle by lexical field theory (e.g. Coseriu and Geckler 1980), which usually assumes that the words in the field stand in paradigmatic opposition to each other. Most frames are deemed to exist in consciousness independently of the language (Fillmore 1985: 230) as are the 'spaces' set up by 'space-builders' in the kindred theory of mental spaces (Fauconnier 1985).

A key issue in hypothesising about coordination and resource use in SI is the possible distinction between a spontaneous and resource-free kind of inference and a more active, perhaps resource-using kind. Fillmore distinguishes between frames which contribute to interpretation by being *evoked* by the text, and those which are *invoked* by the interpreter. A frame is evoked by a word or phrase conventionally associated with it, e.g. in *we never open our presents until the morning,* hearers with a certain cultural background evoke the frame which supplies *Christmas*. A frame is *invoked* when the interpreter, in trying to make sense of a text segment, is able to assign it an interpretation by situating its context in a pattern that is known independently of the text. This distinction, and the Relevance assumption of proportionately increasing effort with remoter contexts, may offer a partial basis for assessing the inferential load component in modelling SI effort and difficulty.

The value of frame theory in the study of SI lies chiefly in its explanation of the interpreters' use of paraphrases reflecting extralinguistic knowledge. In cognitive semantics, context takes the form of structured concepts in the hearer's memory, which are evoked by items in the text. Conventional modular parsing theory based on Chomskyan grammar distinguishes the syntactic-semantic information retrieved for each word (which RT calls its logical entry) from 'contextual' information (in RT, its encyclopaedic entry), or other knowledge evoked by the items. For instance, *The carpenter...* would project the syntactic information 'Noun Phrase (NP)', perhaps projecting a Verb Phrase (VP), and the semantic feature +HUMAN; in frame semantics, automatic evocation would extend to an envisionment involving wood, tools, beams or furniture, as distinct from, for example, the current wage levels of carpenters, which would need to be *invoked* (Fillmore 1985: 234). We will present a model in which the information needed for syntactic assembly and associated conceptual information are retrieved or evoked in parallel.

Fillmore's account is compatible with the other pragmatic theories we have adopted in viewing the output from the parser as an partial blueprint; in Fillmore's terms, the enrichment to a full representation is done through the evocation or invocation of frames. U-semantics takes a maximal view of interpretation (ibid: 233-4), which again seems particularly appropriate in goal-oriented compre-hension. In pragmatic terms, evocation from words or phrases may be seen as 'lexical presupposition', a form of conventional implicature in which lexical and grammatical material in the text automatically indexes frames grounded in shared experience, culture and convention. This usefully complements accounts of how other types of implicature, such as logical connections, are derived through the operation of Gricean or Relevance principles.

RT and frame semantics respectively describe the principles and mech-anisms by which relevant contexts are marshalled for comprehension. However, for a comprehensive account of intermediate representations in an intensive communication task like SI we also need an account of how they are economically maintained and organised. Rather uniquely, conference interpreters, especially freelance ones, have to load large amounts of information into their awareness for periods of a few days, much of which is new to them and will be forgotten after the event. We suggest that for successful SI, a mental model of the situation and the discourse must be built up and updated in the interpreter's working memory.

3.3 Mental models

Cognitive scientists and IP-oriented SI theorists have sometimes been tempted to view SI as a dichotic task involving a process of rapid switching of attention between the two streams (Monsell 1987; Lambert 1989). But the two streams in SI clearly have some features in common, namely most of the context and (one hopes to a large extent) meaning; it would be surprising if, in handling such a task, the system did not maximise the sharing of resources where possible. The better performances obtained in SI than in dichotic listening to two streams of mutually irrelevant material, or tasks with stimuli and responses in different perceptual or motor systems, suggest that it does. To what part of the discourse processing task do these shared resources—processing components in some way bridging comprehension and production—correspond? Mental models theory (MMT) offers a viable explanation.

Mental models theory is a theory of cognition rather than communication. Its starting assumption is K. Craik's proposal (1943, cited in Johnson-Laird 1983: 2-3) that thinking is the manipulation of internal representations of the world, and that humans, as processors of information, make use of three distinct processes in reasoning: a 'translation' of some external process into an internal representation in terms of words, numbers or symbols; the derivation of other symbols from them by some sort of inferential process; and a retranslation of these symbols into actions, or at least a recognition of the correspondence between these symbols and external events.

In Johnson-Laird's account of discourse comprehension, the final and most elaborated cognitive representation is a mental model, a structural analogue of a real or imaginary state of affairs which is constructed in working memory from propositional representations of discourse and other tokens and concepts. Since these propositional representations (PR) are themselves elaborations from a first stage of phonemic decoding and parsing, the complete process of discourse interpretation comprises three stages, along the lines of Marr's influential theory of visual perception via a primal sketch, a 2.5-dimensional sketch[9], and a full 3D representation (Marr 1982, cited in Johnson-Laird 1983).

According to MMT, the construction of a mental model can begin even before a propositional representation (PR) is complete, but the PR, which is close to the surface form of the utterance, can still be consulted if reanalysis becomes necessary (Johnson-Laird 1983: 407). Johnson-Laird is agnostic about how relevant information is retrieved (ibid: 175) but shares the RT and cognitive semantics assumptions of a constructive rather than an interpretive semantics, in which people build interpretations beyond linguistically given meaning, citing as evidence the fact that people do not normally remember the surface form (or deep structure, or D-structure) of sentences. Propositional representations of input discourse, and other tokens and concepts, are mapped into the model by a mental language using logical primitives for identity, set-membership, etc., a set of innate conceptual primitives, and a further finite set of semantic operators (time, space, possibility, permissibility, causation, intention) that occur in every field to build up more complex concepts: the meaning of the verb '*to watch*' for example, is built from perception, time, and intention.

In discourse comprehension, tokens of entities are introduced into the model both by text referents, and automatically to model the perceptual environment and ongoing situation.[10] The logical and relational structure is built up by the addition of successive premises according to their truth-conditions, coherence being maintained by an active search for possible alternative or invalidating representations. In the case of an assertion, if no implicit or explicit reference is made to any entity in the current discourse model, a new model is begun. If at least one entity referred to is represented in the current model, the other entities, properties and relations in the assertion are added in an appropriate way. If an assertion interrelates entities in two or more hitherto separate models, they are integrated. If all the entities referred to in the assertion are represented in the current model, a procedure verifies whether the asserted properties/relations hold in the model (ibid. 247 ff.).

Mental models obey a principle of economy: an initial model is built on plausible, sometimes arbitrary assumptions, and held on to even if it is incomplete or indeterminate, being revised and amended as far as possible, unless it is subsequently invalidated, in which case reconstruction is necessary (which is costly, in part because it means retrieving information from earlier discourse). The model must also have procedures for self-revision, although in practice few people perform them without error. This process of adding new information to the model—updating or revising it—may occur clause by clause or constituent by constituent (ibid: 250 ff.). The need for costly radical reconstruction of models in everyday discourse is limited, because Speakers are generally cooperative in the sense of guiding their hearers through referential and other necessary cohesive devices, even in 'competitive' discourse with asymmetrical goals (Attardo 1997).

Like Relevance theory, MMT recognises that the processes of human reasoning and comprehension cannot be accounted for simply in terms of a mental logic working with a semantic network. A symbolic logical language, such as the bee dance or a computer language, can only represent *correspondence between tokens*, not reference, which has intentionality. Reference resolution and disambiguation are only possible in terms of an additional value, the 'significance' of an utterance, which is not given in the PR, for example in a string like: *Roland's wife died in 1928. He married again in 1940. His wife now lives in Spain.*

Models are assumed to be easier to remember than propositions (PRs), because they are more elaborated and structured, and require more processing, but they encode little or nothing of the linguistic form of the sentences on which they are based, and subjects accordingly confuse inferrable descriptions with the originals (Johnson-Laird 1983: 160-2; Garnham 1987). Johnson-Laird suggests that both the mental model and the PR are accessible, the latter being relied on, but at some cost, for input which is not sufficiently determinate to support a structured conceptual representation. (This is compatible with the IT hypothesis of an alternation in SI between direct translation from linguistic forms, and spontaneous formulation from a synthesis of text meaning and cognitive memory.)

MMT's main contribution to our framework is its account of the *economy* of intermediate representation. Each communicative event, each speaker and discourse, is new to the interpreter, but must be rendered coherently. The efficiency of representation is critical to speed and adaptability: the single revisable model plausibly explains the ability of interpreters to maintain coherence through the discourse. It also suggests a different basis for assessing effort and coordination, at least as far as inferential load is concerned: the relationship between surface form and effort, which is assumed in IP models to be direct, may instead vary depending on whether the representational source for formulation is the more SL-oriented 'digital' PR or the more efficient, 'analog' and less language-specific mental model.

Finally, we can assume that the need for representational efficiency in SI favours stable, structuring features in the model, such as anything that may remain valid throughout a single speaker's discourse. Johnson-Laird views intentional reference as a distinctive feature of human communication; the key to efficient representation and cohesion in SI should be sought in this direction. On this issue the literature on intentionality is instructive.

3.4 Speech-act theory

In addition to dealing briefly with large amounts of new information, conference interpreters also briefly represent many different Speakers. Illocutionary force is important in SI in capturing a vital dimension of discourse which eludes description in terms of surface features: communicative intent. Searle (1983) defines speech acts as the expression of intentional states, which embed or modify propositional content; intentionality is 'that property of many mental states and events by which they are directed at or about objects and states of affairs (essentially the basic attitudes of cognition and volition, or belief and desire)' (1983: 10). In speech-act theory, the informative function of language (stating and describing) has no special status among other types of illocutionary acts (Austin 1955/1962). Grice later acknowledged (1989) that his own statement of the maxims as if the purpose of exchanges were a maximally effective exchange of information was too narrow, and that the scheme needed to be generalised to allow for such general purposes as influencing or directing the actions of others.

To simplify, let us provisionally borrow from Functionalist terminology and distinguish informative, conative ('persuasive'), and social (including perfor-mative and ritual) functions of language. In conference discourse, the conative function, expressed as illocutionary force (IF) and propositional attitude (PA), is as pervasive as the propositional content. Expanding Searle's initial analysis (1969: 29-32) to include a level of propositional attitude, we will suggest that every utterance has the general form [IF [(PA)[P]]], i.e. has an underlying illocution, reflecting a communicative intent; that its basic proposition may be presented under a propositional attitude (belief or desire); and that in spoken discourse, at least one of the two is normally overtly signalled or encoded, and more rarely, both (*Let me say that I believe...; Listen, I think...*).

We should not expect to find a regular correlation between overt expressions or markers and illocutions or attitudes, which may be expressed in many ways or not at all. There is no direct correlation between sentence form and speech-act type: questions and statements may be commands (*Will you (or will you not) shut up/ go to bed?*; *You are leaving tomorrow*); imperatives may be offers, recipes, salutations and warnings (*Have a nice day; Go ahead and ruin my carpet* (Levinson 1983; Sperber and Wilson 1986/1995)). But speech-act theory offers the possibility of distinguishing qualifications of propositional content from those of the illocutionary act, a necessary but subtle distinction in analysing discourse, since these different functions may be performed by the same surface item (e.g. a connective) in different contexts (Sweetser 1990; see Chapter 6).

Interpreters may find clues to the Speaker's intentionality and the general trend of his discourse, allowing anticipatory hypotheses of a pragmatic rather than strictly semantic kind, in utterance-scope indicators of propositional attitude, or degrees of authority or evidentiality, such as the attenuative forms prevalent in the discourse of some cultures. These features are typically expressed in a few classes of expressions, including modals, sentential adverbials, parentheticals or conative phrases such as *I would venture to say.., I do feel.., Basically..., It seems to me, undoubtedly, probably* etc. Similarities of distribution among these items have been noted in traditional descriptive linguistics. Jackendoff (1972) recognised that 'adverbs, PPs and modals make similar contributions to the structure of the semantic reading of sentences', and noted their similarities with parentheticals, which like sentence adverbials, occur anywhere except between the Verb and its direct object, suggesting they are Speaker-oriented; 'epistemic' modals display similar ordering restrictions. All these elements occur before, but not after Subject-oriented adverbs, and none have negative counterparts: compare adverbs like *truthfully, honestly, sincerely*; parentheticals like *I would say, in my opinion*; and epistemic modals like he <u>must</u> *have reached the bridge by now* (1972: 98-9).

Another similarity between adverbials, modals and connectives (including causatives and conditionals), described by Sweetser (1990), raises questions about the mechanisms of disambiguation. Sweetser observes that these items share a three-way polysemy between content, epistemic and speech-act uses. *May, can, should, must,* for example, can express degrees of possibility or necessity in these three different domains: in reality (*you may not smoke*), in reasoning or evaluation (*it may be too late*), or in regard to the felicity of performing the speech act (*that, I may say...*). The fact that such 'polysemy' is fluently and easily disambiguated may be explained by postulating, as a derivative property of relevance, some semi-permanent virtual representation of patterns of illocution or attitude with default scope (rather like discourse topics) over extended passages, cumulatively defining 'discourse genres'; this would provide a more solid basis for the use of this concept in applied pragmatics.

Conversely, a problem might be expected in simultaneous interpretation when the speech-act meaning is elliptical, as illustrated in a sentence like *She's not happy, she's ecstatic,* or *For the benefit of the interpreters I'm omitting paragraph 3;* the ellipsed speech acts must be supplied, in the first case *I would not say that ...rather I would say that...*; in the second, *I am saying this* before the first phrase and *let me warn you that* after it, which makes sense with the knowledge or inference that the interpreters have been given a copy of the speaking text. The distribution of possible domain polysemy is language-specific: the temporary ambiguity of *She's not happy* in the first example above could not, for instance, survive in Chinese translation, where the speech-act contrast would require some overt equivalent of *I would not say ...rather I would say...* (e.g. *yu qi shuo ... bu ru shuo...*). In written translation, the stylistic effect would need to be specially recreated by other means.

Cognitive pragmatics and cognitive semantics, as their names imply, are the accounts of language in use which offer the most promising basis for a cognitive-linguistic model of the kind needed for SI. But to model translation, we need to go further. The conceptual processing and non-linguistic input which seem to be necessary for almost any form of translation suggest that we might ultimately need to project an intermediate conceptual-intentional language—which indeed may correspond to a psychological reality, as suggested by philosophers of language like Fodor (1983)—particularly when confronted with the many 'holistic' but intuitively effective renditions in translation which show no clear equivalence between words and language structures.

4 The phenomenology of discourse

These theories taken together suggest a wide range of determinants of meaning in discourse beyond what is delivered by grammar and lexical rules. A motivated, externally paced task like simultaneous interpretation can be expected to draw opportunistically on any and all available clues to meaning. In sum, on a full psychological account of discourse comprehension, what can a hearer processing a discourse for the purpose of passing it on expect to find?

1. A world of *entities* evoked by the discourse, associated by experience and culture into accessible frames.
2. *Propositions*, ranging from the mere existence of these entities, to complex relations between them in virtue of either text meaning, or the structure of the frames, and embedded under various *attitudes*, i.e. gradations of belief, desire, approval or disapproval, interest, indifference. Both attitudes and propositions may be implicated or presupposed as well as being asserted.
3. *Directions and intentions.* Those propositions and attitudes encoded or evoked directly by the text are marked for the attention of the hearer in various ways (prosody, position, stress) and to various degrees along a focal scale from what is most directly asserted or questioned to what is most weakly implicated.

In studying speech for communication, we have to survey all possible sources of comprehension, but in simultaneous interpretation the *order* in which meanings become available is significant. Pragmatic, syntactic and semantic components of meaning may become available in any order, and some may be able to combine in the absence of others to produce a truthful formulation based on explicit encoded meaning or 'safe' implicature; the order in which information for meaning assembly comes in may be to some extent language-specific, to some extent specific to a discourse type or mode (degrees of impromptuness or preparedness of the discourse, for example), and to some extent specific to individual Speakers.

The processing model we propose for the SI task strives for a plausible balance between interactivity and modularity. In the RT model of comprehension via decoding and inference, logical forms are derived by applying rules of grammar to the linguistic input and elaborated in contexts to meaningful propositional forms. If we allow that logical forms can include small parsed fragments, this account is generally compatible with the incremental assembly and production process which we hypothesise for simultaneous interpretation. The involvement of extratextual context and inference at an early stage is also superficially compatible with both the cognitive semantics view of the limits of parsing, and with the theory of mental models, except for a difference in the account of successive stages of representation: Mental Models theory distinguishes two levels of representation, one of which is propositional, the other (in the mental model) conceptual and not necessarily structurally related to the input language form. The implications are not crucial to the basic pragmatic theory of SI, but it will be suggested later that the two-stage account provides a better explanation of certain patterns in the data.

A simultaneous interpreter must sometimes formulate on the basis of partial meanings, either because the utterance is still incomplete or because, not being addressed, she receives less than the full meaning available to the Addressees. It is clear that the translation of fragments is possible, but it seems that such fragmentary partial meaning is heterogeneous in nature: it may consist of some clue to attitude without a complete proposition, or vice versa; to an envisionment of participants without an event, state or action, 'players in search of a script'; or to a logical form in which the arguments or predicates are obscure, as in Lewis Carroll's Jabberwocky. In describing SI it is inadvisable to start with assumptions about levels of processing, since the partial assemblies which are used for formulation are not likely to correspond to a level of meaning delivered by a given component in the brain.

5 Outline and scope of the study

Chapter 2 presents a review of the current state of SI research through a description of conflicting paradigms, or of differences of emphasis which may yet be reconciled. To this end, a new SI model is laid out (Chapter 3), drawing on speech-processing research and two assumptions in cognitive science: modularity with limited interaction, and the reality of intermediate representation.

Chapter 4 provides a description of the corpus, conditions, discourse types, languages and interpreters, and spells out our assumptions and procedure for reading the data. This first attempt (as far as we know) at a thorough description of SI data in terms of the available cognitive and linguistic apparatus rests on a radical observation phase, a kind of Voyage of the Beagle in which—this is the third key assumption of the study along with weak modularity and intermediate representation—the input (and the interpreters' output, as input to the Addressees) is read exhaustively on the principle that whatever is input to a hearer's decoding and inferencing processes potentially carries meaning. The implications of this position as an epistemological starting point are expanded upon in Chapter 4.

The model and corpus analysis procedure serve as a basis for our inquiry into four issues which are controversial in SI theory. The first three appear crucial to the underlying assumptions and methodology appropriate to the study of interpretation, and the fourth cannot be probed without clarifying these assumptions:

(1)   the nature of intermediate representation in SI;
(2)   the role of the implicit in translation/interpretation, and of dimensions of discourse which are not strictly 'informational';
(3)   the constraints and tolerances of simultaneous processing, in connection with assumptions about intermediate representation;
(4)   the weight of typological, or language-pair-specific factors.

To shed light on these issues, we looked to the corpus for answers to some specific questions: what kinds of cues are used by simultaneous interpreters? to what extent does SL sentence structure affect SI? what kinds of errors or failures reflect coordination problems, which reflect linguistic competence, and which a lack of extralinguistic knowledge? and are differences in structural transformation patterns or the use of cues visible between language pairs, situations (mock/live) or discourse modes (recited vs spontaneous oral input)? These research foci are specified further in Chapter 4.

The study is exploratory in assembling a new framework of contemporary theory for the study of SI, and as such does not try to answer the 'big' questions of immediate interest to the profession, such as how to assess quality. It is also necessarily interdisciplinary, involving both language competence and performance, and significant extralinguistic factors. The corpora involve three languages, eight interpreters and two or three texts and situations, but the linguistic focus required above all the preparation of detailed transcripts of the discourse and careful analysis. The analysis begins (Chapter 5) by testing the common intuition that SI in certain language-pairs depends on the ability to counter structural asymmetries between SL and TL with specific strategies; the findings suggest that the surface structure of input is less constraining than is often assumed. We then try to tease apart the code and inference dimensions of the interpretation process by modelling the extralinguistic context available to interpreters from meanings they express which are not encoded on the surface of the input. Contextual sources for SI, which previous work (especially in IT) had claimed to be crucial, are explored in some detail, but we also examine the visible use of markers of the Speaker's intentionality and other pragmatic indicators which have not previously been analysed in SI as such. (Chapter 6).

The interpreters' versions show clear evidence of the role of judgment, in their simplifications and elaborations, and their exploitation of the relative autonomy of production through prosody, cohesive devices and emphasis, to restore the message to the Addressees (Chapter 7). The mental model approach allows a new view of the economy of SI processing, but reliable 'time-and-motion' models of overall coordination in SI will require further research, and in particular, finer methods for reading hesitancy patterns. However, examples of failure or breakdown in certain conditions give an idea of the type of skills and language competence required for SI, and its inherent limits.

In terms of cognitive modelling, the current consensus in psychology is that behaviour is an interaction of several psychological mechanisms, but we have few complex models to illuminate the extent to which cognitive-linguistic functions can be configured to share resources: the involvement of production and a second language have been avoided in the past as obscuring factors. We believe that something can be learned from observing processes interacting instead of attempting to separate them in controlled experiments. In particular, SI data provides a unique database of externally-paced, on-line paraphrase with examples of how 'starting-points' for formulation (Chafe 1994) may be based on minimal pragmatic and semantic elements which correspond only incidentally, if at all, to minimal syntactic units. This condition cannot be obtained in constructed same-language paraphrase experiments, which would not be distinguishable from shadowing: in SI, the thoroughness of the paraphrase is defined both by the passage into a different language, and by the goal-orientation of the activity. To this extent, SI can suggest something about the nature and course of intermediate mental representation in language processing, and about the cognitive synergies which are possible. In methodological terms, some compensation for the additional complexity of the data is to be found in its relative abundance, since two or more overt texts are available for the study of a single communicative act.

Chapter 2 SI Research

1 Historical background

Interpretation studies have remained relatively isolated from other research in applied linguistics, perhaps because of the methodological challenge posed by the involvement of multiple languages and variable situations, and because its applications concern a tiny community as compared, for example, to the market for research on language teaching and acquisition.[1] The most prolific writing of the early period came from professional interpreters seeking to set out a theoretical basis for training; more recent literature has reflected an increasing contribution from mainstream cognitive science. However, nearly forty years after the first attempts at analysis, a consensus has yet to emerge on the most appropriate paradigm for research (see e.g. Gile 1990, Moser-Mercer 1991).

Because of the unique characteristics of SI, those who have taken up the research challenge have had to make many theoretical assumptions. The main themes of early writing grappled with the implications of SI for existing models: in the first place, the possibility of successful simultaneous speaking and listening, with the additional complication of a translation task, was not predicted by the then current single-channel and serial models of speech comprehension and production (Shannon and Weaver 1949; Broadbent 1958). Secondly, the claim that instant accurate translation of discourse was possible beggared belief among linguists and translators aware of the semantic and structural differences between languages; but at the same time, SI highlighted the inherent differences between written and spoken language, which had yet to be explored in linguistics.

Research on SI has traditionally been pursued according to two different agendas. Practitioners and trainers have taken a normative, sociopragmatic approach, which was to develop into the interpretive theory (IT) of the Paris school, while cognitive psychologists have conducted more detached studies.[2]

The post-war rise of international organisations created a sudden demand for fast, competent language intermediation. According to some writers, when the idea of SI was first mooted there was some doubt about its feasibility (Lederer 1981: 19), but once it was demonstrated, training programmes were set up and the first practitioners set out to establish professional and academic credentials. A number of handbooks published in the early period have remained classics (Rozan 1956, Herbert 1952). But outside the small community of interpreters and users, some scepticism remained. D. Seleskovitch and like-minded early pioneers identified the enemy in prevalent Structuralist[3] and Behaviourist conceptions of language and speech behaviour (Seleskovitch 1968), and set out to demonstrate not only that good conference interpretation was possible, but that its very feasibility shed new light on the nature of language comprehension. Seleskovitch and a close-knit group of IT theorists built a theory and training principles on their own experience and insights, presenting SI as a skilled activity requiring no special linguistic strategies, merely training in speaking while listening, relying on a spontaneity guaranteed by near-native competence in the source and target languages.

The idealisations in IT, and its reluctance to entertain failure in professional SI, can be traced to this early adoption of a defensive position and the need for validation. Cognitive psychologists have not shared these concerns, viewing SI as a source of data for research into speech task coordination. Early studies of SI by researchers outside the profession focused on temporal factors like synchronicity, pauses and input segmentation, adopting structural and semantic linguistic criteria to control for fidelity (Goldman-Eisler 1972; Barik 1973, 1975). This interest is reflected in the low priority which these studies have typically attached to simulating professional or conference conditions.

If traces of these traditional biases are still visible, the dividing line is no longer as distinct. Interpreter-researchers are exploring the contribution of other disciplines and collaborating with cognitive scientists. The information-processing (IP) paradigm, for which its advocates claim a stronger scientific foundation than IT theory[4], is followed by researchers both from inside the profession (Moser 1976, 1978; Gile 1990, 1995) and outside it (Massaro 1975, 1978; Gerver 1976; Lambert 1988, 1990 etc.). There is a lively ongoing debate on the definition of the field and its scope and position with respect to other disciplines. Studies on all aspects of interpretation proliferate, from perspectives as diverse as neurobiology and systemic-functional grammar, while some authors prefer to maintain a link with Translation Studies (Stenzl 1983), or doubt that anything can be learned without placing the activity in its socio-psychological contexts (Pöchhacker 1994). The next Sections trace the history of SI research and outline some influential theories.

2 Temporal and surface variables

Early studies compared the delivery patterns of SI input and output, measuring fluency, pausing, and the lag between the two streams (ear-voice span, EVS), and comparing linguistic structures, in order to discover the mechanisms of simultaneity. This focus on temporal variables was criticised by practitioners for its disregard of both meaning and the psychological aspects of the translation process. In the 1970s, IP-based models were published which incorporated semantic processing; but a landmark symposium which brought the two communities together in Venice in 1977 failed to establish common ground.[5] In the recollection of an IP-oriented participant, the interpreters present were sceptical of the psychologists' theories about the unconscious dimensions of SI processes, and impatient for a full explanatory account (Moser-Mercer, p.c.). IT researchers deplored the unwillingness of linguists and cognitive scientists to step outside their established concepts and terminology and learn from the practitioners, or even to reflect their views in the conclusions (Lederer, p.c.). Twenty years later, there is still little or no dialogue between IT and IP theorists.

2.1 Measuring synchronicity

The ability to listen in one language while speaking in another is usually regarded as the most spectacular and mysterious aspect of simultaneous interpretation. Several early studies by cognitive psychologists (Oléron and Nanpon 1965, Gerver 1969, 1971, 1974; Goldman-Eisler 1972; Barik 1973, 1975) investigated the simultaneity of processing in SI by measuring temporal variables in laboratory simulations.

At first it was believed that listening and speaking could not be truly simultaneous without a performance decrement, and that interpreters must pause to listen and use pauses in the input to speak. Gerver (1971) asked SI students to interpret two passages of pre-recorded French prose, one with minimal stress and intonation and all pauses of over 0.25 seconds removed. The finding that 89% of pauses occurred 'at the same position as source language pauses' suggests that these SL and TL texts were very close structurally, and that translation was virtually word for word. Gerver concluded that normal pausing in input speech helps the interpreter overall, but made no local analysis; on the question of whether an interpreter can really process several sensory inputs at one time, he concluded that the process must involve rapid switching, or 'multiplexing'.

Barik (1973, 1975) made strong claims about the limits on simultaneity, suggesting that Speakers' pauses were used by the interpreter for her output, and assuming limited flexibility or control over processing and storage: 'a pause occurring at an ungrammatical location [...] may be unusable [...] or may cause the interpreter to act on insufficient information, resulting in inaccurate performance' (1973: 273).

Attempts to correlate pause patterns in the two streams have not been successful. Goldman-Eisler's (1968) and Barik's suggestions that Speakers' pauses could be used by interpreters to cram in their own production, and that interpreters had to pause to hear what Speakers were saying, were shown by Gerver to be untenable: the pauses measured by Goldman-Eisler, Barik, and Gerver himself were hardly long enough for an interpreter to utter anything coherent, or to avoid filling if she was already speaking (Gerver 1976: 182). [6]

The assumed difficulty of listening while speaking has since been discounted by repeated findings: Speakers' and interpreters' speech streams overlap more often than not: 64% of the time in Gerver (1972, cited in Gerver 1976: 183), and about 70% of the time in Soviet and Czech studies (Chernov 1992; Cenková (1985), cited in Gile 1995: 40-1). [7] I. Pinter (1969) showed a clear effect of training in the simple ability to talk and listen at the same time: seasoned interpreters and last-year SI students performed much better than beginners and other students in repeating and answering questions about heard sentences in the condition involving simultaneity.

2.2 Ear-voice span (EVS) or 'lag'

Measurements of the lag or 'ear-voice span' (EVS) between source stream and interpreter's output have yielded a wide range of values. [8] Paneth (1957) suggested 2 to 4 seconds, but Oléron and Nanpon (1965) found that EVS could range from 2s to 10s, and ventured that an interpreter 'must grasp a certain amount of material before he can begin to translate, the amount varying with the position of certain key words, such as the verb' (both cited in Gile 1995). Goldman-Eisler (1968) recorded wide variations in EVS, but found no correlation between the mean number of elements (words or word units forming a whole, e.g. *has gone*, *in front of*) and the ear-voice span (1972: 132), thus ruling out the word as a meaningful unit to gauge segmentation. Gerver (1969) also attempted to measure EVS in words, but found only that 'interpreters have significantly greater ear-voice spans than shadowers' and in a later study (1976) recognised that comparative word and syllable counts were irrelevant in terms of translation. [9] It is now generally accepted that structural changes are too great for EVS measurement to be meaningful.

2.3 Segmentation and processing units

Investigating the segmentation of input by interpreters, Goldman-Eisler (1972) recognised that although in normal speech perception listeners had been shown to segment input according to (syntactic) constituents, they have a relatively simple task compared with that of the simultaneous interpreter, where segmentation is based on comprehension rather than perception (1972: 128). Her data on comparative speech rates and fluencies of Speakers and interpreters in several language pairs was nevertheless presented in support of grammar-based theories of segmentation: she concluded that interpreters generally require a predicate before beginning to encode and vocalise a segment for output, stressing the primacy of this level over lexical units:

> 'under high pressure simultaneous translation does not break down into passive, atomistic and lexical segmentation; on the contrary, it is as if, when really put to the test, processing cannot be bothered with *less* [her italics] than predicative expressions' (1972: 131)

Goldman-Eisler implicitly recognised some complex intermediate processing in observing that interpreters impose their own segmentation on input, preferring constructive processes over purely receptive ones (1972: 136), and in noting the possibility of 'a discrepancy between the temporal and semantic fitness' of chunks of input, which might blur language or speed factors in predicting which chunks would be recoded as such, which could be split into two propositions, and which fused. However, some confusion remained in the definition of the chunk as a unit of input (on this account, as a constituent or a speech burst bounded by pauses) or of output.

The relationship of this intermediate processing with memory is unclear. Goldman-Eisler and Cohen (1974) cite two types of memory, 'active verbal memory', which is largely bypassed in SI in their view (1974: 2), and 'echoic memory,' the short-term store claimed to be chiefly involved in SI, in which each stored chunk is 'converted from sound image to meaning when its turn comes to be recoded'; but the capacity of echoic memory is viewed in lexical unit terms (number of syllables) (1972: 136).

Variables such as speech type or genre, and language-pair, were acknowledged in Goldman-Eisler's work, but unfortunately confounded: her conclusion as to the crucial role of the verb in delaying output relied heavily on differences between the samples of SI from German texts, which were all read from written material, and the French or English source texts, which were mixed (spontaneous and read). The same reservation must apply to the conclusion (based on the same data) that output chunks match grammatical input units more frequently from German than from other SLs.

Goldman-Eisler also overlooked task effects, or the possibility of a fundamental difference between a simultaneous listening/speaking task, in which the output is based on the meaning of the input (as in SI), and one in which it is linked with an unrelated cognitive activity, as in a 1974 study (Goldman-Eisler and Cohen

1974) in which subjects performed vocal counting or subtracting tasks while listening to a difficult speech. The phenomenon of articulatory suppression in simultaneous vocalisation of irrelevant material makes it difficult to extrapolate from such studies to the SI situation.

2.4 Speech rates

Interpreters have repeatedly questioned the significance attached to temporal data by authors like Gerver and Barik (Bros-Brann 1976), but implicitly accept that delivery speed is a limiting factor on performance, becoming critical for the recitation of written texts. Seleskovitch (1965, cited in Gerver 1976) suggested that an input rate of 100-120 wpm (words per minute) was a comfortable one for interpreters, with 150-200 as an upper limit (cited in Gerver 1976); this was confirmed in an experiment by Gerver (1969). Lederer (1981) considered 100 wpm a maximum for recited text.

   However, no convincing correlation has been found between Speakers' and interpreters' speech rates, and the method of measurement has been questioned: Déjean Le Féal (1980) found that interpreters' rates varied between 71% and 87% of the source text rate in terms of words per minute, 83% and 102% in terms of syllables per minute; Krusina, comparing rates for Czech speech and SI into English, French and German (1971, reported in Gile 1995) found opposite results for counts by words or by syllables. Stenzl's (1983), Déjean le Féal's and Lederer's (1981) figures show that interpreters often speak faster (more words) than the Speaker, but Stenzl herself (in a corpus of French and English into German) also measured an overall *negative* correlation—a tendency for target texts to become shorter with accelerating source rates (1983: 29).

   The significance of EVS or comparative delivery rates as measured in words or syllables is highly questionable, firstly because of the morphemic differences between languages, but also because in translation, the meaning of a word may be rendered as a sentence or as a prosodic feature (Lederer 1981), or vice-versa, and redundancies may be omitted, or explanations offered; as Gerver points out (1976), syllables are not semantic units, and translation concerns meaning, not words. Professional interpreters agree that the 'writtenness' of the presentation is a far more important factor than the speed of delivery, and that SI from fast recited text is extremely difficult, but this relationship has not been adequately analysed except in general terms of redundancy and information density. IT writers, intriguingly, explain it in terms of (de)synchronisation between speech and thought (e.g. Déjean Le Féal 1982).

2.5 Error analysis

Barik (1973, 1975) analysed SI protocols produced by recent graduates of an interpreters' school, and non-interpreter 'fluent bilinguals', one English-dominant and one French-dominant in each pair, from audiotaped recordings. Texts were non-technical and included semi-prepared lectures, formal speech prepared for oral delivery, spontaneous speech (a story and improvised description of a picture), and recited text. Barik offered even more detailed statistical analysis than did Goldman-Eisler of several formal and temporal variables, such as speech and articulation rates, which he sought to correlate with performance. While this was a pioneering study in its thoroughness, Barik's (like Gerver's) treatment of the material, and his tentative conclusions, rested on strong implicit and explicit assumptions about the nature of translation (or interpretation): his definition of errors ('discontinuities' in Gerver's terms) in terms of omissions, additions and substitutions made no allowance for a pragmatic dimension; for example, one category of Barik (1975)'s 'errors' included changes of order in the presentation of information.[10] Barik also offered guesses about the causes of certain errors, e.g. a unit omitted 'due to inability to translate or comprehend it' or 'due to delay'. These simplifications allowed him to 'cleanse' the text, for correlation purposes, of passages involving gross errors or omissions, and even of all filled pauses (1973: 245-247), thus ruling out analysis of the discourses in their global or continuous aspects, either in terms of quality or processing.

In the absence of a generally accepted yardstick for evaluating interpretation performance, such inventories of local 'non-correspondences', some at the level of individual lexical items, could not serve as a guide to quality, taking no account of prosodic, discoursal or total semantic and pragmatic effect.

3 A computational linguistics approach

A first attempt to build a computational model of SI on linguistic and cognitive assumptions was made by Dillinger (1989), who constructed two texts of a 'narrative' and 'procedural' type respectively, controlled them carefully for 'equivalence' at various levels (e.g. lexical, syntactic, propositional, cohesive), and had them read out onto audiotapes. Subjects from two groups (eight experienced interpreters and sixteen novice bilinguals) were asked to simultaneously interpret the texts into French. The texts were read at a rate (145 wpm) deliberately faster than the comfortable range for interpretation arrived at by Gerver, Seleskovitch and others (110-120 wpm) 'in order to generate deviations'.

Dillinger applied a model described as 'a computational counterpart to the [serial, clause-based] clause-processing hypothesis in psycholinguistics'. This assumed three-stage comprehension: parse trees are operated on by 'proposition generation' (semantic interpretation), either by frame instantiation (the matching of sentences to canonical frames based on information in the lexicon), or by the top-down semantic analysis of clausal segments. Propositions (predicate-argument structures) are output to the 'general cognitive processor', which enhances their internal coherence by inference based both on the text (recovering anaphoric antecedents, etc.) and prior knowledge, generating new propositions and propositional components and linking propositions into larger conceptual structures ('frames' as described in e.g. AI literature). Dillinger hoped to isolate 'frame-level' processing, distinguishing 'rule-based' frame generation from frame instantiation from prior knowledge.

This study, based largely on the AI-oriented work of Frederiksen and others, confidently hypostatises where other research cautiously speculates: all stimuli and reponses are fully quantified; texts are constructed, and their units (text segments), as well as the interpreters' mental processes, are all axiomatically defined and indexed to each other. Meaning-changing responses are assumed to index semantic processing, while paraphrased responses are taken as an indicator of syntactic processing and proposition generation; propositional density is defined as 'the number of propositions that have to be generated for a syntactic unit' (1989: 57-9; 92).

Dillinger's results are difficult to evaluate or extrapolate to real-life conference interpreting, for several reasons:

(1)   The source texts were 'purposely designed to have normal values', so as to reflect 'normal' processing rather than specific strategies for unusual texts. Texts were controlled separately for lexical, syntactic and inference load equivalence, ignoring the possible effects of combined syntactic, lexical and semantic load patterns. Values were computed statistically for the texts overall without reference to local processing or linguistic events. The basis for calculating 'inference load' is not specified.

(2)   Dillinger neither gives examples, nor indeed does he supply any part of the French output protocols or an example of evaluation of the 'responses,' making it impossible to verify the validity of his type-classification of responses, or statistical statements like 'paraphrased responses were only 4% of texts'. Secondly, the analysis is heavily dependent on *a priori* definitions of units such as the 'frame', and the 'proposition', which here subsumes lexical, declarative and relational types. 'Segments' are not defined other than to say they were chosen for comparability; identity of

input and output segments appears to be assumed. In linguistic terms, the distinction made between 'syntactic' and 'semantic' processing reflects the convenient analytical divisions of a structuralist era before linguists came to grips with real discourse; similarly, 'sentence' is defined not in utterance terms (i.e. capturing prosodic contour, pauses and other cues to Speaker intent), but as 'a clause with a finite main verb and any non-finite clause attached to it', making it difficult to apply to most real-life discourse with its afterthought adjuncts, parenthetical comments and ungrammaticalities.

No account is thus taken of possible prioritising by interpreters—especially in view of the artificially high delivery speeds imposed—against their perceptions of intended relative saliency and macrostructure, or in adjusting to task or audience-related factors; this makes it hard to assess the significance of certain results, e.g. that 'considerably fewer responses were given to mid-density propositions in the procedure than in the narrative' (ibid.: 70)

(3)   The frame of analysis ignores most of the factors generally recognised to affect interpretation, which is viewed exclusively through a set of linguistic and computational constructs. Conditions where prior knowledge and situational context are significant are termed 'loaded'; but conclusions are extrapolated implicitly to professional interpreting generally, including suggestions for training. It is claimed that experience had 'only a weak effect on performance', but the basis for assessment of performance is unspecified. Conference interpreters' experience is of manipulating constraints in certain conditions, which were here virtually all absent: the texts are of a narrative and descriptive (procedural) type atypical of conferences, since they lack illocution and communicative purpose; interpreters had no opportunity for preparation; and inappropriate equipment was used, in the form of enclosed headphones.[11]

Dillinger found that trained interpreters performed only 16.6% better than untrained bilinguals, but this conclusion is based only on 'linguistic skills' (syntactic processing, proposition generation and frame-structure processing), which are defined as components of comprehension. Since production data is not provided, there is no way of assessing the author's inferences about processing. Dillinger defines 'interpreting expertise' purely in comprehension terms (ibid.: 85) and explicitly does not investigate production. In this context, the conclusion that 'there is no special set of abilities which constitutes interpreting skill' appears rather circular, since comprehension is assumed to be what interpretation has in common with normal listening (ibid.: 91).

4 Information-processing models of SI

SI theorists in the IP tradition have favoured complex multi-stage serial accounts with an allowance for the overlapping operation of some processes, emphasising the limits on overall capacity shared between distinct processes variously described as listening (or decoding), analysing (converting, rehearsing), storage, and reconstitution (recoding, production).

The earliest attempt at a complete processing model for SI is Gerver's (1976). Both this model and Moser's (1976) are based on Massaro's (1975) model of information processing for speech comprehension, and rely on theories of human cognitive functions, including speech processing, as limited-capacity systems with procedures to increase capacity by rehearsal or recoding (Miller 1956). IP approaches tend to emphasise the difficulty and complexity of SI, viewing it as a case of multitasking in which most or all of the component processes, as well as coordination, are effort-consuming and capacity-constrained:

> 'the central process of interpretation encompasses listening, processing of the original discourse and its restitution in the target language, with operations of linguistic decoding, bringing into play different types of memory, and language production. This [...] implies attention-sharing, and decision-taking, with the management of risks and difficulties' (Gile 1995: 17).

The Message to be conveyed, and the fidelity of the product, are viewed in terms of information, and the grammatical structure of input is predicted to be a significant factor in processing difficulty.

Massaro (1978) claims that 'almost every aspect of IP is relevant to SI: an interpreter must decode the surface structure of the original message, map it into some abstract representation, take this same abstract representation and map it into a surface structure, and finally articulate the translated message'. Some unique or novel skills must be involved in SI in his view, 'since time-sharing and parallel processing are necessary as in normal speech processing, but with two languages' (1978: 300).

Massaro (and Moser) model several steps in speech processing: feature detection is accomplished within 250 ms, then a multiple-stage parsing process, subject to feedback from context, yields meaningful phrases (syntactic-semantic structures) which are recoded and rehearsed, and passed through a LTM-resident network of conceptual nodes with different perceptual attributes for each language, to production. The extra perceptual codes for polyglots require postulating a filter and switching mechanism, since reaction times are no slower than in monolingual subjects. Rehearsal and recoding 'are the workhorses of the

SI task [...] and it is at this stage that the task becomes unique relative to normal language processing' (Massaro 1978).

Meaningful units appear to remain in linguistic or quasi-linguistic form throughout the process: according to Massaro, although working memory[12] is assumed to be abstract relative to auditory memory, 'the nature of the information appears to be tied to the surface structure of the language rather than underlying meaning that is language-independent'. Massaro declines to speculate on the representation of these meaningful units in working memory or their integration with non-text information; but some structural features apparently persist through the process, since success 'depends on how quickly original units of the message can be recoded into their appropriate transformations' (1978: 310).

While the IP source models are basically serial, the SI applications allow some overlap: storage, retrieval and formulation can function in parallel within a processing capacity ceiling. Moser's (1976) model of SI appears to locate both parsing (decoding) and rehearsal processes in working memory, which has a limited capacity of 7 ± 2 chunks of information (Miller 1956; Moser 1976: 44). These processes have access to everything in long-term memory (LTM), including semantic rules, syntactic rules, general knowledge, conceptual knowledge, and situational context.

5 The Effort Model: a processing capacity account

Gile (1985, 1990, 1995, 1997) emphasises the difficulties and efforts involved in the SI task and the strategies needed to overcome them, observing that many failures occur in the absence of any visible difficulty due to environmental conditions, terminology, the Speaker's line of reasoning or syntactic complexity (1995: 88). In line with models of the mind as a limited-capacity information channel, Gile assumes that most of the cognitive processes involved in SI compete for resources, and that the difficulties of SI stem from the pressure of time, the interpreter's short 'horizon' in terms of segments available for processing, and the need to divide attention (ibid.: 91). Gile adopts a wide definition of processes which, according to psycholinguists, cannot become progressively learned and automatic:

'the receipt of a brief stimulus; the recording of an unfamiliar stimulus in unfavourable conditions; the storage of a datum for later use; non-automatic responses; controlling the precision of a gesture; and general cognitive operations involving the symbolic system' (Richard 1980, cited in Gile 1995: 91-2).[13]

He declines to speculate on the nature of intermediate processing, focussing on resources: 'we do not know how the passage from reception in one language and production of another proceeds mentally [...] but we can assume that coordination between the two languages requires an effort.' On this basis he postulates three distinct 'efforts' in cross-linguistic interpretation:

1. Listening and Analysis (L), including

    'all the mental operations between perception of a discourse by auditory mechanisms and the moment at which the interpreter either assigns, or decides not to assign, a meaning (or several potential meanings) to the segment which he has heard.'

2. Production (P), including

    'all the mental operations between the moment at which the interpreter decides to convey a datum or an idea and the moment at which he articulates (overtly produces) the form he has prepared to do so.'

3. Short-term memory (M), including

    'all the mental operations related to storage in memory of heard segments of discourse until either their restitution in the target language, their loss if they vanish from memory, or a decision by the interpreter not to interpret them.' (1995: 93).

Gile claims that listening and analysis, though fast and unconscious, cannot be 'automatic' (i.e. resource-free), since STM storage is required for comparison with LTM data to make interpretive decisions. Memory effort is assumed to stem from the need to store the words of a proposition until the hearer receives the end of that proposition. The storage of information is claimed to be particularly expensive in SI, since both the volume of information and the pace of storage and retrieval are imposed by the Speaker (ibid.: 97-98). Production in SI may be taxed in four ways: by any knowledge deficit, or lexical retrieval, 'especially when a paraphrase is required'; external pacing by the Speaker; 'short-horizon' constraints, such as phrasing neutral sentence openings, and forced reanalysis, or 'struggling with unexpected sentence-endings'; and resistance to linguistic (morphological) interference (interlanguage).

On the other hand, effort may be reduced with respect to normal speech comprehension—although with a potential risk—by following the Speaker's syntax and lexical choices, the latter being possible chiefly with cognate terms, notably in technical meetings.

The Effort Model assumes the general (but not pure) additionality of the efforts L (Listening) + M (Memory) + P (Production) + C (Coordination) in the SI task, it being understood that at any time the various efforts are operating on different segments. The total *required* processing capacity at any time is thus highly variable, depending on the needs of the segments being processed; and the total *available* capacity, though finite, may also vary. Successful performance requires not only that L+M+P+C be less than the Total Available Processing Capacity (TAPC), but also that each of the four specialised capacities is adequate to its allotted task, i.e. that L (Listening) > A(L) (available for Listening), M (Memory) > A(M) (available for memory), etc. Failure may thus occur in the event of either overall saturation of the TAPC, or a temporary lack of capacity for one of the tasks. Gile reports that the latter problem is more common in beginners, due to coordination problems, but may also occur with professionals faced with sudden peaks in complexity.

Recovery before error is possible in both cases by a prompt transfer of resources: e.g. if a current segment is redundant, a previous segment can be kept longer in STM to give time for formulation; or, if a word is missed in formulation but stays remanent, it can be retrieved later during a subsequent lull in the listening effort; or else, to free up resources, the interpreter can fall back on paraphrase instead of the full translation of a string.

Processing capacity failures are predicted to cause a knock-on effect which emerges downstream of the segment concerned; for instance,

- a string may be missed when effort is shifted to the retrieval of an elusive TL word (Production) at the expense of Listening; or
- extra attention to Listening (to a Speaker with a thick accent, for example) may detract from Production, which slows delivery and increases the lag, overloading Memory; or
- attending to Production to remedy this may in turn cause the interpreter to miss some input (Listening) (1995: 102-3).

Gile identifies two classes of 'triggers' of SI processing failure:

(1)   overload due to high capacity-consuming features, such as
- densely informative strings which tax both listening/analysis and production capacity, notoriously in the case of listings;
- pre-composed written texts which are read out;
- unfamiliar accents;
- unusual or ungrammatical linguistic structures, which tax the listening effort; composite proper nouns [e.g. *'National Grain Farmers Loan and Investment Agency'* (my example)] which are dense in information; and
- syntactic differences requiring reordering, e.g. Noun-Modifier order between English (Head-final) and French (Head-initial), as for instance for composite NPs like the one above.

(2)   features vulnerable to lapses of attention, e.g. short non-redundant items
       such as numbers or short proper names, which are very often missed by
       interpreters (Gile 1984; 1995: 108).

Gile acknowledges the difficulty of experimentally verifying the Effort Model,
since observation of these predicted effects is complicated by reaction latencies.
Another possibility, direct measurement by physiological indicators, seems no
more promising, since changes in most of these (heart rate, blood pressure, etc.)
are slow compared to cognitive processes: pupil dilation, for instance, follows
'mental load' with a latency of as long as 0.5s. However, Gile reports correlations
found in Finnish studies between physiological indicators and syntactic
complexity of input discourse (Tommola and Niemi 1985, cited in Gile p. 117),
and EEG studies (Kurz 1992a; Petsche 1993 (ibid.)).

       IP theories of interpretation share the assumption of a complex step-by-step
model of comprehension, storage, processing and production in which linguistic
structures never entirely disappear. In Gile's version, almost every processing
operation is assumed to use attentional resources, and many are described directly
in terms of linguistic features of input or output.

       The positive aspects of IP theories include their consistent approach to SI as
a task, their readiness to consult other disciplines and describe SI in terms
compatible with current models in cognitive science, and the effort to address
possible causes of failure and difficulty. However, they offer no cogent account of
intermediate representation, and therefore no consideration of contextualisation or
the economics of central processes. These accounts also focus rather narrowly on
the informative dimension of discourse, leaving aside the illocutionary and
conative dimension. Lastly, the IP community has yet to present a corpus in
support of its theories.

6 The Interpretive Theory of translation (IT) *(théorie du sens)*

The 'interpretive' school of translation studies, based at the ESIT[14] in Paris (e.g.
Seleskovitch[15] 1968, 1975, 1981; Lederer 1981; Seleskovitch and Lederer 1986,
Déjean Le Féal 1982; Donovan 1990; Laplace 1994) has specialised in the study of
oral translation (interpretation), and places translation studies 'in the space between
the (typological) description of language and the study of intentions, which belongs
to literature, psychology or hermeneutics.' Translation science, in this view, should
return to a focus on the interaction between linguistic forms and memory contents
(Seleskovitch 1981: 264-5). IT sees itself as the theory of the thinking interpreter,
and the Paris school is widely respected for its training programme.

The interpretive theory views discourse interpretation as a natural process in which the synthesis between the semantics of an utterance and knowledge external to it produces states of consciousness which correspond to the message (*sens*) (Seleskovitch 1986: 272), and simultaneous interpretation as being achievable with the ordinary speech functions: the difficulty lies not in translation but in the superimposition of the normally separate functions of comprehension and production.

The Paris school stands out among doctrines of translation by its confidence in the translator's ability to identify intended meaning. The IT model of discourse processing rests on two concepts: *sens* and *vouloir-dire* (Speaker's intended meaning), but these are not always clearly distinguished. The constituent elements of utterance meaning *(sens de l'énoncé)* are its linguistic significations and the Speaker-meaning *(vouloir-dire)*; but the object of translation, the *sens*, is 'what the author/speaker deliberately wishes to express'. The apprehension of *sens* may be more or less complete or accurate, but 'is automatic and precedes the analysis of motivations and intent. Understanding *sens* is the manifestation of ordinary human mental function.' (ibid.: 268-270).

IT views the domain of spontaneous comprehension as encompassing the whole of the Speaker's intended meaning; the assembly process is automatic, and unconscious at any level below the *sens*:

'*le sens [...] n'apparaît pas au lecteur comme le résultat d'une construction pierre par pierre, élément sémantique après élément sémantique: c'est l'ensemble des indices pertinents perçus simultanément qui devient prise de conscience du sens...*' (ibid.: 267).[16]

Lederer (1981) describes the medium for this activity in connectionist terms, citing Barbizet (1964): understanding proceeds in a series of '*mini-revelations*' scattered at intervals along the speech string, where words evoke non-linguistically-coded cognitive associations and spark together briefly and uniquely in a 'meta-circuit', a special neural network which functions as a medium for perception, knowledge and action. Parsed input fragments 'mobilise and slightly alter states in the cognitive network, creating a meaning—or in other words, a cognitive memory—which can be expressed in any form and in any language'. As meaning is built up, the building blocks successively disappear: first sounds, then semes (semantic traits), then conceptual units, which melt into the overall sense of the discourse (1981: 147-148).

In discourse comprehension, two processes are postulated, corresponding to two different memories:

(1)   storage of words 'with only linguistic signification' in the immediate
       [phonological] memory, described as a very short term formal memory
       required for sensory identification and integration to existing knowledge.
       Immediate memory is likened to a scroll on which incoming words and
       sounds are displayed briefly (3s) before disappearing; the information they
       carry, however, contributes to the registration (*marquage mnésique*) of
       ideas, or sense-units, in the longer-term 'cognitive' memory.

(2)   synthesis with other than lexical data, into units of *sens* in 'cognitive'
       memory, a longer-span memory which registers ideas by associating them
       with pre-existing concepts (Fr. *notions*) (1981: 120).

Seleskovitch and Lederer rule out the possibility of sentence ambiguity in actual
discourse: '*sens*' is transparent in the act of speech (*parole*).

The lexical knowledge base for the first step in assembling conceptual unit
meaning is described as the '*updated pragmatic meaning*' of words in the discourse,
accessible to a listener with the same knowledge base as the Speaker and defined as
the unique meaning of tokens (words or sentences) in contexts (1981: 185).
Meaning assembly is seen as the fusion of lexical meanings with knowledge about
the denoted entities and relations: 'semantic charge' + 'cognitive complement'
(Lederer 1981, 1990). Two types of context function as disambiguators: linguistic
context disambiguates by suppressing virtual polysemy, while 'cognitive context',
accumulating through discourse (medium-term memory) and life (long-term
memory) neutralises the effect of deviations such as ungrammatical and infelicitous
expression (e.g. with non-native Speakers) (1981: 195-7; 1990).

Lederer's (1981) account of interpretation rests on a three-stage model of
discourse comprehension in which the first two stages are considered to be reflex or
automatic processes, and the last, conscious. These processes are not all clearly
separated, since word-meanings appear to be derived in all stages, and text-external
or prior knowledge is involved from the auditory stage:

1.   sound and word identification (*identification des sons, des vocables [...]
       accompagnée de l'attribution à ces sons de traits significatifs ou sèmes*)
2.   parsing (*construction de la signification linguistique de la phrase compte
       tenu de l'apport sémantique de sa structuration grammaticale*)
3.   synthesis of the input with previous knowledge into successive units of
       '*sens*' (*construction de l'ensemble conceptuel (unité de sens)*). (Lederer
       1981: 115).

Lederer (1981) illustrated this account in a large German-French corpus of
spontaneous or at most semi-rehearsed speech. In SI, all three discourse

comprehension processes are considered to overlap at times in immediate memory. Units of *sens* in SI are either

(a)   semantically self-contained, and can thus be immediately understood and translated, e.g. the word *Further(more)*, by which a Speaker announces he is about to give new information, or

(b)   formed at the '*déclic*', a 'trigger' of comprehension, or moment of dawning, as an item bestows meaning on hitherto unconnected elements.

The synthesis of a meaningful unit (unit of *sens*) from parsing information combined with other knowledge occurs suddenly (ibid.: 144); the exact moment of dawning depends on knowledge, and is therefore predicted to vary between different interpreters working on the same string. As the discourse advances, the synthesis of sense units rests increasingly on information from prior discourse (ibid.: 139). A total of eight mental operations are postulated, with constant switching, but two or more operations are running concurrently at any time. Lederer does not offer a diagram, but the operations are grouped into three categories:

1. Successive and continuously overlapping operations:
   a) hearing
   b) language comprehension
   c) conceptualisation: 'the construction of a cognitive memory by the integration of successive fragments of the speech string with previous knowledge';
   d) enunciation from this memory.
2. Processes which are constantly operating but not always visible:
   a) awareness of situation
   b) self-monitoring.
3. Occasional operations:
   a) transcoding (*transcodage*) of the few technical or proper terms which display one-to-one equivalence across languages, or of opening strings where a unit of *sens* has not yet crystallised;
   b) retrieval of specific terminology from the mental lexicon.
   (adapted from Lederer 1981: 50).

Translation, in the sense of transcoding, is only an occasional operation. 'Translatable' words are defined as only those which 'pass from language into speech without taking on any meaning other than that conferred by the code' (Seleskovitch 1975: 31; cf. Coseriu and Geckler 1980: 48).

Lederer found that the interpreters' production largely reflected a wave-like process marked by successive sudden moments of comprehension (*déclic*), usually preceded by silence or hesitant production and followed by fluent delivery, corresponding to an alternation between phases of linguistic transcoding and spontaneous enunciation of understood concepts. In normal conditions of Speaker delivery, this succession is said to correspond to the alternating use by the interpreter of phonological and cognitive memory in a pendular rhythm. A short EVS (2-4 secs) indicates that information is new and is being treated at a linguistic level; while a longer lag (*décalage*), evidence of anticipation, and formal independence in wording, reveal that understanding is either instantaneous or anticipated, or beyond auditory memory (3-4 s), and that transcoding has been superseded by interpretation proper, which is the expression of integrated concepts (1981: 149-157). In general, Lederer found 'transcoding' to be in operation as Speakers begin new idea units, with interpretation coming fully into play at the ends of such units, and increasingly as the text progresses.

Production may not be completely transparent to these alternations and the engagement of different memories, since the trained interpreter may stall and utter neutral filler material, or compress to avoid falling too far behind. There may be extended strings of words with no clue to *sens*, during which an interpreter may either utter non-committal words, or wait in silence. The non-correspondence between the hesitancy and fluency patterns of synchronous SL and TL passages is explained by the fact that the fluent production of a fully-grasped idea (*unité de sens*) by the interpreter coincides with the hesitant beginnings of the Speaker's next sequence, and vice-versa. Comprehended units, having been cognitively assimilated, can be kept in storage for far longer than the surface-based transcodings, so that for an input string ABCD, where D is a decontextualised or non-associable item, output based on the content of A, B and C may not appear in output until after the equivalent of D.

According to IT, attention is switched partly to either input or production as a function of the interpreter's knowledge: interpreters spontaneously *hear* information, reasoning and affect, and *listen* only for low-probability items to be transcoded, such as unknown proper names, or numerals, as opposed to predictable items such as *'Ladies and Gentlemen'* (Lederer 1981: 75-80; Seleskovitch and Lederer 1989: 154); while a Speaker is summarising known information, predictability is increased, so that attention can be devoted to improving style and fluency, and preferred reordering. The only 'strategy' described is stalling, i.e. uttering non-committal material, guided only by the lexical and syntactic information in the text, until the point at which understanding dawns.

Interpretation proper is seen as the dominant process, and in order to distinguish it emphatically from the occasional transcoding imposed by the SI condition, the IT theorists are reluctant to describe the process of intermediate representation. IT writers generally favour the 'metacircuit' account of Barbizet

(Lederer 1981, Donovan 1990), but in general prefer to say that the message is 'deverbalised' in the association of text meaning with cognitive memory, and that speech is produced from these successive crystallisations of *sens* by an unconscious programme at non-verbal level. Seleskovitch recognises the operation of automatic parsing, but rejects the idea of a deep (linguistic) structure: 'instead, there is a sensorimotor intelligence which coordinates speech as it coordinates muscles for movement.' (Seleskovitch 1986: 276). The model deliberately leaves the inter-mediate stage of cognitive processing unspecified, in contrast with IP theories which see a conceptual-semantic network, integrated with a cross-linguistic lexicon, through which the interpreter has to find her way.

IT does not break down SI processing into separate efforts: SI is tiring to the extent that the interpreter maintains coherence by attending to all the 'cognitive indicators' in the previous discourse (Selekovitch and Lederer 1989: 151). The only specific effort mentioned is resistance to interference from the SL forms, to which self-monitoring must be specially attuned (1981: 105). Good interpretation may in fact be more difficult from close cognate languages like French and Italian (Seleskovitch, p.c.).

There is no general discussion of failure in SI, but some errors in the corpus are reported as evidence of the dominance of global cognitive over linguistic processing, in which 'the interpreter is reasoning as much on the basis of what he has said as on what he hears, consulting the input only episodically.' However, the theory of the '*déclic,*' as a kind of watershed between decoding/stalling and fluent confident production, also predicts more on-line recasting than appears in the corpus.[17]

A second idealisation lies in assumptions about language proficiency: IT does not entertain the possibility that limitations in the interpreter's expressive ability might bias production toward what he is able to express most comfortably (cf. Le Ny 1978). IT is therefore of limited application in the training of interpreters working into non-native languages.

7 SI in *Allgemeine Translationstheorie* (ATT) ('General Translation Theory')

Writers in the German-speaking community have largely been concerned to preserve a link between interpretation research and general translation studies (*Translations(wissenschaft)*) (e.g. Wilss 1978; Stenzl 1983). Pöchhacker (1994) analyses a substantial SI corpus from a three-day international conference with the tools of the influential *Allgemeine Translationstheorie* (ATT) against the background of the event and local discourse situations.

ATT has developed in the last ten years from broadly Functionalist and text-linguistic origins, as a fusion of *skopos* theory (e.g. Reiss and Vermeer 1984) and the *gestalt*-like theory of 'translational activity' (*translatorisches Handeln*) which views translation as an act of communication 'set in a web of functionally structured elements' (Holz-Mänttäri 1981, 1984 cited by Pöchhacker). *Skopos* theory postulates a hierarchy of universal principles of translation 'beyond time and culture', the highest being the *skopos* rule: translation is action, the main driver of which is its purpose (*Zweck*).[18] At a lower level, a 'sociological' sub-rule states that purpose is dependent on the receiver, and a 'coherence rule', which determines comprehensibility, is ranked accordingly: a translation must be coherent, first and foremost in itself, and as far as possible, with the original. The last level of rules are non-universal specifications of translation procedures. In ATT, translation is defined as 'a functionally-oriented act (*Handlung*) of (imitative) cultural transfer' and authors in this tradition generally approach text through its function in a top-down approach (e.g. Nord 1993).

Pöchhacker (1994) adopts the main ATT principles—translation as action, the criteria of purpose and receiver orientation, and the priority given to the *intratextual* coherence of the target text—and their methodological consequence: the need first to identify the overall sphere of action (*Gefüge*), and thence the goal of the specific communicative act, and the requirements for its translation. The stated objective of the study is to offer a 'macroprocess and product-oriented' analysis, to counterbalance what the author sees as some researchers' fixation on the mental microprocesses of SI on line, and to address the issue of interpretation quality. But as he moves down in the analysis of the conference from the 'Hypertext' or *skopos* level (the Conference event) through the Situation (each conference session) to the Text, he finds ATT short on methodology for the analysis of oral texts produced in a shared situation. Examples from the SI corpus demonstrate the effect on interpretation of conference conditions (e.g. the interpreters' access to information) and situational factors (e.g. paraverbal events in the meeting room). At the lowest level, Pöchhacker proposes a typology of oral texts based on features like spontaneity, information density, 'mediality' (e.g. the use of audiovisual aids), speed of delivery and speech errors.

This honest, global approach demonstrates the inadequacy of text-bound, 'equivalence' measures of quality, but does not quite achieve a counter-proposal: the notion of functionality *in* texts is not specified clearly enough to compare the content and impact of the 'Message' in input and output, and Pöchhacker does not attempt it. The missing link appears to lie at ATT's second-level principles of receiver orientation and coherence: the coherence of a text to its hearer depends on cognitive and volitional variables, summarised in Pöchhacker's terms as the hearer's 'horizons' (knowledge and socio-culture) and 'perspective' (orientation and intentionality), which cannot be reliably determined. The impasse is reflected in the discussion of 'context': ATT offers no theoretical way of deriving the 'subjective' context defined in part by the participants' horizons and perspectives, from 'objective' context (as recorded on audio, video and in other documentation). Ultimately, then the Functionalist approach comes up against a familiar dead-end when applied to a communicative situation: so many factors are perceived to contribute to understanding (external knowledge, situation, culture, world, individual disposition etc.) that the analyst must fall back on taxonomic descriptions of the text or the event with illustrations of their influence, losing the baby (an account of interpretation) with the 'cognitively impenetrable' bathwater.

8 SI research: evaluation and prospects

The emergence of a 'superdiscipline' of cognitive studies augurs well for interdisciplinary projects on complex phenomena. It is not clear whether research on interpretation can gain recognition as a discipline in itself, or whether this is appropriate. As things stand, the field remains divided as to objectives, methods and assumptions about language and mind, and hence on issues with direct implications for interpreter training and qualification (the traditional driver of the field) such as the 'specificity' of interpretation skills and the influence of typological differences between SL and TL. Before proposing our own 'interdisciplinary' model and methods for corpus analysis in the next two chapters, we conclude this review with some observations on past methodology, a précis of current controversies, and a closer look at the underlying assumptions of existing models in critical areas such as memory and the nature of language in communication.

8.1 Methodology in SI research

Recently the debate has intensified over methodological prerequisites for the plausible study of a phenomenon as dense and complex as SI (Pöchhacker 1994; Gile 1994, 1995; Moser-Mercer 1997). A general consensus appears to be emerging around certain key points: more corpora are needed; observational and experi-mental studies are both necessary, but neither are very useful without some theoretical underpinning; and at least some input from practising interpreters is advisable. The problem remains of handling the multiple variables (text, subject, environment): if too many are excluded, findings cannot be validly applied to actual conference interpretation, while insufficient control or weighting yields at best only vague generalities.

The most influential contemporary approaches (IT, IP, ATT) are explicit about their theoretical premises and their treatment of the different classes of variables, amid lively mutual criticism. In contrast, some research has strayed too far from ecological validity and is difficult to build on or apply because of the loss of control over important variables. Temporal and 'constructed' studies, in particular exhibit the following weaknesses:

1. *Inadequate simulation of conference conditions.* Extrapolation to SI generally is not safe from experiments which confound the following variables:

    • *discourse characteristics and mode of delivery*: some studies have overlooked the difference between pre-recorded readings of written material and spontaneous or semi-prepared speech (Goldman-Eisler 1972; Dillinger 1989);

    • *choice of subjects (interpreter competence)*: performances by beginners or untrained bilinguals (Gerver 1971) are not a safe basis for hypothesising about SI processes;

    • *apparatus*: the use of inappropriate equipment, such as enclosed headphones (Dillinger 1989), which have proven effects on performance (Lambert 1989).

    • *situation*: the effects of the presence and visibility of Speakers and Addressees (real or simulated), and the interpreters' opportunity for contextualisation, are not taken into account.

2. *Inappropriate performance criteria*, lacking a pragmatic dimension, particularly in the definition of errors (Barik 1975; Lambert 1988, 1989). Some psycholinguistic studies have been content with little or no specification of norms for evaluating the translation, making it difficult to interpret certain assertions, e.g. that 'the most successful verbatim translations' came from texts with input rates in a range of 13% to 40% pausing (Goldman-Eisler 1968). Some studies assume comparability with tasks like dichotic listening, recall or shadowing, disregarding the effects on performance of task-specific goals and training (Gerver 1974, Lambert 1989), or extrapolate from findings based on isolated sentences lacking illocution and discourse context (Darò, Lambert and Fabbro 1996).

3. *Impossibility of verification or replication in the absence of a detailed corpus.* This is still a weakness of even the most developed IP-oriented models (Moser 1976, 1978; Gile 1995).

The various schools can be distinguished by the attention given to different classes of variables. Interpreters themselves viewed the early studies focussing on temporal and surface features with a disfavour which went beyond the usual scepticism of the practitioner for the theoretician. Practitioners, even when IP- (or AI-) oriented, stand out in their attention to the situation, the Speaker, the mode of presentation of the discourse, and the professional competence of the interpreter;[19] they insist on the importance of criteria such as the preparedness of the discourse, distinguishing impromptu speech from the recitation of written material (which some IT writers do not even consider to be an act of communication (Déjean Le Féal 1982)); environmental and technical conditions; access to extralinguistic information through documentation, contact with participants and direct visibility of the conference floor.[20] On the other hand, interpreter-researchers tend to downplay or eliminate subject variables (notably the interpreter's competence).

The most influential studies can also be roughly placed along a continuum from the observational to the experimental. IT and ATT-for-interpretation both rely on the analysis of real situated corpora. In IT, the observations feed the theory; in ATT, they test its power. IT is quite explicit about its decisions to control or ignore a particular class of variables: the scope of the investigation is defined *a priori* so that interpreter competence, working conditions and the quality of the product can be taken for granted: it is only interested in analyzing successful interpretation 'experienced by users as a full rendition of the discourse with all its shades of meaning' (Donovan 1990: 19), which is assumed to be achieved when professional interpreters—trained in the necessary skills on a basis of total language competence—are working in proper conditions and with adequate preparation. Lederer's (1981) and Donovan's (1990) corpora address canonical situations in which the input is impromptu (albeit informed) speech, and interpreters are trained, experienced, informed about virtually every aspect of the discourse except the upcoming sentence, and working into their native languages.[21] These environmental and subject variables are thus 'controlled' by choosing conditions in which they fall within an acceptable range of tolerances, rather than attempting to vary them experimentally. IT proposes a cognitive model with some modular features, but its operation in SI is assumed to be too interactive for anything but holistic treatment: 'the most important operation in interpretation, the apprehending of *sens*, would be distorted in any experimental study which aimed to dissociate its components' (Lederer 1981: 114).

In the ATT-inspired approach, as in IT, the variables are held in place, as it were, by the theory, in this case a taxonomic framework of social and psychological relationships. However, Pöchhacker prefers to explore the effects of less-than-ideal aspects of the situation and task conditions: product quality, in particular, is not taken for granted, although the emphasis is still on external factors rather than variations in interpreter competence. But the data reveal a complexity which challenges both the descriptive and explanatory power of the theory.

Gile offers a mix of observational, theoretical and experimental work. He is still less inclined to take interpreter competence for granted, and proposes his theory in part as an explanation for failures. Gile is aware of the complexity of the material, and cautious about methodology and experimental results, recommending a programme of 'small steps', or targeted empirical studies, to advance interpretation research (Gile 1995).

Traditional IP- or AI- oriented work makes do without systematic observation or experiments. Machine interpretation (MI) research rarely refers to human interpreting at all, proceeding directly from theory to implementation (e.g. Kitano 1993), although recently, some MI-oriented papers have appeared which cite human T & I research (Jekat and Klein 1996; Lonsdale 1997).

At the extreme 'empirical' end of the continuum, the most prolific writing on interpreting in the last decade has come from the SSLMIT[22] in Trieste, from perspectives ranging from neurolinguistics to Hallidayan discourse analysis. Some of these studies have been criticised for a lack of ecological validity, or the use of materials, subjects or measures discarded by most researchers as inappropriate (e.g. Barik's error-based fidelity measure). These criticisms may reflect prejudice against work independent of any general theory of translation or interpretation; it remains to be seen what impact such studies will have as contributions to other disciplines.

8.2 Outstanding issues and controversies

The remaining sections of this review examine the state of the art on some key controversial or outstanding issues for an SI theory, and conclude by identifying some of the recurring modelling 'primitives' common to SI theory and cognitive science.

8.2.1 Intermediate representation

Competing theories of SI differ radically in their assumptions about cognitive function and language. IT and IP differ over the process of meaning assembly and the passage from one language to another. IT sees meaning as crystallising in non-linguistic units of understanding, at irregular intervals, in an executive 'metacircuit'; comprehension and production are connected, as are Speaker and interpreter, by a quasi-infallible spark,[23] in which meaning is objective and unambiguous: 'only one interpretation appears, and it is relevant since it is prepared by the shared knowledge and anticipations arising from the unfolding of the discourse' (Seleskovitch 1986: 303). In short, the concept of *sens* is underspecified, and unassailable in that it tacitly conflates utterance-meaning and hearer-meaning (i.e. interpreter-meaning), implying full determinacy and perfect symmetry between brain states; there is no account of how relevant contexts are chosen.[24] The underlying assumption resembles the 'conduit metaphor' according to which

> 'language provides a vehicle for thought, [and] connected words express thoughts, and do so uniquely. You have a thought, you put it into words which will carry the thought, and any sane and sober person who knows the language will be able effortlessly to behold your thought, to get your idea' (Green 1989: 10)

This has generally given way in cognitive linguistics to the view that utterances are more like blueprints, from which much can be inferred, but with no assurance of correctness, and that divining what a Speaker intends the hearer to understand involves real work (Reddy 1979; Green 1989: 10-11).[25]

IP models describe the Message in terms of information and/or linguistic structures. In Moser's model, representations appear to remain close to linguistic form throughout multiple stages of parsing, rehearsing and recoding, and passage through a conceptual network of nodes, with separate language entries (Moser 1976, 1978); it is not clear how compositionality and contextual factors operate. Gile (1995) assumes a two-store model of memory (STM and LTM) but does not speculate on the shape of any process between the perception of words and the involvement of long-term memory.

8.2.2 SI skills and strategies

IT and IP models differ over the psychological mechanisms of SI and over training. IT, for which both central and peripheral processes are spontaneous, does not refer to specific strategies, and sees training essentially as a process of habituation to overlapping speaking and listening. There is no discussion of coordination between analysis, translation and production, nor reference to a resource-consuming storage process, since no limited-capacity store is postulated between short-span auditory ('echoic') memory, and cognitive memory in which 'the synthesis of new information and prior knowledge allows the elaboration of a delayed memory of almost unlimited capacity' (Barbizet 1964: 6, cited in Lederer 1981: 147-8). Attention is assumed to be fully controlled in professionals, as are decisions on output and timing. Errors, other than those due to environmental conditions, are not attributed to failures in on-line coordination, but to either language weaknesses (comprehension or expression), poor SI technique, or (in professionals) a lack of background information.

IP writers are more concerned with the allocation of resources in SI, particularly attention and storage; errors and failure are largely attributed to attentional imbalance caused by problems in listening, memory or production, and resulting bottlenecks. Some writers (not usually interpreters) see SI as a dichotic or multiple task made up of components like listening-while-speaking, analyzing, memorising and translating, and recommend separate training in these sub-tasks (e.g. shadowing) before combining the components (Lambert 1990).

It has become commonplace in the training community to define SI skills (beyond language, listening while speaking, and general knowledge) in terms of a number of acquired 'strategies'.[26] The terms in which they are described reflect the assumptions about how language works which underlie much of contemporary writing on translation and interpretation.

The on-line strategies are commonly defined in terms of the temporal dimension of SI and/or the structure of input. Most textbooks and training programmes (with the exception of IT) teach that SI from SOV languages requires specific skills, which are usually formulated as strategies for countering word-order differences. The four most commonly cited, which we shall address in Chapters 5 and 6, are waiting, stalling, 'chunking' or *saucissonnage* (Ilg 1978) and its Beijing variant 'preserving linearity' (Zhong 1984); and anticipation.

1. *Waiting*: One tactic for handling left-branching or temporarily indeterminate strings in SI is described as 'waiting' for certain constituents, or more context; a simultaneous interpreter may pause for a few seconds without making users feel uncomfortable, especially at 'ideal' (e.g. sentence) breaks in her own discourse.[27]

2. *'Stalling'* involves delaying output by slowing delivery and/or 'padding', the 'production of a string which contributes no new information but fills a silence' (Gile 1995: 130). 'Stalling' is often cited in the literature as a technique by which an interpreter can deal with long-distance dependencies, such as left-branching structures (especially verb-last SL syntax), by 'buying time' without subjecting her listeners to a long and uncomfortable silence.

3. *'Chunking'*, also called *saucissonnage* (Ilg 1978) or 'preserving linearity' (Beijing School), is presented by several authors as a cornerstone of SI technique, and involves producing sentence openings without waiting, or uttering neutral, non-committal material. Gile cites it as a tactic which is used 'when faced with major syntax differences' (1995: 130), but the structural element in the definition varies. Ilg borrows the Prague functionalist framework which divides utterances into Theme and Rheme:

   '[in German-French SI the simultaneous interpreter must] segment the Rheme into little independent, descriptive, circumstantial chunks (*phrasettes*) so that the punchline will also come as an independent, highlighted proposition [...she must] unload whatever comes in with the German sentence in an acceptable

order for a French listener [...] in most cases (according to Martinet) a complex
sentence can be rendered as a series of simple ones' (Ilg 1978).

A form of *saucissonnage,* or pre-emptive segmentation of the input, has been
the main strategy recommended by the Beijing school (Zhong 1984, Zhuang
1991) which trains interpreters in Chinese-English.[28] The technique of *shun yi,*
'translating with the flow' (e.g. Zhuang 1991), or 'preserving linearity' (Zhong
1984), is described by Zhuang as one of three essential techniques for
interpreting from Chinese into English, along with anticipation (*yuce*) and
storage (*chucun*). Zhuang defines *shunyi* as 'flexibly selecting English words
and phrases to follow closely the order of the Chinese original; this sometimes
sounds awkward, but it is still tolerable' (1991: 24; my translation). In
Zhong's terms (1984),

> 'the peculiar condition of simultaneity [...] virtually rules out the possibility of
> a drastic recasting or restructuring of the sentences in the target language [...]
> the interpreters should as far as possible [...] put across the idea without
> recasting, which invariably affects one's listening to the next part of the speech
> [...] in other words [...] wherever possible the simultaneous interpreter should
> try to follow the basic sentence structure of the original—chopping and
> interpreting one sense group after another and making the sense groups
> coherent in the meantime' (Zhong 1984: 236).

In this technique, the interpreter does not wait for a Noun Phrase (for
example) to be complete, with the result that the final NP Head, when it
comes, is expressed in another form:

Dangqian   guoji   jushi   de zhuyao biaozhi shi....
[NP present international situation [*de* main feature [VP is
(the main feature of the present international situation is...]
.... '*the present world situation is marked by* ...

IT does not talk about 'strategies', but its training manual (Seleskovitch and
Lederer 1989: 148)) gives examples of a similar kind of operation, here
described as '*travailler par sous-unités de sens*' ('working with sub-units of
sens'):

Speaker: **Since the UN was founded over three decades ago...**
*Interpreter: Les Nations-Unies ont été fondées il y a plus de trente ans. Depuis
cette époque ..*
(The UN was founded over thirty years ago. Since then...)

However, it is not clear why in another, similar example, the rendition of the first segment is described as 'transcoding', while the second is 'the re-expression of an idea' (interpretation proper) (ibid.: 155):

> **From the time the General Assembly adopted Resolution 1514, 19 years ago...**
> *Interpreter:La Résolution 1514 <u>a été adoptée</u> il y a 19 ans par l'Assemblée Générale...*
> (Resolution 1514 <u>was adopted</u> 19 years ago by the General Assembly)
>
> **many countries, including mine, have joined the ranks of free and independent nations**
> *...Depuis cette époque nombre de pays, dont le mien, ont accédé à l'indépendance.*
> (...Since that time many countries, including mine, have gained independence).

4. *'Anticipation':* simultaneous interpreters often produce a sentence constituent—a main verb, for example—before any equivalent constituent has appeared in the SL input. Anticipation has been described in SI research as a strategy typically used for countering verb-last or Head-noun-last structures. Most authors (e.g. Lederer 1981, Gile 1992, 1995) distinguish two different types:

    (a)   'linguistic' or 'syntactic' anticipation, based on the prediction of source discourse continuations from a knowledge of either collocations and formulas (Wilss 1978, Lederer 1981, Gile 1988, Zhuang 1991, e.g. *chengdan....de yiwu* undertake an obligation to...); or 'predictor' words (function words, connectives, and subordinators which provide clues to the role of proposition in the sentence); or selectional categories and case morphology (Gile 1995); or more generally from 'transitional probabilities related to phonological, grammatical, stylistic and other language-related rules' (including, according to Gile, the length of lexical units).

    (b)   'extralinguistic' anticipation, which is based on external knowledge, or 'cognitive complements' (Lederer 1981). In Gile's view, this kind of anticipation, being 'a function of the rhetoric of the discourse and the interpreters' extralinguistic knowledge [...] varies according to situational and personal factors which have been little explored' (ibid.).

In SI, predictive or 'probabilistic' processing—the ability to predict downstream structure or meaning—is viewed by some authors as an indispensable and normal part of discourse comprehension (Kade and Cartellieri 1971; Seleskovitch 1986: 272; Chernov 1992). According to IT, anticipation follows (besides possible predictions from text or language factors) from capturing the *sens*, and is observable in a sudden increased confidence in output (smoother and faster delivery)—the interpreter is liberated from the constraints of input structure and may 'free-wheel' (Lederer 1981: 279). Lederer attributes anticipation to one of three eventualities: (a) the early recognition of a formula; (b) a 'logical sequence of ideas which makes the perception of words almost unnecessary'; and (c) (discursive) arguments or logical sequences which have been heard before, albeit expressed in different terms; she gives several examples (ibid.: 248-9).[29]

Anticipation and chunking are described by IP theorists, and indeed almost all non-IT writers with experience of typologically contrasting languages, as essential strategies for countering left-branching structures (Wilss 1978; Zhuang 1991; Dawrant 1996).

The identification of distinct strategies which might be acquired and applied in SI, and particularly the definition of these strategies in terms of input sentence structure, may result in too constrained a model of SI performance. This 'strategies-against-structures' analysis is tested on our corpus in Chapter 5, and compared in subsequent chapters with a more incremental model of SI as the mature use of two existing abilities: pragmatic competence and cognitive mobilisation.

8.2.3 Language-specific factors

One of the most notorious controversies in interpretation research is the question of whether SI is more difficult in some language pairs than others. IP writers assume a significant effect of input word-order, particularly verb-last structures (Moser 1976), and other language-specific effects (Gile 1995), while IT claims the universality of meaning and effability, and denies the existence of such factors provided only that the interpreter is competent in the two languages.

Of the ten most common SI languages (probably Arabic, Chinese, English, French, German, Italian, Japanese, Portuguese, Russian, Spanish),[30] three (Chinese, German and Japanese) have a significant amount of left-branching or SOV structure, while Arabic exhibits Verb-first forms. Most authors believe that SI is feasible for any pair of languages, but the research community is split into two schools of thought, which we may call the 'bilateralists' and the 'universalists'.[31] The 'bilateralist' view is that SI from a language like German, Japanese or Chinese to English or French is more difficult than the reverse (or French-English or English-French), and requires special strategies. Sentence structure is not claimed to be an *absolute* difficulty for professionals. No-one doubts the role of predictive processes in SI, but the universalists believe that language-specific structural asymmetries are naturally cancelled by the predictive and projective nature of understanding, while 'bilateralists' claim that special strategies are required (Wilss 1978).

Typically, anticipation and *saucissonnage* are recommended as strategic responses to word-order conflicts, and are the main focus of pedagogical writing on SI from these languages (Ilg 1978, Zhong 1994).

IP-oriented theories describe intermediate processes in terms of rehearsal and recoding, in which transformations are never entirely independent of linguistic structure, and so predict a significant effect of SL and TL structural asymmetry (Moser 1976). Gile claims that left-branching structure, and embeddings generally, force 'mental gymnastics' and slow comprehension due to larger STM loads; indeed, outside the IT school, almost all writers on SI with the relevant experience consider SI from such a source language to present particular problems (Wilss 1978, Le Ny 1978, Ilg 1978, Zhong 1984, Kurz 1983, Strolz 1992, Dawrant 1996; and (cited in Gile 1995) Fukuii and Asano 1961, Kunihiro, Nishiyama and Kanayama 1969).

The IT 'universalist' position is that only factors which impair normal comprehension should impair SI, and since no language can be more difficult to process or produce incrementally than any other, typology is irrelevant given the interpreter's competence and some practice. For IT, surface structures disappear and are replaced with non-verbal concepts and 'a meaning is formed in the brain which can be expressed in any language' (Lederer 1981: 147); Seleskovitch defends a position close to the Effability Hypothesis after Jakobson: 'anything which can be said in a language can be expressed in any other, provided that the two languages belong to civilisations having reached a comparable level of development' (1968: 144; cf Coseriu 1980: 48). In the IT view, verb-final structure presents a problem only when processing is reduced to 'decoding' on the basis of grammatical and lexical rules, i.e. 'in conditions of [either] unfamiliarity with the language, [or] lack of background knowledge; due to a wrong technique (word-for-word); or [due to] a lack of prosodic accompaniment, as in recited written discourse (Lederer 1981: 260; Seleskovitch and Lederer 1984: 193, 184). Support for this position is adduced from an experiment conducted by Lederer in which she read contextualised German speech to students, stopping at points in each sentence where the sense seemed to be clear. She found that all the German native-speakers in the class, but only the most proficient non-native-speakers, could fill in the semantic content of the sentence ending (1981: 259).

Other typological factors which have been mentioned as complicating SI include minor word-order differences, such as the left-branching internal structure of complex English NPs (e.g. for SI into French), sparse inflectional morphology, predictable strings or formulas,[32] similar or contrasting etymology or combinatorial semantics, the different latitudes of register and formulation said to be tolerated in different cultures, and cross-cultural or institutional differences (Gile 1995: 200-206).[33] One limited corpus study has addressed the issue of conflicting sentence structure directly in Chinese-English (Dawrant 1996) but empirical investigation is hampered by problems of multivariate comparability across languages, discourses, events and interpreters. Strong claims for or against language-pair specificity therefore remain intuitive and 'holistic' (Gile 1992: 13).

In the linguistics literature, the problem posed by language differences for translatability has been addressed by Keenan (1978a), who examines the case for inferring an Exact Translation Hypothesis (ETH)—'anything that can be said in one natural language can be translated exactly into any other language' from the Effability Hypothesis (EH) according to which 'anything that can be thought can be said'.[34] Keenan demonstrates convincingly that semantic equivalence is not possible in translation, and argues that at most a Weak Effability Hypothesis (WEH) can be defended: 'anything that can be thought can be expressed with sufficient precision for efficient communication'.

Keenan argues that the fundamental limits on exact semantic translation are inherent in the nature of human languages. A human language must be both expressive and efficient: it must 'permit the communication of thoughts in a way that is reasonably efficient relative to the lifespan and cognitive capabilities of human beings'. To be capable of expressing anything which can be thought entirely through overtly encoded linguistic forms (in other words, with no reliance on the hearer's extralinguistic knowledge), a language would have to be impossibly complete and inefficient. Explicit reference assignment would require full NPs throughout instead of pronouns, or an infinite number of pronouns with the obligation on the hearer to remember each assignment code throughout a discourse. Instead, of course, languages use just a few placeholders, and count on hearers' knowledge and inferencing. This naturally leaves scope for referential ambiguity. Similarly, natural languages must display some lexical ambiguity: if all words were required to be semantically unambiguous 'the size of the basic vocabulary would be increased by several orders of magnitude' (ibid.: 162). In order to be efficient, therefore, human languages must be imprecise, but this imprecision in itself assists communicative efficiency: 'not only [must we be able to] talk about an unlimited range of phenomena, but we must be able to do so in an even more diverse range of communication situations.' Only in a formal or artificial language like that of Euclidean geometry, with a small closed set of predicates and a further small set of operations for their combination, is effability traded for precision—a trade that natural language cannot afford and still be useful in communicating in novel situations (ibid.: 163).

Keenan demonstrates that there is no formal unit—word or sentence—at which an Exact Translation Hypothesis could hold. At the individual *word*-level, certain entities or concepts (and the words to describe them) may exist in one but not the other speech community, and in Keenan's view not all these 'semantic gaps' can be handled by explication (ibid.: 175). The *sentence* might be thought, through compositionality of meaning, to provide enough scope to compensate non-equivalence between individual word meanings in the two languages. But in practice, the grammars of some languages allow the explicit encoding in a single sentence of what in others must be left to inference. An attempt to preserve all the semantic properties by factoring them out results in asserting what in the original is only presupposed, or of losing a presupposition. In terms of the semantic properties of sentences, then:

> 'any attempted translation either undershoots or overshoots [exact translation] [i.e.] either the given sentence has certain semantic properties which the purported translations do not, or else [....] the purported translations have certain properties which the original fails to have' (ibid.: 157).

The inevitable changes affect the relationship between the explicit and implicit, as in the case of certain conventional implicatures: the address terms *tu* and *vous* justify different inferences about the Speaker-hearer relationship, so that 'if an utterance of *tu es malade* is a true utterance, we know more about the world than we do from the utterance *you are sick*. Again, the additional information could only be fully translated by explication, or by asserting what in the original is only presupposed.'[35] So

> 'in general, if a putative translation of some sentence into another language presents some of the presuppositions of the original as assertions, we may agree that the translation is not exact (although it may well be good enough for many ordinary purposes...)' (ibid.: 170)

Keenan concludes that regardless of all the skill and talent of a translator in selecting words and structures, in many cases it will be impossible, by dint of the very nature of natural languages, to preserve semantic properties exactly: exact translation is blocked by the double asymmetry between languages (different lexica plus different semantic operations). However, a translation where (inevitably) some meaning is lost, or the information perspective is altered (e.g. a presupposition is either overtly asserted, or sacrificed), may be 'adequate for most purposes'.

Keenan's argument shows that The Weak Effability Hypothesis (and hence a Weak Translation Hypothesis) is therefore the best we can hope for at the semantic level: exact translation is not possible since the message conveyed by a given utterance depends on the hearer's and Speaker's knowledge. We are left with a rather unsatisfactory conclusion as to the potential fidelity of translation, that it can at best be 'adequate for most purposes', which is another way of saying that translation must be 'pragmatic' in the vulgar, unconstrained sense. However, since Keenan's paper, pragmatics has been developed into a more rigorous and precise set of principles; and indeed it follows from his arguments that the cognitive dimension—knowledge—is precisely what can be exploited to make translation effective.

In interpretation, where on-line processing is a factor, a typological principle, also due to Keenan (1978b), tends to support the universalist position on processing different languages if it is extended into a pragmatic dimension. The Principle of Covariation of Functional Equivalents suggests that, even at the semantic level, languages cannot vary as dramatically in the processing strategies they require as purely morphological differences might suggest:

> 'the more a language has of one of the [syntactic or morphological] processes, the less it
> need have of the other. [...] By 'have the same function' we mean 'code the same
> semantic or syntactic information [...]; for example, case-marking and word-order
> restrictions [...] have somewhat the same function of coding grammatical relations, e.g.
> Subject-of, Direct Object-of, etc. The principle predicts that the more we have of one the
> less we need have of the other' (Keenan 1978b: 120, cited in Hawkins 1983: 41).

Thus the rich case-marking and free-word-order of German, for example, 'co-vary' with the opposite characteristics in English.

The two source languages in our corpus, Chinese and German, provide sufficient examples of left-branching and embedded structures to explore the relations between input and output structures in typologically contrasting languages, and illustrate a number of features of Chinese whose effect in SI has not previously been studied. Of these various factors, the significance of sentence morphology can be studied in a corpus, as can the effect of unexpected continuations such as afterthoughts and late modifications to utterance meaning.

9 Old and new concepts in T & I research

Interpreter training and quality assessment are very different objectives from those of pure cognitive science research, and the methods applied to the study of SI will no doubt continue to reflect these different interests. But some conceptual convergence might be achieved through more research into the sources and the details of meaning assembly on line. Some theory of intermediate representation in translation, and closer specification of the pragmatic factors in SI, should improve our understanding of vexed issues such as the mechanisms of simultaneity and the significance of typological factors.

The standard approach to investigating the mechanisms of simultaneity has been to try to characterise the typical EVS, or generalise about what an interpreter needs to start formulating. Opinion seems to have become polarised between those who claim that segmentation units can be defined in terms of linguistic structure (Goldman-Eisler 1972; Wilss 1978; Davidson 1992) and those who insist on an irreducible subjective element (IT). An intermediate and more specified position is possible. In terms of comprehension, if situational and Speaker-related variables have any significance in SI, their role must be traceable in a corpus, and specifically in cues which may guide production, and therefore underlie segmentation.

Against surface segmentation accounts of EVS, IT stresses the importance of context, but has not yet identified it in a corpus in terms of specific cues for formulation. This can be achieved by a more rigorous use of pragmatic concepts such as presupposition, implicature, deixis and intentionality, on which IT remains vague. Lederer (1986: 44) identifies three types of context, all of which are subsumed under 'the implicit': linguistic (compositional meaning), cognitive (ideas which have been evoked by the discourse) and situational (perceptual information accompanying the discourse). In terms of Speaker-related variables, although IT has the concept of *vouloir-dire*, intentionality is confused with perlocution (the *effect* sought), and so is excluded from the theory: Seleskovitch suggests that 'intentionality' is not the preserve of the translator (1986: 132).[36] But the distinction between 'explicature' and 'exegesis' may be less clear-cut and more scalar.[37] As Sperber and Wilson point out, there may be no cut-off point between assumptions strongly backed by the Speaker, and assumptions derived from the utterance but on the hearer's sole responsibility: 'the fiction that there is a clear-cut distinction between wholly determinate, specifically intended inferences and indeterminate, unintended inferences cannot be maintained' (1986: 199).

The dimension of Speaker-related variables may also be obscured or neglected in narrow 'information'-based definitions of the Message adopted by some IP-oriented writers. Gile (1993) distinguishes between 'primary' information, and three kinds of 'secondary information' that is not part of the Message. Under 'secondary information', he cites two categories of involuntary information ((2) and (3)) alongside a dimension which, far from being secondary, is a vital part of intentionality in discourse (1):

1. 'Framing information', the purpose of which is to help guide the receiver towards the message;
2. Linguistically-induced information required by language-specific convention (e.g. 'Mr.', 'Mrs', or 'Ms.' give information about gender and/or marital status, whereas Japanese -*san* does not);
3. 'Personal' information introduced unwittingly by the Speaker ('accent, certain errors, a choice of terms, etc., may reveal information about the Speaker which has nothing to do with the message he wants to convey').

Gile observes that interpreters exhibit strategic priorities, apparently 'conveying information secondary to the Message only in so far as it does not detract from the effect sought' and that in this case, 'framing' and 'personal' information are conveyed first (1995: 125). However, a close analysis of interpreters' responses reveals that 'framing information,' quite unlike involuntary information, is not only useful to interpreters, but is used autonomously by them in their role as speakers; in contrast to the other two categories, it reflects ostension and can be tracked in discourse in the form of ostensive devices, pointers, and constraints on relevance.

The more sophisticated approaches to modelling interpretation reviewed in this Chapter have not been recognisably in step with developments in linguistics and cognitive psychology. The interpretivists (IT) rejected Behaviourism and American Structuralism at the outset, but drew no inspiration from their successors in TGG or experimental psycholinguistics, keeping their sights firmly on *parole*. With pragmatics still in a formative stage, they remained fairly aloof in their convictions about constructive, context-dependent interpretation, recognising affinity only to some work in European structuralist semantics (such as the work of Coseriu or Pottier) and, in line with their pedagogical mission, the developmental constructivism of Piaget.

Research in the information-processing paradigm reflects key principles of the AI-oriented parsing and comprehension models of the 1970s, notably the distinction between automatic and strategic (controlled) processes, and the mixture of rule-based decoding and heuristic strategies which combine in a 'recoding' or 'rehearsal' phase. IP theorists of SI accept the need for parallel processing (Moser-Mercer 1997), but have not drawn on more recent theory, either in regard to cognitive architecture—somewhat surprisingly leaving it to machine interpretation research (e.g. Kitano 1993) to propose distributed parallel models—or speech processing, via models of inference (e.g. Haviland and Clark 1974), cognitive grammars, or prototype, frame or script theory (Fillmore 1982 etc.; Schank and Abelson 1977).

Translation theory has responded to the problem of formal semantic equivalence with attempts to define the 'viability' of translation at some informal level, through parameters such as the text, the situation, equivalent effect on the target language (TL) addressees, or the goal (or '*skopos*') of the communication.

For Chomsky,

'the existence of deep-seated universals [...] implies that all languages are cut to the same pattern, but does not imply that there is any point-to-point correspondence between languages. It does not, for example, imply that there must be some reasonable procedure for translating between languages.' (1965: 30).

Translation theorists do not consider this a deterrent, but have shifted the emphasis from the sign to either the text, the situation, or the response. In Nida's view, the message can be determined and can be rendered in such a way that the message received by the reader is 'the same as that perceived by the original receptors' (Nida and Taber 1969: 202). The German text-linguistics school explores the idea that texts can be classified in terms of their dominant *'skopos'* (goal) expressed in terms of a few basic functions (representative, expressive, and appellative), and that these properties could be identified as pertinent in different discourses, thus guiding prioritisation and the translation process itself (Reiss and Vermeer 1984).

Situation and context are precisely the domains available in SI to bypass the structural-semantic binds inherent in the switch between languages. The observation that translation is possible 'for all reasonable purposes' (Keenan 1978a; Jackendoff 1996), an admission of failure in an idealised formal semantics, is the beginning of translation in the real world, where situation and purpose are integral to communication. The tension between the coding of languages and the novelty of situations is an instance of the tension between any codification and the variations of reality, which (as in the analogous relationship between the law and the unpredictable permutations of human behaviour) must be negotiated by interpretation.

As explained in the introduction, this study presumes to rethink existing cognitive and linguistic models for T & I to begin the analysis of SI afresh with new tools, drawing (for example) on both Chomskyan descriptive theory and pragmatics. But we find ourselves united at a more basic level in grappling with the same recurring primitives. If the inspiration for theories and models of interpretation has been diverse, we find the same problematic characters from the ancient debate on the relations between language and thought returning in different guises. The notion of intentionality recurs in the *vouloir-dire* of IT and the goal-orientation inherent in *skopos*, individualised in Pöchhacker's 'perspective'. Attempts to identify it in the actual speech product find it entwined with Content (Information for IP, *charge sémantique* for IT), and must fall back on a conceptual composite of intent and content: the 'Message' or *sens*. But as we venture from this comfortable theoretical landscape to approach the data, and try for empirically-based models of comprehension, translation and text production, we come up against towering challenges: Knowledge, and its still fuzzy relationship with Context, which in previous usage, seems ambivalently to straddle the objective and the subjective, smeared across the text and the rest of the environment.

Having recognised that a Message comprises Content and Intention, that its reception depends on individual Knowledge and a multilayered Context, and that its transmission through speech must obey different rules in each language, the would-be modeller of interpretation finds that most linguistic models fall rather short. The Chomskyan revolution has transformed our understanding of language, but its powerful ideas about a universal substrate of language have yet to be implemented in a theory of comprehension. Researchers on interpreting have had to reach for conceptual tools from various neighbouring disciplines, but in so doing have used models or concepts which conflict with their own intuitions, and indeed with contemporary knowledge about language—such as the segmentation of the surface speech string, or the classification of figures of speech and text types, which belong to the infinitely variable superficial realisations of speech rather than the conceptual and structural features of the thoughts which drive it. In short, interpretation research has ample room to develop, since it has not really tapped the resources of modern cognitive linguistic theory. In the next Chapter we propose a basic model drawing on some modern theories of meaning and speech processing.

Chapter 3 An Outline Model for SI

1 Introduction

In this Chapter we propose a model for SI based on current theories about the relationship between perception, cognition and action in speech. Such a fundamental inquiry is necessary, since empirical and theoretical studies of translation and interpretation rely inevitably, and sometimes explicitly, on specific models of cognitive function and discourse comprehension. Indeed a significant rift persists within the interpretation research community over what is automatic and what is controlled in the derivation and assembly of meaning, and in expression.

SI demands interdisciplinary treatment, and it seems there is sufficient consensus about human cognition in linguistics, psycholinguistics, and psychology to license some fundamental assumptions at the outset. However, on some aspects of SI, popular mainstream theories may fail us because of unresolved controversy, or too narrow a focus: in the present state of knowledge, a special effort of creative and constructive modelling is needed to describe how cognition adapts itself to complex communication involving extended discourse and multiple participants. This provisional model is therefore necessarily a hybrid of best available theories.

Much of the trouble in agreeing on a basic paradigm stems from the gap between the strong intuitions of practitioners and the apparent predictions of findings in cognitive science, resulting in polarisation between those who have insisted on starting afresh on a holistic basis, and those who have tried to explain SI in terms of findings in related fields. But all the existing accounts of SI, whether they are based on corpus observation or information-processing models, are vague as to how knowledge is integrated with source text meaning.

In dynamic terms, a model for SI must accommodate overlapping comprehension and production at the speed of ordinary discourse, and be equipped with input and output parsing mechanisms valid for any human language, bearing in mind that more meaning is derived and transmitted than what is overtly coded in the surface form of utterances.

It is fair to say that in the current state of knowledge, our assumptions about the workings of peripheral systems, like word recognition and articulation, are more secure than those concerning central processes, which are less accessible to experimentation. The next Section outlines the main sources for the model. Section 3 fixes some basic assumptions about cognitive function which currently enjoy consensus and to some extent reflect biological and evolutionary requirements: they concern constraints and flexibilities in the interplay between perception, cognition and action, and a hypothesis about presentation and representation as the mind's media. The ontogeny of human cognitive function (e.g. developmental and language acquisition issues), and its physical layout (local vs. distributed memory, for example) are set aside as issues on which this study will remain neutral.

SI is a motivated speech comprehension task drawing on all types of audiovisual and cognitive input (Section 4). Speech comprehension must include processes for recognising words and assigning to strings whatever meaning follows from a knowledge of the language and from other indications. The degree of interaction between these processes is a vexed issue and efforts to distinguish the use of language knowledge and context in parsing have had mixed success. After a brief overview of speech processing research in psycholinguistics, Sections 4.3-4.4 describe word recognition and the multilingual lexicon. Section 5 places parsing within a wider process of meaning construction in an 'Assembler'. Sections 6 and 7 describe the role of the mental model in further contextualising the discourse. Section 8 describes the features of a possible language of intermediate representation. Section 9 postulates an Executive as the seat of overall task coordination and judgment. Section 10 describes speech production in SI. Finally, the question of the overall dynamics of SI, and of processing capacity and effort, are foreshadowed in Section 11.

2 Sources for the model

Models of monolingual speech comprehension and production based on findings in psycholinguistics provide us with an initial framework. The human cognitive apparatus has been represented by consensus for over a century as a structure in three tiers, corresponding roughly to sounds, forms and meanings.[1] Modern inputs from cognitive psychology, neurophysiology and linguistics (with the possible exception of Connectionism[2]) have not shaken this basic model: standard texts in psycholinguistics describe language processing in terms of sensory registration, recognition and interpretation on the comprehension side (Clark and Clark 1977), and conceptualisation, encoding and articulation on the production side (Levelt 1989). Our composite SI model (Figure 3.1) reflects this consensus.

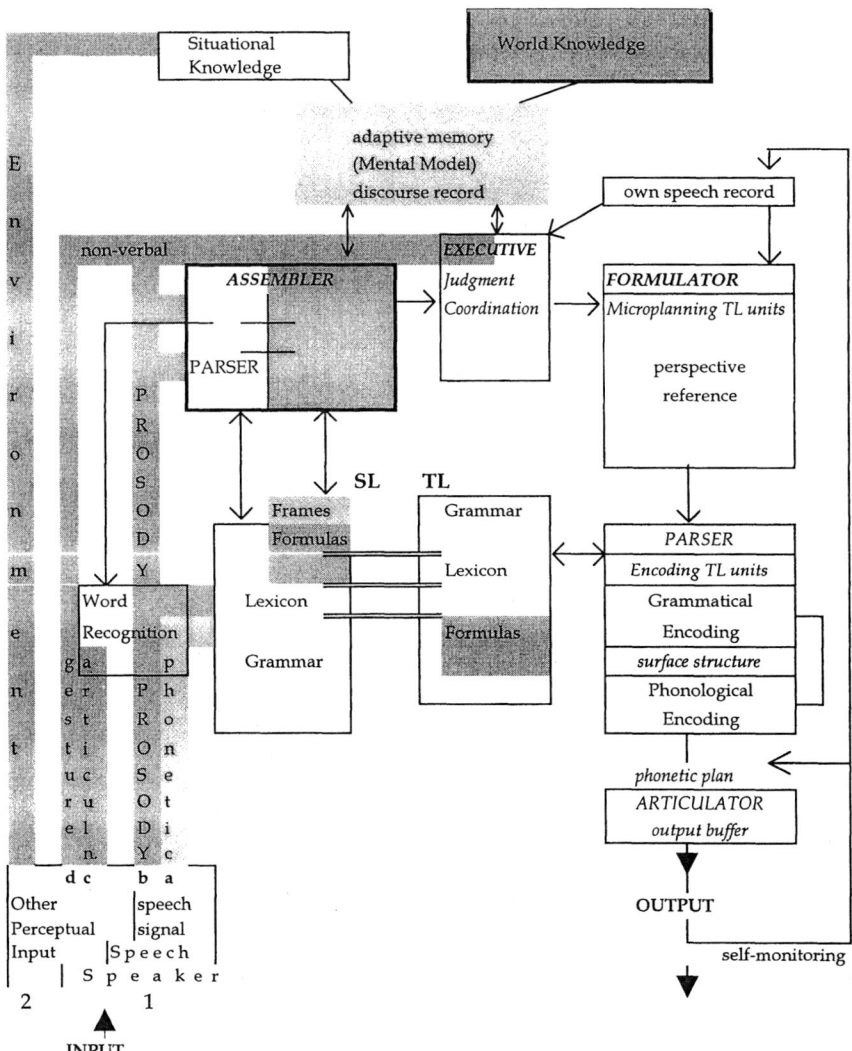

Figure 3.1 A model for simultaneous conference interpretation

The sensorimotor level, shown at the bottom, comprises audiovisual input, on the left, and the articulatory system, to the right. The recognition-retrieval level comprises any and all components which identify basic linguistic units after perception, or select and implement them for production. The upper central level provisionally encompasses whatever contributes further to meaning assembly, including memory, world and local knowledge, and a record of previous discourse.

On this basis we can construct a shell with boxes for perception and phoneme-word recognition and parsing/disambiguation on one side, and formulation-articulation on the other. We can also sketch in stores for grammatical rules and lexica, and world and local (situational) knowledge, whose role in discourse processing is not disputed. It is assumed that discourse comprehension in normal conditions, and *a fortiori* under strong task motivation as in SI, is a fine-grained incremental process, drawing on all available inputs (Marslen-Wilson and Welsh 1978; Altman and Steedman 1988; Garman 1990; etc.); secondly, that the task requires some form of adaptive working memory with powerful selective, representational and mapping functions; and thirdly, that input and output functions are encapsulated, in the sense that the influence on them of central conceptualising processes is limited, i.e. that reanalysing a parsed fragment received, or altering an already assembled articulatory plan, carry a cost.

The architecture of the model draws on several sources. The description of inputs to comprehension is adapted from Garman (1990). Word-recognition is presented as a black box sensitive to some feedback from context (Tyler and Marslen-Wilson 1982). The Assembler subsumes parsing, modelled on the parallel-processing account of Altman and Steedman (1988), and the further enrichment and disambiguation of propositions, which has access to context and frame knowledge (Sperber and Wilson 1986/1995: 180-191; Fillmore 1985). The contents of working memory in the SI task, and the economy of their representation in the form of a mental model, are based on Johnson-Laird (1983) and Garnham (1987); its capacity is flexible along the lines suggested by Just and Carpenter (1992). The production system is adapted from Levelt (1989).

The SL and TL grammatical rule-bases and lexica used for word-recognition and syntactic parsing for input and output are as described in GB theory (Chomsky 1981, 1986), and extended to include stock phrases and formulas. Lexical items also index and evoke frames (Fillmore 1984, 1985), which constitute the socio-cultural and conventional level of competence, or the necessary shared Background for communication (Searle 1983, 1992); frames are therefore pictured as residing in close contact with the lexicon, insofar as they are automatically evoked by input. Further encyclopaedic or world knowledge, which may be invoked to support interpretation, is shown as a long-term memory store in the upper-right-hand corner of the diagram, and is also thought to be organised in frames (Fillmore 1985: 232). Finally, in addition to peripheral processes, an Assembler, a mental model and information stores, the model contains an Executive, located at the junction between input and output. These components are summarised below:

INPUTS:
- Speaker input
- Other audiovisual input
- Interpreter's own speech

PROCESSES:
- Word recognition (including acoustic discrimination of speech, feature detection)
- Assembler, including Parser (captures fragments)
- Executive
- Formulation
- Articulation

ADAPTIVE (WORKING) MEMORY (short to medium-term):
- Activated 'space' encompassing a task-oriented mental model, the Executive, and very short-term echoic memory (not shown), which briefly (3-4s) represents fragments of the contents of the Assembler as auditory traces with whatever elaboration they have achieved within its span.

STORES:
- Linguistic knowledge for SL and TL: rules of grammar, lexicon (linguistic information for words and phrases) and formulas, with cross-linguistic connections.
- Situation knowledge
- World (encyclopaedic) knowledge

The model is a strictly functional and synchronic one, representing the interpreter's competence and functional potential at the time of performance: it is neutral as to the ontogeny of mental function, or its neural architecture; SI data as such does not justify any position on these issues.

This arrangement appears superficially satisfying but remains vague on all the crucial questions: the possible interaction between sub-systems, or competition between them for resources; the absolute and relative limits on their operation; the processes involved in intermediate representation; and the involvement of extralinguistic knowledge, specifically in relation to the passage from one language to another. We must first fix some assumptions about language processing, to clarify the interface between the comprehension and production systems which we have coupled together to model SI, and about the relationship between the peripheral (de/encoding) and central (inferential) levels of the model. These horizontal and vertical relationships are addressed below in two hypotheses.

The issues which we hope to clarify through corpus analysis largely concern details of the contents and operations of parts of this model, patterns of throughput, or the apparent effects of linguistic structures and other discourse features, and so will not greatly affect the general outline. However, some proposals about pragmatic processing, metarepresentation and judgment emerging from the corpus analysis will be presented in a complementary diagram at the end of Chapter 7.

3 Basic assumptions about cognitive function

3.1 The representational hypothesis

Our first assumption, which is relatively uncontroversial in modern cognitive science, is that some form of intermediate representation in the mind[3] is necessary to processing spoken discourse.[4] This follows from two uncontested basic features of human language first demonstrated respectively by Gottlob Frege (1952(1892)) and Ferdinand de Saussure (1972(1916)): the compositionality of meaning derived over language strings, and—a fact dramatically obvious to all translators—the lack of one-to-one correspondence between signifiers in different languages.

The combined effect of these two principles in the process of translation, as singularly revealed in simultaneous interpretation, requires that the mind construct some form of intermediate representation. To render the complex NP *surface diamond drilling program* into French (M. Lederer's example), the translator must select the relevant extensions and assemble them as *programme de forage au diamant en surface* ('program of drilling with diamond on surface').[5] Here the correct relations are inserted as required by the TL with the help of previous knowledge, which might suggest that intermediate representations can be computed in terms of linguistic units corresponding to semantic primitives derived from the text and additional knowledge. That this is not enough is shown by a second example:

Il savait que la vengeance est un plat qui se mange froid.

which might be translated, in a conceivable narrative context, as

Don't get mad, he thought, get even.

In this case, constituents, lexical meanings, semantic features and propositional forms all disappear, suggesting that intermediate representation in language processing cannot be conceived of in purely linguistic terms. Whether or not the representations built in comprehension and translation employ, or correlate with, a 'language of thought', conceived of as a pre-existing or virtual store of concepts and attitudes which has mediated the acquisition of the first language (Fodor 1987), or what it might mean to say that utterances are 'deverbalised,' as claimed in the interpretive theory, will be further discussed in Chapter 6 in connection with the way in which some linguistically less crystallised dimensions of meaning, i.e. attitudes and intentionality, are perceived and expressed in language, as is directly revealed in simultaneous interpretation.

We shall suggest that the processes observed in SI can be partly explained by the hypothesis that a mental model of the situation and the discourse is built up and updated in the interpreter's working memory. The consensus in cognitive science is that such intermediate representations are formed by 'central processes' which are distinct from the peripheral (input and output) systems which analyze speech or encode sentences for speaking or writing.

3.2 The Modularity Hypothesis (MH)

The distinction between input systems and central cognitive processes was accepted at least as early as the last century by pioneers of research into aphasia. The most influential modern version of the modularity hypothesis is given in J. Fodor's *The Modularity of Mind* (1983), and is based on observations of the relationship between cognitive activity and different kinds of perceptual input, including the visual, auditory and tactile systems. Research on language processing, for which modular organisation is proposed at the peripheral stages, must define this division of labour more closely for language-related functions.

The main claim of the MH is that there is a fundamental distinction between the systems which register sensory input and central cognitive functions which infer, evaluate, reason and decide. Central processes are non-modular, but are embedded in, and fed with readable information by, a matrix of subsidiary input systems (perceptual analysers, transducers), one for each of the five senses plus one for language. These input systems are modular in the sense of being computationally autonomous, i.e. not sharing resources with other modules, and informationally encapsulated, which means that they process their specialised inputs without access to other information. This direct route from perception to awareness guarantees that an approximate representation of the organism's environment is rapidly available for evaluation and decision, or reflex action: a trade-off between speed and accuracy which is argued to be the most efficient arrangement from the viewpoint of self-preservation. Strong arguments for informational encapsulation are given from the existence of perceptual illusions.[6]

In language terms, while some processes, like word-recognition, may not be fully informationally encapsulated (see § 4.3 below), speech recognition on the whole remains a highly autonomous process. We know that some mechanism effectively (and not in any way we are aware of) picks out speech from non-speech sounds and other background noise; we cannot *not* perceive to some level of meaning an utterance heard in a language we know. Such automatic perception can only be avoided by deliberately not attending, e.g. by concentrating on something else, and dichotic listening experiments show that even then, unattended systems may continue to operate, though losing access to some central systems (e.g. for memory and recall) (Fodor 1983: 54). Feedback theories of word-recognition concede that contextual constraints cannot prevent the initial accessing of words that do not fit the context (Marslen-Wilson 1987: 87).

Regarding the extent of modularity, it is clear that while a basic representation is delivered automatically, most of the work of utterance interpretation, including the recovery of both the content and speech-act potential of utterances, is done by central processes, which in contrast to input systems, are non-modular and global, drawing on the entire belief system. However, as explained in Chapter 1, we need not conclude that central processes are impenetrable to cognitive modelling, except perhaps for complex reasoning, as in the formation and confirmation of scientific hypotheses (Fodor 1983: 107). We follow Sperber and Wilson in allowing that in the case of utterance interpretation, some hypothesis about context formation and inference is possible, specifically (as outlined in Chapter 1) in the case of the directed temporary use of external knowledge for an interpretation task.

In modelling language-related tasks, we are also concerned with the relationship between the formation of representations and the use of resources of memory or attention. On the one hand, we know that peripheral systems can function simultaneously with little decrement in performance, since we can see and speak at the same time, but it is also widely accepted that mental processes often compete for access to resources variously characterised as attention, short-term memory, or work space (Fodor 1983: 72). The MH recognises that, while the basic architecture is modular as between input and central processes, input may be probed in a directed task when special attention is required. Input systems compute a series of intermediate representations ('interlevels'), of which the lowest levels are completely inaccessible to central processing, and the higher ones only at a cost in memory and attention. In speech comprehension, for example, details of syntax and choice of vocabulary are lost within moments, leaving only the gist, but these details can be recovered within certain limits when there is pressure to fill in gaps in the perceptual input, as may often occur in tasks like memory experiments, or involving special parsing problems such as ambiguities, or in conditions of noise or degraded stimuli. The psychological mechanisms deployed in such conditions are 'not necessarily the same as those which mediate the automatic and fluent processes of normal speech comprehension' (ibid.: 75-6).

In sum, the evidence suggests that some input system, largely informationally encapsulated and autonomous, irresistibly and rapidly delivers a very shallow product of linguistic utterances for further processing, a logical form[7] which probably does not integrate word-definitions, but uses placeholders recognised as morphemic units in the language; and that comprehension beyond this point has access to central processes, which are highly interactive (nonmodular). Parsing, like other input systems, computes immediate, working representations on the basis of minimal data, which are then corrected in light of information in memory and of the simultaneous results of input analysis in other domains. Relevance theory identifies three such complementary processes as disambiguation, reference assignment, and enrichment.

It must be stressed, in view of assumptions found in some accounts of SI and inferences from experiments in cognitive neuropsychology, that the modularity of mind conceived of in this way does not imply either an exact fit between components in the Assembler and linguistically-defined levels of processing, or that any task can be broken down into component sub-tasks.[8]

To illustrate the steps in the SI model, we will take an utterance from our data (Appendix W1/W3: Würzburg S7, lines 87-90) and in the next few Sections, track it through the process of understanding and translation (a key to symbols and abbreviations can be found at the front of the book):

meine kurzen /Worte - @ gliedern sich deshalb auch in diese beiden \Teile
[Gloss: my short words   are-articulated hence also   in   these   two   parts]

4 Inputs to discourse comprehension

4.1 Audiovisual input

Understanding makes use of all available information, including the linguistic signal, other signs from the Speaker, the environment, and information in the hearer's memory about previous discourse and the world in general (Garman 1990: 107). Perceptual input channels are shown as shaded bars in the lower left-hand corner of the diagram (Figure 3.1)[9]; conceptual inputs come from boxes shown at the top.

(1) *Input from a Speaker* comprises the speech signal, with its phonetic and prosodic components (a and b), and other Speaker-related input, including articulatory movements (c), and gestures and facial expressions (d).

The *phonetic string* alone (a) is not generally sufficient for comprehension.[10] *Prosody* (b) accompanies the phonetic string conventionally, as in our example in which the rising and falling contours of /**Worte** and **Teile**, and the pause, are supporting markers of sentence topic and closure respectively. But word-recognition and sentence parsing also use prosodic features: words are distinguished by pitch and tone in many languages, and the intonation contour of an utterance may affect its semantic value, distinguishing for example, in a common British dialect, between different quantifier readings:

> *They don't take out the family silver for* *anyone*
> *They don't take out the family silver for* ~*ANY* /*one* (implying 'not just anyone')

Prosody includes speed and rhythm, which affect perspective and emphasis: a speaker may signal the relative importance of elements by contrasting slow, deliberate articulation with 'throwaway lines'. In short, prosody may affect the interpretation of words and sentences, but also, at the extended utterance (illocutionary) level, contributing rather as the non-verbal accompaniment does to a general impression independent of parsing. In the diagram, the prosodic 'channel' (1b) therefore feeds directly into all these processes.

SI may be severely affected at the speech input stage by acoustic conditions, but far more frequently, in practice, by variant pronunciation or diction. With delegates from over 200 nations obliged to communicate in only six languages, an increasing proportion of speech in international fora (except in the EU) is delivered by non-native speakers of the language concerned.[11]

Speaker-related input may also include (c) *articulatory and associated facial movements* which may influence auditory perception (McGurk and Macdonald 1976), and non-verbal signs like (d) *gestures, facial expressions and posture*, which may carry information relevant to the linguistic message. A Speaker may rely on these expressive resources to express additional sincerity or irony, or simply for emphasis (Garman 1990). In the diagram, the Speaker's articulatory movements are represented simply as contributing directly to word-recognition at some unconscious level.

The interpretation of non-verbal signs from Speakers involves the integration of images, as well as affect and instinct, with conceptual and propositional representations; to simplify, this complex process is shown in the diagram as a channel feeding directly into the Executive (see below) where all input to the SI act converges for selection and commands to the production system. An interpreter may produce words to render the meaning of a gesture; for instance, when a Chairman points to 'recognise' a delegate, and not all listeners are visually attending, she may say 'Guinea-Bissau' or 'yes, Madam (you have the floor)'[12] (The model does not attempt to address the interplay between code and inference in the interpretation of sign languages.)

(2) *Input from the environment*: people, objects and events need to be monitored for clues to comprehension. For example, at the most direct level, an invitation to 'Saito-san' to speak can be rendered felicitously as *Mr.* Saito (not *Ms.*) if the Japanese delegation are seen to be all male. In conferences, discourse often refers deictically to slides and graphic presentations (e.g. '*this* shaded area'; 'on the last slide,' etc.) A clear view of the meeting room is also a condition in standard professional contracts.[13] (Of course, there are several highly competent blind interpreters in the profession; but a discussion of the role of vision in interpreting would take us beyond the scope of this study into the question of the reconfigurability of resources to offset temporary or permanent impairment.)

In the diagram, the 'situational knowledge' box represents a virtual store comprising all accessible local knowledge which may be activated by the interpreter. Much of this is usually acquired deliberately by a study of the conference documents and the conference setting. A professional simultaneous interpreter is assumed to come to her task with some knowledge of the participants and subject-matter of the event, besides a native-equivalent comprehension of the language of the source discourse (SL) and native proficiency as a Speaker of the target language.[14] In standard professional practice such knowledge should be fairly extensive, based on a study of the agenda and programme and written texts provided by Speakers, records of previous meetings and some personal revision of any relevant technical knowledge and terminology.

In the absence of clear evidence that hearers do *not* in any circumstances use any one of these sources to interpret discourse, the potentially useful input would seem to be abundant, and probably, in most circumstances, redundant. This is not to prejudge the relative importance of these different sources under different conditions. In certain forms of communication only some channels may be used: A may ask *How are you feeling?* and B may reply by simply pulling out and displaying a bottle of aspirin (Sperber and Wilson 1986/1995: 26-7). Again, a Speaker may signal the relative weight he wishes to attach to parts of his message simply by varying the speed or volume of articulation (1b); last but not least, the relative contribution to understanding of external knowledge and information from the speech signal itself varies constantly, as we hope to demonstrate for SI tasks.

4.2. Speech processing in psycholinguistics

Psychology and linguistics have converged on contemporary theories of speech comprehension in fits and starts: a brief overview (based largely on Tanenhaus 1988), provides some historical background to the arrangements in our model.

In the 1950s, both linguistics and psychology remained under the extreme empiricist influence of logical positivism: linguistics was largely taxonomic, while behaviourist psychology studied associations of stimulus and response. (Early studies of SI reflected these paradigms, but without quite resisting the temptation to guess at internal psychological events (e.g. Barik 1973)). Following the Chomskyan revolution, psycholinguists tried to show how parsing might use the competence grammar and to analyse sentence comprehension in terms of constituent structures and transformations. But transformationally complex sentences were soon found to be no harder to process than 'simple' ones in which deep and surface structure were close (see Appendix A on parsing theory).

The next generation of models postulated parsing strategies only loosely related to the theoretical grammar, to account for the difficulties experienced by subjects with embedded, ambiguous or 'garden-path' sentences. The link with TG theory was further weakened by experiments which showed that representations for recall do not necessarily reflect clause boundaries, that meaning is remembered better than words, and that subjects' recall reflected their own construction of meaning from inference and other knowledge (Johnson et al. 1973).

The late 1970s and 1980s saw a proliferation of whole-text and 'whole belief system' approaches to language processing alongside the ongoing Chomskyan programme, as cognitive psychology challenged the view of language as a special and distinct faculty (Tanenhaus 1988: 11). The linguistic-conceptual and syntax-semantics boundaries appeared increasingly fuzzy, and various studies on levels below and above it seemed to challenge modularity. Word-recognition experiments showed (e.g. Marslen-Wilson and Welsh 1978) that listeners integrate *all* available information from sensory input and linguistic context within microseconds to identify each incoming word; this research also highlighted the lexicon as the locus of many such interactions. At a 'higher' level, studies on discourse phenomena like anaphora and text cohesion led to more global attempts to model comprehension, which now had to integrate syntactic parsing with a model of the available knowledge and an account of how sentence meaning is affected by context.

In short, while the idea that a set of fixed, hard-wired structures underlie language remains strong, the variations in its use are increasingly seen through our representations of our cultural and interpersonal environment—the proper domain of cognitive psychology—both in a new semantics, related to our models of the world and the culturally determined organisation of our lexica, and in the development of pragmatics, in which aspects of language which do not fit neatly into sentence grammar, like non-literal and implicit meanings, are being explained in terms of our interactions with each other.

The next Sections describe the components we have assembled for the SI model, from the recognition of words, through the syntactic and semantic information they deliver, to the integration of other contextual, non-linguistic information and the formation of conceptual representations.

4.3 Word recognition

The 'informational encapsulation' of linguistic input systems prescribed by a strong version of modularity must be qualified to allow for findings on word-recognition. Marslen-Wilson and Welsh (1978) found that fast shadowers[15] (latency 250 ms— 1s) fluently restored phonemes which had been excised or obscured by noise, and concluded that the primary lexical interpretation is the result of immediate combined interaction between top-down (context-driven) and bottom-up (sensory input-driven) processing:

> 'the fundamental importance of top-down processes, especially those deriving from the sentential and discourse context, is to maximise the efficiency of [...] word-recognition. Word-recognition is thus a self-optimising interactive process; the system uses top-down information to allow it to devote the minimum feasible processing capacity to the detailed interpretation of the incoming acoustic-phonetic input [...] thus processing resources are released for the primary business of understanding the message being communicated.' (1978: 61).

Numerous experiments (e.g. Tyler and Marslen-Wilson 1982) have shown that, in an utterance context, words with an average duration of 400 milliseconds (ms) are recognised within 200 ms, or about half-way through, indicating that contextual effects must be involved in selecting the word among a cohort of several dozen in the language, on average, which begin with the same phonemes. Modern versions of the cohort model (Marslen-Wilson 1987) have clarified the interaction between bottom-up and top-down effects: in a first step, a word-initial cohort is activated from the lexicon, then both sensory and contextual constraints contribute jointly to recognition (1987: 79-80). These findings can be accommodated by viewing the word-recognition box in the diagram as functionally autonomous in the sense that only sensory input initially activates a cohort from the lexicon, and showing the contribution of context to the converging process of selection (within 200 ms of word onset) in a feedback loop from the Assembler, which has access to context. Some contextual effects may act faster than prosodic information (ibid.: 74).

The accuracy with which our data is timed does not authorise any discussion discriminating between processes at this level; word recognition and to a large extent, syntactic parsing proper, must be viewed as black boxes. This study addresses SI processes which begin from the automatic delivery of syntactic representations with immediately evoked basic lexical definitions. In the diagram this point corresponds to the transition from the white to the shaded area in the Assembler.

4.4 The (multilingual) lexicon

Before addressing the most controversial area in speech comprehension—the interplay between syntactic and semantic information—we must specify the contribution of the lexicon and mention some apparent effects of its internal structure on language processing by multilingual subjects.

Evidence from language impairments and speech errors suggests that words and phrases ('listemes') are stored in our mental lexicon in distinct but cross-referenced layers containing semantic, syntactic, morphological, phonological, and orthographic representations for each item (Emmorey & Fromkin 1988). Entries are also partially connected through semantic fields (*type, genre, kind, sort, token...*), derivational links (*type, typical, -otype*), and phonological or visual similarities (*type$_1$/type$_2$, typist, typing > tiepin...*). As we process utterances, many more words are activated, if only temporarily, than those which enter into parsing, and the potential activation does not stop at language boundaries. Comprehension should not be slowed by a knowledge of other languages, since phonetics and phonology filter out words in other languages from their initial phonemes; but lexical activation and suppression are likely to be significant in production (Section 10-11 below). The lexica for the input and output languages are therefore shown in Fig. 3.1 as interconnected (and, as false cognates in the corpus show, there are also unwanted links to words in other languages known to the interpreter: see Chapter 6, note 2).

These associations—both useful and 'parasitic'—are morphological, phonological, orthographic, derivational, or semantic: there is no evidence to suggest associations between words through their syntactic similarities (Emmorey and Fromkin 1988: 124-5). There are therefore strong grounds for distinguishing the syntactic/logical entries for words, which are part of the grammar, from their semantic/conceptual entries, which shade off into world knowledge, in line with the Fillmorean view outlined in Chapter 1. While syntactic lexical information is delivered to the parser automatically, semantic information belongs to a 'negotiated' domain: the first meaning evoked by a word will only be its most publicly shared meaning (its dictionary definition, say) *by default*: the most relevant meanings in a particular discourse will soon acquire the greatest saliency.

Finally, for reasons of efficiency, the Assembler may sometimes short-circuit fragmentary parsing when it recognises a formula or collocation by its first components, just as a word may be identified by its first phonemes. In the diagram, a stock of formulas (stock phrases) is shown as a structured compartment of each lexicon.

5 Assembly: syntax, lexicon and context

Traditionally, the knowledge used to understand utterances has been divided into linguistic and non-linguistic knowledge. Language knowledge is assumed to consist of a grammar and a lexicon, and to be implemented for the decoding (or encoding) of sentences by a parser. In the Chomskyan scheme, the competence grammar is said to be rooted in a universal template ('Principles') for the structure of sentences in all possible human languages ('X-bar' structure with later refinements), adjusted by a set of Parameters defining the particular language concerned. The lexicon specifies rules for the structures words may enter into according to their category (Noun, Verb, Determiner etc., i.e. 'subcategorisation'); and semantic information, which specifies how they may or may not combine in virtue of their meanings ('selectional restrictions'). In Chomsky's famous sentence *Colourless green ideas sleep furiously*, subcategorisation rules are observed (it is 'well-formed') but not selectional restrictions (it is 'semantically anomalous').

Experiments in sentence comprehension have shown that, when any of the syntactic or semantic indeterminacies which are common in language occur in the course of a sentence, we cannot possibly generate all the possible readings and keep them equally available until the ambiguity is resolved: subjects processing 'garden-path' sentences show 'boggle' effects when a contradictory sense emerges, as if one reading was originally committed to, and they then had to backtrack and reanalyse the sentence. Other experiments, however, have shown that some apparently ambiguous sentences are processed without difficulty.

These results have been generally interpreted to mean that speech processing, like the processing of visual perception, is subject to some degree of modularity, although clearly an incoming sentence is not simply fed serially, clause by clause, into modules for syntactic, semantic and contextual processing. However, successive proposals in the vast body of literature which has accumulated over the last half century have not been able to devise a model of the 'context-free' application of language knowledge (rules for lexical subcategorisation and selection, referent indexing and so on) to account satisfactorily for all the data (see Appendix A). Most of these models had attempted to preserve a distinction between syntactic and semantic processing, or at least, between linguistic and non-linguistic knowledge; and most assumed some sort of closure or commitment at the level of each clause or sentence. In recent years, models have been proposed which combine linguistic and non-linguistic knowledge, and admit that elements for comprehension may be carried over from one clause to the next.

We can safely assume that syntactic and semantic information somehow constrain each other and combine in assembling sentence meanings; many suggestions have been advanced about the details, and it may ultimately fall to neuroscience to specify the process exactly. One idea for the 'next', cooperative stage in assembly from logical (syntactic) and lexical-semantic information is thematic structure: for example, if a word is recognised as a Noun in a certain position typical of Subjects, and it could be Animate, it can be projected as the Agent of an action; a Noun with a certain case ending or suffix which begins a German or Japanese sentence can be projected in the role of Patient, Beneficiary, or Instrument. Thematic structure may even have some reality in evolutionary psychology: we may have a small, old, hard-wired set of 'who-does-what-to-whom' templates used in first approximations to a Speaker's meaning, making comprehension faster and more efficient, subject to specification and refinement of the Message by the syntactic and semantic facets of language. Be that as it may, thematic structure is useful as a propositional format combining syntactic and semantic information, and is used in many theories of both competence and performance, from TGG to discourse grammars (e.g. Kintsch and van Dijk 1978; van Dijk and Kintsch 1983), and in Levelt's (1989) account of speech production, where it is proposed as the format for conceptualisation before speaking.

Altman and Steedman (1988) and colleagues have shown convincingly how sentence comprehension may be immediately and strongly affected by factors outside the sentence at hand, and outside the text altogether,[16] and cast doubt on the very possibility of 'context-free' data by demonstrating that choices between alternative readings in cases of attachment ambiguity are loaded by presuppositions about the different referents involved. On this account, not only semantic interpretation but also thematic reference—'integration of the utterance meaning with the discourse model itself'—is incremental: alternatives are initially offered in parallel, and discriminated among by appeal to higher-level referential and contextual information (1988: 192).

This arrangement of parsing and Assembly is 'weakly interactive' in the sense that syntax proposes alternative analyses, from which a reading is selected after consultation of contexts: interpretive processes judge on contextual appropriateness, causing some readings to be abandoned (in contrast to the 'strong' interactive hypothesis in which semantics can *instruct* syntax to pursue some analysis). The course of assembly is 'fine-grained', allowing semantic or cognitive plausibility to weight parser outputs positively or negatively (or rule them out) by the constituent, or even by the word, without compromising modularity (Altman and Steedman 1988: 192; 205-6).

The conventional distinction between linguistic and non-linguistic knowledge is reflected in the hypothesis that the primary human speech-processor is a 'parser' which takes strings of recognised words and phonemes as its input and delivers parsed units to central processes for further interpretation. Various accounts have tried to preserve a serial modular arrangement by proposing subsequent stages, such as a semantic or a thematic processor. Assuming the fine interplay between these processes described above, we propose to call the primary module for building propositional meaning from recognised words and morphemes the 'Assembler'.

An autonomous parser may survive within a module like our Assembler as a sub-component which projects syntactic information for each incoming word, building partial structures which are then either upgraded to thematic structure or ruled out as impossible or implausible by selectional information (semantics) or other knowledge (pragmatics). The parser represents what information it can from the input immediately, but words in the sentence are simultaneously evoking conceptual structures (frames) and 'assumption schemas' (RT) which will then become available to bias representations delivered for enrichment to propositional forms. Automatic syntactic parsing should therefore be viewed as 'prior' to other assembly processes only in the sense that some connections are made automatically and delivered to them for further interpretation.

The syntactic contribution can be represented in TG notation as a parse-tree or bracketed sequence (an abstraction in processing terms, since the whole tree cannot be built, bare of meaning, before semantic information intervenes):

Meine kurzen /Worte - @ **gliedern sich deshalb auch in diese beiden \Teile**
$[_{CP}[_{IP}[_{NP}$ D   A   N$_P$ - $[_{VP}$V-N $[_{I'}$ Adv   Adv $[_{PP}$$_p$ D   Q   N$]]]]]$

The labels on the brackets represent clauses and constituents in the GB (Government-Binding) version of Chomskyan syntax which can be projected from lexical (subcategorisation) information. The first word **Meine**, a Determiner, projects a Noun Phrase (NP) with optional slots for whatever is allowed to intervene in German grammar (adjectives, or an embedded adjectival/participial clause). Its Case (Nominative, Accusative or Vocative) marks the phrase as either

Subject, Object or identifying an Addressee. The meaning of **Worte** rules out 'Vocative', so the phrase can be assumed to be either Agent or Theme. The 'unaccusative' form of the verb **gliedern** <u>sich</u> rules out any Subject-Object relationship, encoding a Property predicated on 'my short words' (Theme).

Syntactic and semantic information combine in this way to build thematic structure, as well as a logical structure or 'anticipatory logical hypothesis' (in RT terminology) as can be illustrated in more complex propositions: words like *If* or *Although*, for instance, would project two clauses. We assume that for each word, recognised within 200 ms, the information presented to Assembly within about half a second (500 ms) includes its syntactic or logical projections (if any), and for a 'content' word, its most salient semantic meaning (by default, the most stable, common, publicly shared meaning, but subject to revision in context).

Let us now assume that basic word meanings have been retrieved, in addition to all available syntactic rules, so that semantically-labelled parsed fragments can now be assembled (again, a complete sentence resolved to this 'level' is a theoretical abstraction, since each word and phrase immediately becomes available for reference assignment or enrichment against the assumptions already in place around the parser):

meine kurzen /Worte 75.6- @ gliedern sich 77 deshalb auch in diese beiden \Teile 78.6
$[_{CP} [_{IP} [_{NP} D \quad A \quad N_P -$ $[_{VP} V\text{-}N$ $[_{I'} Adv \; Adv \; [_{PP\,P} \; D \quad Quantif. N]]]]]$
my short words   are articulated   ('so') ('also')   ...in these two parts

Context (conceptual representations originating from outside this text) is now needed to relate this form to the world: for example, to fix the reference or boundedness of 'my short words' (although the collective plural **Worte** encodes 'connected discourse', as opposed to individual detached words (*Wörter*)). Which discourse? in the past, present or future? The verb **gliedern sich** is in the grammatical 'Present Tense', but that can be used to describe past, future and present events; and German verbs (unlike English) do not distinguish ongoing from completive actions (Aspect). Also, **deshalb** ('because of this') and **auch** indicate the dependence of the relevance of this statement on something in the prior discourse, but on what or how much of it is not encoded.

(It may be objected at this point that many words, phrases and formulas can be translated directly through reliable equivalents stored in the experienced interpreter's memory. Without denying this, we know, from earlier examples and from the limits on exact semantic translation, that such translation of individual items can at most be an accessory to producing a Message which achieves fidelity to the Speaker. Since we also know (from recall experiments, if nothing else) that interpreters understand (can paraphrase) what they have been hearing and saying, we will in any case need a complete account of how a phonetic string is worked up to conceptual representations, and how these are then formulated in another language, even if observation later suggests ways in which this process may be short-circuited.)

The general account of understanding we are following is that of Sperber and Wilson (1986/1995), in which the output from linguistic decoding needs to be enriched to full propositional forms somehow related to the world. One of the necessary operations is the assignment of reference. The grammar provides rules for deciding which pronouns, proper nouns and so on refer to the same or different entities within the sentence, and cognitive or functional grammars propose rules to link them to items elsewhere in the discourse (e.g. Givón 1990); but non-linguistic information is necessary to relate those sentence entities to people and things in the world, helping to choose the most plausible reading in case of ambiguity.

We shall call what can be decoded from syntactic and semantic information as described above the 'semantic representation' (SR) of the sentence. Now as discussed in Chapter 1, the default ('context-free') lexical and logical meanings of the items in a *sentence*, combined and semantically interpreted according to the rules of grammar, fall well short of describing what is communicated by an *utterance* (which includes, of course, a written sentence in context); the SR of a sentence forms a blueprint which does not stand in a one-to-one relation to the situation it describes on any particular occasion it is used (Garnham 1987: 17). The final representation built by a comprehender relies not only on logical and lexical meanings, but also on the inferences and pre-existing assumptions he brings to bear. This observation has been the starting point for modern attempts to model utterance comprehension, from model-theoretic semantics to pragmatics.

Perhaps the most fundamental idea in pragmatics is that it is the presentation of a sentence in a communicative setting (conversation, lecture, book or billboard) which allows a hearer/reader to make use of it. According to Relevance theory, the additional contexts which allow a hearer to 'fill out' the meaning of an utterance are made available to an Addressee with the help of the Speaker. Recent work suggests we can usefully distinguish two phases of pragmatic input to understanding (from inference in contexts). In the primary phase, context and expectations contribute along with syntactic and semantic information to building basic propositional forms, in which the referents and basic truth conditional relations are resolved. In the secondary phase, clues to the communicative intentions of the Speaker, and roughly, to what he considers to be important, complete the understanding of the (extended) utterance, with all its explicatures and implicatures, as a relevant communication.

Primary and secondary pragmatic inputs, though significant theoretically to describe levels of understanding, do not necessarily become available in that temporal sequence. Some elements may be pragmatically enriched while others are still semantically ambiguous (and as already suggested, others yet are still unresolved as to syntactic status). But unresolved material can be translated. To model SI, we have to track all clues, insofar as they can contribute to understanding *and/or* support formulation, in the order in which they become available.

The incremental assembly of meaning over a string of incoming discourse is not an easy process to model graphically. Fig. 3.2 attempts to show some of the ways in which utterances may deliver incomplete information, using the DRT (Discourse Representation Theory) format of Kamp and Reyle (1993) for convenience, but adding an on-line (incremental) dimension and some other features. The examples are chosen to illustrate the various contributions to meaning from (i) syntactic structure, (ii) lexical semantic information, (iii) logical functions like quantification and scope, and (iv) illocutions and attitudes expressed by the Speaker towards the proposition. The first three dimensions are represented in the 'main box' from top to bottom ((i) above, (ii) and (iii) below the string).

The main box in each case shows the core proposition, i.e. in the first example (a), *he was chasing her at the time.* This may fall under the scope of a propositional attitude and/or an illocutionary force (PA and IF brackets at top left). In the first example, the first word *Maybe* encodes an attitude (to the evidentiality of the proposition), and an illocutionary force (a suggestion). The second word, *he*, points to an unknown male referent outside the discourse (animate or inanimate), the Subject of *was chasing*: a pursuit or courtship in the past (e1, durative aspect), although *her* still doesn't tell us if either or both were cats, dogs, or people, or a man and a ship. *At the time* tells us that this action overlapped with some other event or state of affairs (e2).

Parsing proper is straightforward, the syntactic status of each word being resolved within a word or two at most. Semantic information becomes available word by word,

(i)　　from lexical and encyclopaedic entries, shown in bold in the boxes below the words, which tell us only that *he* is masculine, but not that it is human; and that *chasing* involves an (animate) Agent with one or more intentions, and a Goal, both of which must be moving; and

(ii)　　from rules of grammar, for features like Tense, durative aspect, and so on, which are shown at the bottom.

This exhausts the information available automatically to someone *overhearing* the utterance; he may squeeze it for some relevance to himself, and perhaps generate some amusement at the cost of a mild effort imagining ships or past courtships; but he will not get the Message intended, lacking knowledge of the rest of the discourse, and not being the Addressee. He has not been given access to the information required either to relate the basic proposition to a representation of the *(a)"Maybe he was chasing her at the time"*

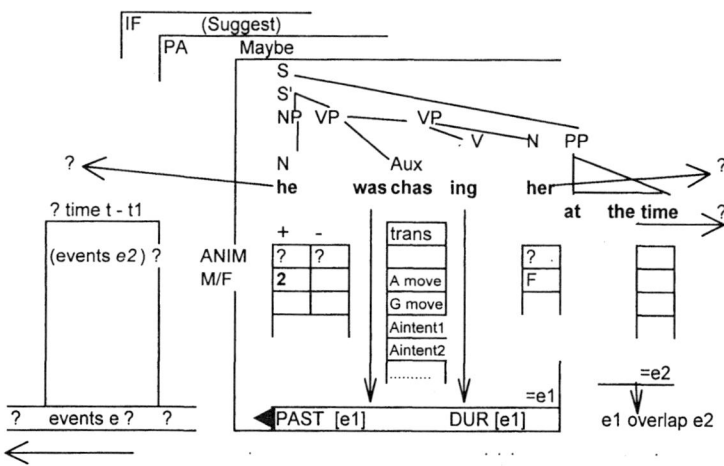

(b) "Funü de canzheng - lishi shizai shi hen duan"
  ('Women participate- politics - history actually very short')

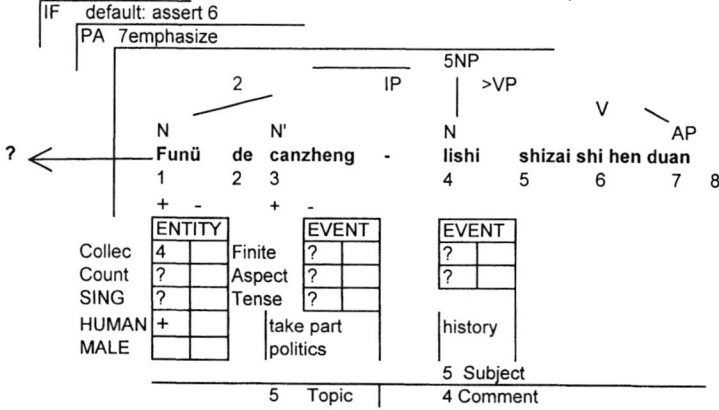

Figure 3.2 Indeterminacy of semantic representation

(c) "Meine kurzen Worte gliedern sich deshalb auch in diese beiden Teile"
('My short words are therefore articulated in these two parts')

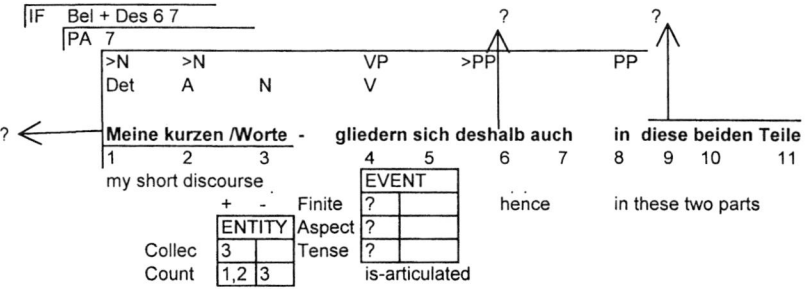

Figure 3.2 Indeterminacy of semantic representation (continued)

world as he knows it (primary pragmatic support), nor to compute its relevance to him (secondary pragmatic support).

Speech strings unfold in ways that allow 'filling in' of different elements of the utterance meaning in different orders. Attitudes and illocutions may be revealed in the first word, e.g. *Maybe,* or only later (*auch; shizai*), and sometimes even in a final verb phrase, e.g. '*.....que bu shi zheyang* (...however is not the case') or some other expression: *'...., frankly.'* In our familiar utterance (Fig. 3.2c), the slots are not filled in such a linear sequence. Its dependent relevance is not made explicit until the 6th and 7th words, **deshalb auch**. The string also contains two NPs with under-determined reference ('my brief remarks...' and 'these two parts').

Different languages tend to leave different aspects of meaning to inference. The second example in Fig. 3.2b, from Chinese, '*Funü canzheng lishi shizai shi hen duan...*' ('Woman participate-in-politics history indeed is very short') was the first line of a speech at a Women's Summit about the history and outlook for the women's movement. A propositional attitude appears at the seventh word *shizai* 'in fact/frankly'; but a range of semantic features which we usually get in English are left unencoded, such as Number, Definiteness, and Collective/Mass/Count status, unmarked on the Noun *funü*, and Tense, unmarked on the Verbs *canzheng, shi.*

The representations in Fig. 3.2 are also incomplete with respect to another dimension which can encode or point to meaning: prosody (and to a far lesser extent, punctuation in written text). Different contours (particularly in English where intonation is a favoured device) could give these strings the force of a question (IF), encode an attitude to all or part of the proposition, or license a range of implicatures—but again, in the absence of context these added features, far from resolving the indeterminacies, would actually raise more questions and virtual boxes outside the SR: *maybe he was chasing HER at the time*; *maybe he was CHASing her at the time*; *maybe HE was chasing HER at the time*; etc.

To return to the model (Fig. 3.1), we can now imagine parsed fragments and skeleton logical forms being passed into the Assembler proper for disambiguation, reference assignment, enrichment and further assembly to fuller propositional forms. This is accomplished by consulting the contexts in the mental model, to which the Assembler in our model has access; these include information not contained in or evoked directly by the immediate utterance, integrated into larger, more permanent conceptual structures established in working memory for the duration of the task.

It should by now be clear that this scheme for comprehension, using top-down and bottom-up information incrementally to build valid but fragmentary representations, removes any special status from syntactic information, as supplied by a clause, for instance. One may at a given point, for instance, have an inkling of the participants in the incoming proposition and the Speaker's attitude towards it (or them). A simultaneous interpreter would prefer to work on whole propositional forms, but this is not always possible, and it is plain that in the case of long sentences, logical structure must be held even while the words have begun to evoke complex associations and contextual matching is in progress. This incremental view of parsing and propositional assembly does not require that structure precedes content, but allows for the appearance of thematic and logical information in varying order for different constituents; no segment can be defined for which a logical form must be assembled before reference is assigned, or vice-versa. In other words, logical and thematic structures are built in parallel, so that either placeholders (as free variables—*something, someone*), or thematic entities are available for early formulation, for example by topicalising them.

In this SI model, the mental model is essentially a dynamic (updatable) store of thematic and relational structures to support the deductive and inferential operations performed in the Assembler. Roughly, it holds temporary beliefs about participants, scenarios, time and place. Access to the mental model, and to frames and formulas, allows incremental strong guesses based on words, phrases and prosodic features.

6 The mental model

A mental model, as briefly described in Chapter 1, offers a good account of the organisation of useful contextual support to utterance interpretation in SI, in maintaining an updated record of the entities, relations and propositions most salient and relevant to the discourse, regardless of whether their origin is implicit or explicit in the text, evoked or invoked as part of a frame, confirmed by direct perception (e.g. objects in the room), or assumed by the interpreter or speaker on evidence of different strengths.

The contents of a mental model are constrained only by our conceptualising ability: it can embody tokens and relations between them; spatial relations; temporal or causal relations (events); or 'content and form adapted to function (e.g. to explain, predict or control)' (Johnson-Laird 1983: 411). Models are assumed to be easier to remember than propositions, because they need more elaboration, but less determinate in that their efficiency depends on assimilating concepts received to those already resident in the interpreter's long-term memory. A mental model deriving from perception is assumed to be simpler than one built from discourse, which has more indeterminacy. This efficiency constraint also leads to some merging of like propositions, and may be a source of error. A crucial point about the mental model is that it does not 'receive' concepts, percepts, or affect from an interlocutor, but builds analogue representations with its own percepts, concepts and affect: communication depends on the quality of this simulation, which in turn depends on the richness of this resident stock of experience.

With access to the mental model, interpretation proper can begin:

Meine kurzen /Worte - @ gliedern sich deshalb auch in diese beiden \Teile
my   short   words   are-articulated hence also   in   these two   parts

In the first phrase of our example, the Definite determiner **meine** signals that the referents are accessible: 'Speaker = self' (the interpreter identifies with the Speaker) is a token in the mental model; as for **Worte,** the only familiar connected discourse associated with the Speaker is his current speech, which is a good candidate for the referent (subject to some qualifying continuation, e.g. 'last week at the Yacht club...'). Indeed this is the maximum determinacy which can be attained for this referent (except perhaps, later, by inference after the Speaker has completed his speech). The definite **diese beiden Teile,** 'these two parts', directs the hearer to search for the most recent compatible 'doublet', installed in the model by '**zwei Komplexe**' 30 seconds previously (S4), and then developed in the two macro-propositions in segments S5 and S6: 'two problem areas in particular (S4) ... the first (S5)... the second... (S6)'. This information about the dependent relevance of all these propositions is necessary to resolve the reference and intentional value of **deshalb** and **auch.** Access to all these discourse features must be postulated to account for the translations produced by the three interpreters:

L90-91   *and I \hope that my - brief presentation will deal with BOTH of these \aspects*

A89-92   and what I have to say -fits - under BOTH of those
         - concepts and \ISSues
B90-92   and therefore I will make -m my- divide my statement into- two PARTS

'My statement', 'my presentation', and 'what I have to say' are based on the same 'Speaker=self-speech' token. The superordinate entity in the discourse model corresponding to the original **Komplexe**, the elliptical NP of 'the first ø' and 'the other ø', and now evoked by **Teile** 'parts,' has acquired attributes in the course of segments S4-S7, which are selected as naturally as the attribute mentioned in the text ('parts'): *those aspects;* those concepts and \ISSues.

The connectivity in **deshalb auch** is recognised in the use of sentential *and*, rather than the VP-attached readings '*also' or '*too' licensed by the logical form and lexical value of **auch**. The intentionality in **auch** is realised in the use of *I \hope that..*, and less directly in what I have to say and I will make...

7 Contextualisation for SI

The overall course of discourse interpretation in this model is 'top-down' insofar as a context is already available to interpreters in advance of input, forming a background for the operation of the parser on successive utterances. This predicts that the interpreter's promptness and confidence in formulating from the output of the Assembler will depend to a considerable extent on its familiarity or compatibility with the context.

Contextualisation is ongoing on the basis of the discourse model and other knowledge, and specified, for each successive utterance, by the previous utterance and by connectives or conative prefixes, sentential adverbials etc., which embed its main proposition.   Contextualisation is part unconscious, part conscious. It is unconscious to the extent that, in communication, and probably all cognitive activity, a mental model is maintained and relevance is sought as a matter or routine:

> 'Speakers and hearers need no more know the Principle of Relevance to communicate than they need know the principles of genetics to reproduce' (Sperber and Wilson 1986/1995: 162).

It is conscious in so far as a simultaneous interpreter knows (increasingly with experience and training) that the context is a (more-or-less) safe source of material for formulation in advance of a full propositional assembly of the current utterance.

This context includes the 'set of assumptions' described in Relevance theory, consisting of assumptions constructed on the basis of previous discourse, against the background of general assumptions about the world and the situation, then the assumptions based on the previous utterance, and finally the partial assumptions currently taking shape, from utterance-initial cues, about the illocution and/or modality of the impending utterance, the authority the Speaker wishes to attribute to it, its intended weight in the ongoing argument, or other indications of how it should be processed. This Speaker-related level of contextualisation may be supplied by a connective (conjunctive or subordinate), by a sentence-adverbial, a prosodic feature, or indeed by the Speaker's facial expression or body-language. These verbal and other cues may prefix the new utterance or be interwoven with it, usually in the opening words.

The mental model integrates and 'saves' those elements of the discourse, and related information from percepts and knowledge (including the interpreter's own beliefs, tagged as such), which are marked as important by the Speaker, or by their successful integrating function—e.g. a piece of extralinguistic knowledge which has served as an essential bridging inference. The discourse record is a vanishing scroll of propositional representations, which fade as its key relations and referents are established in the mental model.

The MM thus presents to the Assembler a set of probable referents, including the current discourse topic (and in a Topic-chain language, the sentence topic) and other salient candidates for the main roles in the next proposition, with their evoked frame information, including local combinatorial lexical meaning and associated encyclopaedic knowledge which has been accessed. The Assembler presents elaborated propositions to the Executive (see arrows in Fig. 3.1) for the final interpretation of their intentionality.

In SI, in which an interpreter identifies with successive Speakers, the mental model must also to some extent represent the Speaker's attitudes and communicative intentionality. The immediate source of production is the last utterance, which is processed in the Assembler, but production draws on both this propositional form and the representations in the model, so the two must be compatible. A common format is proposed in the next Section.

Short-to-medium term memory must retain some logical properties of each clause, or of several previous utterances, for co-processing, such as: an antecedent (protasis) of a hypothetical conditional, to be held until the consequent is parsed; a dependent quantifier; a question (*wh*-operator) with scope still open, etc. Information of various types which has been generated, assembled or retrieved in the process of comprehension may remain and be integrated into the model, with the result that percepts, transitional inferences (including presumably, in order of priority, entailments then stronger and weaker implicatures) may all potentially be reflected in the output.

More than in the case of most ordinary conversation, contextualisation for SI begins before input: the interpreter starts assembling pieces of a situation-discourse model before entering the booth (perhaps weeks before), adding features at an accelerated rate as she gets the agenda, the minutes of the previous meeting, and the list of participants, then sees the meeting room; finally, if her colleague ('booth-mate') starts working first, she is fully contextualised by the time she begins.

8 The language of representation

The Assembler and the mental model must use compatible languages of representation. We suggest that the mental model organises knowledge as assumptions under attitudes, while the Assembler deals in variations on a template utterance compatible with SL grammar and able to accommodate these conceptual structures.

In the mental model, the body of assumptions used for interpretation (context), deriving from both perceptual and conceptual sources, can be seen as a set of propositions under attitudes, with the typical structure

$$\{PA\ \{epr\}\}$$

where PA stands for 'propositional attitude' (*believe that, desire that, hope that* etc.), and {epr} stands for entities-properties-relations. Assumptions or propositions can be entertained as beliefs or desires, e.g.

BEL {epr}: 'the belief that {proposition consisting of *e* and/or *p* and/or r in any combination}';

and indeed as objects of the beliefs and desires of others, by the recursive embedding of mental models.

Structures from the model can be substituted under the illocutions, predications and directives of Speakers if we imagine that the Assembler works within a template universal utterance, parametrised for different languages, and conventionalised by different speech communities, of the form:

$$S \, [\text{Dir} \, [\text{IF} \, [\text{PA}^*[\, \varphi^* \, (\theta \, \{\text{epr}\}) \,] \,]$$

where a Speaker S presents an optionally recursive structure φ^* involving predication(s) of Entities (e), Properties (p) and Relations (r) associated in thematic structures (Agent, Time, Theme, Location, Patient, Instrument, Beneficiary, etc....), part or all of which can be embedded under a propositional attitude, carry an illocutionary force (IF: assertion, request, question, advice, command, suggestion etc.), and be marked by a processing 'directive' Dir (discourse connective/conjunction, focus, prosodic or word-order feature) for its dependent relevance within or beyond the utterance, or its relative strength (evidentiality).

·   Structures in the MM have different inherent strengths depending on whether they originate as percepts, concepts or attitudes. Percepts, as direct evidence for entities and relations from the audiovisual sphere, offer the highest degree of certainty. A dimension of the mental model for the discourse can thus be envisaged—we can call it the 'situation model'—which has the special robust property of being kept salient by analogy with perceptually-sourced imagery (e.g. positions in the conference hall). All deictic indices, including time, place (visually verifiable) and personal (verifiable for the participants present) are monitored automatically, as well as social deixis, 'the encoding of social distinctions that are relative to participant-roles [...as in] choices between pronouns, summons forms or vocatives' (Levinson 1983: 63, following Lyons 1977: 667 ff. and Fillmore 1975) and discourse deixis: 'the use of expressions [...] to refer to some portion of the discourse that contains that utterance [or...] other ways in which the utterance signals its relation to surrounding text.' Elements rooted in the situation, which enjoy the highest degree of strength (verifiability) in that they are backed by percepts, are among those which show the highest degree of autonomy in their use in output by interpreters.

9 The Executive

The Executive in this SI model differs from various Executive or supervisory centres conjectured in cognitive science literature in that, in addition to task coordination, it performs functions related to meaning assembly—specifically, secondary pragmatic processing—but is only a short-term user of working memory, rather than its seat.

Conscious behaviour or action is widely held to require a cognitive component which can plan, learn from mistakes, make decisions, and deal with novel situations.[17] Existing models differ in the degree of control and centralisation of such a component. The Working Memory (WM) model (Baddeley and Hitch 974,

Baddeley 1986, Gathercole and Baddeley 1993) attributes attentional control and task coordination to a core component of WM itself, named the 'Central Executive.' But Norman and Shallice (1980) and Shallice (1988), working mainly from neuropathological data, reject a fully centralised executive system as being too expensive in terms of time and resources, and propose (with evidence from frontal-lobe impairment studies) a three-tier control structure in the cognitive system, comprising two higher levels of supervision and coordination, which have access to representations of the environment and of the organism's intentions and cognitive capacities, and a lower level at which most simple control functions are decentralised to sub-systems, such as phonological, syntactic and semantic processing in the language system (Shallice 1988: 326-7).

This view of language functions as semi-automatic and distinct from decision-making does not adequately cover the pragmatic dimension of a language-related task like SI. The differences between languages mean that text input and other knowledge must necessarily be integrated at a fairly abstract level. But if an interpreter is to be coherent, what she says, and how, when and how much, depend not only on this integrated meaning, but also on the form and content of what she has just said, the plausibility of the representations she receives, the time she has available, the attentional demands of the current input, and her own perception of her task.

In our model the Executive is the only component with access to all these inputs, and is responsible for overall control of the delivery of meaning for action, specifically:

(1) *Secondary Pragmatic Assembly*: evaluating the match between propositions and the Speaker's assumed intentionality, and their plausibility in this light. The strengths of assumptions not directly perceptually-based are adjusted according to Relevance theory. Decisions to give voice to inferences are in part conscious and subject to judgments, although given the possible permutations of language, they could only very exceptionally become generalised as strategies. Such judgments may be driven by task imperatives, as suggested in Chapter 1: in producing an SI version, bits needed for a satisfactory whole utterance may be delayed, while implicit material or evoked frame information may at times be available and seem appropriate for formulation. 'Omissions' may therefore be due either to judgments about relevance or importance, or to processing failure.

(2) *Addressee Orientation*: elaborating, or eliminating redundancy, based on a record of own previous speech, adjusted in the light of any particular task parameters, such as a knowledge of what is expected by Addressees.[18] A simultaneous interpreter has some control, and her

responsibility is enshrined in her working conditions.[19] This involves decisions to select, eliminate, tone down or highlight elements. Whether an item is worth incorporating in production depends on the interpreter's own conscious or unconscious definition of her task (which elements are deemed redundant seems to vary individually), but also on some specific local factors, including her own previous discourse; she may, for example, already have anticipated something by natural inference.

(3) *Compensation*: compensating on-line as far as possible for any vagueness or dilution of the Speaker's meaning due to the interpreter's own forced approximations to incoming meaning, for instance by instructing the production system to assign focus or intonational stress;

(4) *Production Control*: directing other production parameters such as speed, volume, voice modulation, etc.

To what extent does an interpreter, who is both more and less than a hearer, become a Speaker? Our hypothesis, in line with recent work in Relevance theory, is that hearers do not incorporate the directive and procedural elements in speech, like *but, after all, let's remember that,* and stress or word order variations, into their conceptual representations: such elements merely adjust the saliency of the content and direct us to inferences. The natural tendency for interpreters *qua* hearers (trainees, for example) is therefore not to represent and carry over this pragmatic dimension. Their success in delivering speech with appropriate ostensive direction will be a function of professional skill, comprising both passive (SL) and active (TL) pragmatic competence as well as SI coordination: the ability to derive the range of implicatures and provide access to it using the ostensive devices of the target language. Hence many trainees at first either merely report what content they have extracted, losing the ostensive guidance, or translate the SL procedural devices as if they encoded content, with infelicitous results.

10 Speech production in SI

Speech production has been less studied than comprehension, being much more difficult to manipulate experimentally. A symmetrical arrangement of speech perception and production is inadequate, since hearers and Speakers have access to different kinds of information.

Production in SI cannot be straightforwardly modelled from accounts of sovereign speech. Before Levelt (1989) the most influential account was perhaps Clark and Clark (1977), in which speaking was described in a number of steps: a speaker

(1)   conceives an **intention** to convey a message;
(2)   forms a **discourse plan** in line with the type of discourse (genre) he/she is participating in;
(3)   forms a **sentence plan**, deciding on formulation as a direct or indirect speech act (e.g. a request by means of a question, or a complaint by means of a question), on the item to occupy Subject role, the position of the given and new information, and any subordinations;
(4)   forms **constituent plans** for phrasal constituents, picks words and phrases to inhabit each constituent and arranges the constituents in the right order: 'although the global form may be planned, subjects normally select specific words only phrase by phrase';
(5)   as words are selected, forms a **programme for articulation** in a memory buffer capable of holding all the words of a planned constituent at once, with representations of phonetic segments, stress and intonation pattern.
(6)   **enunciates** according to the articulatory program. (1977: 226)

An interpreter could only be said to *conceive an intention to convey a message* (1) in a setting in which she has been given special responsibility and latitude, for example as a negotiator or facilitator, in which case she may choose to add information of her own, for instance to help the case of an applicant for legal aid or asylum. In other cases, major differences in reference or discourse organization norms in the two cultures may require a new, Addressee-oriented *discourse plan* (2) to be formed for the material. Only if this latitude or these differences were very considerable would this voluntary information take the form of a whole 'message', requiring a discourse plan . Such situations may arise in consecutive interpretation and translation, but not in SI.[20] A simultaneous interpreter may frame a whole sentence autonomously (form a *sentence plan* (3)), but may also follow the speaker's sentence plan to the extent that is compatible with her previous sentence, TL rules, etc. But even if she is more or less following the Speaker's structure, she will often be forming *constituent plans* (4) before having a sentence plan (3). However, a constituent may be very long, and she may have to begin *enunciating* a part of it (6) before having the *phonetic programme* for the whole constituent (5) or indeed any part of it (4).

The production side of our model (Fig. 3.1) is based on Levelt's 'blueprint for speaking' (Levelt 1989). This account does not assume that speakers make a discourse plan before speaking, or that pre-verbal messages are necessarily propositional; they may be simple function/argument or thematic structures. Levelt also begins with a Conceptualiser, in which a speaker plans a speech act and a communicative intention, selects and orders appropriate information, and decides on modes of politeness or directness (1989: 5). This pre-verbal message—comprising intentional or motivational forces shaping utterances—is accessible to interpreters and other hearers only via inference. In SI, this 'Conceptualiser' is replaced by the whole apparatus of comprehension (input, contextualisation and assembly) plus that of willed action, judgment and coordination, which we have called the Executive. This marks the turning-point in the interpreter's active autonomy.

The next stage in Levelt's model, **Formulation**, is in two stages, Micro-planning and Encoding. *Microplanning* includes planning an informational perspective for an utterance, by choosing among possible word orders and variants for marking the focus of the utterance against its background, and among possible forms of reference (reduced, definite, anaphora) (ibid.: 1989). All such decisions are based partly on the speaker's (in SI, the interpreter's) record of his (her) own and the interlocutor's (in SI, the Speaker's) previous speech. This is followed by *Encoding*, in which items are retrieved from the lexicon with their syntactic and semantic information ('lemmas' in Levelt's terminology) and assembled into phrases and sub-phrases using parsing sub-systems.

In our model the structures, words and intonations of output are selected to express the combined propositions, attitudes and intentions finalised in the Executive. The precise mechanism of the passage from thought to language is, of course, a holy grail of cognitive science. According to one working hypothesis (in RT for example), concepts index lexical and logical entries containing words and structures for their expression. However, problems remain, firstly, for specifying how attitudes and intentions might index language; and secondly, for accommodating the 'many-to-many' property of concept-language correspon-dence. Our own account, like RT and others, assumes that our potential for conceptual representation is far richer than the vocabulary of any language: the number of concepts we have far outnumbers the words we know, and concepts formed for understanding and speaking (as for thinking) are not confined to those which exactly fit words in the public shared lexicon, but include *ad hoc* concepts to which the available language resources must approximate afresh for formulation (cf. Sperber and Wilson 1998). [21]

These philosophical issues aside, in simultaneous interpretation it is unlikely that all formulation is based purely on representations abstracted to the level of the intermediate 'language' outlined in this chapter. Although we expect the main processing route in successful professional translation to be via conceptual and intentional representations, there must also be several partial short cuts (as there are also multiple additional sources for understanding feeding into stations on the main route). One arrow in our model shows a short cut through which the Executive may take uncontextualised fragments from the Assembler to feed Formulation. In an extreme case of 'mixed-level' operation (which we might call Jabberwocky processing), even a bare phonetic string, assumed from its syntactic position to be a name, acronym or other entity in an unknown language, can be parroted (consciously) into a corresponding syntactic slot in output. Mixed-level processing presumably also yields mixed results; but in our model, these 'half-baked' inputs to formulation transit the Executive and are thus accessible to consciousness (recognisable as such to the interpreter). Other short-circuits may be unwanted and unconscious, requiring special monitoring. The main short-circuit of this 'interference' type of is thought to be lexical, via wanted or unwanted cross-language connections.

Certain reliable correspondences probably stabilise in an experienced interpreter's or translator's multilingual lexicon over the years, in addition to the external lists of specialised terms which she may compile and review for conferences. But interlinguistic activations in our lexica (Section 4.4.) can only partially be brought under our control (for instance through training), and may interfere, since they correspond not only to those SL-TL equivalences which might be useful in translation, but also morphological and phonological affinities independent of semantic correspondence, the famous *faux amis*. Consequently, in polyglots appropriate connections for translation have to be selectively reinforced and maintained. Smith and Tsimpli (1995) describe a 'polyglot savant' with severe impairment to Executive reasoning functions (as shown on other tasks), who, when asked to translate between his many languages, produces false cognates routinely and uncritically.

However, healthy but untrained bilinguals, and to some extent every bilingual, including professional translators, also produce *faux amis*.[22] Most writers on SI have described on-line 'interference' on line between SL and TL. Even the IT theorists, who postulate 'deverbalisation' in all good SI, recognise the pressure due to unwanted activation (perhaps structures as well as individual words), particularly when interpreting between cognate languages, by source language linguistic forms which remain present for a few seconds in auditory memory (Seleskovitch and Lederer 1989: 141). Even L3-based forms appear occasionally in L1-L2 interpretation (for an example in the corpus, see Chapter 5, endnote 2). The intuition that a significant effort is spent resisting such interference is supported in some recent writing on suppression in interpreting (Williams in Moser-Mercer et al. 1997; Gernsbacher and Shlesinger 1997). The cross-linguistic lexical links pictured in the model can be inhibited only imperfectly and at the cost of some training and effort.

IT theory sees production as spontaneous for an interpreter who knows what she wants to say. But the conversion of concepts to words—or of words to words—also depends on pure linguistic performance. Selection and formulation are limited (and probably biased, according to Le Ny 1978) by TL proficiency, i.e. the actual operational range of available constructions, words, phrases and formulas, which will vary significantly between interpreters working into their native language and others. In IP, Gile has modelled lexical retrieval in a gravitational model (Gile 1988, 1993) in which the relative availability of expressions is represented in terms of their distance from a 'nucleus', with each instantiation having a centripetal effect; the active lexicon of interpreters working into a non-mother tongue 'takes on a peculiar shape [...being] both more and less than that of native speakers' (1995: 193). Gile also found that well-formedness drops off in native speakers in the SI condition (Gile 1987 cited in 1995: 195).

Phonological encoding of the string into a *phonetic plan* with a prosodic contour is postulated by Levelt, on the basis of abundant speech-error evidence, as a separate process, with some possible feedback to grammatical assembly. The result, 'internal speech', a phonetic plan consciously accessible to the speaker, is briefly held in an an articulatory buffer, then produced as overt speech. Internal speech may thus be somewhat ahead of **Articulation** (Levelt 1989: 12). In Levelt's model, a syntactic buffer holds the results of grammatical encoding; and an articulatory buffer holds bits of the phonetic plan.

In terms of the cycle of SI production, both IT and IP writers have described the basic rhythm of SI processing as an overlapping, canon-like pattern. In Lederer's account, a fragment W is produced while an incoming fragment X is conceptualised and marked in memory, then this concept (based on X) is formulated while listening to and conceptualising Y, and so on. Levelt's model postulates parallel and incremental processing even in ordinary sovereign speech: word order may not be able to follow thought-order, since the Formulator applies language-specific rules. Kempen and Hoenkamp (1982, cited in Levelt 1989) describe the incremental production cycle in a simple example: *John played / last week / in Amsterdam*. As *John played* is articulated, *last week* is being encoded and *in Amsterdam* is being conceptualised.

Both internal and overt speech are monitored by the Speaker's speech comprehension system. While formulation and articulation are deemed to be largely automatic (wired-in innately or by learning), non-resource sharing, and capable of running in parallel without mutual interference, **Monitoring** is controlled in the sense that it can be enhanced or neglected, and is subject to attentional resources.

In SI, the selection for formulation, and the microplanner's choices (reference and perspective) also depend on the interpreter's immediate previous speech, delivered by a self-monitoring loop shown on the left side of the diagram. There is evidence to suppose that self-monitoring may operate at two levels, pre- and post-articulation. Gerver (1976) observed that interpreters 'appear to be carrying out a monitoring procedure similar to Miller, Galanter and Pribram's (1960) 'test-operate-test-exit' (TOTE) model, i.e. 'generate TL response, test, if approved, utter, test again, if unsuccessful, make a new response''. This hypothesis is supported by evidence from repairs, which are 'usually of the 'retraced false start' type' (Gerver 1976: 199). Accordingly, a self-monitoring loop with these two branches is included in our model. However, we have shown the interpreter's own output as being available to her before she starts formulation, enabling her to make appropriate choices of sentence perspective and reference (full NP, pronoun, etc.) in the Microplanner. The Executive must therefore access some linguistic features of this previous speech. It is reasonable to suppose that this linguistic processing does not interfere with awareness of the conceptual representations in the mental model, but it is less plausible that two directed linguistic processes can run concurrently, i.e. that attention to linguistic coherence in production can coincide with deliberate probing of linguistic features on the comprehension side.

11 Processing capacity and coordination

The mental model account blurs the distinction between short and medium-term memory. It does not assume unlimited capacity of working memory, but does predict wide variations, firstly, in the amount of speech input to which a model can correspond, and generally in the efficiency of representation, with experience. This is compatible with a model like Just and Carpenter's (1992) dynamic constrained-capacity theory of working memory. Just and Carpenter do not see working memory as a component in the traditional sense, but as the sum of elements activated at a given time; the model attempts to accommodate both connectionist and symbolic accounts. Capacity can be expressed as the maximum amount of activation available in working memory to support either storage or processing, so that as long as an element's activation is above some minimum threshold value, it is considered part of working memory (1992: 123). The model provides for a budget-allocation scheme, in which some partial results are forgotten when processing demands are high, and mechanisms for pre-empting such failure by selectively retaining 'only the most recent and most central clauses in an activated form' or 'only the most relevant aspects of world-knowledge'. The effects of practice are explained by increased efficiency in the allocation of the resource (activation), rather than an increase in total capacity. Contextual support is also described in activation terms: 'the stored context might facilitate the processing of the ensuing sentence by pre-activating some concepts, relations and schemas relevant to its comprehension'. What is here presented as a fail-safe mechanism may be seen rather as the main function of working memory in SI, as a mental model which adapts to variations in the saliency of elements in the discourse.

In a coordinated task like SI, processing capacity probably depends on the economy achieved in intermediate representation, provided that attention is not distracted by peripheral problems requiring special efforts. This study focuses on the role of this central, *discourse processing* performance in coordination, via mental modelling and pragmatic competence, which is not to deny the special constraints of certain peripheral, mechanical efforts in SI. For example, Williams suggests that simultaneous interpreters must handle at least one more processing load than sovereign speakers in terms of suppression, since they must selectively suppress both production in SL, and partially (except for self-monitoring), reception in TL (Williams in Moser-Mercer et al. 1997: 138).

This completes our hypothesis about the configuration of understanding and speaking in SI, which has been broadly drawn to accommodate cases in which the interpreter is fully contextualised. The simultaneous interpreter has been presented as highly dependent on inference and hence the availability of contexts, and therefore a greedy user of input cues and other knowledge. It remains to be seen whether a close analysis of corpora confirms this picture and allows an account of SI 'strategies' in terms of more general cognitive and pragmatic principles.

Chapter 4 Research Issues, Corpus, and Methodology

The many variables which might interact in SI make it a methodological challenge. We may adopt Austin's common-sense principle that speech phenomena should be approached globally, but are faced with a dizzying array of possible factors.[1] Gile (1990) lists as parameters whose influence on performance is claimed by professionals: source language, speed of delivery, style, degree of specialisation of the speech, Speaker pronunciation, environmental noise, temperature in the booth, visibility of the Speaker and the conference room, prior knowledge of the subject, general mental condition and state of health of the interpreter, his physical condition, talent, honesty, personal relations between team members, the number of delegates listening to the interpretation, and organisers' and delegates' attitudes towards the interpreters.

Obviously a researcher must choose a focus and a strategy. Most approaches have sorted these factors, implicitly or explicitly, into a few classes of macro-variables and addressed them according to their disciplinary bias. We can roughly distinguish variables related to the speech input ('language-in-text', including style, presentation, delivery etc.); the subject (the interpreter: her competence, intelligence, preparedness and motivation) and the environment (size and character of the audience, feedback, comfort and technical conditions). This study aims to describe cognitive operations in SI and correlate them with texts. We assume that a basic set of such operations can be modelled, and that they can be reliably inferred (if at all) from corpora in which all three classes of variables—interpreters, input and environmental conditions—are in a range of values representative of professional practice. Some natural or deliberate variations, such as the interpreters' preparedness (contextualisation), or the writtenness of input, and the possible role of different languages and discourse structures, are then explored through the interpreters' production. The aim is to establish a core cognitive-linguistic model, a kind of competence baseline for SI, leaving it to other disciplines and projects to establish the effects of different conditions on performance.

There is some controversy about what constitutes scientific method in the study of interpretation. Past approaches to an explanatory account of SI have included:

(a)   introspection by practitioners, which though valuable, is limited to the conscious component;

(b)   top-down adaptations of models of cognition, speech or information processing; and

(c)   the bottom-up recording and commentary of speech products obtained in the defined conditions.

IT has favoured inference from the analysis of corpora; IP, the extrapolation to SI of models in cognitive psychology. An epistemologically 'soft' object of study like human discourse interpretation calls for an approach from both directions: meaning-in-language (based on the data) and functional architecture (based on theories of human cognition). The theoretical sources must be adapted to the object of study: we cannot ignore existing theories of language, but we must embed them in a theory of communication; we cannot ignore current hypotheses about the architecture of cognitive functions, but must allow that these may be configured in a task-specific way for SI.

This study sought to combine bottom-up and top-down approaches, with the help of introspection where appropriate. We concluded from our review of SI research that, firstly, the total corpus base is still too meagre to make progress towards a real explanatory theory; and secondly, that the main differences between researchers stem from fundamentally different assumptions about language processing, and in particular, some hesitancy in addressing the nature of intermediate representation for translation. Our own small contribution to the corpus base highlights structural and typological contrasts between the source and target languages. Like other studies, we shall read the data against our own framework of assumptions, which we have tried to make as explicit as possible in the last Chapter.

We recorded and analysed several SI samples in two language combinations, German-English and Chinese(Putonghua)-English, and compared features of input and output with reference to their relative timing as fixed on the superimposed recordings and synchronised interlinear transcripts. The study as reported here in fact telescopes several abductive steps in the refinement of methodology, in parallel to the development of the model hypothesis. The linear dimension of speech is perhaps the feature which makes SI so interesting and potentially fertile for cognitive studies, since it provides a clear and absolute processing constraint which is absent from reading or translation. Once again, to start from a linguistic segmentation of the speech would be to prejudge the psychological processing reality in *performance* of a theoretical construct describing language *competence*: as we have seen, this correspondence has yet to be demonstrated. The crucial step was therefore the realisation that 'segmentation' must be approached in cognitive terms even though decoding and encoding are constrained by linguistic rules.

This Chapter begins with a summary of the issues explored, followed by a description of the corpus (German-English and Chinese-English) covering the events, discourses, subject matters, languages, SI conditions, recording and transcription procedures, and profiles of the interpreters. Section 3 outlines the methods used in the study and the approach adopted to comparability.

1 Research issues

Many of the controversies in SI research can be traced to assumptions about the central process of transfer of meaning from one language to the other. Does linguistic structure survive in intermediate representation, or does it dissolve? Simply put, the premises for this study against the background of SI research are that if a viable structural correlation can be found between SI input and output, then one must accept the possibility of an intermediate process that manipulates (converts) syntactic structures, perhaps labelled with meanings; in which case the contrasting structures of typologically different languages would be significant, and the doctrine of strategies would have a solid empirical basis. If, on the other hand, the process by which SL becomes TL^2 cannot be reconstructed or modelled in any systematic way, then one is compelled to accept that it is subjective and impenetrable.

The primary aim of this study is to show how SI can be more closely modelled by integrating the operation of context and the intentional, communicative dimension. The following questions—some of which are *leitmotivs* of SI research—address potential indicators accessible through corpus analysis:

1 What kinds of cues are used by simultaneous interpreters ?

Goldman-Eisler (1972) found that interpreters' EVS almost always contained a predicative expression, usually NP + VP; while IT theorists (Lederer 1981, Seleskovitch and Lederer 1986) claim that chunks produced by the interpreter cannot be defined in terms of input, since they are based on a synthesis of text-based meaning and other context. In tracking cues which can be clearly shown to be used by interpreters, we can obtain a more complete view of the SI process. The use of such cues can be inferred from timing and the output; even IT writers, for whom cues are subjective, claim to identify them in the input (Lederer 1981: 121). Evidence can be gathered from any pattern which might be visible in such cues, whether syntactic, as Goldman-Eisler claims (1972), or pragmatic.

2. To what extent does sentence structure affect SI ?

Claims for word-order asymmetry as a major source of difficulty in SI have not been supported by corpus studies except on isolated sentences. Gibson's parsing model (Gibson 1991) assigns processing loads to certain structural properties of sentences, but he recognises that pragmatic and contextual factors might assign other, equally significant loads (or, presumably, relief) which cannot be quantified in the present state of knowledge. We do not attempt to assign such loads, but examine responses to left-branching or embedded structures with special attention to apparent hesitation, boggle effects or processing breakdown, the timing of formulation with respect to input clause boundaries, and semantic dilution as a result of unpacking complex sentences.

3. What kinds of errors or failures reflect coordination problems, which linguistic competence, and which a lack of extralinguistic knowledge ?

Simultaneity is usually assumed to limit interpreters to handling successive (major) propositions as they emerge in the SL string. Difficulties may arise either from the internal complexities of each proposition, or from any re-ordering of the propositions, which burdens short-term-memory. For conference interpreters, in whom SL competence is assumed, problems are not predicted in deriving *proposition-internal* meaning encoded in lexical items and grammar, even if it is complex or technical, given the necessary background knowledge, good acoustic conditions within certain input rate limits (100 wpm for recited written text, 150-200 for spontaneous discourse). This leaves two possible causes of failure: coordination and pragmatic competence. Gile (1995) explains SI failure primarily in terms of coordination problems due to processing effort overloads initially triggered by input features like structural complexity or information density, or by lexical equivalence problems (Gile 1995). Our corpus contains a number of speech and well-formedness errors, and some more serious cases of information loss or communicative failure. Three such cases are analysed, one on recited written text from our corpus, and two from the SI literature.

4. Are differences in structural transformation patterns or the use of cues visible either between language pairs, situations (mock/live) or discourse modes (recited vs. spontaneous oral input)?

The influence of the first of these three variables (language pair) is, of course, controversial; the other two (situation and discourse mode) are interesting in that no-one denies their significance, but they have not been widely investigated. Documenting such differences is a methodological challenge; here they are secondary issues included in the hope of finding some interesting phenomena. They may offer additional insights into the relative importance of pragmatic and syntactic factors.

5. What is the nature of intermediate representation in SI ?

As we have said, SI research has scarcely ventured into this area. In language processing research, the types of representation hypothesised include phonological form, logical form, semantic representation, propositional form, mental models, a language of thought and others besides. Formulation in SI can begin from different levels of representation, as evidenced in lapses into interlanguage ('interference'), the substitution of set formulas for the input (Chernov 1992), or the intrusion of pre-formed ideas (Lederer 1981) (see Chapter 2, note 15). Context-poor logical forms can be processed and understood in SI, and time factors in SI force the selection and formulation of 'half-baked', relatively unenriched material. Micro-analysis of the samples, and timing, reveal different sojourns in memory, and certain errors reveal translation without conceptual support. But renditions with no trace of contextualisation are rare.

More details about the experimental stages in developing a corpus analysis methodology, and a precise description of the procedure which was finally adopted, are given below in Section 3, after a description of the corpus and a summary of the main typological features of German, English and Chinese.

2 The corpus

The corpus consists of tape-recorded samples from real and simulated conference sessions with transcripts for reference. The main corpus comprises two samples from different source languages, German (Würzburg corpus, prefixed W) and Modern Standard Chinese (MSC: 'Mandarin'/Putonghua) (Taipei corpus, prefixed T), involving three original Speakers and five different interpreters (three for German-English, two for Chinese-English). Further examples are taken from later segments of the Taipei corpus; a third Chinese sample with three different interpreters (Fang corpus, prefixed F); and a second text from the Würzburg conference (two interpreters).

Sample transcripts of the main corpora are provided in Appendices: an interlinear presentation, timed and synchronised to $< 0.5s$ accuracy and marked for pauses, primary pitch contour, stress and speech errors (W2 and T3); and a second-by-second tabular presentation, with input and a bracketed gloss in the first column, and a partial symbolic representation of semantic and inferential assembly of meaning (W1, W3 and T2a). Chinese discourse is transcribed in standard Hanyu

Pinyin romanisation; a *hanzi* (Chinese character) transcript of 'Taipei' is provided in Appendix T1). Lastly, 'fluent' interpreters' versions, with pause, stress marking and speech errors eliminated, are given for the German-English corpus in Appendix W4.

In all, detailed analysis was made of about 14 minutes of discourse, or a total of about 30 minutes of TL versions (Würzburg: 3 mins, 3 interpreters; Taipei: 9 mins, 2 interpreters; Fang: 2 mins, 3 interpreters), of which about two-thirds is used in examples. This is comparable to the 30-35 minutes of German-to-French SI (approximately 18 mins by two interpreters) selected for analysis by Lederer (1981) from an hour of bilingual discussion. Longer and shorter corpora have been subjected to different types of analysis in the literature. Barik (1973, 1975) recorded 6 versions of 8 SI discourses lasting about an hour in all, with detailed analysis of temporal and error data in two 3-5 minute texts. Goldman-Eisler (1972) reports having examined syntactic input segmentation in a total of 28 versions of 9 texts of 3-6 minutes each. Larger corpora with rougher annotation and synchronisation have been used for more general statistical analyses (Gerver 1974; Pöchhacker 1994) or as sources of examples to illustrate situational factors (Pöchhacker 1994). For the present corpus, exhaustive analysis and annotation of both syntactic and prosodic features were necessary, since the research issues required an examination of both structural and pragmatic dimensions.

Samples were recorded, or already available, in various language combinations. Since one of the main research issues was the possible effect of typological differences, contrasting source and target languages were chosen. German and Chinese are both partly SOV, contrasting with rigid SVO English. German as SL (which in addition to having final verbs, is a 'free-word-order' language) has been a main focus of studies making claims about the significance of SL-TL structural asymmetries (Wilss 1978, Lederer 1981, Stenzl 1983). Chinese has been little studied as an SI language, and no corpus study has hitherto been attempted; it displays other typological differences, in addition to sentence structure, with respect to all the other major international conference languages. English was chosen as the common target language, being accessible to most readers, and on the grounds that a common language on one side of the equation was necessary for expository clarity and comparability.

The corpora were selected for their representativity of professional practice, exemplifying semi-rehearsed, discursive speech[3], and their comparable subject-matters and levels of technicality, as well as for other technical reasons described further below. Many different recordings and transcripts were made by or made available to this author, both of mock and real-life conferences and sessions, but most were ruled out as inappropriate or unmanageable for various reasons, including

(a)   poor acoustic conditions (e.g. crosstalk);

(b) insufficient quality of the interpretation (student interpreters);
(c) uncertainty about documentation available to interpreters (much of the Würzburg sample); and in some cases the certain knowledge that a Speaker was following a supplied text, introducing complicating factors like reading, which we did not want to address in this study; or
(d) discourse not representative of mainstream conference genres in terms of style (e.g. pedagogical) or content (e.g. pop sociology).

Some samples were all too typical of real-life conference conditions, but ill-suited to an exploratory study, being too metalinguistic or allusive, or so improvised and disconnected that what cohesion there was virtually disappeared in the transcription (cf. the sample of the Watergate transcripts in Pinker 1994). An example of a rejected sample is given in Appendix B: the input is so redundant and disconnected that one cannot deduce whether the source of any TL string is the last·utterance, the remoter discourse record, or background knowledge; in such conditions sophisticated task performance variables, specifically the need for pragmatic manipulation, or packaging in TL, become so dominant as to obscure other factors, such as possible difficulties arising from linguistic structures and content.

The main German-English and Chinese-English corpora are provided in Appendices. A supplementary Chinese-English corpus ('Fang'), and extended interlinear transcripts of the main corpus, are given in Setton (1997).

2.1 German-English: 'Würzburg'

(a) Live on-site recordings

Audiotape recordings were made[4] of several speeches in German, French and English, with some SI versions, at the Founding Symposium of the Association for European Criminal Law held in Würzburg, Germany in 1992. An extract from a panel discussion on the second day of the Symposium was selected for detailed analysis. The interpreter, WL ('Würzburg-Live'), is an English native speaker and professional conference interpreter of about five years' experience (350-400 conference days) largely within the European Union system.

(b) Mock (simulated) session

To obtain several interpreters' versions of the same speeches, it was necessary to organise a mock session with a reconstruction of some of the speeches of the original Symposium. This was mounted at the Ecole Supérieure d'Interprètes et de Traducteurs (ESIT) in Paris, with the kind permission of the Director, Prof. M. Lederer.

The mock session was organised as follows: two conference interpreters, WA and WB, both English native speakers and professionals of 15-18 years' experience (about 2000 conference days), volunteered their services. A lawyer was retained at a fee and given texts of two or three speeches and extracts, transcribed from tapes of the Symposium, to prepare for delivery as an actor prepares a part. In the event, these presentations were interspersed with some appropriate impromptu conference discourse in German by the same Speaker and another pseudo-participant.[5] A tape of the corpus sample (Chairman and Dr. Odersky's speech) was then played as if in continuation of this discourse. WA and WB interpreted into English throughout. The interpreters agreed that pace and delivery did not differ from a live situation in any significant way. Original and interpreters' versions were simultaneously recorded on a Fostex X18-H multi-track tape recorder (transcripts and analysis in W3-4), and on separate single-track cassette tapes to obtain clearer versions for transcription.[6]

The situation, and the amount of available background knowledge, differed completely as between WL and WA/WB. Interpreter WL was present at the event, where she had interpreted speeches during the entire previous day, and also had ample documentation. WA and WB were sent the programme and Prof. Odersky's text a week before the simulation. It was therefore possible to hypothesise about the effect of these different backgrounds on the versions of the 'live' and 'mock session' interpreters (Chapter 6, section 2).

The discourse sample chosen is unscripted material, including Prof. Odersky's remarks, which show no formal correspondence with the supplied text, except for one similar sentence (lines 87-97 of transcript). Later, the Speaker began paraphrasing his text closely or reading verbatim from the text, but these passages are not included in our sample.

Reference documents: *Appendix*
Live original speech and interpreter WL (analytic tabular presentation)   W1
Live original speech and interpreter WL   (interlinear synchronised transcript) W2
Simulation and interpreters WA, WB (analytic tabular presentation)   W3
Interpreters' versions presented as 'fluent' punctuated texts   W4

The main sample consists of an extract of about three minutes from the panel discussion on the morning of the second day of the Symposium, on the theme 'The Future of European Law'. Three Speakers have described different aspects of the fight against trans-border crime and EC fraud in the European Community. The Chairman, or Moderator, now introduces Prof. Odersky (Chief Justice of the German Supreme Court), to speak on problems of jurisdiction. The extract comprises the Moderator's thanks and introduction (1 minute) followed by Prof. Odersky's introductory paragraph (1 minute) and the first substantive section of his speech (1 minute). This three-minute section was selected for analysis because

(a) it covers two different Speakers in different roles,
(b) the discourse comprises semi-rehearsed speech, i.e. is positioned at a point on the written/oral scale which we believe on the basis of personal experience to be most typical of conference discourse, between the spontaneous discussion analyzed by Lederer (1981) and recitations from written text;
(c) the first minute of the Main Speaker's remarks are a spontaneous preamble to the content of his supplied written text. Only this far can the supplied text can be safely treated as background knowledge and ruled out as a second version supporting the on-line interpretation.

The Moderator takes the floor after applause, thanks the previous Speaker (Dr Rump) with a few complimentary and descriptive epithets ('up-to-date overview') and emphasises its relevance to the discussion and the foreign guests; this serves as a link (M2-3) to the next Speaker, Prof. Odersky, who is deferentially introduced (M4) and his career summarised, with dates and titles of posts held (M5).

The style is correct and formal with no colloquial constructions or usages, but not stilted; there is 'cooperative' redundancy, with frequent pauses, the longer ones matching discourse topic shifts: three extended pauses introduce segments M3, M4 and M5. Delivery is smooth, slowing from a brisk 124 wpm/238 spm (M1-2) to a comfortable 107 wpm/201 spm (M3-7).

After the standard greeting, the (invited) Speaker hesitates before beginning extempore. He first invokes his duty as Speaker and outlines his intended remarks (S1-S3), then summarises the issues which have emerged in the discussion so far (S4)—the concerns of the European Community and Member States to protect themselves against subsidy fraud (S5-6)—and confirms that he will address these issues (S7). Falling intonation and a long pause signal a shift: he now embarks on the prepared part of his presentation (S8), beginning with the first words of the supplied text (**Der europäische Subventionsbetrug..**), but then digresses, producing a long and complex sentence, the first clause paraphrasing the opening text statement, about the satisfactory legislative situation, the second (S9) extending it to describe the equally satisfactory consequences: equal protection of national and Community interests is assured in German law.[7]

2.2 Chinese-English: 'Taipei'

The Chinese-English SI corpus consists of two samples recorded at the Graduate School of Translation and Interpretation Studies (GITIS) of Fujen Catholic University in Taipei. The first and main sample for analysis is a speech on Taiwan's prospects for rejoining the United Nations, which was prepared for delivery by a teacher at the Institute (a native Speaker of Modern Standard Chinese-

Putonghua), on the basis of an article in an academic journal, and delivered in the framework of a mock seminar. The presentation was simultaneously interpreted into English by two professionals, TA and TB, and all three versions were simultaneously recorded on a Fostex 280 multi-track recorder.

The supplementary sample, from which some examples are taken, consists of a videotaped television interview with a well-known Chinese dissident, Prof. Fang Lizhi, and English SI versions by one professional and two trainee interpreters. Details of these two samples are given below.

Reference documents: *Appendix*
Chinese (Hanzi) transcript of original speech (without annotations)   T1
Analytic transcript (Romanised) with gloss, and interpreters TA, TB   T2a
Tabular transcript (continued), without assembly analysis (S11-S28)   T2b
Interlinear synchronised transcript of recited segments (S29-39)   T3

The interpreters, TA and TB, are both professionals, each of about 2 years' (200 days) experience. TA is a Chinese (Putonghua) native speaker with English acquired in tertiary education and about one year's residence in the United States. TB is considered a near-bilingual with English dominant, of Chinese native-speaking parents, but having spent much of her childhood and adolescence in English-speaking environments.

The main Taipei sample consists of the first five and a half minutes of the speech, prepared on the basis of a text which was not supplied to the interpreters. The transcript was divided for convenience into 28 segments (S1-28); the remaining segments (S29-39), consisting of recited text without preparation, were analysed separately (see below).

The Speaker first establishes the objective, Taiwan's re-entry to the UN, and the recommended method (via the financial organisations) (S1), then refers briefly to current opinion on this issue (S2-3), and hints at the difficulties (S4-5). He then presents and rejects (S7, S15) two possible approaches, with facts and arguments for and against: through a vote in the Security Council (S7-S8) or in the General Assembly (S9-14). From S16 he introduces the third, preferred option (via the financial organisations), contrasts it with the first two (S17-S20), and develops a favourable argument based on Taiwan's strengths in trade and finance (S21-23), but concedes the difficulties (S25), and now moves back into a discourse-directive mode, drawing attention to his written text and stating his intention to discuss the main obstacles to this strategy in more detail (S26-28). Delivery seems somewhat faster than the German sample (it was measured at 129 wpm, but wpm speeds are not comparable across languages).

As preparation, the interpreters were given a general briefing in advance and asked to accept the simulation of an event described as 'a seminar on Taiwan's prospects for rejoining the United Nations'. They were then given the title of the presentation *'Woguo chongfan lianheguo jinrong zuzhi zhanwang'* ('Our country's prospects for rejoining UN financial organisations'). They first interpreted the Moderator's short introduction (counter times 0-21, about 25s) from English into Chinese ('prospects for Taiwan's entry into the UN'[8]), then the main body of the speech from Chinese into English.

At segment S29 the Speaker of 'Taipei' switched without warning from semi-rehearsed delivery to reading, slowly but directly, from the written text (Segments S29-39), which was not supplied to the interpreters. This passage, lasting a further three and a half minutes, describes a trend towards politicisation in the IF and the World Bank, with examples (citing names, dates and organisations) of financial pressure exercised by various countries and blocs to political ends. The passage also contains long, substantive and syntactically heavy structures, and little or no phatic or rhetorical material prefacing sentences or added as parentheticals or afterthoughts. Some problems of SI from written text delivered orally are discussed in the analysis, with examples from these segments.

2.3 Supplementary Chinese-English corpus

Three interpreters (one professional, FC, and two final-year students, FA and FD, produced SI versions of a videotaped TV interview with an exiled dissident, Prof. Fang Lizhi. The interview was conducted in the United States in 1992 (one year earlier). The Moderator and interviewee are seated facing the camera and audience; their names and titles appear on screen for about 10s as the Moderator begins his prepared introduction (not interpreted). The subject-matter of the interview is Fang's own career and recent experience, and his views on Chinese current affairs. The audience, seen in brief camera pans, is described in the Moderator's opening turns as comprising Chinese students and teachers. Interpreters were asked to begin from the interviewee's first words, but FC began when the Moderator turned to address his first question to Fang (M1), while the others (FA,FD) waited for Fang's reply (F1).

Interpreter FA is a trainee interpreter and Chinese native Speaker having acquired English at school. Interpreter FC is a professional interpreter (5-6 yrs/300-400 days experience), and is considered a near-bilingual, with Chinese dominant and English acquired from adolescence. Interpreter FD is a trainee interpreter, considered a near-bilingual, with English dominant and Chinese acquired through contact with her extended family, tertiary education, and employment.

As preparation, interpreters were given a preliminary briefing about twenty minutes before the session, in which they were told the circumstances of the interview, the interviewee's name, the place and date, etc.; all three knew something about the interviewee. In his introduction (not interpreted), the Moderator summarises Fang's career and reputation and recent events in Taiwan-PRC relations, and mentions the place and situation of the interview. In this case, interpreters were removed in time and space from the original speech event, and so had only a thin background of expectations. Like most televised interviews, this comprised overlapping turns, probing questions and humorous banter. The Moderator's discourse is more rehearsed, faster and denser and with more 'stage-effects', while the interviewee talks modestly and spontaneously about himself. Since the present study focuses on professional SI, and the acoustic conditions were uneven, only a few selected examples are used from this additional sample.

2.4 Comparison of SI corpora

The two main samples (Würzburg and Taipei) are of a similar level of technicality, each assuming at this stage only some superficial familiarity with institutions (the European Union (Würzburg) and the United Nations (Taipei)). Some names and titles occur in Würzburg, and some simple statistics in Taipei. The rate of delivery is faster in Taipei, but the discourse is less formal, contains fewer stylistic and interpretive usages than the Würzburg speech, and is more repetitive and redundant, notably in the amount of phatic, evidential and connective material at the beginning of each sentence. Both texts contain left-branching grammatical structures not found in English. The amount of Speaker ungrammaticality is about even.

Oral and written (recited) modes

Both the Wurzburg and Taipei samples are assumed to be formulated on-line, from notes (semi-rehearsed speech). The Würzburg Moderator's discourse was at least semi-rehearsed, as shown in the low proportion of non-ideal (mid-constituent) hesitations and the higher incidence of stylised rhetorical devices. The opening extract of the main Speaker in Würzburg is a preamble to a prepared text, edited by reference to the discourse record of the previous two days. In the Fang interview, the questions were probably thoroughly rehearsed, if not read. Prof. Fang's replies are probably spontaneous, or at most semi-rehearsed discourse, with numerous after-thoughts, qualifications, repetition and expansions, Topic NP editing, false starts and recastings, and interpersonal prefatory phatics and planning markers.

Taipei S29-39 (read from written text), in contrast to all other samples, is highly formal and structured and contains no parentheticals, rhetorical openings or afterthoughts.

2.5 Equipment, recording, timing and transcription

Technical conditions and interpreters' equipment were as used in professional practice. Acoustic conditions were mostly good, but not sufficient for precise sonograph, phonetic or pause measurements. Mock sessions were recorded on multi-track recorders (Fostex 280 for Taipei and Fang, Fostex X-18H for the mock Würzburg session) and played back and timed on a Fostex X18-H portable model; one counter number is equivalent to approximately 1.2 seconds.

Synchronisation

The Würzburg 'live' recordings of the source and interpreter's version were made at the actual conference on separate tapes. The source speech is audible at several points not more than 40 seconds apart on the interpreter tapes, enabling synchronisation to virtually the same degree of precision as with dual-track recordings. Repeated stopwatch measurements were made to confirm that possible fluctuation between these points does not exceed 0.5 seconds. In the interlinear transcripts, the input (with an extra line for the English gloss) and interpreters' production were aligned by the use of tab and space, after checking synchronicity against repeated simultaneous audition of the two tapes. In the tabular presentations, each line is equivalent to approximately one second.

Even with multi-track equipment, there are limits to the accuracy with which the streams can be reliably synchronised by an observer; wide between-subject variations are usual in experiments requiring subjects to locate 'clicks' in sentences. Lederer (1981) superimposed the regular clicks of a metronome on dual-track recordings, but recognised the limitations of the method. Her transcriptions are accurate to the order of the 3-second units used, and to 1s for selected examples.

It is not possible to establish unequivocally what an interpreter has 'heard' at every point, not least because words are recognised before they are complete (Tyler and Marslen-Wilson 1982). Consequently, for safety, none of the examples used in the study rely on an accuracy of less than 0.5 seconds, which is, however, safely within the margin of error for timing and synchronising two clearly audible tracks, as on a multi-track recorder.

Transcription

Transcripts are annotated with the cumulative time elapsed in seconds (checked against occasional audible background fragment, or with Fostex counter numbers); empty and filled pauses (e.g. 'er' or 'erm', glossed @, @m); pitch, with rising, falling and 'modulating' intonation peaks,[9] syllable-lengthening; stress by articulatory force or loudness; indistinct phonation, etc.; and rustling noises indicating consultation of documents in the booth. A key to notation is provided at the front of the book and with each transcript.

Source discourse appears in Times New Roman bold face in the original language, plain face for glosses (with or without bracketing of syntactic structure). Different fonts and styles are used throughout to distinguish individual interpreters' versions: *italic* for Interpreter WL, `Courier New` for Interpreter WA, Book Antiqua for Interpreter WB, Century Gothic for interpreter TA, Arial for TB, as illustrated in the following samples:

WÜRZBURG (live):
'Tagung 10.5 -   auf diesem - Be'REICH 12.3 des - Subventionsbetruges. 13.9
meeting -   on   this   area   of-the -   subsidy fraud -
WL: *@ /fraud- 10.6 -   which is. as I have said.12.4 one.   of-   the - 13.8*

WÜRZBURG (mock)
H als   Präsi'denten -   des 34.7 -   deutschen 'Bundesgerichtshofs 36.3 -
as . President $_{ACC}$ of the   German   Federal Justice Court

`WA:tsky's 33.5 going to address precisely that` /THEME 35.4 -   <R
WB: an ISSUE. 33.6   that 34 -   <R> Doctor Walter ODERsky will speak /to 36.6

TAIPEI:
S5: NA- - 80 dajia ye tongyang- - 81 renshi dao yi dian. jiu shi 82   +
so[$_{CP1}$ well[$_{IP1}$ everyone *ye*[$_{VP}$ likewise V realise   one thing   F>dm *shi*

TA: ment/ 80   -   and. 81 from the opposition \party -.
TB: +   80 in-   H   +   Taiwan's 82 NEED to re-enter

Extracts and examples in the analysis (Chapters 5 to 7) are cross-referenced by Segment (TS-, WM-, WS-) or by line numbers in the analytic (tabular) presentations.

2.6 Segmentation of the transcripts for analysis

The input texts were divided into segments for convenience. The sentence was taken as the basic unit for the German corpus, except for the longest ones, which were divided into one- or two-clause units using labels based on Halliday's system of clause-chain analysis: M2 is divided into a first subordinate clause (M2), a root clause (M2α) and its *Wh*-complement clause M2$\alpha\beta$. Similarly, M5 is subdivided into a root and subordinate clauses; but S2α consists of a subordinate including a succession of three complement clauses, and a conjoined 'afterthought' clause, which are taken together as a discourse unit. Finally, S8 is divided from its complement of result S9.

The Chinese corpus is divided heuristically into discourse units, each of which usually consists of (a) conative/phatic or rhetorical lead-in material; (b) one or more adjuncts and other preverbal phrases; (c) one or more verb phrases, and in some cases (d) an afterthought. In some segments this 'afterthought' is a whole sentence, as in S4 **'zhe shi buke fouren de yige shishi'** ('this is an undeniable fact').

2.7 Linguistic descriptions

The aim of the initial analysis is to investigate what correlations, if any, emerge between the *linguistic structure* of the input and output versions. The salient characteristics of the two corpus source languages, German and Chinese (Putonghua), and the most obvious contrasts with the output language, English, are summarised here.

German

Typologically, German is considered an underlying SOV language, in which surface directionality is mixed: CP and PP are Head-initial, while AP, and VP/IP in the subordinate clause, are Head-final. In the Noun Phrase, participial and Relative Clause modifiers may precede the Head Noun in addition to quantifiers, determiners and adjectives, while PPs attach to the right.

Table 4.1 German and English: morphological and word-order contrasts

Clause	German	English
Main	SVO, OVS	SVO
Subordinate	SOV	SVO
Elements between finite and nonfinite verb	arguments and adjuncts (almost unrestricted)	adjunct, adverbial, parenthetical (one or two only)
NP		
Pronoun Gender	yes	animate only
Number (Sing/Plural)	on Det, Adj, Pron and N	on Pron and N
Case	Ternary system (Nom/Gen/Dat) on Det, Adj, Pron and N	Binary system (Nom/Oblique) on Pron only
Complex modifier position	participial, relative: left or right	participial, relative: right only
VP		
Mood(indicative/subjnctve)	yes	no
Person, Number	yes	3rd person only

German differs from English chiefly in its rich case-marking morphology, and its surface word orders. Traditional German sentence grammar distinguished the *Vorfeld* or 'initial field' ahead of the finite verb or Auxiliary, containing exactly one constituent (either an argument, an adjunct or a non-finite verb), and the

Mittelfeld or 'middle field' situated either between the finite verb/Auxiliary and non-finite verb, or after the finite verb (Rambow and Joshi 1994: 268-9). In the root clause, a long 'middle field' may separate finite and non-finite verb components, or split a compound verb. In subordinate clauses, it may distance the verb from the Subject. The finite verb or auxiliary can occupy three positions:

- initial, in yes-no questions and some conditionals;
- second, preceded by a Subject, Complementiser or another element, in declarative Main clauses; or
- last, in subordinate clauses (although phrases can 'leak' past the verb in less formal registers) (Hawkins 1983; Haegeman 1991).

German is considered a 'free-word-order' language: in this example (from Haider 1991: 12, cited in Rambow and Joshi 1994) all 120 (5!) permutations in the order of the five 'middle-field' items are theoretically grammatical:

dass [eine hiesige Firma] [meinem Onkel] [die Möbel] [vor drei Tagen]
that [a local firm$_{NOM}$] [my uncle$_{DAT}$] [the furniture$_{(ACC)}$] [three days ago]
[ohne Voranmeldung] zugestellt hat
[without warning] delivered *past-Aux*

However, the movement rules[10] which allow these permutations in syntactic theory overgenerate possible orders: acceptability levels vary widely. 'Free-word-order' languages like German are said to use these optional variants for pragmatic purposes, i.e. to mark given vs. new information, or topic vs. focus. Some authors claim that this allows a 'tighter fit of form to meaning' via the syntactic expression of pragmatic functions which are vague or ambiguous in a fixed-word-order language like English (Hawkins 1983: 364-5). In our corpus, segments WS8-WS9 provide good examples of the protracted 'middle field'.

In the 'initial field,' Topicalisation may delay the Subject by fronting an argument or adjunct e.g.

Fronted expletive (Lenerz 1977, cited in Olsen 1985)
Es klappert die Mühle am rauschenden Bach
'it/there' clatters the mill at the gurgling brook

Fronted locative PP (Lenerz 1977, ibid.):
Am rauschenden Bach klappert die Mühle
at the gurgling brook clatters the mill

Fronted Object (from our corpus, WM4):
Als Präsidenten des Bundesgerichtshofs brauche ich Herrn Odersky nicht vorzustellen
as President$_{ACC}$ of the Federal High Court need I Mr$_{ACC}$ Odersky not to introduce

Fronted Dative NP, marked for oblique case (supplementary corpus):
Der illegalen Ausnutzung solcher Gesetzeslücken[...] muss ...rechtzeitig vorgebeugt werden
the$_x$ illegal$_o$ exploitation of-such legal loopholes[...] must therefore - timely   prevented be

Fronted Dative NP marked as dative, with focal stress (supplementary corpus):
DIESEM ANLIEGEN ist das Gründungsymposium für [...] gewidmet
(To) this$_{DAT}$ concern is the$_{NOM}$ founding symposium for [...] dedicated

Germanic languages have been adduced in support of incremental parsing theories, in which 'the sentence processor operates in such a way as to maximise the interpretation and comprehension of the sentence at each stage of processing, i.e. as each lexical item is encountered' (Crocker 1994: 250; Bader and Lasser 1994), and against Head-driven theories which assume that structure is built exclusively from Heads in the input string, and that every attachment must be licensed by an element in the already existing structure (see Appendix A).

Modern Standard Chinese (Putonghua)

The features of MSC (Putonghua) which contrast most saliently with English include

- the pervasiveness of Topic-Comment structures;
- the apparent fluidity of lexical categorial distinctions;
- the virtual absence of inflectional morphology;
- high lexical homophony;
- sparse referential tracking (zero anaphora).

In Chinese, the traditional 'predicate - internal/external argument - adjunct' analysis, and the distinction between phrase, clause and sentence, are blurred by several features:

1. *Topic-Comment structure*,[11] and the sharing of a Topic by several successive 'clauses' or sentences, which may include a Subject and a Verb. A Topic Chain is a series of 'Comments' sharing the same Topic, which appears as a full NP only once, thereafter taking a null form or appearing as a resumptive pronoun:

    zhei tiao yu Mama shuo bu xinxian, ø wo bu chi le.
    this *cl* fish Mother says not fresh, I [do] not eat *pfv*

Topic chaining involves neither coordination nor subordination in the usual sense, and the 'clauses' can be connected without overt markers or parallel structure. The shared Topic can be linked to any grammatical function in a given clause, but each clause in the chain has some 'Aboutness' relation with the Topic, and adds some information about it (Shi 1992):

> zhei ke shu,   hua xiao,   yezi da,   hen nankan, wo meiyou mai.
> this *cl* tree, flowers small, leaves big, very ugly,   I didn't buy

The Topic Chain has been defined as a discourse rather than a syntactic unit, leading some authors to classify Chinese typologically as a 'discourse-oriented' (Tsao 1979, 1990) or 'Topic-prominent' (Li and Thompson 1981) language. But even if the Topic Chain is treated as a syntactic category (the largest category in Chinese, larger than the conventional maximal unit [NP-VP]), both discourse factors and syntax are required to explain how the Topic is disambiguated, since it can function as a declarative, interrogative, verbal complement, oblique object, subject, adverbial clause, NP modifier or complement (Shi 1992: 39; 330-1).

2. the frequent *deletion or ellipsis of the Subject*, in serial verb constructions: when there is nothing in Subject position, interpretation of the Subject is anaphoric.

3. the moot *categorial status* of certain lexical items which may behave as verbs or prepositions, e.g. **dao** '(go) to, as far as'; **gen** 'accompany/with'; **jingyou** '(go) via', which have consequently been termed 'coverbs' (Li and Thompson 1981). In the corpus, certain such items whose dependence on a downstream verb is not immediately clear are treated as 'prepositional verbs' (PVP).

Morphology and word order

Chinese is a mixed-Headed language. Main Clause (CP) order is largely SVO, but Verb-oriented PPs and adverbials usually occur to the left of the Verb, which may also be preceded by a direct or indirect Object marked with the preposition **ba** or **jiang**.[12] The Noun Phrase is strictly left-branching, and may contain demonstrative, possessive or quantifying determiners, a classifier, and participial and relative-clause modifiers. PPs may be Head-final, Head-initial or both.

Several features which are mandatorily marked in English (and most Indo-European languages to varying degrees) may be unmarked in Chinese, notably the 'Finiteness' of both Verbs (Tense and Aspect) and Nouns (Definite/Indefiniteness and Number). Aspect may, but need not, be marked by a suffix such as perfective **le** (glossed pfv), durative **zhe** (dur) or completive **guo**. The Definiteness or Number of Nouns may optionally be marked by determiners, e.g. **yige** (a, one) or **yi xie** ('some'). Chinese Nouns are not marked for Case or Gender. Possessive and relative-clause determiner phrases are attached to the left of the Head Noun with the 'attributive' particle **de**, which can also function as a Nominaliser.

Table 4.2 Chinese and English: morphological and word-order contrasts

	Chinese	English
Clause	(S)VO, (S)OV, OVS;	SVO
	Topic chain	
Scope in multiple quantification	largely determined by linear order	ambiguous
NP		
Def/Indef Article (Det)	no	yes
Pronoun Gender	no	yes
Number	optional (determiner)	yes
Modifier position	all precede N	PP, participle, relative follow N
VP		
Person, number	no	3rd person sing.
Tense	optional (suffix)	yes
Aspect	optional (suffix)	yes

However, **de** particles are also found in the VP, as (1) an adverb suffix, rather like English *-ly;* and (2) as a resultative or causative particle linking a predicate to its complement of result. In writing, three forms correlate with *de* in these different roles. The attributive NP use is probably the most frequent in discourse.

Many Chinese verbs are optionally transitive, and Chinese has no expletive, so that e.g. the verb **chu** in a string like **Sulian chule yige Suokelafu** ('Fang' sample) can be analysed as transitive 'produce' ('the Soviet Union has produced a Sakharov') or as an unaccusative preceded by a locative phrase and followed by its argument ('in the Soviet Union there emerged a Sakharov').

Logical and information structure

Chinese logical form is rather transparent, since the scope of quantifiers largely follows constituent order (Huang C-T. J. 1982, cited in Li Y-H. 1990). The scope of the Topic, or of semantic values like negation, is marked by the presence or absence of the copula *shi*, particles like *ne*, and pausing in spoken discourse.

Descriptions of Chinese tend to appeal more than do those of European languages to discourse and information-structure factors. With the relative poverty of markers of subordination and coordination (Topic-chains and serial construc- tions are often connected only by pauses), and of morphology marking definite- ness and referentiality (absence of articles, zero anaphora), an account of how the language works for communication invites the investigation of other guides to coherence, such as focusing devices. Chinese has a rich system of focusing devices which direct attention by foregrounding certain items directly, or by attenuating other elements by deleting, topicalising or repeating them. Cheng (1983) describes several common devices (focus is underlined and preceded by F>):

- Topicalisation of elements out of the predicate, and their nominalisation (by *de*), sometimes with an added generic, e.g.

> *Zuotian shanghai tade (ren) shi <u>Laowang</u>*
> Yesterday-harm-him-*de* person is F><u>Laowang.</u>

In discourse, the topicalised string is often marked off by a pause and/or a particle (e.g. *ne* or *a*), which we have glossed 'p':

> *Zuotian shanghai tade (ren) ne, shi <u>Laowang</u>*
> The person who harmed him yesterday p, (that) was Laowang.

- Parallel constructions (two juxtaposed clauses sharing a referent) with the repetition of unfocused elements, e.g.

> *Dianying <u>ta</u> yao kan, <u>wo bu</u> yao kan*
> movie <u>he</u> want watch, <u>I (do) not</u> want watch

- *Shi* is commonly used to mark off a string containing a Focus, and may accompany other focus devices; only one *shi*-focus is possible per clause. When *shi* precedes a whole VP, focus on an element other than the verb is additionally marked by a second device, e.g. repetition of the non-focused part in the Topic:

> *wo yao shi yao* F> <u>*zidian*</u> '(what) I want is (I) want (a) <u>dictionary</u>'.

Cheng suggests that within a whole VP prefaced by focal *shi*, focus is on the leftmost, 'outer' element of the VP after *shi*, if there is one (usually the Subject or a time/place adverbial). Only a Topic or Subject, a sentence adverbial (e.g. *xingkui,* 'fortunately') or a Time/Place nominal, can (precede) or modify *shi*:

> *Ta xingkui shi zai jiali dengzhe*
> He fortunately is at home waiting (Cheng 1983: 85).

Thus *shi,* when not a copula, can be seen either as a marker of a logical scope boundary, or as a (pragmatic) focusing device.

2.8 English gloss

An English gloss accompanies both the Chinese and German input texts. For readers working in the current dominant paradigm of structural analysis, constituent bracketing is provided based on a simplified state-of-the-art syntax with functional projections confined to CP and IP.

The glosses include a few SL particles and other language-specific features which have no transparent equivalent in English, e.g. Chinese *de* (attributive/ resultative/adverbial particle) *shi* (copula/affirmative predicate) *yao* (Auxiliary (want/need)/conditional marker) or the adverb/discourse particle *ye*. Chinese also uses nominal classifiers (glossed 'cl'). Some items are glossed simply as discourse marker (dm), discourse connective (dc), particle (p), or filled pause (fp). The word **zhe(i)ge** ('this...') for example, is often used as a filled pause. German Case, Number and Gender inflections are shown in the gloss, where significant, as subscript indices, e.g. 'President$_{DAT}$,' or in more abbreviated form, as shown in the key to symbols.

These details are supplied to allow readers to follow the course of assembly of 'semantic representations' from the morphosyntax of the input. This meant composing a word-for-word gloss using 'basic equivalents', an invidious task which inevitably finesses and may appear to prejudge issues of lexical and compositional semantics: for the sake of clarity it was necessary in some cases to let context leak into the choice of an equivalent. However, the choice of words in context is not a central issue of this study. In short, the gloss is an entirely virtual construct, serving as a window on the assembly of meaning for expository purposes, and not implying correspondence to any actual stage in processing.

3 Methodology

Empirical studies often appear more scientific and reliable because they use crisp, clear units for comparison and measurement, but there is the risk that units established for analytic convenience, or for a static system, are then imperceptibly assumed to be psychologically real in a dynamic performance. Units of analysis or segmentation which have been used for temporal studies include syllables, words, pauses (Goldman-Eisler 1972, Barik 1973, 1975), speech bursts, syntactic constituents (Goldman-Eisler 1972, Davidson 1992), subjective units of under-standing (units of *sens*) (Lederer 1981), and heuristically-defined units (e.g. David-son found 1006 meaning units in 99 Japanese sentences (1992: 7-8)). These units are all defined by the language system, or the articulatory and respiratory system, or by the researcher. We did not therefore pre-define segments for processing, leaving it to the data to reveal any correlation between the surface speech strings.

The first task of an empirical study is to establish what actually occurs, which requires a descriptive apparatus calibrated finely enough to capture the pertinent features, in this case temporal and linguistic, within the accuracy achievable by the observer and his instruments. If the descriptive tools are calibrated in only one dimension, the findings will be too, so we attended to pragmatic as well as structural characteristics of the texts. The most general or preliminary aim of the study was to determine the relative contribution of decoded and other information to the interpreters' formulation; to try to distinguish between information contributed by the syntactic structure, lexical items, and other perceptual and cognitive input.

The general method adopted was simply to deduce what information was needed for the formulations at specific points in the interpretation and compare it to the information assumed to be available at that same point from these different sources—decoding, inference, perceptual and cognitive—assuming native-like comprehension of the speech input, visibility of the conference room, and prior documentary knowledge about the event and situation (participants' roles, etc.). This general method was itself developed in steps.

To explore the effect of sentence structure (Chap. 5), we first identify features of the SLs which contrast with English, e.g. verb-last sentences, heavy left-branching NPs with embedded participials, and (for Chinese) Topics and Subjects and other initial elements of uncertain status, and compare them with the structures used by interpreters to carry the same propositional content. Each instance of such structures was checked to see whether a pattern of segmentation could be found and described in terms of a minimum sequence of constituents required before starting formulation, as suggested by Goldman-Eisler (1972), who claimed a NP-VP structure as the minimum unit, or Davidson (1992), who found differing results for novices and seasoned interpreters on the basis of subjectively defined 'meaning elements.'

This also gave imprecise results, since interpreters often begin with a connective, a pause and/or a conative or rhetorical phrase of the type described in the literature as 'neutral' or 'filler' material. An attempt to solve the problem by matching these to equivalent items in input revealed that the correspondence relations for these items were even more elusive than for the core propositions. This experience of trying to match structures and contents led to a second stage of the analysis (Chap. 6), based on a simple theoretical principle: that *all* linguistic production within an intentional communication, even a secondary one such as interpretation, carries a semantic or pragmatic meaning, or in other words, has a procedural (ostensive) or conceptual source. This brings back into the analysis all those items which are traditionally set aside as 'empty' or 'neutral', or as 'stylistic' or 'rhetorical' on the grounds that they do not visibly contribute to propositional content, and assigns them a source. To describe and model the range of sources identified for these items, features or 'paraphrases', we had to draw on cognitive semantics (for the 'frames' of associated encyclopaedic knowledge which seemed to be evoked by the input), and a cognitive pragmatics—Relevance Theory—to show how output items which could not be matched on the surface were not aberrations from faithful translation, but were reflections either of strong implicatures and higher-order explicatures which were indeed communicated, or procedural methods to ensure that they would be communicated in the interpretation. In short, it became clear that the output could only be properly accounted for in terms of complex combinations of semantic and pragmatic meaning, for which it would be necessary to assemble a vocabulary of primitives; that the sources for these meanings were by no means all to be found in the previous utterance, and in many cases not in the text; and that to explain them, it was necessary to postulate some highly organised and constructive process of intermediate representation.

This led to the development of an experimental vocabulary of (logico)-semantic and pragmatic values, to supplement the GB-based syntactic notation, along with the occasional references to 'frame' or extratextual knowledge. These symbols are used in some of the examples and in the 'Assembly' columns of the analytic tabular transcripts. Blow-by-blow microanalysis was done of two long and complex sentences from each corpus, and the interpreters' incremental renderings, by identifying quanta or qualia of meaning derivable from the successive words, pauses, orders, inflections and suprasegmental features, in order to reconstruct the basis they had for their formulations at each point. Other segments of the German and Chinese texts were analysed in the same way. The result is offered, in largely symbolic notation, in the second column of the tabular presentations, to show the interplay between syntactically, semantically and pragmatically derived meaning in a smoother course of incremental comprehension than is predicted by accounts focusing on only one or two of these levels.

To find out how SI is affected by sentence structure, we also examined the treatment of SL structures which could not be rendered sequentially phrase by phrase, then of those which could be so transposed with only minimal rewording and adjustments for syntax at phrase level; and reviewed the degree of paraphrasing (forced or voluntary, as defined above), signs of effort or breakdown over the non-compatible structures, and evidence of different kinds of autonomous processing by interpreters in restoring semantic values or rhetorical effects for their Addressees.

To diagnose possible causes of errors or failure we looked at the position of boggle effects or partial breakdown, then at the quantity of input preceding the failure and its nature in terms of structure, number and familiarity of referents, redundancy, pragmatic or illocutionary packaging and any rare words or unusual usage. Such cases also offer indirect evidence for a reading of hesitancy profiles in terms of attention and coordination. Three cases of failure in SI (two major, with compound loss or distortion of semantic and/or pragmatic meaning) are diagnosed

(Chap. 7), one from our own corpus (over the recited written input in S29-39) and the others from the literature (Gile 1995 and Pöchhacker 1994). A timed and synchronised transcript of the former sample (from Gile 1995) was not available, but the errors are obvious in transcription. A Relevantist analysis is offered of the successive implicatures available from the source discourse to a native comprehender.

Language typology, written/oral mode and situatedness are three factors commonly claimed to influence SI, but each is extremely difficult if not impossible to isolate, so that their influence can probably only be suggested by the weight of indirect evidence. The corpus includes two source languages, live and mock situations, and both recited and semi-spontaneous text. Over the recited segments, errors and partial breakdowns in the interpreters' renditions, and changes in their fluency patterns, lend support to the widespread claims about the relative difficulty of this kind of input.

The main focus of the study was of course the nature of intermediate representation in SI, a question which we approached in stages as successive units of analysis failed to account for all the data. In a processing model, both psychological and semantic features are needed. To analyse holistic renditions, an adequate analytical vocabulary requires both minimal semantic notions, such as 'a quantum of information evoking a link between any two of an entity (e), a property (p) or a relation (r)', and pragmatic operators: intentionality and attitude primitives, and relevance pointers, such as 'projection of belief/desire/evaluation', *realis/irrealis* etc. Finally, it would seem that the cognitive and linguistic-communication aspects of interpretation are inseparable, making it difficult to determine the limits of SI processing (effort, capacity etc.) without considering representation.

Our tentative progress through the methodological jungle might be described as an 'abductive' process. Researchers in social and behavioural sciences, including those who insist on a psychological approach to linguistics, have identified with a method described by C. S. Peirce (1955) as *abduction* (or *retroduction*),

'the first starting of a hypothesis and the entertaining of it, whether as a simple interrogation or with any degree of confidence [...;] an inferential step which [...] will include a preference for any one hypothesis over others which would equally explain the facts, so long as this preference is not based on any previous knowledge bearing upon the truth of the hypotheses...'

Unlike induction, which requires units to test a hypothesis by experiment, abduction must estimate some values according to their significance. In abduction, a hypothesis is first admitted on probation, as an interrogation, and the researcher proceeds by making observations, and at each stage modifies the theory, preferring always the simplest account which will fit.[13]

Chapter 5 Structures and Strategies

The challenge in modelling SI lies in squaring what we know about language with our understanding of psychological tasks: existing accounts reflect assumptions from linguistics and psychology as much as the researcher's own intuitions. In linguistics, the dominant contemporary paradigm originated in the description of language structures, while in psychology the renascent evolutionary perspective favours 'strategic' explanations of human behaviour. Observing SI against this background it is easily inferred, from the premises that languages differ in structure while speech is linear, that there must be significant asymmetry in the way that different languages deliver meaning, and hence—on the further assumption of limited cognitive capacity—that successful SI must involve strategies for countering this asymmetry.

However, this inference involves a leap over areas which are still relatively uncharted in cognitive science, and yields models of SI which are at best incomplete. In its crudest form, the structure-based, information-processing paradigm views language as a medium for encoding information by generating predicate-argument structures, connected up as clauses, using a grammar and lexicon; speech processing research has suggested the development of this basic competence model into a complete performance model by grafting on a semantic component and a knowledge base for contextual processing. Ignoring any distinction between language as a code for cognition and language in communication, this scheme would license the formulation of speech processing (or translation) as explicit, operational procedures capable of computational implementation—for SI, as we have seen, this has been done by simply postulating cognitive components corresponding to these linguistic 'levels' of syntactic, semantic and contextual (or frame-based) processing (Dillinger 1989).

However, speech data, not to mention our own intuitions as language users, suggest that performance is more complex, and that the representational paradigm has some way to go to capture semantic and contextual factors, the operations of memory, and the wide variations observed in speech production. These irregularities are currently addressed in assorted theoretical superstructure in linguistics, such as lexical semantics, rhetorics and functional theory, which still appears marginal, controversial or exploratory in contrast to the mainstream structural descriptions. Pragmatics seems to offer the most promising avenue to unify these ventures by building on existing descriptive linguistics, rather than starting afresh (as seems to be required in Functionalism, for instance).

If some observers of SI sense that the 'irregularities' or 'performance variations' in comprehension and production are part of a communicative dimension which accompanies the information content in discourse, they lack a model of how it is cognitively processed: modelling SI reveals the absence of an integrated framework capable of supporting the analysis of communicative discourse in different languages. Accordingly, those who feel no pressure to produce an operational algorithm at this stage in SI research leave a gap between the linguistic and cognitive phases. IT, for example, discounts any obstructive effect of input structure on the grounds that 'cognitive memory' (for concepts) quickly takes over from 'auditory memory' (for morphophonology), but does not venture to describe the shift in representations. In IP, the underlying assumption that structure is the main determinant of meaning is reflected in the belief that SL-TL syntactic differences are a potential obstacle or memory-loading factor; but authors who claim some language-pair specificity of SI, due in part to structural asymmetry (Moser 1976; Gile 1983, 1995, 1997), describe no explicit representational step between working memory, said to retain linguistic structure, and TL formulation. Some IP-based accounts recognise 'secondary' and 'framing' elements in discourse, but these are treated as residual to the primary information-processing task or attributed to personal stylistic variation (Gile 1993 and *passim*).

The immediacy and density of SI as a cognitive operation, and the performance variables involved, pose a huge challenge in fitting theory to data. Corpus analysis has traditionally approached the material by observing the temporal shifts on the one hand (the lag or EVS), and the linguistic shifts (content and structure) on the other, and introducing theory to explain them. SI corpora invariably show a complex relationship between input and output, even (perhaps especially) when the interpretation seems intuitively of high quality. Lederer (1981) and Donovan (1990) explain interpreters' departures from input forms by placing the source of formulation in a non-linguistic cognitive memory, with inter-subject variations reflecting differences in its contents, hence differences in the moment of understanding of each meaning unit which allows formulation. On the IP side, Gile explains the time-and-formulation profile of SI as the reflection of complex patterns of cognitive effort management between memory operations and peripheral pressures, implemented through various preventive and corrective strategies; quality is achieved when coordination is successful in capturing all the content, with surplus capacity allowing attention to lexical choice and style.

The notion of SI 'strategies' is now widespread (Lonsdale 1997, 1998; Kalina 1998). However, the theoretical status of 'strategy' in a cognitive-linguistic task like SI is unclear. The use of the term in psycholinguistics to describe automatic processes like parsing has made it ambiguous as between more or less conscious, deliberate or learnable levels of performance, and between forced and voluntary behaviour. In SI research, the identification of 'strategies' is based on introspection (which is notoriously poor at distinguishing conscious from automatic behaviour) validated by the subsequent 'recognition' of the patterns in recordings and transcripts. These patterns are then postulated as learnable or automatable procedures to be applied, in functions as varied as semantic projection (anticipation), time management (shortening or lengthening the EVS) or production (chunking), to counter irregularities in information input due to semantic density, syntactic encoding or logical structure. Since these features are largely language-specific, so will some of these automatic learnable procedures be (Gile 1997). But the idea that such information management procedures can be learned or automated for application to fresh speech input certainly needs further validation; according to some psycholinguists, 'implicit, highly automatized strategies [...] cannot be enhanced through explicit strategies, since practice does not convert explicit knowledge into implicit competence' (attributed to Paradis (1994) in Moser-Mercer et al. 1994: 145).

The second problem concerns the quanta or qualia on which such strategies are supposed to operate. An operation on the syntax of a string necessarily involves both its logical structure and the semantic correlates of its constituents; but logical structure is often cued by prosody and connectors, whereas semantic correlates must involve encyclopaedic knowledge (on which any management or relief of semantic density also depends). This is the basis for our claim that both pragmatic analysis of the texts, and a model of the accessible knowledge base, are needed to account for the wide range of expressive variation (in word order, prosody and lexical choice) which an appeal to stylistic preference, or background, leave unexplained in other than subjective, individual terms. A combination of syntactic-semantic processing focusing on 'information' and stylistic adjustments for its 'presentation' seems inadequate to account for the communicative dimension of discourse as it is passed on in translation; in corpus analysis, it leaves a significant residue of phenomena which must be ascribed to the 'unusual logic' of the input, stylistic choice, error, or 'neutral' padding.

Our aim is therefore to integrate three of the variables invoked in existing models—subjective knowledge, on-line strategies and stylistic preference—into a more comprehensive model including linguistic processing but grounded in general cognitive and pragmatic principles; and ultimately, to attempt to couch it in representational terms. But to find the appropriate level of description, we have to begin by artificially unpacking the processes along traditional lines, i.e. in terms of 'syntactic', 'semantic' and 'contextual' processing. In this chapter, the terms 'word order strategy' and 'strategies-for-structures' will be used provocatively to illustrate the implications of the suggestion, which we believe to be implicit in some writing, that an SI strategy can be an *operation on syntax* (as traditionally described). A second straw man is then erected—a 'semantic chunking' principle—to show why an SI strategy cannot be defined as an *operation on semantics.*

The following questions are addressed directly in the first part of the corpus analysis: Can we detect any trace of a correlation between structures in input and output that might reflect a re-ordering strategy, triggered for instance by the appearance of an embedded or left-branching constituent? Is the semantic content of output words and phrases given by that of input words and phrases, and if not, what are its sources and composition? what does the order, timing and content of output tell us about meaning available at given points of the input?

This first stage in the investigation should help us to assemble the various sources and drivers of formulation into a picture of the intermediate represen-tations serving the conversion task, and perhaps, to deconstruct general and phenomenal concepts like paraphrase, and 'idiomatic' as opposed to 'literal' rendition.

1 Introduction to the corpus analysis

To assess the impact of input sentence structure in professional SI from German and Chinese to English (given adequate background knowledge), we first established the constraints and tolerances of English sentence structure, then examined the interpreters' output for those German and Chinese structures which resist phrase-by phrase treatment, either because they postpone certain constit-uents which must be produced early in English, or because the syntactic status of their initial strings cannot safely be assumed. Most accounts of SI (except IT) predict that such input structures (verb-last, for example) force waiting or stalling, loading short-term memory and taking capacity from other functions, unless countered by certain paraphrasing strategies, which are not always available.

Sentence-by-sentence comparison of the speeches and interpreters' versions reveals patterns which cannot be accounted by a structure-driven analysis. The German sentences are considerably longer than the Chinese (average 12 seconds as compared to 5.8), and not surprisingly, the interpreters routinely build their own structures without waiting. However, no regular pattern of structural trans-formation emerges, raising the question of the semantic basis for the interpreters' autonomous structures. In the Chinese-English sample, clauses are shorter, so that they are usually available *in toto* as a basis for formulation; but pervasive paraphrasing and other phenomena still suggest a complex process in which inferences and external knowledge, traceable in the output, confirm the use of information from various sources.

Chapter 6 explores these sources and tracks the pragmatic dimension of SI through evidence of the interpreters' use of various kinds of extratextual contexts, including knowledge about the discourse situation, the participants, previous discourse, conference and social conventions, and other world knowledge. Evidence of the effective exploitation of a variety of cues in SI places the effects of linguistic structure, and language factors in general, in a broader pragmatic perspective. This evidence also justifies a hypothesis about the contents of a discourse model which is built up in an interpreter's working memory to support the SI task.

Comparing input and production over complex sentences involving various kinds of indeterminacy reveals the significant role of pragmatic markers, or indicators of intentionality, and other directions to relevance, a dimension of communication which has only very recently begun to be described in formal terms. Idiomatic and free renditions, in particular, cannot be analysed without recourse to these values; a basic vocabulary is proposed at the end of Chapter 6. The need for such an analytical apparatus suggests that, if any valid processing unit for analysing translation is conceivable which is not infinitely variable from one individual's comprehension processes to the next, and yet allows latitude for paraphrase and style, it would have to be much smaller than the clausal proposition, and not tied to language forms but to *both* semantic entities *and* communicative microfunctions (although it is hard to see how any kind of atomistic analysis of this kind could be credible and robust enough to handle stylistic, literary text). This might be conceived of as the vocabulary of a 'language of thought' but including communicative functions.

Chapter 7 turns to production. We suggested in the introduction that an interpreter has to recreate the ostensive-inferential dimension in communication along with the recoding of content. This implies, on the one hand, an executive or decision-making function, which we have located at the interface between input and the interpreter's own speech acts; and on the other, the possibility of taking the Addressee's inferential abilities into account in compensating for any distortions. The question of SI fidelity, competence, and inherent limits on performance are reviewed in this light, with examples of SI failure from the corpus and the literature.

2 SL-TL asymmetry in SI: obstacle or epiphenomenon?

Many writers on SI have been concerned with the contrasting surface structures of source and target languages, notably word order. This is widely assumed to be a significant challenge to SI, and much normative writing (including introductory textbooks) focuses on heuristics and strategies for handling SL/TL asymmetries (Ilg 1978, Wilss 1978, Zhong 1984). German as a source language has traditionally been the main focus of interest in this respect, but similar and new difficulties have been claimed for emerging conference languages like Chinese and Japanese, and language typology has thus been assumed, willy-nilly, to be a key factor in SI.[1] Some authors claim that any useful account of SI processes must necessarily be 'language-pair-specific' (Wilss 1978).

Models which focus on processing capacity (e.g. Gile 1995) also assume some direct link between input structure and effort. On these accounts, interpreters are sometimes forced to wait for certain sentence constituents before being able to formulate and produce, entailing a load on storage capacity, or else to apply special linguistic and attentional strategies to overcome the asymmetries.

We will argue that the emphasis placed on syntactic asymmetry in some information-processing accounts artificially isolates and magnifies the significance of one feature of discourse, producing a limiting view of the possibilities of SI. Our argument turns on the semantic and pragmatic correlates of word order changes and the possibilities inherent in the flexibility of language. In this Chapter we shall test the impact of input syntax, as traditionally described in constituent-structure terms, by looking for correlations between SL and TL structures, or failing that, between SL structures and any strategies which could be described in structural terms. This will raise several questions and point the way to the investigation of pragmatic factors.

Word order is not the only dimension in which languages differ, even in terms of long-distance dependencies. Languages also vary in the way they encode logical scope (e.g. quantification or negation), features such as Tense, Aspect, Boundedness (the Finiteness of predicates or the Definiteness of referents), modalities (Givón 1984, 1990), illocutionary force, and speaker attitudes (Fillmore 1984), not to mention the different arrangement of the universe embodied in each language's lexicon.

As discussed in Chapter 2, theoretical work has suggested that the interplay between these factors restores the balance in the overall efficiency and flexibility of meaning delivery in different languages (Keenan 1978a, 1978b, Hawkins 1983). But the spontaneity of formulation of the source discourse is another important parameter in any consideration of the effect of typological factors on SI processing. Pragmatic functions can be performed largely suprasegmentally, by prosody and contrastive stress. For spoken language, then, it is surely perverse to isolate the word order parameter for special attention and ignore the supra-segmental dimension: if Keenan's Principle of Covariation is extended to functions that encode 'pragmatic and discourse' information (e.g. prosody, stress, focus), as seems reasonable in connected oral discourse, such contrasts are placed in a different perspective, so that in oral comprehension, the 'different processing strategies' conjectured for different languages (Hawkins 1983: 217) would be largely cancelled.

To address the typology issue, therefore, we must look at the combined impact and implications for SI of the whole range of differences in the ways that languages associate form and meaning.

3 Word order

An interpreter receiving the following string will have no problem in converting it sequentially into an SVO structure in a language like English:

Vielen 'Dank Herr Doktor - @'Rump für diesen - AKtuellen 3.5 'Überblick 4.5 +
Many thanks Mr Doctor   Rump for this   topical   overview
- - - - - - - - - - - *2.9 THANK you very much indeed- 4.6 Doctor Rump*

zu dem 5.6 -   Spe'zialthema des-   Subven'tionsbe'truges 8.3 +
to the -   special theme of   subsidy   fraud
for having given@   us this. 6.2 UP-to-date@   overview-   of. the.@ 8.5 specific.
topic. of@   SUBsidy -   /fraud- 11.4

But to produce a well-formed sentence in English—a fixed-word-order language with Head-initial VP—an interpreter cannot follow word orders such as:

in dieser Tradition. fügen sich auch die Bestrebungen des Kollegen *Sieber* - in Würzburg
in this tradition   fit also the   efforts   of-the colleague Sieber in Würzburg
ein Forschungszentrum für europäisches Strafrecht einzurichten - ein Vorhaben -
a   research centre   for European   penal law   to establish   a project
für das er sich - der vollen Unterstützung der Universität - gewiss sein darf
for which he self   the$_0$ full   support   of-the University   certain be may

In English, long VP-oriented PPs and adverbial phrases cannot usually be placed before the verb, as they can in Chinese:

name jintian xiawu ne   gen - hen duo de Zhongguo jiaoshou   yiji gen Zhongguo
- well-so today afternoon p - with - very many *de* Chinese professors - and with Chinese
tongxuemen jiu youguan liang 'an - Zhongguo de wentine - jixune - jiaohuan yijian
students -   p regarding two shores - China *de* question(s) - continue p - exchange view(s)

Even between cognate SVO languages, SL discourse may be full of structures which are tolerated in SL but dispreferred in TL, e.g. adverbial phrases inserted between a verb and its direct object (not to mention inelegant parentheticals in all languages), and so require re-ordering for stylistic reasons:

la question que je me pose est de sav/oir. EST-CE \QUE il ne serait \pas - à L'ÉTAT ACTUEL.
the question which I ask myself is to know   qn-marker   it wouldn't be   at the state present
euh- de la discus/sion euh-- nécess\aire. première\ment - d'élargir - au besoin euh-
er   of the discussion er -   necessary   firstly   to enlarge   if necessary er
\ce groupe de TRAVAIL
this working group

...attir\er l'attention euh - des différentes délégations - sur le fait qu'il y a. au niveau de-
.....attract the attention er -   of the various delegations   - to the fact that there is at the level of
ce- membre de- parag/raphe - DEUX CHOSES qui sont proposées
this segment of   paragraph -   two   things   which   are proposed [2]

French word order is often thought to be more rigid than English (and therefore more difficult as a TL from German) but it is more flexible in some respects, as seen in this SI example from Lederer (1981: 118) (with my English gloss), again showing a tolerance of adverbial phrases between a main verb and its complement:

Ferner beabsichtigen wir dem Verwaltungsrat gelegentlich der Sitzung
further   we intend   [to the$_{DAT}$ Board of Directors [on the occasion of the meeting
Interpreter: D'autre part nous avons -   l'intention -
                                Besides this we have   the intention
am achtundzwanzigsten März in Basel - je einen Prototyp -
on the twenty-eighth   March in Basel - [each one$_{ACC}$ prototype
            le vingt-huit -   - mars à -
                (on) the twenty-eighth   March in
mit jeder der beiden Varianten der Inneneinrichtung -   vorzuführen
with each of the two   versions of the   internal furnishings [to present
        Bâle   à   l'occasion de la   reunion   du comite   de
        Basel [on the occasion of the   meeting   of the Board of

direction de montrer chacun des prototypes aux directeurs généraux
Directors [to show each of the prototypes to the directors (From Lederer 1981: 116 ff.)

English word order rules and tolerances

For the purposes of this corpus analysis, we must first establish the formal constraints on English, as the common output language. Let us assume that to produce each well-formed English sentence, an interpreter needs a Subject, then a Verb, then an Object; that determiners, possessives, adjectives and- so on, if present, must precede Head Nouns; and that there are limits on where she can place adjuncts and adverbials. Possible variations allowed are as follows:

(1) *Ahead of the Main Clause Subject*: certain PP or Adv phrases, conjunctions and connectives; S-level recursion allows complementation, with insertion of a 'higher' S, or in modern GB terms, (a) constituent(s) in COMP(lementiser-CP Head) position, including a subordinate clause first (e.g. a conditional, concessive, causative etc.).

(2) *Within the Main Clause* (i.e. below S, or from Subject on), she may employ XP-level recursion within certain limits: Adv and Adj phrases can be expanded with adverbs and adjectives, and PPs with other PPs, while a Noun phrase can only hold one determiner (not counting quantifiers and numeral phrases).

(3) *Adjuncts, adverbials and certain PPs* may occupy several positions, depending largely on whether they qualify the whole utterance or only part of it (Jackendoff 1972; Huang S.F. 1975).

Semantic marking of certain features is compulsory in English: Verbs must be marked for Finiteness, and if Finite, for Tense; Nouns are marked for a combination of Definiteness and Number.

Theoretically, using the recursive tolerances of TL structure creates a problem for translation: new structure means new content, since in principle constituents and structures have semantic values. Insertion of a higher S (Comp recursion), of initial adverbs and phrases (IP recursion), or XP-level expansions to produce VP- or NP-internal delays all modify the semantics of the utterance.

If the recursive flexibility of language is used in SI, where does the content come from, and what is its effect on the interpretation?

4 Word order asymmetry and indeterminacy

To test for any tenable correlation or pattern in *structural* terms in the way interpreters handle conflicting word orders, we can look for examples of structures in the input discourse which delay the appearance of a constituent needed at a certain point to construct a well-formed English sentence, such as the following (1-2 for SI from Chinese or German, 3-4 more generally):

1. a *delayed main verb*, as in left-branching VP structures (found in Chinese and German);

2. a *delayed fixed-position argument* (e.g. Subject, Object) such as
    (a) the Head of a Subject or Object NP delayed by left-branching material (determiners, possessives, adjectives, reduced relative clauses (also found in both Chinese and German);

   (b) a Subject delayed in other ways, by fronting of an oblique-case
       argument (German); or by *uncertainty about its Subject status*
       (Chinese Topic);
3. a *Main Clause delayed by a subordinate clause*, or by adjunct or other
   material;
4. other *empty positions* in SL which must be filled in TL. Languages differ
   in the ellipses they allow: zero anaphora in Subject position is common
   in Chinese; verb ellipsis may occur in German, as in Würzburg M5: '**dass
   er 1983 Präsident [des ...] V ø und dann 1988 Präsident [...] war.**'

'Left-branching' structures are attached to the left of the constituent which
governs them, i.e. they occur in the speech string before the item they qualify or
modify. In English, long Verb-attached phrases follow the Verb; in German and
Chinese, they often precede them. In German and Chinese, a whole 'participial'
relative clause may precede and modify a Noun, and may itself contain a left-
branching phrase.

The strategies proposed to deal with SL-TL syntactic differences include:

(1) waiting for the predicate or phrase Head;
(2) stalling by producing neutral 'filler' material;
(3) recasting the content of the left-branching phrase as a constituent which
    can be produced immediately ('chunking', or 'preserving linearity'); or
(4) guessing at the Head (Verb or Noun) before it occurs ('anticipation')

Inasmuch as all the first three options, and 'stylistic' rephrasing, are said to
increase memory or production efforts, and guessing carries a risk, the logic of an
account linking restructuring to effort predicts that parallel structures, such as the
following constituents (in Comp and IP positions), when marked as such, would
be rendered immediately (see e.g. Shlesinger and Massaro 1997: 37):

(1) an initial NP (Nom-marked in German, or simply initial in French), as
    English Subject;
(2) an initial subordinate clause (Comp position);
(3) a sentence-initial pre-Subject PP or adverbial phrase.

Paraphrasing such structures would need to be explained in terms of some benefit
expected to outweigh its cost. In the remaining chapters we hope to show why
such structures are not as transposable as they seem, and why their transformations
do not necessarily carry a processing cost.

Let us first examine what interpreters do when encountering word order which cannot be accommodated by the rules of the output language. The examples in what follows can be found in the Appendices and are referenced by segment and/or line number in the analytic (tabular) presentation (Appx. W1, W3 or T2). The interpreters are WL, WA and WB for the German corpus, and TA and TB for the Taipei corpus.

Since a simultaneous interpreter's output usually lags a few seconds behind the Speaker's, NP or VP Heads often become available in time for complete clause structures to be processed together. There would therefore be no call for special strategies for left-branching items lasting less than 1-2 seconds (typically pre-V adverbials, and pre-N adjectives and determiners), which interpreters receive fully before formulating their content.[3]

4.1 German-English

Examination of the German-English corpus shows that interpreters do not usually wait in silence during left-branching constituents. However, short silences are sometimes noticeable (if the interpreter has finishing producing an earlier segment) when a downstream dependency is signalled in the current string, as here in Würzburg S2-WA (Table 5.1) by the cataphoric copy-pronoun **darauf** ('thereon') and the pre-verbal PP: 'when the representative of a court ... is asked to make a speech, he is - no doubt... thereon advised [about legal issues....> *VP*':

Table 5.1 Würzburg S2 (Interpreter WA) Pausing at left-branching structure

@mm wenn 6 @ - ein Räpräsentant einesGe'richts. [CP?when/if - [IP a NN representative of-a court	+
zumal eines Revis'ionsgerichts 10.7 [especially of-an appeal court	when 10 - somebody. -
@ refe'rieren soll 12.2 - [VP make-speech M supposed]]]] -	who represents a /court. 12.3
dann- ist - [CPthen Aux is -	particularly a court of
er wohl 14.3 [IP he [Adv I-guess	apPEAL.13.8 is asked.
'schwerpunktmäßig @ [Adv focally	to give a SPEECH 15.5
darauf angewiesen 17.6 - [PP thereon] advised -	+
über -@ 'Rechtsfragen 20.6 - [PPabout/over - law questions -	+
und zumal- [& especially	obviously- 21.7 he- is going
'darüber 22.9 zu berichten [PPthere-about[VPtoreport	to talk

The issue is whether certain patterns in SI are strategies in response to structural triggers, or simply reflections of natural processes which can be re-interpreted in linguistic and cognitive terms.

An interpreter can only stall usefully, or 'pad' credibly with filler material, to the extent that she has something to say. Interpreters sometimes fill gaps and silences with something which the Speaker *might* plausibly have said, but usually only a social or communicative lubricant, as in the addition here of the word 'colleagues':

Vielen Dank Herr 'Vorsitzender meine sehr verehrten Damen -
Many thanks   Mr Chairman   my   very honoured ladies -
GERMany   H THANK you very much @Chairman.

meine 'Herren 2.6   + @mm wenn 5 @ -   ein Räpräsentant
my gentlemen   if/when -   a representative
ladies. and. gentlemen 3   +   colleagues 9   +

4.1.1 Autonomous syntax

In the Würzburg sample, a fairly regular pattern emerges. Where interpreters encounter left-branching structures they usually 'enter' (begin a sentence) as soon as the first left-branching phrase begins. Table 5.2. shows left-branching sentences in the German corpus with the three interpreters' 'entry points', i.e. the point at which they commit themselves to a sentence form at CP or IP level. (S9 is more complex, and is analysed in detail later). Responses are timed to a precision of around ± 0.2 s for WA and WB, and ± 0.5s for the live recording (WL).

As a rule, once constituents in CP, and particularly IP, have been uttered, a speaker is committed to expressing a proposition with some semantic content. At several points in the table, two successive entry points have been shown (superscript [A, B,] or [L]), usually corresponding to the production of some initial element, roughly in Comp position, followed by the first IP element, such as the Subject, which more firmly commits the interpreter to a syntactic and propositional form; for example, interpreter B in S2α:

$[_{CP}$ then of course + $[_{IP}$ [B]he has - MAINLY. to discuss...

The structures produced at each left-branching string (initial subordinate clause, prepositional or adverbial phrase, initial adjunct (**als**...), and embedded 'participial' P, are summarised in Table 5.3. They can all be classified as one or more of the following (see Table 5.2. for the examples cited, and Apps. W1-3 for WS9):

Table 5.2 German-English left-branching structures (superscripts show interpreters' 'entry-points')
Subscripts: case/gender/number (Dative, Genitive, Oblique, Plural...); @ filled pause. (See key to symbols, page xii.)

W-M2 H Da einer der .Schwerpunkte - dieser - 'Tagung -

[CPAS [NP oneN ofthe focal-points [NPof this - meeting]
auf^L diesem^A - Be'REICH des^B - Subventionsbetruges. liegen soll
- [IP[PPon[NPthisD - area   [NP ofthe -   subsidy fraudG   [VPlie should]]]]

L: *which is. as I have said.   one. of- the- main@ points@*
A: one of the - M MAIN points of our symposium - WAS
B: and that is-@ one of the important points   - of.

H ist es -   vor allem auch für unsre \ausländischen 'Gäste

[CP is it - [IP [above all   [also [PPfor [NPour   foreignP   guests]]]]
- von^AB GROß^Lem Inter'esse -   WIE. ....
- [PPof   great   interest -   [how.....

L: *is a point which is. of- great. interest@ - to. our ...*
A: and I think. that - this is of great interest [to our...
B: and.- its very important   I think for...

WM4   als Präsi'denten -   des -   deutschen 'Bundesgerichtshofs

[CP?as/when/if [NPPresidentP/A[oftheG - German Federal Court]]]
brauche^A ich Herrn^B Professor Odersky - hier - NICHT VORzustellen (...^L)
V need   I [NPMrA - Prof. Odersky] -   here -   not   V introduce

A: he - hardly needs any introduction I think.@ for as you know
B: he's President and Chief Justice of the [...] I hardly need..

Table 5.2 German-English left-branching structures (continued)

WS2α dann- ist er wohl-. 'schwerpunktmäßig @

[C then is [IP[NPhe[I-guess -[focally

darauf angewiesen - über + L**'Rechtsfragen** B - **und zumal-**A   **'darüber zu berichten**

[PPthereon] V advised -[PPabout/over - law questions - [& especially   [PPthere-about [VP to V report

          then I think- L*he- @ has been@ asked to speak principally about...*

L: obviously- Ahe- is going to talk [about..]

A: Bhe HAS-   MAINly. - [to-- discuss-@....]

B: then   of course-   +

wie Rechtsfragen   DURCH

[CPhow [IP[NPlaw questioI.SP [PPby/through

die GerichteA **bereits entschieden 'wurden** B -   L**oder welche** *sich* **Probleme sich da \ stellen**

[NPthe courts [already [VPdecided were]]]] -   [or[IP[NPwhich F/P # [NPproblems *unacc* there V pose

           L*he- @ H   -is   asked.   to talk.   on-*

L:*...and in particular*   -

A:.......... -   Aand the way in which. legal issues ....

B:.................. -   Band HOW legal issues ......

WS4 [In Ihrer Tagung hat sich bereits her'ausgestellt] daß sich # unter dem 'großen Feld das

   In your meeting has ?Reft already   emerged - [CPthat[IP[NP#[I-[PPunder theO largeO field[CPthat

unter dem General thema - L **er'faßt ist - insbesondere zwei Komplexe** A**her'auskris**A **tallisieren -**

[IP[PPunder theO general-theme]] - [VPsubsumed is]] -[I- especially [NPtwo groups [VP P -out Vcrystallize

L: [*it has become. quite \clear.that.*] L*there is a very*@   *LARGE. RANGE of QUEStions*@ [....]

A: [in the symposium so far] ...   +   it has emerged. that there are

B: - [your meeting] +   Bh-has @ alREADy - discussed@   @TWO   -   speCIFic

WS6: das 'Andere - vielleicht mehr von

[CP[NPthe other - [CP[IP perhaps[more[PPof/ from/by

der[B] **'Mitgliedsstaatsseiten**[A] **@**[L]   [L]**betone Anliegen ist das-**   **der-**   **@Ver-**   **der Ver'besserung** -

the[O]   member-states-side[D]   [stressed [concern[VPis[that- ([NP(of)the   # -   [NP(of)the improvement -

L: *and@ - Member States \also- have- quite. leGITimate concerns. which THEY .....*

A: and@ the OTHer.issue. that @ per/ha@s is a concern more for the member..

B: and the OTHer - which comes from member /STATES ......

WS8: Der europäische Subven'tionsbetrug[A] [The European subsidy fraud]

'wird -   **das ist**[L] **hier in**   [AB]**Ihrem Kreis schon ge'sagt worden** [B]   **in** [B] **der Bundes**[A]**republik**

'fut/pass -   that is   here in   your circle already said   been -   in the Federal Republic

L....+   *H* [L]*European subsidy @ - ~fraud- -*   *as has been said. already*

A: [A]I'm going.to address. [A]fraudulent obtention of subsidies.- IN Europe.and [A]it's alREADy

B: ....H   [B]European-   @ -   [B]subsidy fraud. - [B]as alREADy been SAID@

'Deutsch [L]**land** [B] **durch /** [L]**den -**   **##**[A] **in den siebziger** [L]**Jahren EIN'gefügten Paragraphen zwei hundert**

Germany -   by/through the   ##   in the seventies y   years   inserted   paragraph twohundred

L: [L]is@ a- - @ @   [L]crime-   which- -   [L]has been- en /shrined -   in -   %   is   @

A: -   been pointed out.@ that - [A]this is something. that   +   <R

B: -   [B]in. this particular semi/nar   +   is-@ -

B[L]**vierund'sechzig**[A]   **des Strafge'setzbuches** [L]   **-gegen -**   **Subven'tionsbetrug -**   **'MITerfaßt** -

fourandsixty   of-the penal-law-book -   against -   subsidy fraud -   also-covered

L : [L]*the- legal* *system of the Federal Republic of Germany* [L]*by means of its insertion. in paragraph twosixfour - of the. H*

German. penal \code.   the.   penal /code. there're. specific /paragraphs...

A[A]regulated in   federal Germany BY@   in /article -   two six \~FOUR - of @. the criminal /CODE

B: R>[B]/TREATed -   in German law -

(a)   'anticipation', i.e. early output of a Main Verb or predicate ('antic MV' in the table), as in S8 for all three interpreters;

(b)   expansion of a Subject, as in S8-WL 'European subsidy fraud *is a crime which...*' or WA in S8 and again in S9, '*this is something that...*', or insertion or expansion of parentheticals, as in M2-WL, M2α-WA, or S8-WB 'as already been said - *in this particular semi/nar*'

(c)   creation of a presentative (copula) or existential Main or Relative Clause (MC or RC) which in effect simply asserts a presupposition of the embedded input structure, as in S4-WL '*there is a very large range of questions*'.

Table 5.3 Interpreters' output structure over German left branching strings
RC: relative clause; MC: Main Clause; conn: connective; MV: Main Verb; exp: expansion

Seg	Int	Structure produced at left-branching input	Left-br. structure	Interpreter's structure
M2	L	[IPwhich is. *as I have said* one. of- the- main@ points@	SubCl , PP	RC + parenth
	A	[IPone of the - m MAIN points ..- [WAS		MC
	B	[and [IPthat [is-@ [one of the important points of...		MC
M2α	L	[*and* @ [*this* @ [*is* [*a point* [*which*...	Adv, PP	MC + exp
	A	[and [I [think. [CPthat - this is		conn, MC
	B	[and.- [its very important...		antic MV
M4	A	[IPhe- hardly needs any introDUCtion for	adjunct	antic MV
	B	[IP he' s President and Chief Justice of the [...]		MC
S2	L	[then [I *think-[he-* @ *has been*@ asked [to *speak* ..	PP	repetition and antic MV
	A	[obviously-[he-is going to talk..		antic MV
S4	L	[*there* [is [a *very*@ *LARGE. RANGE of QUEStions*@	PP	MC exist
	A	[there are ...		MC exist
	B	[YOUR- -m\MEEting + [h-has @ alREADy - disCUSSed@ [@ TWO - speCIFic		MC
S6	L	[and [*SECondly* - [*Member States* *also- have-*	AP	MC
S8	L	is@ a- /crime- which- -has been- en/shrined-	PPs, AdvP	exp Subj , RC, antic MV
	A	[this is something. that - is @ regulated ...		exp Subj, antic MV
	B	as alREADy been SAID@ - in. this particular semi/nar + is-@ /TREATed -		expand paren, antic MV
S9	L	are@ - now @m + protected@ -	PPs, AdvP	antic MV
	A	+ + and. @ basically + this is something that ...		pause, Adv, expand Subj
	B	... is-- there-fore. + @dealt with...		antic MV

However, interpreters also pause and make apparently redundant insertions or expansions at other points (underlined in Table 5.3). The flexibility of spoken language allows an interpreter to stall at little or no cost to the product by various expedients in addition to simple pausing, such as more or less gratuitous parenthetical comments or expanded qualifying forms (underlined), or slow, deliberate articulation: drawling (_ or -) and short or long 'schwa-suffixing' (glossed "." and "@") lengthen the articulation of vowels and consonants respectively (WL-M2β):

...**einer der .Schwerpunkte - dieser - 'Tagung 11.6 - auf diesem - Be'REICH 13.2**
... one of-the focal-points -   of-this meeting -   on this   'area
                        /*fraud- 11.4 - which is. as I have said. 13.1 one.*

des - Subventionsbetruges. liegen soll 15.4 + H ist es - vor allem auch für unsre..
of-the - subsidy fraud - lie should   is it - above all   also for   our ...
of-   the -   main@   points@ 15.9 which we- wish to deal with - in this...

Such initial elements, filled pauses ('er(m)', glossed @) and 'gratuitous' expansions can indeed help to delay syntactic commitment at IP level until the source predicate is available, as in the above example where WL's *which we- wish to deal with* is a further expansion not traceable to anything in the source text. WA also fills the next gap, until the PP predicate *of great interest*, with the insertion of 'and I think. that...'.

Another form of expansion is the redundant reiteration of constituents, which can allow even more material to come in, as in S2αβ, where WL's repetition of '*he is asked. to talk*' allows her to process the two conjuncts together:

wie Rechtsfragen DURCH 22.9 die Gerichte bereits entschieden 'wurden 24.8 -
how law questions through/by   the courts   already   decided   were
(*he has been asked to speak principally about questions of the law, and in particular*)

oder welche sich Probleme 25 sich da .stellen 27.3 -
or   which [#unacc] problems [Refl/unacc] there pose
he- @   H   25.7 -is   asked.   to talk.. on- 28.3 decisions. already taken. bycourts. 29.3 and   the difficulties which the courts. 31.5 experienced. in taking these decisions

In summary, there are various phenomena in the interpreters' versions which seem gratuitously to delay the output of something more meaningful, but which have varying cognitive and communicative significance:

(1)   utterance- or sentence-scope elements: adverbs reflecting a modality expressed in the original discourse (*obviously, of course, I think, in*

particular); conjunctions; conative or formulaic phrases (*I think*); parenthetical additions, and discourse connectives (*Secondly,...*), some of which have no overt origin in the source discourse; or the deliberate use of longer forms for certain referents (WL and WB 41-43; WB 97-8 'in this <u>particular</u> seminar')

(2)   the functional apparatus required to generate new clause structure ('new' with respect to the original), i.e. complementizers, relative pronouns; and reiterated, or 'copied' elements (which would normally be candidates for ellipsis).

(3)   articulatory phenomena: filled pauses, solecisms, extended phones (drawl, schwa).

The second and third categories are purely linguistic devices allowed by the flexibility of spoken discourse. To account for the first type of element, however, a cognitive-pragmatic account of SI is needed, regardless of whether they are dismissed as translation errors (cf. Barik 1975), or accepted as a natural part of the target language version.

But the same passages from the text also show more complex syntactic and semantic processes behind the interpretation which cannot be dismissed simply as stalling tactics. Table 5.4 shows how the three interpreters handle Würzburg S4, in which the Subject **zwei Komplexe** ('two complexes') of an unaccusative verb **(sich... herauskristallisieren)** is delayed by a long PP and relative clause.

Interpreters **WL** and **WA** deal with the first clause in simple successive chunks, rendering '**In Ihrer Tagung** ('In your meeting...') immediately as an independent sentential phrase (WL: *I think during the course- of. this seminar-* /WA: in. the. symPOSium so /far' /).

Interpreter **WB**, in contrast, ventures 'Your meeting... ' as a Subject, forcing her tentatively to generate her own predicate, and indeed an entire clause, independently of the text syntax. Having departed from the original syntax, she now has to build an entirely different sentence, requiring a predicate expressing some action, state or attribute, on the Subject 'meeting'. There is no help from either the input grammar (a presentative verb with so far only a left-branching PP as complement) or its rather uninformative lexical content:

'...it has emerged that - within the broad domain covered by the overall theme..... '

In short, she must create a predicate from some known attribute of 'Your meeting' or of meetings in general. The text indicates past tense (WA: *so far*) and something becoming clear (WL: *it has become quite clear*). The most basic activity of meetings is discussion, and the next words fit the category of its likely

Table 5.4 Würzburg S4: complex restructuring in SI

	Input	*Interpreter WL*	Interpreter WA	Interpreter WB
67	**In Ihrer Tagung hat** In [NPyour meeting [has	*/ by way of intro* *DUCtion*	+	and THAT's basic ally what I shall try and do/HERE
68	**sich bereits her'ausgestellt -** [IP[NP *refl* [already [emerged	+ *I think*	in. the. - sympₒsium	y-
69	**daß sich #Fe# unter dem** **'großen Feld** [cpthat[IP[NP*refl* # [PP under the large field	*during the course-* *of. this seminar-* *it- has@*	so /far	/Y_OUR- - m\MEEting +
70	**das unter dem Generalthema** **- er'faßt ist -** [IPthat [vp[ppunder the general- theme [subsumed is -	*become. quite* *\clear - that.* *there is a very @*	+	h-has @ alREADy -
71	**insbesondere <u>zwei Komplexe</u>** **her'auskristallisieren** [respecially [two groups[out - crystallize]]]] -	*LARGE RANGE* *of QUEStions*	it has emerged. that there are	disCUssed@ + @TWO - speCIFic
72	**das Eine ist** [cp[IP the one is......	*@m -*	TWO MAIN -	issues@ -IN - the OVERall
73		*under- the-*	ISSues -	ISSue that
74		*@ main topic -* *of subsidy \fraud*	@%	you're - re/FERRing -

objects ('subject-matter': theme, field...), so there is little risk in generating 'discussed' as predicate. By this time the vague 'subject-matter' is specified as 'two complexes' ('within the broad domain covered by the overall theme').

WL, having followed the structure of the first clause, now prefers 'chunking' to waiting. She can project a downstream Subj-V-O structure, qualified by 'within the broad domain...', but not its content, so first she simply asserts the existence of this domain:

> [*there* [*is* [*a very@ LARGE. RANGE of QUEStions@....*

i.e. a minimal presupposition licensed by its status as Definite.[4] But she can enrich it with her own knowledge about the identity of this 'general theme', i.e. that it is in fact, although this is not specified in the text, the *main topic* [of the meeting].

> ... *under- the- main topic - of subsidy \fraud*

When the SL Subject appears she continues in this 'presentative' mode,

> <u>*and there are*</u> *TWO - MAIN - points of con\cern (-firstly....)*

the simple conjoining of the two statements being deemed sufficient for listeners to infer, for what it's worth, that the latter (*points of concern*) are ranked 'under' the former (*main topic*).

WA and WB use the referent of **zwei Komplexe** ('two complexes') according to the status of their current sentences, WA in a presentative ('there are two main issues'), WB as an Object ('has discussed two specific issues'); WB then attaches the earlier qualifying phrase ('...in the overall issue...'), while WA discards it. Whether such elimination is due to a relevance judgment or to failure (e.g. a processing or memory overload) is not knowable; this issue is discussed in Chapter 7.

This example appears to show a variety of 'strategies', including pausing, added qualifiers and conatives and other rhetorical dressing (*I think, during the course of, quite clear*), the extra spelling-out of a referring expression *the main topic - of subsidy \fraud;* and 'chunking' with the use of a neutral existential construction based on a simple presupposition '*there is a very LARGE. RANGE of QUEStions*'.

4.1.2 German-English SI structural patterns: summary

So far, we have established that these German-English interpreters

(1)   start building their own TL structure on encountering word order in input which cannot be followed sequentially;

(2)   often expand or insert structure with respect to the original discourse;

(3)   express simple existential presuppositions licensed by the text as well as its explicit assertions;

(4)   use text-external knowledge, of the situation or conference event, in their versions;

(5)   use connectives, conjunctions, conatives and other interclausal or Composition elements rather liberally with respect to the original.

We have also seen how the choice of outputs is constrained by the interpreter's ongoing sentence. Similar patterns can be observed in the Chinese-English corpus, insofar as similar asymmetries are found.

4.2 Chinese-English

As explained in Chapter 4, to test the assumption that SL-TL correlations can be observed at a structural level, and their significance, and in general to support a discussion of the structural aspects of SI, at least for German-English and Chinese-English, we have adopted a conservative GB-based account of phrase structure assigning various elements to CP, IP and other positions.

Chinese contrasts with English in other features than word order. Most accounts also recognise important differences of Chinese with respect to Indo-European languages in both logical form (e.g. the marking of logical scope) and the encoding of thematic and case relations, e.g. the distribution or deletion of sentence Topics, Subjects and anaphora (Li and Thompson 1981).

Whereas German clauses may begin with direct or indirect Objects or adjunct phrases marked for their status by case inflection or preposition, the opening strings of Chinese clauses offer little or no grammatical clue to dependencies being set up within the proposition. Pre-verbal strings typically include elements which may be Topic and/or Subject, and prepositional or adverbial phrases. An initial Topic may be marked off as such by a particle (*ne* or *a*), but there is no overt semantic indication of its relation to the subsequent 'Comment', and the Subject may be deleted. Clauses or V-O constructions can be sentence-topics, because Chinese verbs are not marked for Finiteness, whereas in English, for example, *-ed*, *-ing*, *to* V, and zero inflections on an early occurring verb show its syntactic status:

Zhangsan hui jia qu, bu shi hen fangbian
*Zhangsan return home is-not very convenient
Zhangsan('s) returning home is not very convenient

The only corresponding garden-path in English might be the gerundive/participial ambiguity of *-ing*, as in

Returning to the old homestead is every cowboy's dream
Returning to the old homestead, he vowed never again to leave

On the other hand, Chinese Topics and other segments are often logically marked off by a scope marker like *shi*, or a particle like *ne*, and are relatively short. A language with this arrangement—marking logical or thematic units for processing—may have fewer long-distance syntactic dependencies than a language like German. But the need to supply arguments which are dropped, especially Subjects in new clauses, clearly means that comprehenders must maintain an array of likely entities accessible over the medium term to be supplied in various roles: Subjects and Topics may be deleted over several sentences.

At discourse structure level, not all differences between the source texts can be extrapolated as differences between languages, or culture-specific discourse patterns. For example, the higher frequency of prefatory or parenthetical items (*I think, I feel, that is to say*) in our Chinese text, or of 'afterthought' strings, cannot safely be attributed to a typological difference. On the other hand, the clustering of such elements with modal and sentential adverbs in utterance-initial position, with explicit marking of the boundary (by particles, *shi*, etc) between these clusters and predicate-containing strings, is at least partly language-specific.

We shall examine whether the interpreters' handling of the utterances, as traditionally described in terms of tactics (waiting, stalling, chunking or anticipation) can be re-interpreted in more general cognitive or linguistic terms.

An 'incremental' parsing grammar gives us the following approximate framework for the Chinese utterance, with brackets around optional constituents which can be deleted in surface form (e.g. the Chinese Subject), and * indicating a recursive constituent (recursion can be accommodated at almost every point):

$$*SM - (*Adjunct) - (Subject) - *[P/VP] - [_{VP} *V-(*O)]$$

(1)   SM: SENTENCE MODIFIERS (in CP) like conative phrases, prefatory discourse markers, discourse connectives etc., which usually appear in initial position, are primarily a feature of *spoken* discourse. They are signally absent from the written text segment of our sample (S29-39), which was read out as it stood.

(2)   Initial ADJUNCTs and PVPs (prepositional verb phrases): any phrase(s) for which provisionally no more precise relation with the main predication can be inferred than 'Aboutness' (for a Topic), or in the case of a PVP, than whatever is suggested by its Head preposition or coverb (see 'Verb Phrases' below). Such constituents may appear in any categorial form (NP, IP, VP, CP, AP, PP) and are candidates for realisation in an English sentence as argument, adjunct, or secondary predicate. They may also include or coincide with a Subject of the main VP.

Selecting the status of such a phrase for production of an English sentence—e.g. as clausal Subject, verb complement or PP adjunct—must therefore involve an element of semantic(-pragmatic) inference. A pre-verbal argument may be marked by *ba* (or *jiang*).

(3)   (Main) VERB PHRASE(s), usually comprising a Verb and its Object. Like the PVP, these are recursive: serial verb-phrase constructions with deleted Subjects are a common feature of Chinese sentences. Some types of Chinese phrase Heads which have been variously analysed as prepositions or verbs (a distinct category, 'coverb', has been proposed (Li and Thompson 1981)), are glossed as 'preposition/verb phrase (PVP)' and treated in general as preverbal PPs.

4.2.1 Parsing Chinese

Generative linguists recognise that the 'theta-role' (Chomsky 1981, 1986) of an argument in a fixed-word-order language cannot be predicted from its position (Radford 1981: 378). The role of a phrase (including, if relevant, its status as argument or adjunct) is established either by assignment from an available marker, via case morphology, or a θ-role-assigner, such as a verb. But constituents are not always marked as complements or adjuncts, or for their roles. In the Chinese Topic position, a wide range of constituents may appear, and neither morphology nor word order can be relied on to yield information. In everyday spoken discourse, ungrammaticality and false starts may also impair the reliability of morphological marking, which suggests that constituency must often rely on relations strongly assumed to hold on the basis of frame or discourse knowledge. To our knowledge, there are no parsing accounts of how Topics are handled on-line; indeed, little or no parsing literature has addressed Chinese corpora, even at the level of individual sentences.

We shall treat Topic as an initial Adjunct signalling a priori nothing more in terms of its semantic relation with what follows than 'Aboutness'. In the absence of other clues, nothing more can be assumed by a parser to support the attachment or 'association' (Frazier and Clifton 1996) of any such material appearing in advance of a predicate or other material which disambiguates or specifies the relation. (Aboutness as a relation in its own right is explicitly encoded elsewhere in expressions like English *about, regarding, as far as* ...(*is concerned*), Chinese *youguan, dui(yu), guan(yu)*, and less formally in a large class of expressions such as *on (the subject of)..., in terms of..., ruguo jiang dao... (de wenti)*, which are often but not always used to signal a change in discourse topic.)

4.2.2 Left-branching structures in Chinese-English SI

Structures which might conventionally be analysed as left-branching in Chinese are of two types: VPs and NPs; but if unmarked initial adjuncts as defined above are included, then virtually every sentence in the corpus contains a pre-verbal string of uncertain status.

Only after having established the approximate size of input segments which can form the basis for processing does it make sense to look for apparent strategies. Our first finding is that—predictably given this low level of reliable syntactic clues to roles and relations in Chinese utterance form—interpreters usually do not formulate and produce predicate-argument structures on less than one clause (defined as a predicate and at least one argument).

In other words, the interpreters' lag with respect to a strictly clausal analysis of the input is generally such as to allow production after each clause is complete, with or without some waiting or variations on tentative openings ('stalling').

The examples below are referenced either by Segment (e.g. S1, S2...) or by the line number in the tabular presentation in Appendix T2. The interpreters are TA and TB for the main Taipei corpus, and FA and FC for the Fang samples.

Some examples of left-branching structures in the Chinese source discourse are given in Table 5.5. Clear instances of the interpreters waiting in silence for input can be seen in S2-TA, during a left-branching PVP, S6-TB, over the complement to a Wh-question, and S10 (see Appx T2), where both interpreters wait out the Speaker's own hesitations.

· More frequently, over left-branching or other pre-predicate strings (as indeed over other strings), the interpreters are either still finishing a previous sentence, or beginning a new utterance with a prefatory conative or adverbial phrase. Such tentative sentence openings may include conative or resumptive openings like *you know, I think, so, as such...* (S6, 14, 15, 17, 21), and may be accompanied by pausing or hesitant delivery (S1-2, TA). However, they do not always correspond to the opening used by the Speaker, raising again the question of the source and generation of such elements. Table 5.6 lists the utterance openings used by the Speaker and the interpreters. Of 86 responses, over half involve additions, deletions, expansions or enrichments, simplifications or abridgements, or meaning-changing paraphrases. Over the recited written text (S29-39), which contained no rhetorical openings, four connective openings were inserted.

The lack of formal correspondence between such conative or discourse-directive items in the Speaker's discourse and the interpreters' versions, where they often seem to function as tentative or 'neutral' beginnings or continuations, suggests that rather than trying to model processing of such material in structural or formal terms, we should look for some more general cognitive account. This is explored in Chapter 6.

Time may also be bought, or commitment postponed, by generating a 'dummy' constituent or structure, for example by expanding a Subject or Object with a relative clause, as seen in the German-English corpus. In TS1, interpreter A has already begun I've been invited..., calling for a Verb-Object complement continuation, when the pre-verbal adjunct is introduced (by *yi...*, underlined). She inserts a generic object (a topic), then attaches a rather redundant relative (focusing on...)

When SL recursion lengthens the clause beyond what can reasonably be waited out or stalled over, these interpreters sometimes produce temporary approximations of predicate-argument cores. Sometimes (though rarely in this sample) an interpreter may tentatively start on the VP using elements current from

Table 5.5 Chinese-English left-branching structures (superscripts show interpreters' 'entry points')

de : attributive/possessive particle; ([unclear syntactic status; *shi*, F> focus/emphasis; p particle; fp filler; ~ 'modulating' intonation.

TS1: (Thank you Chairman, good afternoon] **wo - jintian ... yao. gen gewei tan tan** (today I would like to discuss..)
@^A jiushi yi woguo jiaru^AB - Lianheguo JINRONG ZUZHI - de ^B zheige cengmian ne -
[that is [by Taiwan join - UN financial. organisations.   *de*   this   aspect   p
TA: ^A| been invited - ^A to talk - on -   a topic -   focusing -
TB: today/ - ^B| will be talking to you about - H ^B Taiwan's -

lai gen gewei tan tan - wo guo chongfan Lianheguo ^A de - zheige kenengxing\ +
to with you-all discuss - our country return UN *de* - this   possibility
TA: on -   +   ^A Chinese Tai\pei's -   re-entry ......
TB: |entry into   UN's   financial   institutions   +

TS2 : cong - gang gang de ji wei - lai zi. guoneiwai de JIANGZHE - de zhe yanjiang dangzhong
from - just now   [several - [come from country-in-out [speakers' - [speeches] -   within -
jiu keyi faxian....^A, B
thus can realize....
TA: +   ^A speakers from home and abroad who spoke before me have shared with us their \views....
TB: ^B from the |speakers that we have heard so \far we /know. that the speakers have reached a consensus...

TS3 : (now today what I particularly want to stress is...)**women ru-he - touguo - canjia -** [how we... via join(ing)]
^A@^B Lianheguo de. zheige jinrong zuzhi - nenggou DADAO - women ^A - chongfan Lianheguo de - zheige mu^B biao^A
[United Nations'   thisfinancial organisations]] - can reach - ([[we - rejoin   UN]   *de* -   this   goal]

TA:[.|'d|ike to|^A stress   ~more-   -on   +   ^A how -   we can   +   ^A ob\tain.
the \goal....[of...
TB:[..|mgoing to]^B emphasize   + H   H   the-   +   ^B reentry (of -
Taiwan into the United Nations - VTA - the financial institutions of the UN)

Table 5.5 Chinese-English left-branching structures (continued)

TS4: (on the question of rejoining the UN...)
zai... YIYUAN **fangmian .. zheige chaoye .... yijing shi dadao yizhi de gongshi le** (^A, B)
- on   intention side ...   govt & opposition ... already *shi* reached unanimous consensus p

TA: ....   politicians [....] have [...]all made a
consensus... that re-entry to the UN..   .. is necessary
TB: ....   Government and private sectors have...
reached a consensus   ...in (SIC)..Taiwan's NEED to re-enter the UN

TS5: (everyone also recognises one thing, i.e. ... **zai** DANGQIAN **de ...guoji qingshi zhi xia ne** - [under present international
conditions] - **chongfan**[B] **Lianheguo - shi xuyao - chang shijian de qu-**[B] **jingying @ chang shijian de qu-**[A] **zuo**[B] **jihua**
                          [rejoin   UN]   - [F> [need -   long   time   [go-   busy   -   [long time   [go -   make plan
                                                                                            how/ever] -   ^it is _   [B]to- plan/-   -
TA: ....
TB: (...we all know that]   [B]under the   current   international situation/   - [B]we   will   need

bu shi shuo. yi xiang QINGYUAN **de - jiu keyi mashang -**[A]**jiu cucheng de +**
[not F> say [just think wish   [then [can [instantly -   then accomplish

TA: a TASK that requires -   long-term PLAN.NING -   ^and its (not something that can just be completed - by our OWN wish)
TB: and WORK -   for a long time - in order to achieve our GOAL   of re-entering the UN\   -

---

TS6: (I think most important today is...) **women yong yige shenmeyang de fangshi - nenggou** (we use   what kind of method - can)
ZUI YOUXIAODE ^**- hui dao Lianheguo** -[B](... ^)
[most effectively -[return to United Nations]]]

TA: ....   ^there/fore. the ISSUE today - is how can we re\ENTER the United Nations - through the most. efficient \way
TB: +   H .   +   [B]we need to lknow how we can - most \EFFICIENTLY - be come a UN member a\GAIN

TS9: suoy-. dangran women jintian - yao y- nenggou chongfan Lianheguo de hua ne - bixu nenggou RAOguo -
so of course [we today -([if/want able rejoin UN- -if p [must able [bypass

Anlihui - zhege TUJING - nenggou- ba women de zhege SHENQING'AN ne - kan shi bu shi nenggou
([SecCouncil this route] - able ba >Obj [our fp application] p - see [whether [[able

ba ta ^{B} **zhuan dao. zhege** ^{A} **Lianheguo de DAhui shang** ^{B} **mian** ^{A} +
ba >Obj it [divert -to fp ([[UN Gen.Assembly]] -on]]]]]

TA: .... ^{A} therefore it is necessary to ^{A} BYPASS the Security Council [by going to the General
ASSEMBLY directly +
TB: (so) ^{B} we need to see - if we. can. ^{B} apply. through the General ASSEMBLY of the UN INSTEAD of the
Security Council

TS14: dangran zheige yao. juli -   dadao zheige SAN FEN ZHI ER -
of course [this [shall[distance(from)- reach fp [two-thirds -

duoshu @ ^{B} **juedui zheige BIAOZHUN ne - shi hai xiangcha - jiangjin yibai piao - zhi duo** ^{AB}
majority - absolute fp criterion p - [F>[still lack - nearly 100 votes -so-many]

TA: ....   you know. ^{A} we are - a long /way from.
obtaining. majority. support. from the UN.....
TB: (so) - ^{B} it's not LIKELY that we will be able to- reach - a two-thirds majority- vote. - ^{B} we need. more than. a hundred
VOTES in our FAVOUR

TS15: (so seen in this way, clearly...) **jingyou. Lianheguo DAHUI de zhei tiao lu ne** (via this UN General Assembly route...)
shuo shizai ye BUSHI name de RONGYIDE ^{AB} +
[say-honestly [also[not > [so easy]]]]

TA: ....   as such - ^{A} if's not so - EASY - to obtain - membership in the United Nations. - bygoing
through the General As\sembly
TB: an- -so- I conclude here that - ^{B} it won't be EASY for us to - re-lenter the UN/ - \through the General Ass/embly

Table 5.5 Chinese-English left-branching structures (continued)

TS17 : ... yinwei women zher zai - zai Lianheguo - zai Anlihui limian ne (because there in the Security Council...)
Zhonggong you foujuequan[B] ~ - **wo gang gang shuoGUO le** (...[A])
[Communist China [has   veto right   -   {[I   just   said   pfv] }

TA: ....   (CHINA commands voting POWER in the Security COUNCIL)
TB: H   we know that   -   [B] \inthe Security /Council Mainland /China has. a right.....

TS19: xianzai - zai - Lianheguo de - tixi zhi xia - xianzai (at present in the UN system there are (now) ...)
zonggong you [B] - **SHIBAGE - ZHENGFU JIAN**[A] **DE - @- ZUZHI @ zhezhong ... ZHUANMEN JIGUAN**
[altogether [(there)are [eighteen intergovernmental. organisations [this kind .. special bodies

TA: ....   +   [A]there are EIGHTEEN - intergovernMENtal - SPECIALISED - (organisations or
agencies under the umbrella of. UN)
TB: .... [B]under the UN/system - h there are EIGHTEEN intergovernmental organisations (- @ specialized AGENCIES)

haiyou -   san ge -   yinhang zuzhi[B] **- x- xing de -** [A]**zheizhong zhuanmen jiguan**
and(there)are [three   -   (([bank orgs   -   type *de* -   such   [special. agencies

TA: ....   [A]there are ALSO   - THREE -   BANK - TYPE - organisations
TB: ....   [B]there # three -   H   H   \BANK-@   organi sations
-    a - nd.

the previous utterance (Subject) or inferred (Tense and Auxiliary). Here the preverbal PPs are clearly marked by prepositions 'with...' and 'about [regarding..':

FANG M1/3-4:
name jintian xiawu ne 22.7 - gen - hen duo de Zhongguo jiaoshou 24.8 -
well-so today afternoon p - [with - very many China/ese professors
FC: .... *23.5 - and   this   after/noon 24.6*
yiji gen Zhongguo tongxuemen 21 - jiu youguan liang `an - Zhongguo de
and with China/ese fellow students - [about [regarding two shores - China *de*
                  - you   -   were   ~able 27.6
wenti ne -   jixu ne - jiaohuan yiJIAN 29.8   + name jintian zaizuo ne...
question(s) p - [continue p - exchange view(s)   well-so today sitting p...
                              - to. dis\cuss 29.9   - problems concerning
Chi/na 31.9 and Tai.\WAN with many professors and students 35.6 ....

Anticipation in SI is not reserved for delayed verbs, but is seen for other delayed or absent constituents, like Subjects, Objects or a delayed question focus (Wh- *in situ*). In S1 (see Table 5.5.) both interpreters select an Object early, at odds with the input structure. TA, with some pausing, produces a 'virtual' Object and relative clause expansion 'talk - on - a topic - focusing - on...', but the nominalising particle '*de*' signals a further delay to the Head of the Object NP:

S1: (Thank you Chairman, good afternoon..)
wo- jintian ..yao. gen gewei tan tan @^{A} jiushi yi woguo - jiaru^{AB}- Lianheguo
I today -   intend [with you-all discuss [that is [by Taiwan join United Nations
TA: .... ^{A}I been invited - ^{A}to talk -   on -
TB: .... today/ - ^{B}I will be talking

JINRONG ZUZHI   - de ^{B}zheige cengmian ne -
financial. bodies.   - *de*   this   aspect p
TA: a topic -   focusing -   on -   +
TB: to you about- H ^{B}Taiwan's -\entry

TB selects the first proposition 'Taiwan's entry...' as the Direct Object. It is an Indirect Object, but is all that is so far available. In truth-conditional terms this is not false: to say that the Speaker will talk about 'our entry into UN's financial institutions' is a valid entailment of '...discuss [pvp in terms of/by our joining the UN's financial institutions [DO the possibility of] our rejoining the UN.' Of course the focus of emphasis is wrong, so TB produces an entirely new sentence, with repetition, to correct it: 'I will be looking at the possibility of the ROC's[5] re-entry into the UN from this point of view'.

TA, on the other hand, merges the two propositions ('re-entry to international financial organisations'), producing an uncorrected distortion.

Table 5.6 Rhetorical openings in Chinese-English SI

Key to symbols: - no opener; ≅ paraphrased; • simplified /abridged; ° dropped; <> expanded or enriched; + inserted

	Opener	Interpreter TA	Interpreter TB
S1	thank you Chairman	thank you Chairman	thank you very much Mr Chairman <>
	hallo all	ladies and gentlemen <>	good afternoon ladies and gentlemen <>
	today I intend with you discuss	I've been invited to talk on a topic focusing on <>	today/ I will be talking to you about
S2	I think you from just now several come from home and abroad speakers' speeches realize	Speakers... who spoke before me have shared with us their views on ≅	from the speeches that we have heard so far we know that ≅
S3	today I esp. want to stress- *shi*	today I'd like to stress more on	but today I'm going to emphasize <>
S4	I think	- °	I think that
S5	well everyone likewise realise something *shi*	however •	however we all know that •
S6	most important today *shi*	therefore the issue today is.. <>	I think most importantly <>
S7	of course many speakers also mentioned	many scholars who spoke before me mentioned ≅	- / we know that •
S8	Why? - because	as •	because we know that ≅
S9	so of course we today	therefore •	so •
S10	and that is to say	- °	- °
S11	but we also know	- °	maybe +
S12	we all/also know	we also understand that °	we know that •
S13	so this means	- °	we know that ≅
S14	of course	you know ≅	so •

	Opener	Interpreter TA	Interpreter TB
S15	so from this point, of view we also know	as such •	so I conclude here that <>
S16	another possible go route p *shi* what? p	the other approach that we can consider is	another alternative is ≈
S17	why? because	- °	we know that
S18	but p	but	yet
S19	-	-	-
S20	I think	- °	and I think that <>
S21	I think	- °	so ≈
S22	I just mentioned	as I mentioned •	-
S23	so I think	therefore •	so •
S24	but I still must stress again one point, *shi* that is	again I'd like stress that	however I must also stress that
S25	presently I want to stress to you all	perhaps I will say a few words more about ≈	and i must stress - I will stress...later
S26	you all in your hands have	I'm sure that you have... <>	I'm sure that you have... <>
S27	-	-	so +
S28	I directlywith you-all address *shi*	and I'd talk about	-
S29	-	-	-
S30	-	-	because +
S31	-	-	-
S32	-	and	but +
S33	-	but +	-
S34	but	however	as for... ≈
S35	-	-	-
S36	-	-	-
S37	-	-	-
S38	-	-	-
S39	-	-	-

In a language like Chinese where the *Wh*-focus of a question may not occur until the end, the interrogative force is nevertheless often cued at an early stage, just as a preposition occurring in the course of a VP or NP may signal a left-branching structure. Here the interrogative mode is cued by the words **ni juede** 'you feel,' the Speaker's role as the interviewer, and the polarity adverb **daodi**, but the *Wh*-focus is delayed by about 8-9 seconds of VP and other material including adjuncts, Subject, and modal auxiliary ('Fang' supplementary corpus M1-5):

> **Ni juede zai ZHEIge shihou 38.4 - daodi zheige Zhongguo zhishifenzi 41 yingdang**
> you feel   at   THIS   time   - [Qn-marker] this Chin/ese   intellectuals   ought
> +   · ·   *39.4 and*

> **zai zheige shihou yijiujiuling niandai 43 - dui Zhongguo yehao Taiwan yehao Dalu**
> at   this   time   nineteenninety age - as-to China- be it Taiwan -be it Mainland
> -   *to\DAY 41.2*   -   *what do you \feel   43.9*   - *the Chinese*

> **yehao 45 - you shenmeyang de yizhong zeren huozhe shenmeyang de shiminggan?**
> be it   have what kind *de* one-type responsibility or what kind *de* mission-feeling?
> *intell/ectuals 46   whether   they   be.   in*
> */China or in Tai/wan +   should   +   take on as their*
> *responsi\bility*

After stalling with *and - to\DAY,* the interpreter opens a cleft construction, choosing for the *wh*-word which is now compulsory in English one with as neutral a focus as possible (*what*), and a recursive insertion which in effect multiplies the scope options: *what do you feel...* When the actual *wh*-element is revealed about 4s later ('what kind of responsibility ... sense of mission'), she post-edits by further specifying this focus '*(what) .....as their responsibility*'.

In the above example, the verb is enriched in the process ('take on' as compared to the neutral you 'have'), but there are considerable distortions: *dui...* more probably has its ordinary root meaning of '*towards...*', and there is some further simplification, or dilution, in the merging of 'at this time [...in the] nineteen-nineties with 'today' and 'what kind [of] responsibility and sense of mission' in *what [...] responsi\bility.*

'Chunking' or quasi-anticipation of this kind may therefore have different implications for strict semantic equivalence than inserting a conative 'I think' or 'as I have said'. In the first example (S1) the prepositional Object (subordinate) argument 'Taiwan's entry into UN financial organisations' was, at least temporarily, presented as the Direct Object (the main, focussed proposition). In the second example, F-M1-3,' *you were able...*' commits the interpreter to a Tense for the main predicate. 'Chunking', for example by asserting the existential presupposition of an embedded string, and anticipation, by producing all or part of a predication, are therefore more likely to affect the propositional semantics of the clause as a whole.

In terms of syntactic structures, however, no regular pattern of transposition emerges (Table 5.5 and Appendix T2): sometimes the material of a pre-verbal PP is rendered in the same initial position, either in a form close to the original (S5, TB; S9, TA), or abridged or paraphrased (S6), sometimes as a postposed PP (S8, S15, S17, S19), although often with some variation or enrichment (S3, S9 TB), or in a Relative Clause attached to a dummy NP (S5, TA); sometimes it becomes the Subject (S2, S4), sometimes the Object (S1), sometimes a Verb complement of the main predicate (S7); sometimes it disappears altogether (S5, first clause, TA; S5, second clause, TB) or appears to have been semantically fused with other elements (S4); sometimes it becomes a Main Clause, again in 'enriched' form (S14).

4.2.3 Subjects

Another major difference between Chinese and English, as described in the introduction to this Section, lies in the surface realisation of the Subject. Attempts to find a structural relationship between input and output are frustrated by the fact that Chinese often deletes the Subject, and as explained, an initial NP in a Chinese utterance cannot safely be interpreted as a Subject.

Since Chinese may have Topics, and delete Subjects, an utterance may begin with an NP or Clause which is a Topic, and/or an NP or Clause which is a Subject, or (according to some grammarians) an item which is both Topic and Subject. Examples are found in the second initial NPs of S5 and S7. How is Subject/Topic constituency recognised and parsed?

Table 5.7 shows Subjects in input and output. Formal input-output matches are not always possible, since there is no one-to-one relationship between structures (they may be fused or expanded in interpretation). Otherwise, the same wide variation in operations is found as for left-branching structures: interpreters may select as Subject, apart from the first animate NP (S4):

1. a dummy or expletive, e.g. for a cleft construction (S9)
2. an anaphoric pronoun (S5-TA)
3. an NP from an original PP (S2, S4,S11-TA)
4. an NP from a VP embedded in a PP (S11-TB)
5. a sentence topic or current discourse topic (S5),
6. a current Subject which is null in the present clause (S6-TB),
7. a null Subject (*pro*) (S9 TA-3).
8. an NP supplied to stand for an [AP[null Subject]] (S6-TA: the issue)

Table 5.7 Subjects in Chinese-English SI

	Subject in source discourse	Interpreter TA	Interpreter TB
S1	I	I	I
S2	all of you	speakers	we
	they/every speaker (3 verbs)	...who...	the speakers
S3	what I want to stress	I	I
	we (2 verbs)	we	-
S4	ø	-	I
	'Government and opposition /rulers and people'	politicians within the Govt and the opposition	Government and private sectors
S5	everyone	-	we
	? rejoin(ing) UN ? ø (2 verbs)	re-entry to the UN	we
	ø (2 verbs)	it ('s not something that...	-
S6	the most important (thing)	the issue	- (most importantly....)
	we	we	we
S7	many speakers	many scholars	-
	we ....if ø	it's very difficult to	if we were to....
S8	Communist China	Mainland China	Mainland China
S9	(if) we	it (is necessary to)	we
	ø (3 verbs)	....	we
S10	we / ø (4 verbs)	(by ....) it ('s possible to)	we ...to *pro*... to *pro*
S11	countries with dipl. relations with Taiw.an	we	only twenty eight countries
	there are 25... which...	only twenty-five	only twenty-five
S12	(there) are	there are	there are
S13	those 25 UN members which have relations with us	those 25 UN members which maintain diplomatic ties with Taiwan	the 25 members that have diplomatic ties with us

	Subject in source discourse	Interpreter TA	Interpreter TB
S14	this (still short of ..)	we	it (s not likely that) we
S15	this route through....	it ('s not easy to...)	it (won't be easy to....)
S16	another possible route	the other approach (that we can consider)	another alternative
S17	Chinese Communists	China	Mainland China
S18	ø	but not ø in...	Mainland China
S19	(there) are	there are	there are
S20	the power we can best command	we (make the most use of our strength)	the most concrete strength that we have
	we	we	we
S21	thus ø is a good method	this	this
S22	our best weapon	we	our greatest advantage
S23	ø	we	we
S24	this road	the road to..	this. (is not an easy path
	obstacles	there are	there are
	chances for success	-	-
	ø	-	this path
S25	its main obstacle	I	the main obstacle
	its main obstacle	one of the hurdles	these organisations
	these organisations	-	you
S26	you all	I / you	I / you
S27	I	I	I
	everyone	-	-
S28	I	I	I / I
	this	which	you
	everyone	-	you

or may supply Subjects when inserting 'higher' clauses (S7). Conversely, initial NPs which might be candidates for Subjecthood may be ignored in favour of a current topic, become sentential adverbs (S6-TB) or be rephrased as VPs (S11).

In the main Taipei corpus (S1-S28), only 37 out of 90 Subject-selection responses are structurally and semantically equivalent, of which 15 are 'we' or proper nouns. As seen in the Table, certain Subjects appear largely inter-changeable, e.g. within the set *we, Taiwan, my country, everyone, you all*; most utterances can apparently be framed with either *I, you* or *we* as Subject; one interpreter favours expletive (impersonal pronoun) constructions, while the other favours personal pronouns.

4.2.4 Asymmetries and moot constituency in Chinese-English SI: Summary

This wide assortment of rearrangements and transformations of sentences involving two major typological differences (left-branching constituents and Subjecthood) shows the futility of seeking generalisations about SI processing, such as the definition of a 'processing unit' traceable from SL to TL, in terms of constituent or categorial structure.

The difference between the entry-points of the German-English and Chinese-English interpreters with respect to clause structure—the German-English interpreters more often begin their own structure in the middle of an SL clause—is attributable to the different size of the 'clause' in the two languages (an artifact of the syntactic conventions), and to the difference in register between the discourses (the Chinese is more spontaneous and 'oralised').

4.3 Left-branching Noun Phrases

Long left-branching NPs afford another test of possible strategic responses to structural asymmetry between SL and TL. Typologically, German, Chinese and English NPs all branch to both left and right.[6] But while English NP Heads may only be preceded by nominal and adjectival modifiers,[7] both Chinese and German Head Nouns may be delayed by long, complex constituents such as participials and relative clauses. In spoken discourse, even these are usually not long enough to be troublesome (e.g. W-S8, T-S22, S33). Over longer such embeddings, however, the interpreters proceed smoothly with their own formulation, as shown in the following synchronised extracts.

In WS6, WL embarks immediately and resolutely on an autonomous structure, using an NP in the embedded clause as a Subject without waiting or stalling:

das 'Andere -   vielleicht mehr von der 'Mitgliedstaatsseiten @
the other -   perhaps more   from the   Member-State-side
positions. to-   *protect their own.* *- H   financial interests and SECondly -*

betonte Anliegen   ist das-   der-   @Ver-   der Ver'besserung
stressed concern -   is that/the (of-)the   imp-   of-the improvement
Member States - \also- have- quite. leGITimate concerns.which THEY have
emphasised

A delayed NP Head, like a delayed verb, can be 'hedged' by producing a
reasonable inference (I am skipping the first part of my paper >> this part is long
>> 'I elaborated'):

S 27: wo tiaoguo qianmian de# ... jiushi jieshao- Lianheguo - yiji woguo - jiaru
    I   jump past[front (first) *de* - [that is ([describe [UN   - and[our-cntry - [join
Lianheguo - ^Acanyu Lianheguo gen tuichu Lianheguo ^Ade...LISHI de bufen
UN   -   participate UN   and withdraw UN]   *de*   history] part]] p

TA: +   ^in beginning of the /pa per -   ^ I elaborated. on the
~history. of...

Long complex left-branching NPs are longer and more frequent in written text,
such as segments S29-39 of the Taipei discourse. Here the interpreters produce a
predicate from the embedded relative '(reason... is based on [detest...': TA: the US
is antagonistic towards...; TB: the United States does...not like...):

S32:
Meiguo fandui daikuan de liyou -   biaomian ·shang shi JISHUXING de
USA   oppose loans [*de* N reason   on surface   is   technical
   +   shiji shang ne. ze shi. jiyu   YANWU. zhexie guojia JIJIN
     in reality   p however *shi* ([ₙₚbased on [ᵥₚ detest [ₙₚthese countries ([ₙₚextreme

TA: and Nica\ragua - and the United States has- technico#- \reasons -
TB: loans by these - \countries - based on technical reasons but basically

shehuizhuyi de zhengquan - he. choushi Meiguo taidu·de - zhengzhi kaolü   +
socialist *de* regime   - and [ᵥₚabhor USA ([ )attitude]] political consideration]

TA: but   in   FACT - the United States is antago\nistic - to/wards
- the- m - socia\listic approach of these \countries - and they#
\attitude....
TB: it's because - the United States does n- is n-   -   does not -/like
the ani\mosity of these countries towards the United.   \States -

Unforeseen extensions to an NP may require the interpreter to generate a new VP or clause, as here to deal with 'politicisation' attached with attributive *de* (S29):

Shijie Yinhang - he Guoji zu- Guoji Huobi Jijin 299- liangge jinrong 300 zuzhi
[CP[IP[NP World Bank - and int'nl org-#   IMF   -two cl finance organisations
TA: ....   +   World
TB: 299   -   World 300 /Bank -

de ZHENGZHIhua 301 -   yu Lianheguo -   tixi xia 303 -   qita daduoshu
orgns *de* [politicisation]]] [PP with [NP UN   system -under   [other [majority.....

TA: Bank   - and -   \I M /F 303 - <u>are under - a</u>
<u>trend. of.</u> -   <u>politiciz\ation</u>
TB: and. the   IM/F 301 - h- <u>have become -</u>   <u>highly po\litical</u>

Of course, in English this new predicate needs Tense and Aspect, which must be inferred, differently by the two interpreters in this example. Furthermore, as in S2, the semantic effect of such an advance assertion on a half-finished sentence may call for a new, corrective sentence or phrase downstream, with some repetition. The interpreters carry out the adjustment as follows:

...zhuanmen jigou   zheng[B]zhihua - you qi. genben[A]- bu tong. zhi chu +
.... [specialised [agencies[politicisation   - [have[its [basically [different   points

TA: ^the politiciz\ation of \these
two (agencies. is different - from. that. of the \other agencies in\nature -
TB: + h   [B]as compared. to the - h other insti\tutions - the-
political- isation of the \other institutions

Although there are few examples of long left-branching NPs in the corpora, no uniform *structural* strategy is visible: rather, any generalisation accounting for these different treatments would have to refer to other information evoked by the text.

5 SL-TL compatible structures: paraphrase and re-ordering

Any account of SI must explain the extensive paraphrasing and re-ordering of strings which appear to encode meaning transparently and in an order permitting easy sequential output in TL. If re-ordering requires a memory or production effort, then either such paraphrases are forced by formulation difficulties (which seems unlikely in professionals dealing with relatively easy material) or the apparent 'closeness' of syntactic structure is only part of the story, concealing a logical and pragmatic level which may even out the difficulty of interpreting between structurally cognate and contrasting languages. The following examples show voluntary paraphrasing or recasting of strings whose word order could easily be followed in TL (e.g. right-branching Noun Phrases), either on-line without hesitation, or when rendered 'consecutively' (after one or more whole clauses are available). In other cases, material from several phrases or clauses is fused or otherwise rationalised. In particular, we see a recasting of structures like conditional and causative subordinate clauses, or interrogatives, which would seem to be logically transparent and easily transposable into equivalent TL forms.

Right-branching NPs which could be transposed directly into English are often recast: in WS9, for example, a right-branching string of Nouns is converted to verb and complement structure:

dürfte - der - der 'Schutz - der- des Finanzsystems - des des Mißbrauchs der
might   the the protection of-the of-the finance system ofthe ofthe abuse   of the
WA: +   +   +   the   point
Subven'tionen -@   **der europäischen Ge'meinschaften -**
subsidies   of the European   Communities
WA: being to -   @ pro/DECT - the European community's
finances
in unserem Land -   **in Kern -**
in our country   in core
(...from being misused)

Similarly, in W-S6 (synchronised extract below), the input structure turns out to be simple and TL-compatible once past the embedded relative, ie: 'NP is [NP N of N of N of N]', and could have been handled by a short pause after 'interests', followed by (for example) 'the other concern, which [...] have stressed, is (for) the improvement of ...' etc. WL's structure is quite different, again with verbs expressing the content of the NP material:

das 'Andere - **vielleicht mehr** **von der 'Mitgliedstaatsseiten @**
the other -   perhaps more   from the   Member-State-side
positions. to-   *protect their own. -* *H* *financial interests* *and SECondly -*

betonte Anliegen   **ist das-**   **der-**   **@Ver-**   **der Ver'besserung**
stressed concern -   is that/the   (of-)the   imp-   of-the improvement
Member States - \also- have- quite. leGITimate concerns.which THEY have
emphasised

@ **der** **der** **Zusammenarbeit** **in** **der** **Kriminalitätsbe'kämpfung -**
  (of)the (of)the   cooperation   in   the   crime-   combatting
@- they wish to \ensure -   *that.* *they can imPROVE*   *cooperation -*
in the area - of the fight against@ \crime

The parallel structure is committed to immediately, the incoming information being recast on line with no apparent difficulty: the product is fairly fluent, with its own prosodic contour, etc. This fluency and the added material, e.g. '*they wish to ensure that they can improve...*', suggest a more dynamic process than simply retrieving and assembling entries for '**Anliegen**' (concern) and '**Verbesserung**' and '**Mitgliedstaaten**' (Member States).

The Head or Modifier status of NP components is theoretically useful in language description in the interests of postulating uniform directionality of a given category of constituent in a given language, but seems to be less significant in on-line processing terms than the semantic relationship between them. In SI, the processing of recursively 'possessive' attributions to an NP depends on knowledge about the properties of their components, which licenses decisions to produce them as Subjects or Verbs, or to omit or fuse them on the basis of their informativeness. This is seen in Würzburg WS6, where WL takes 'Member States' immediately from a left-branching NP modifier phrase as her Subject, confident that she can say something about it.

At sentence level, certainly phrase order may be followed when, for instance, an initial adjunct is semantically clearly marked for 'sentential' scope by the meaning of its Head preposition and/or a final particle or pause, i.e. specifying the general circumstances, time, place, or some epistemic or relevance value of the whole subsequent utterance, as in Taipei S5 and S12:

S5: (now everyone also realizes one point,..) **zai DANGQIAN de zhe** + [in   present
guoji qingshi zhi xia ne **85 chongfan Lianheguo 86 - shi xuyao 87**
intnatn'l conditions -under] p -[rejoin   UN]   - [F>[need -
TB: however - we all KNOW 85 that   - under the 86 current international 87situation/ 88 -
we will 89 need .....

S12: **na women dou zhidao** - **zai Lianhe 159 guo ne** @-   160 zhege zonggong
TB: of them are   UN me-   158 UN   MEMBERS -   we know that 160 at the UN ....

But many sentences whose word order almost exactly fits TL structure, and which are wholly available when the interpreter begins her rendition, come out in a different order. The interpreters' renditions of such 'consecutively' interpreted segments—the majority of core clauses and sentences in the Chinese corpus (not counting 'openers')—shows greater structural freedom. An independent initial place-PP is not necessarily rendered in the same position:

S 18: (but at United Nations...)
de zhuanmen JIGOU limian ne -   **que MEIYOU** -   **zhei xiang WUQI** (^{AB}...)
special. agencies]] -   in   p - [however [not have - [this cl weapon

TA: China commands voting power in the Security Council) but NOT - <u>in the other. specialized</u> - AGENCIES
TB: (yet Mainland China does not HAVE this adVANtage <u>in the</u> SPECIALISED AGENCIES -

In some cases, an utterance may simply elicit a formula, as in the set phrases from conference jargon used here ('handouts provided to the organiser'; 'conference packet'):

S26: **na gewei - zai nimen de. shou zhong** (well everybody - in your hands -)
wo xiang dou you wo ...zheici wei -dahui - suo xie de zhege LUNWEN.
I think [all have [I ... this time for meeting wrote *de* this paper

TA: ...I'm sure you have obtained the HANDOUTS - that I provided - to the /organiser
TB: ...and I'm sure that you have - my- PAPER - in your - CONFERENCE PACKET

Sometimes several clauses which have become available are fused in output, as in S2 where TA and TB each fuse four clauses (*'you can realize - they have a consensus - have a consensus on method - but also have differences'*) differently into three (TA: *they have shared their views - their views converge somewhat - they have some differences*; TB: *they have a consensus - there are slight differences - on how we should re-enter*):

S2 T13-16:
cong - gang gang de ji wei - lai zi. guoneiwai de JIANGZHE - de zhe yanjiang
from   just now   [several -[come from country-in-out [speakers'   [speeches]

dangzhong jiu keyi FAXIAN ne[A, B] **- tamen gege @ jiangzhe ne**
-within - thus can realize p -   they each   speaker p
TA: ....   [A]speakers from home and abroad -
TB: ....   [B] from the \speeches that we have heard so

tamen duiyu women chongfan Lianheguo ne @m- - jiben shang
they   [as-to [we   rejoin United Nations   p - [$_{VP1}$ basically
TA: who   spoke before   me   -   have shared
TB: \fa~r -   we /know - that the   speak50 ers -

you yi xie 51 gongshi - @ zai 52 zuofa shang you 53 xie gongshi -
V have some consensus [$_{VP2}$ approach-wise [V have some N <u>consensus</u>
TA: with us 51 -   their \v i e_w s 52.5   -
TB: H   have   52 -   /reached 53 -

@- 54 dan ye you xie butong de difang 55   + ...
but [$_{I'}$ also [$_{VP3}$ V have some N different *de* points]

TA: on Chinese Taipei's re-entry to international financial organisations: their views converge somewhat, but there are some differences among their views.
TB: a consensus, even though there are slight differences in HOW we should re-enter the UN

When a whole segment is processed as a unit, the result is often more fluent and concise than the original:

S22: (well as I just said..)
women xianzai - zui nenggou yingyong de yige WUQI ne - jiushi women
we   now - [most able   use   *de* one [weapon p - is F>   we/our
PANGDA de zheige - MAOYI SHILI - ^Bhaiyou women de caijin de shili   +
huge *de*   this   trade power]   and-also our finance power]

TB: .... ^Bour greatest adVANtage is our economic - and financial STRENGTH

Paraphrase in SI cannot be explained as a forced response to SL-TL asymmetries. At the beginning of W-S8, WA is offered a clear, unambiguous Subject with which to begin—an initial Nominative-case Noun Phrase—but prefers to use it as an Object in her own formulation:

WS8:
Der   europäische   Subven'tionsbetrug - 'wird   83 - das ist hier....
The   European   subsidy   fraud   is/PASS   that is here ...
TA: - I'm going.to
address.fraudulent   obtention of *sub*sidies - IN Europe.-

6 Simplification of semantic structure

Where several clauses connected in a complex structure are available for processing together, they are often simplified and streamlined (Square brackets in the gloss show items not expressed in the Chinese. The convoluted syntactic-semantic structure of this segment is shown below with labelled bracketing.):

T-S9 (77-90): suoyi dangran women jintian (so of course today we ...)
yao nenggou chongfan Lianheguo de hua ne - bixu nenggou RAOguo - Anlihui
[if we] want [to be] able [to]rejoin [the] UN - [we]must[be] able[to] bypass Security
- zheige TUJING - nenggou- ba women de ... SHENQING'AN ne - kan shi bu
Councl route - [and] be able [to take]   our   application p - [and] see
shi nenggou ba ta^B zhuan dao. zhege^A Lianheguo de DAhui shang^B mian^A   +
whether[_{IP}[V able F> *ba* it [divert - to ([dm   [UN Gen.Assembly]]   -on

TA:.. ^therefore it is necessary to ^*bypass* the Security Council - by \going to the General *Assembly* directly +
TB: H so - ^Bwe need to see - if we. can. ^Bapply. through the General ASS\EMBLY of the UN INSTEAD of the Security Council

[_{CP1} so of course today [_{IP1} we [_{CP2} if [_{IP} ø [_{VP} Aux want V' able V rejoin UN [_{IP} ø [_{VP} must V' able [V bypass ([N UN SecCouncil N <u>route</u>] V' able F> *ba* Obj [our <u>application</u>] - V see[_{CP}whether[_{IP}[V' able F> *ba* it [V' divert - [_{PP} to UNGen.Ass.]]]]]

Interpreter TA begins during the preverbal object, abridges the opener to therefore, ignores the Subject **women** 'we' and the 'premise' topic, which are by now redundant, having persisted over five segments, and addresses the first VP 'it is necessary to bypass..' then summarises the remainder ('see whether we can take our application and divert it to the General Assembly') in 'by going to the General Assembly directly'. The output follows the original order with editing and abridgements, at about 8s. An example of such simplification from the German-English corpus (WS-8) is analysed in Chapter 6.

7 Marked subordinate and non-declarative structures

Another indicator of how surface structures are interpreted in SI is the treatment of interclausal relations marked as subordinate (conditional or causative in these examples), and interrogatives.

On encountering a fronted subordinate clause, the interpreters often substitute a Main clause even when the complementiser appears to mark the semantic dependency (e.g. causative or conditional) with a downstream proposition (W-M2):

Da einer der .**Schwerpunkte - dieser - 'Tagung - auf ^L diesem^A - Be'R E I C H**
[_{CP}since [_{NP}Q one_N ofthe focal-points [_{NP}of this - meeting] -[_{IP}[_{PP}on[_{NP}this_D - area **des^B - Subventionsbetruges. liegen soll**
[_{NP} ofthe subsidy fraud_G [_{VP}lie should]]]]

L: *which is. as I have said. one. of- the- main@ points@.*...
A: one of the - m *main* points of our symposium - WAS....
B: and that is-@ one of the important points - of....

'Antecedent' subordinate clauses marked with 'if' (*ruguo, - de hua, yao(shi)*) in the Chinese text (S7, S9) are usually not rendered as real conditionals, but are either treated as rhetorical openers ('givens'), or integrated into the sentence as adjuncts. In fact, when they are rendered as real conditionals, the result is less

successful. In S7, TB places the conditional initially as a real hypothetical antecedent, but is then forced to repeat herself:

T-S7: na dangran - hen duo de jiangzhe ganggang ye dou tidao guo le -
[$_{CP2}$dm of course   [$_{IP}$[$_{NP}$ many   speakers [$_{VP}$ just now also   mentioned
   women - chongfan Lianheguo ne - yaoshi   yao   touguo   zheizhong -
[$_{CP3}$[$_{IP}$[$_{CP}$ we   return   UN]   p - [$_{CP4}$<u>if</u> [$_{IP}$[$_{VP}$Aux want [$_{P/VP}$through   such
   @   JINGYOU ANLIHUI - lai -   jueding de zhege lutu de hua shi
([$_{NP}$[$_{I}$ p4 [$_{PP}$<u>via [Sec.Council</u> [Aux come - [decide *de* this path]   -if] [$_{VP}$ Ø F>*shi*
xiangdang kunnan de -
fairly   difficult

if we were to follow the path of having the Security Council vote for us
FIRST , we know that <u>it would be very DIFFICULT</u> , because.....

TA produces the 'conditional' as a final PP (*by*...):

it's very difficult to re-enter the United <u>Nations by obtaining support
from the Security Council</u>, as....

Again, in the following passage (from the Fang corpus) the *ruguo* (pseudo-'*if*')
clause is somewhat more successfully handled when treated cautiously as an
unspecified adjunct, and integrated (FC, FD) than as a conditional (FA):

F4: ruguo zhishifenzi. yao   - guanxin   ziji   SHEHUI -
   if intellectual(s) want/need concerned self/own society
[A]**xiwang**[D] **- faxian ziji shehui cunzai de WENti he KUNnan**[C] **- tuidong ta JIEjue**
hope/wish realise own society exist *de* problem and difficulty. - promote its solve
   wo xiang. zheige shi- yige - shehui jinbu de yige BIYAO de- yige tiaoJIAN
   I think   this is   one - society progress *de* one necessary *de* one condition -

A:[A] *if intellectuals are concerned about - their .soCIety - and@- to- -find. the PROB
lems   - so as to find a soLUtion - <u>I think this is</u> - a precondition for this soCIety. to--
C: +   *C*an \intellectual \<u>HAS the
responsibili/ty.</u> to disCOVer the -problems in society - and to - attempt to SOLVE H
those problems <u>and this is an -</u> indispensable ELement of social \progress
D: + *D* intellectuals should \care about - their own society - and when they - discover
PROBlems existing- in the so/ciety - they should find so\LUtions a think - this is.
essential to the. progress. of a soc\Iety*

This suggests that Chinese 'if' phrases are often not real conditional antecedents,
but simply a form of clausal (propositional) Topic, which often emerges in
interpretation as a verb complement. Contrast the German 'conditional' opening
clause in Würzburg-S1:

+   **@mm wenn @** - **ein Räpräsentant eines Ge'richts...**
    if/when -   a representative   of-a court....

The Indefinite new discourse entity '**ein Räpräsentant**' does not license any presupposition, and German '**wenn**', unlike *ruguo*, has no speech-act use by itself, so the clause is truly hypothetical in semantic terms (though a false rhetorical one on a pragmatic level). is followed by all three interpreters. This semantic transparency means that the interpreters can proceed directly with an equivalent conditional subordinate structure in English, as they all in fact do.

These examples reflect the fact, well known in pragmatics at least since Grice, that logical structure, particularly the relations between propositions, is not transparently given either by syntax or fixed values of function words like subordinate markers. Subtle differences exist between the values of 'conditional' markers in different languages, as seen above with Chinese *ruguo*, German *wenn*, and English *if*; French *si* does not necessarily mark a subordinate clause as the antecedent in a true conditional, but may simply attach a scalar epistemic value to a premise (cf English *if he was a good Governor, he was a better President.*)

Similarly, the only interrogatives[8] in the corpora, the rhetorical question-and-answer forms in T-S8 and T-S17 (**Weishenme (ne)? yinwei...** 'Why (is this)? Because....') are ignored by the interpreters who replace them with simple causal connectives (....αs..., / because...) or conative/evidential openings (because we know that...).

Sensitivity to this property of language is part of native-like competence, as shown by the way in which the interpreters approach these structures: they are sensitive to the pragmatic values of forms like interrogatives and conditionals in which there is domain ambiguity (Sweetser 1990): conditional, causative and interrogative forms often do not express real conditions, causes or questions. The same applies to other items with this type of ambiguity or polysemy, like connectives, as will be seen in Chapter 6.

8 Discussion

In this Chapter we took a first step in looking for the appropriate level of description for a model of the process of simultaneous interpretation, which we believe must ultimately be both linguistic and cognitive. We began by comparing the syntactic and semantic profiles of SI input and output with reference to their time course as provided by the synchronized protocols, resulting in the following observations:

(1)   neither the C-E nor the G-E interpreters render phrase-for-phrase or clause-for-clause versions of the discourse. In the German samples, in which sentences last 12 seconds on average, and clauses[9] overall 7.5s, interpreters start building their own sentence as soon as the input departs from English word order, if not before. In the Chinese samples, the content of most sentences, which last 5.8s on average (not counting short rhetorical openers like *I think, what is important today is*), is rendered after the sentence has been fully received. In both cases, the interpreters often add clause structure, and at other times render the content of more than one input clause in a single clause.

(2)   in building their sentences, interpreters frequently render rhetorical opening phrases and clauses by a single word (a discourse connective or conjunction), omit them altogether, or insert their own rhetorical and connective, and in some cases, parenthetical material. They produce place-holding approximations, in the form of superordinate or generic terms, for Subjects, Verbs or Objects. They also frequently render content in different word order and/or constituent structure even where SL and TL order and sentence constituency are compatible.

These observations raise the following questions:

(a)   what is the source of the material inserted by interpreters? is it relevant and appropriate in the discourse, and if so, how is it generated?

(b)   what are the implications of these findings for the question of a processing 'unit' in SI, or translation in general; and is there any hope of finding some formal input-output correlation algorithm in terms of the traditional linguistic categories (syntax and semantics)?

(c)   what is the effect of the recast structure, and the use of temporary approximations to downstream text constituents, on the accuracy and fidelity of the final product?

In Chapter 6, two types of sources for the interpreters' formulations are identified beyond what is encoded in the input discourse:

- thematic sources, in knowledge of the event and situation of the discourse, other world knowledge and generally, attributes and properties which are evoked by and associated with the words of the input speech; and
- logical sources, in inferences and deductions carried out by the interpreter on the propositions of the discourse.

Secondly, we propose a language of intermediate representation to accommodate minimal features which might be derived from a SL discourse and integrated and assembled for TL formulation.

First, however, we must look closely at the potential of syntactic and semantic description to account for the data, provisionally setting aside the constructs of cognitive psychology such as memory and attention. Research in that paradigm continues elsewhere, and a range of models are under examination based on different theories about procedural and declarative (or implicit and explicit) memory, automatic and conscious processes, etc. We are chiefly concerned here to find a plausible linguistic description to interface with these theories, which in turn must constrain them; the notion of interpretation 'strategies' offers a convenient window on the assumptions about linguistic processes which underlie current thinking about that interface. We have looked at purely syntactic correspondences between input and output. How far does a semantic analysis take us towards a plausible model of processing for SI?

Some writers have stressed that SI, unlike translation, processes text at a 'molecular' level (word-group or phrase) (Gile 1995: 125), and certainly interpreters are not at liberty to wait indefinitely for possible disambiguating information downstream. It is of course possible to produce target-language equivalents of words and other fragments, but 'semantics' refers to logical as well as lexical information, and production can also draw on anticipatory logical hypotheses which are not necessarily realised in input lexical items: free variables, for instance, can be rendered by placeholders, both for arguments (*something, someone*) and for predication (existential forms, e.g. *there is a...*).

Is it possible to generalize about SI strategy in terms of any formal properties of input and output at all? Even IT recognises a 'self-contained' type of sense unit, e.g. 'Furthermore,...' (Lederer 1981). To fix the interface between semantics and pragmatics a little more closely in preparation for the next Chapter, let us examine the prediction that an interpreter is dependent at any point on some *semantic* content supplied by the text:

Straw man: a hypothetical 'SI Semantic Chunk Principle'

'Subject to superordinate Preference Principles, on identifying a *semantic chunk*, a simultaneous interpreter formulates and produces an equivalent structure as soon as possible. On identifying a constituent presumed to be dependent on a downstream predicate, or for which attachment is unclear, an interpreter either *waits* until the predicate occurs before formulating output, or *stalls* by producing 'neutral' material.

A *semantic chunk* is one which licenses a partial representation deemed adequate, structurally and semantically, to provide a basis for immediate formulation in the output language. Semantic chunks in this sense include:

(1)   a predicate with all its arguments filled, or
(2)   any element presumed to have sentential scope, to embed another CP, or otherwise to license production as an independent clause or phrase.'

Unfortunately, a generalisation in these terms fails both empirically and theoretically. Empirically, it makes the wrong predictions: in practice, interpreters sometimes wait or stall when input order poses no problem, suggesting that 'semantic' completeness is somehow not enough; secondly, interpreters re-order and rephrase when the input order is compatible with TL tolerances; and thirdly, their output includes material not traceable in input.

Theoretically, the generalisation wants a definition of 'neutral' material; but more fundamentally, it depends on an assumption of the strong predictability of downstream dependency relations from syntax. In discourse, subordination is not always marked, and when it is the predictive power of such marking is very weak. Within-clause prediction from syntax is restricted to predicates and arguments which are subcategorized; adjuncts, a very large class of constituents, are not predictable. Interclausal dependency is often marked, if at all, not by a semantically reliable connector, like a 'causal' or 'conditional', but by a complementiser, topicaliser or conjunction encoding no clear relation. Subordination or 'cata-dependency' may be signalled, but with no inherent clue to its semantic or pragmatic value as a real-world, epistemic or speech-act relation (Sweetser 1990) In this utterance (spoken at a conference)

For the benefit of the interpreters I'm omitting the second paragraph on page 2 of my paper...

the initial PP qualifies the main clause on a speech-act level: the Speaker is not omitting the paragraph for the interpreters' benefit, but rather letting them know his plans so that they can follow his remarks in the text he has given them. (The appropriate output, once this is recognized, is silence or a gesture of thanks from the booth).

A generalisation framed in structural terms would have to define elements in terms of constituency or scope (e.g. as having 'sentential scope') or by distinguishing within-clause (VP-level) and interclausal (CP-level) dependencies. In most languages, phrases with sentential scope occur initially, or finally after a pause, while VP-phrases usually occur near the verb (or predicating expression), generally between it and its Subject (or its direct Object). But position is not a reliable guide to scope (Jackendoff 1972); in practice, there is a gray area in the scope of many modifiers, qualifiers, adverbials etc, as between CP, IP (including Subject) and VP levels, requiring interpretation on the basis of semantic and pragmatic factors, as even Chomskyan linguists recognise (Jackendoff 1972). Parentheticals, which are common in certain types of discourse, are the prototypical case of the 'portable' adjunct.

Structural shifts from SL to TL occur even when not forced, because a strategy based on structural transformation would be derailed so often as to make it inefficient. The variety of responses to left-branching input suggests that interpreters cannot afford to be attuned to the structure of the input language, and that if any structural factor influences the interpreter's production, it is the status of her current sentence, which as often as not has been begun independently of the input structure—plus, of course, as Gile points out (p.c.), production performance variables such as delays in retrieving or assembling the right word or structure. Even without this performance variable, however, formulation is clearly not predictable from the incremental syntactic and semantic meaning delivered by input without an analysis of the contextual effects it licenses, and hence the interpreters' degree of confidence in expressing propositional material and directions to relevance at each point. We must therefore look more closely into the cognitive and pragmatic sources of representation and formulation.

Chapter 6 The Pragmatics of Interpretation

The observation that interpreters formulate largely independently of input sentence structure, and that the content of the last utterance is not the only source of their ongoing production, confirms the important role of contexts in the SI process. As discussed in Chapter 1 and modelled for SI in Chapter 3, contexts introduce situational, Speaker-related and other extralinguistic information into the inter-mediate representation. The first part of this chapter presents evidence of these sources and their role in the disambiguation and enrichment of the propositional content, and the resolution of basic indeterminacies like deictic indexing to time, place and situation, and referential features such as boundedness and set-membership. Frame theory provides some account of how more conceptual information is brought to bear than is available from basic lexical entries. There is also evidence of active modelling during SI of extended deductive and discursive structures involving multiple successive propositions. Later in this Chapter, these multiple cognitive sources and the structuring they require in intermediate memory, on which primary Assembly draws, are presented in schematic diagrams of evolving mental models for the sample discourses, and the language of Assembly is formalised as a kind of language of thought.

The examples in sections 2-5 of this chapter show how pragmatic processes contribute alongside linguistic rules to the primary Assembly of propositional forms. It is proposed that a second level of pragmatic processing, operating 'around' and 'across' propositional content, can be identified as a distinct cognitive process: in the second part of the chapter, further evidence is presented to show how an interpreter may derive intentional values, embedding both individual propositions and extended discourse, from the expression of specific and generalised illocutions and attitudes; and how she may be directed to strongly licensed implicatures by certain discourse devices which we can view in relevance-theoretic terms as local modulations of a Speaker's ostension. Both clues to attitude, and signalled implicatures, allow anticipatory production gambits before the full syntactic realisation of the basic proposition has unfolded.

1 Contexts

A rule-based account of discourse comprehension which computes meaning by applying a grammar, a lexicon and inferential rules, is faced with the difficulties of defining what information is provided in the lexicon, and modelling the effect of various types of context. 'Context' is variously defined in discourse analysis and translation studies to encompass all local influences on meaning, from the compositional linguistic environment to the wider social and ethnographic background: context of discourse and context of situation (Brown and Yule 1983). Since nothing can influence the derivation of meaning that is not first represented in the hearer's head, in a psycholinguistic model of comprehension for a task it is appropriate to define context as that subset of the hearer's assumptions which contributes to the interpretation of an utterance:

> 'Grammars and inferential abilities stabilise after a learning period and remain unchanged from one utterance or inference to the next. By contrast, each new experience adds to the range of potential contexts. It does so crucially in utterance interpretation, since the context used in interpreting a given utterance generally contains information derived from immediately preceding utterances. Each new utterance [...] requires a rather different context.' (Sperber and Wilson 1986/1995: 15-16).

According to Relevance theory, it is the act of ostension which allows a hearer to infer which of the assumptions newly made manifest are relevant. A communicative act must comprise two layers: the content itself, and the ostension that it has been intentionally pointed out. Ostensive acts form a continuum according to the strength of the evidence, from 'showing' to 'saying that' (indirect evidence) (ibid.: 50-54). Although this is not explicitly specified in *Relevance*, we take the procedural features of discourse—those which encode various degrees of suggestion or assertion and point to contexts which will generate the desired cognitive effects, by strengthening, weakening, creating or cancelling assumptions—to be the local modulations of ostension.

We may suppose that the pressure and immediacy of the SI condition limits the search for possible relevant contexts so that the previous utterance is an even more dominant source of relevant context than in conversation. The protocols show that is by no means the only source.

2 'Frame' effects

Context so defined includes any knowledge used to construct an interpretation from the blueprints offered by the parser to the Assembler, in particular the frames or conceptual structures which organise background knowledge and which are evoked, or can be *in*voked, by the interpreter (Fillmore 1985: 233). The hypothesis that knowledge is organised in frames and scripts explains how, in comprehension and recall, people confuse things inferred in the course of 'envisionment' with what was actually said; for instance, a probable instrument in *he posted it up with a drawing pin,* or *he banged on the table with his fist* ; or a highly significant proposition, such as a consequence, which has not been stated: subjects who hear *he slipped on a wet spot and dropped the delicate glass pitcher on the floor* remember that the pitcher broke, but not that this had been inferred (Johnson, Bransford and Solomon 1973, cited in Garnham 1987: 90-104). We therefore expect to find 'insertions' and additions in any recall or SI protocol involving more than close shadowing or verbatim recall (i.e. more than a 3-4s lag).

Secondly, the intersection of the frames evoked by the words in an utterance narrows down their relevant extensions, which is necessary to the choice of appropriate superordinates. The choice of a superordinate or generic term by an interpreter must be appropriate in the discourse context. Consider two examples of expansions supplied by interpreters, already mentioned in the last Chapter:

> WL: [European subsidy fraud] *is a crime which* - *has been enshrined....*
> TA: [re-entry to the United Nations] is a task that requires...

The knowledge that subsidy fraud '*is a crime*' might be given in the common lexicon; but 'is a task' can only be said of 're-entry to the United Nations' with reference to particular knowledge about the Speaker's objectives. Similarly, the lexicon as conventionally defined, whether monolingual or bilingual, is not usually held to include lists of actions which Subjects may perform, so that even the autonomous selection and insertion of Subjects like 'we', 'Taiwan', 'everyone' and so on for predicates expressing certain actions and intentions depends on extra-textual knowledge which can safely attribute those intentions to those Subjects. This knowledge is held to be organized for on-line use in the shape of a mental model.

The SI samples contain prima-facie evidence of the interpreters' use of their knowledge of the conference situation, of certain scripted conventions, and of the world in general. In the following examples, underlined segments of the interpreters' versions have no source, or only a partial source, in the original discourse.

3 Situation and scripts

Comparison of output to input shows the direct contribution of encyclopaedic or local situational knowledge, both to certain 'informed' paraphrases and to the deictic modelling of time, place and audience. A paraphrase like WA's from W-S10 relies on 'script' knowledge about what courts do:

> **[Bundesgerichtshof] hat sich mit dem Tatbestand [...] befassen müssen**
> '[the Federal Court] has... had to concern itself with the case material...'
> WA: ' .... handed down verdicts..'

Similarly, autonomous rhetorical introductions with 'I' 'you' and 'we' rely on assumptions about audience-Speaker relations, while assumptions attributing knowledge to the audience inform the interpretation of certain deictic anaphora, like **hier** in W-M4 (25):

> **brauche ich Herrn .... - hier - NICHT VORzustellen**
> 'I do not need to introduce Mr..... 'here' '
> WA: he hardly needs any introduction for as you know he is..

In general, renderings of individual words may contain additional information known to the interpreter but not given in the input, like a name or a specifying detail. In W-S1, for example, the Chairman thanks '**Herr Doktor Rump**', but WL uses his first name, '*Jürgen Rump*' which she may know from previous discourse or the conference documents. Again, **Tagung**, a general word for 'meeting', is rendered specifically by WL as '*(this) symposium.*'

There is also evidence of differences in the resource-base for interpretation between an interpreter steeped in the situation (WL), and those working only with synthetic and not fully integratable briefing information (in a simulated event). WL, who interpreted the Würzburg conference 'live', shows more familiarity with various aspects of the event than WA/WB, who were called in for a brief mock session four years later.[1] Only WL identifies **Generalthema** ('general theme') as 'the main topic' in Würzburg S4 (L70-75):

> **In Ihrer Tagung hat sich bereits her'ausgestellt - daß sich unter dem 'großen**
> In your   meeting has *Refl* already emerged -   that [ ]   under the large
> **Feld - das unter dem** <u>Generalthema</u> **- er'faßt ist - insbesondere zwei Komplexe**
> field - that under the <u>general theme</u> - subsumed is - in particular two complexes
> **herauskristallisieren**
> out-crystallize
>
> *I think during the course- of. this seminar- it- has@become. quite \clear - that.*
> *there is a very@ LARGE. RANGE of QUEStions @ - under- the-<u>main topic</u> - of*
> *subsidy \fraud*

The term 'subsidy fraud' is immediately accessible to WL, who has heard it used countless times since the conference began on the previous morning, but not to WA or WB:

WA6-8, 94-5:   fraudulent obtention[2] of subsidies
WB 7-8:   FRAUD. - in SUBsi/dies.

WL also knows without being told by the grammar that 'subsidy fraud' is one of the main points of the symposium: the identity relation in 'which is...' is anticipated (she even tells us how she knows it: '*as I have said'*) (W-M2):

M2:(M1: Thank you...for that up-to-date overview on <u>subsidy fraud</u>...)
Da einer der .Schwerpunkte - dieser -'Tagung - auf ^{L} diesem - Be'REICH des^{B} ...
[$_{CP}$as[$_{NP}$Q one$_{N}$ ofthe focal-points [$_{NP}$of this -meeting] [$_{IP}$[$_{PP}$on[$_{NP}$this$_{D}$ - area[$_{NP}$ ofthe -

WL: .... - ^{L}*which is. as I have said. one.*
of- the- main@ points@ which we- wish to deal with - in this. sym\posium

WA and WB had only the written programme for the symposium, and Judge Odersky's written text. Rustling noises in the booth ($^{<R}$..... $^{R>}$ in the transcripts) reveal where WA and WB tried to supplement this knowledge on-line by consulting these documents at three points: for biodata, at a reference to 'the general theme', and when the Speaker seems to be starting to read his printed text. (Still, many names of institutions, dates, and the numerical reference to an article of legislation, were wrongly rendered or omitted: this will be addressed in Chapter 7).

Moreover, in the mock session the previous Speaker's remarks, which precede the Moderator's thanks, differ from those of the real Dr. Rump in the actual event. The real Dr Rump had just given a long talk on recent developments in subsidy fraud, as announced in the programme and referred to by the (recorded) Chairman; the mock 'Dr.Rump' makes some brief remarks about extradition. Predictably, WA and WB are rather vaguer than WL in rendering the Chairman's comments about the last Speaker: ·

Vielen Dank ...für diesen AKtuellen Überblick
many thanks ....for this   up-to date overview

WL   ...*for having given us this UP-to-date overview...*;
WA 3/5   ..that@ clear overview...;
WB 3/5-6 ... for- that. VIEW of @ - the view of...

General world knowledge is sometimes contributed by an interpreter to expand or explain a reference:

tebie   bajiu-   yiHOU 35.8 -
especially eight-nine [=1989] after/since -
after - the nineteen. eightynine <u>*Tiananmen Square- \incident 42.9*</u>

Sometimes the added information appears in the conference documentation (although WB would know that the German Federal High Court is located in Karlsruhe):

W39-40:   **...und dann - 1988 Präsident - des Bundesgerichtshofs wurde**
          ...and   then   1988 President of the Federal- High-Court became
WB41-43: and he- .in NINEteen ninety two. he became. President and
          Chief Justice of the Federal High Court of Justice in \ KARLsruhe

At the same time, information about the situation overrode the input, causing an error: 1992 was the date of the symposium (WB was interpreting a simulated replay, for which she had been given the original programme).

The interpreters use their knowledge of conference procedure to anticipate set formulas: at the start of Judge Odersky's remarks (W46), all three German-English interpreters say '*ladies and gentlemen*' ahead of (or simultaneously with) the corresponding source discourse greeting. (There is no clear evidence of this in the Chinese samples, but the Chinese formula is much shorter).

Familiarity with the script of an international symposium, or the agenda for the current session, generates other additions (underlined) based on knowledge about conference procedures and organisation, the audience or the planned sequence of events:

WL12   *one of the main points* <u>*which we wish to deal with*</u> *in this symposium*
WL24   <u>*we have invited*</u> *Professor Doctor...*
WL47   *ladies and gentlemen -* <u>*colleagues*</u>
WA18-19   <u>now</u> Professor....is going to speak

T3-4:   **wo- jintian shi - yao. gen gewei tan tan..**
          I   today *shi* intend with you-all discuss
TA5-6:   <u>I been invited to</u> talk - on a topic...

For the Chinese-English session, the mock-up arrangements and interpreters' briefing were less elaborate than for the Würzburg simulation. The event described was hypothetical: a 'symposium on Taiwan's prospects for joining the United Nations'. The Speaker's name and the title of his presentation were given orally half an hour before the session. Little evidence of situation-specific knowledge is therefore predicted, but the interpreters' assumptions about standard conference arrangements are apparent (T-S28-222-3):

na gewei - zai nimen de. shouzhong - wo xiang dou you wo
well you all - in your   hand   -   I   think all have [I
zheici wei dahui suo xie de zhege LUNWEN
this time for meeting wrote [this paper

WA(226-8)   I'm sure you have obtained <u>the HANDOUTS - that I provided</u>
           <u>to the /organiser</u>
WB: and I'm sure that you have my- paper <u>in your conference packet</u>

These examples demonstrate sources of information outside the input which allow interpreters to be 'cooperative' speakers in the Gricean sense by adding information they may feel is useful to their audience, or introducing cohesive referential links: in RT terms, enhancing relevance by reducing the effort required from their audience to derive the intended cognitive effects.

They also show how, for routine or ritual items in the discourse, scripted formulas are evoked and readily used in lieu of a literal translation. Problems can arise, as we shall see, when these auxiliary sources for interpretation conflict with the text itself.

4 Inference

As recalled in Chapters 3 and 5, some sentences may not plainly encode certain semantic features which are required either for a full propositional form—the minimal object of most logical operations and relevance judgments—or for mandatory encoding in another language. For adequate formulation of an utterance in TL, information about the relevant extensions of the referents in the context may be needed: for instance, English surface forms require more explicit marking of Boundedness than is encoded in Chinese, including Finiteness, Tense, Aspect and *realis/irrealis* mood on predicates, and Number, Definiteness and 'Mass/ Count' features on Nouns.

Following recent discussion in cognitive pragmatics (Carston 1995, Turner 1997), we shall call this use of pragmatic inference to supply semantic features (elements of a basic proposition affecting its truth conditions) *primary* pragmatic processing, which in our model contributes alongside syntactic and semantic information to the derivation of a primary viable propositional form in the Assembler, as distinct from *secondary* pragmatic processing, which makes more general and synthetic inferences about the Speaker's communicative intentions, on the basis of multiple propositions and the illocutions and attitudes under which they are presented taken together with other, non-linguistic input (Chapter 7).

In early model theory, a context was conceived of as a possible world which could be described in a set of indices for place, time, and audience. However, the 'indexical expressions' appearing in discourse only do part of the job of contextualisation. The concepts introduced are already biased in their extensions relative to each other by the relationship between the frames which they evoke, but must be further narrowed down in a given situation by intersection with a temporary discourse model built up on the local perceptual and linguistic input. The examples given below (section 5) reveal inferences about these referential features which require some such explanation.

The following sections provide examples of inferences of various types which license anticipation or chunking, such as existential presuppositions, and inferences from the previous discourse structure, or from general pragmatic (felicity or relevance) principles. Instances of long-range deductive anticipation (§6.1.3.) entail some representation of relationships between multiple propositions, demonstrating that SI is compatible with the maintenance of complex logical structure.

5 Inferred referential features

5.1 Boundedness and set-membership

The basic claim of mental models theory is that mental representations in comprehension model aspects of the world rather than aspects of linguistic structure, and are constructed from both knowledge and linguistically conveyed information; in other words, representations centre around tokens standing for things that the discourse is about. Mental model theory has focussed mainly on referential processes, like the resolution of lexical ambiguities, the instantiation of words in context and deictic phenomena.

An item like a plural or generic noun delivers only a basic lexical entry, under-determining the relevant bounds of the set in context, which must be inferred (W-M2):

> W16   **'WIE - die Er'fassung dieser 'Fälle - die Dr Menenz und Dr Rump -**
>   how   the   apprehending of these cases - that Dr Menenzand Dr Rump -
>   **ge'schildert haben**
>   depicted   have
>
> L19   *how cases <u>such as those</u> described by [Dr Rump].... <u>are dealt with</u> ....*
>
> A17: how <u>such cases - as</u> presented by... are regulated..
>
> B16-17 HOW <u>CASES</u> - @ which ... has referred to...

The interpretation of **die Fälle** as *such cases* requires applied knowledge, at least of probabilities: it is unlikely that the next Speaker will address the <u>same</u> cases as Dr Mennens and Dr Rump, so a set is projected to accommodate both subsets. The unboundedness may also be derived from the non-specific nature of the process, evoked by '**die Erfassung**', which allows WL to produce an imperfective *are dealt with* in advance of the final input verb **geregelt ist** ('is regulated').

A second example shows how an inanimate abstract noun (**Rechtsprechung**) evokes a conceptual structure comprising at least an Agent, a Predicate and a Theme, for example:

JUDGE {AGENTcourts, THEME cases} ⇒ HAND DOWN {AGENTcourts, THEME verdicts}

and is hence thus represented in the model which may inform formulation. The collective noun, **Tatbestand** (the 'stock of deeds', or case material) is also represented as being made up of individual instances:[3]

W-S10: 130-134
Der Rechtsprechung des Bundesgerichtshofs hat sich mit dem Tatbestand
The jurisprudence   of-the Federal High Court has self [with the case-stock
wenn auch nur in einzelnen Beziehungen befassen müssen[AB]   -
[though indeed only in individual aspects/relations concern must

```
A135-7: (courts).... HAVE handed down a number of /verdicts
- not very many but some - \in this /field
B135-6: the. highest @ federal COURT has had to DEAL with cases of this kind
```

5.2 Anaphora and deixis

Some anaphors with indeterminate reference, like the cataphor in '**<u>das</u> ist hier in Ihrem Kreis schon ge'sagt worden**' ('this has already been said here in your group'), may either simply be reproduced in the same form (WA) or left open (WB):

```
WA: this is something that...
WB:  ...as (has) already been SAID...
```

An SL anaphor with no formal equivalent of equal scope in TL, e.g. **da** 'there' which can mean 'in this', 'in so doing' etc., may invite special inferencing and explication (WL), or may disappear in a paraphrase (WA, WB):

W57-61 (how law questions [by/through[Nthe courts[already[decided were...)
        oder welche sich Probleme   sich   da   stellen
        [or which   #[4] problems   *unacc* 'there' are-posed

L65   (*decisions already taken by courts*) *and the difficulties which the courts*
        experienced <u>*in taking these decisions*</u>
A59-65 [...] and @ – the way in which the cases. are \dealt with
B60-66 [...] and how they go about treating these cases

A more sophisticated inference is apparent in WA's interpretation of '**hier**' as connoting 'to this audience (who, being the legal *élite*, <u>must know</u> the Chief Justice of the High Court)' (W21-26):

Als Präsi'denten... brauche ich Herrn Professor Odersky <u>**hier**</u> **nicht vorzustellen**
As   President$_{ACC}$ ...   need   I [Mr$_{ACC}$ - Prof. Odersky <u>here</u> - not introduce
WA: *he hardly needs any introduction I think for* <u>*as you know*</u> *he's the....*

Of course, **da** and **hier** in these examples could have been rendered as 'there' (or omitted, e.g. 'problems which arise') and 'here'. That they are instead made explicit in this way reflects the richness of contextualisation in the model, and shows how readily available such inference products are for formulation.

5.3 Tense, Aspect and realis/irrealis

Tense-Aspect morphology and overt marking probably differ across any language pair. Among Indo-European languages, English and Russian, for example, have quite distinctive (but not symmetrical) durative/habitual and (im)perfective marking; and in modern spoken Romance languages like French or Italian, perfective Aspect is degenerate to varying degrees, so that additional information is needed to translate *il fume* or *il a éternué* into English, in which time-deictic and aspectual relations are rather clearly encoded, as either *he smokes/he's a smoker*, or *he is* (now) *smoking*, and either *he sneezed* or *he has sneezed*. As for Chinese verbs, they are not obligatorily marked for Tense and Aspect at all, while English verbs cannot omit Tense features.

In the light of the contrastive facts of Tense/Aspect marking, translation itself must require some intermediate representation in which features like spatial and temporal coordinates, and boundedness, among others, are somehow autonomous or at least 'portable'. In addition, since marking of such features is not *always* mandatory, it also requires a context-sensitive way of deciding when and where they are so *significant* as to merit overt expression.

Time indexing in an interpreters' discourse model is necessary, not only because features like Tense and Aspect sometimes need to be marked in TL output where they are lacking in the original. Even in a language like German which marks Tense on the verb, time relations may be underdetermined or ambiguous in the surface form (W64-66):

Das soll   auch die Leitlinie für meinen - einführende n@ Worte 'hier 'sein
That shall/should indeed the directing-line for my - introductory # words here   be

L65-67 *that- so much. - by way of introDUCtion* (implicit PAST)
B67:   and THAT's basically what I shall try and do /HERE (FUTURE)

Semantically, this expresses the intention (**soll**) that the 'general thrust' (**Leitlinie**) of some recent item (default assignment of **das**) should be the same as that of the Speaker's 'introductory remarks';[5] we can infer that **das** refers to some structure evoked in recent discourse. But the time frame is unclear: there is no Aspect on the main predicate **soll sein**, and both terms of the equation—**das** and 'my introductory remarks'—are vague as to their extension; in fact the Speaker is himself unsure of what referent to choose: he reviews his choice of noun in mid-phrase (**meinen** has Accusative-Singular inflection, whereas 'words' is plural), and only the rising intonation on the last words suggest a forward link. Interpreter WL focuses her proposition on the 'past' segment, the link to the future being left to hearers to infer from the meaning of 'introduction'. WB makes the most of the minimum elements of which she can be sure—intention ('I shall try and do'), equation ('and that is what'), and the use of two vague 'placeholder' referents ('that' and 'what')—and hedges the vagueness with 'basically' and 'here'.

Other formulations show that time indices are routinely represented (available) independently of the immediate text:

W87-89: **meine kurzen Worte gliedern sich [...] in diese beiden Teile**
         my short   words are-articulated [...] in these two parts
L90-91   *my@ - brief presentation will deal with BOTH. of these \aspects*
B90-92   I will ... divide my statement into- two PARTS

39-40   **und dann ... 1988 Präsident.... wurde**
         and then in 1988 Chief Judge... became
L41-42   *and as of 1988 he has been.....*

In Chinese neither Tense nor Aspect are mandatorily marked, and so sometimes have to be inferred for formulation in English. Both the Tense and the *realis /irrealis* index of propositions like 'Taiwan rejoin UN' are available from elementary world knowledge (Taiwan is not at present a member of the UN), but time-frames are often given by adverbs or adjectives, word-meanings (plan, prospects for...) and/or aspectual particles:

TS1-2:   **jintian... yao tan tan** (today.. I want to talk about...)
         cong ganggang de jiwei jiangzhe de yanjiang...
         from (the) [just-now... [Speakers' speeches...

TS42-4: chaoye ...   <u>yijing</u> shi dadao yizhi de gongshi   <u>le</u>
[govt & people] ... <u>already</u> F> <u>reach</u> unanimous consensus *perfective*

In the Taipei discourse, three time indices are current: immediate here-and-now past or future for reference to the speech, the Speakers and the current session; general present for the real world situation described; and future-hypothetical (expressed by present intent). These times are often marked in the text by phrases like **ganggang** ('just now' S7, S17), **zai dangqian de zhe guoji qingshi zhi xia** (in the present international situation, S5), **jintian** ('today' S6, S9), **xianzai** ('now', S19, S20); **daihuir yao...** ('in-a-moment intend'). S10 gives a date (1971) for the event mentioned, and S11-14 and 17-19 describe a current reality: voting strengths in the UN General Assembly (existential verbs **you**). In short, Tenses and *realis/irrealis* indices are usually either

   (a)   explicitly marked in each sentence by time words or phrases;
   (b)   supplied in the meanings of intentional and volitional verbs and adverbs which embed the proposition concerned; or
   (c)   manifest to all those present, when the reference is to an aspect of a shared situation.

Where these indices are not encoded in successive utterances by verb inflections or other devices, they must be represented by default—say, in terms of the DRT-like format of Fig. 3.3., in a future-*irrealis* 'box', containing the Goal and predicates on it, set up at the first instance of the material under a (present-tense) verb of *hoping* or *wanting*.[6] This allows TB to supply Tense in S5 (lines T50-60):

zai dangqian de zhe guoji qingshi zhi xia ne - chongfan Lianheguo - shi xuyao
in present   international conditions - under p - [rejoin United Nations - [*shi* [need
chang shijian de qu- -jingying - chang shijian de qu- zuo jihua - (...)
[long time   *de* [go - busy - long time   *de* go - make plan]]]

TA: how/ever - it is a TASK that requires long term PLANNING
TB: we <u>will need to</u> - plan and WORK for a long time in order to achieve our GOAL of...

These different time and *realis/irrealis* indices must be permanently assigned to superordinate concepts or relations salient in the discourse, since they are inserted correctly even when not marked in the present sentence:

S15: jingyou. Lianheguo *Dahui* de zhei tiao lu ne - shuo shizai
     via   UN Gen. Assembly   this route p - say-honestly
     ye BUSHI name de RONGYIDE
     also[not-*shi* [so   easy

TA: as such - it's not so - EASY - to
TB: an-d - so- I con\clude here that - it won't be EASY for us to - re-\enter..

S20:
..women yinggai - YONG ZHEIZHONG SHILI -... qu xuanze yige yige zuzhi -
we   should   - use   this kind (of) power... go choose an organisation -
ranhou ne - zuo wei women - chongfan Lianheguo de yige TIAOBAN -
then   p   -   treat [it] as [we -   rejoin United Nations *de* [a springboard

TB: ~DESIGNATE.. a- financial insti\tution which would serve as a
SPRINGBOARD. for our \entry...

S24 (210)
[zhei tiao lu ne -] ... ta ye bu shi wanquan .... meiyou ... zhang'ai de -
this route p - ....   it also not is   wholly   not-have obstacles p

TA: the road to IMF - or World Bank - will not be as smooth -as [....] expected

S27-28
wo tiaoguo qianmian de - jieshao...   wo zhijie gen gewei tan tan
I   jump past front *de*   introduce   I   direct with everyone discuss

TB: I'll skip a few pages .... I'm going to skip the portion describing...

Where none of these conditions obtain, and Tense cannot be inferred by
association as in the above examples, it must be guessed for obligatory deictic
marking in English. For the recorded videotape interview with Fang Lizhi, the
deictic situation was not shared with the interpreters and they were not told at
what time of day the event was being held, so that, even given *absolute* time
coordinates in expressions like **jintian shangwu, jintian xiawu** (this morning,
this afternoon) plus perfective/completive aspect, they could not guess at the
appropriate Tense (*relative* to the present):

name jintian shangwu Fang jiaoshou ne yuanlai # yingwen. zuole ge yanjiang - ...
well-so today morning Fang Professor   p originally [in] English made a   speech - ...
name jintian xiawu ne   - gen - hen duo de Zhongguo jiaoshou - yiji gen
well-so today afternoon p - with - very many China/ese professors - and with
Zhongguo tongxuemen - jiu youguan liang `an - Zhongguo de wentine - jixu ne -
China/ese students   -   p regarding two shores - China   issues(s) - continue p -
jiaohuan yiJIAN
exchange view(s)

FC: *and this mor/ning - you. have. alrea/dy - made a speech in /Eng/lish - and this*
after/noon - you - were ~able to. dis\cuss - problems concerning Chi/na and
Tai.\WAN with many professors and students +

In fact this discussion was just *about to* take place, i.e. the time was early afternoon. (The term 'discuss with' used by the Moderator is really a euphemism for 'be interviewed in front of').

There are noticeable differences in the overt expression of Tense and *realis/irrealis*: predictably, interpreter TB, a native English Speaker, marks these features more fully than her (Chinese-native) colleague TA:

    TB 71-2: if we were to.... 79 it would be very difficult...
    (TA: it's very difficult to re-enter... by obtaining support);

    TB 139:   it won't be easy for us to re-enter
    (TA: it's not so easy to obtain...);

    TB 104-8: the Resolution... that admitted China
    (TA: which excludes Taiwan and admits China).

6 SI strategies or natural inference products?

As explained in Chapter 2, most accounts of SI predict difficulty with non-isomorphic (SL-TL) sentence structure unless it is countered by certain strategies. Two strategies described in SI normative literature, in particular, involve pre-emptive on-line manipulation of the discourse structure: these are *saucissonnage* (or 'chunking'), and anticipation. *Saucissonnage,* or pre-emptive segmentation of the input, is recommended by European and Chinese authors on SI technique (Ilg 1978, Zhong 1984, Zhuang 1991). Anticipation is usually classified into two types:

(a)   linguistic, based on predictable collocations or formulas, or syntactic: Gile (1995: 115) also claims a major predictive role of grammatical function and predictor words, connectives and subordination markers;

(b)   extralinguistic, usually from the discourse record (Wilss 1978; Lederer 1981).

If surface and linguistic clues play an important role in prognosis, and hence SI, then ill-formed grammar, as well as languages with sparse inflectional morphology and verb-final languages, would be more troublesome due to a lack of such 'predictor' clues and 'the syntactic importance and informational load carried by the verb' (Gile 1995: 115). This view also predicts difficulty with listings, since one 'cannot predict when the predicate will occur', and embeddings, which 'interrupt the logical flow of a proposition' (ibid.).

Prognosis in SI has been defined more broadly. Chernov (1992) proposes a 'multichannel information processing' model for SI based entirely on concurrent prognosis at different levels—sound (phoneme, syllable, word), syntax and categorial semantics (phrase and utterance level), 'semantics proper' (phrase, utterance and text), and sense (utterance, text and communicative context)—and suggests that the reliability of SI is a function of the number of 'tiers of prognosis' concurrently involved.

6.1 Anticipation

We have seen anticipation based on a formula, or the knowledge of scripted conventions, in the immediate output of *ladies and gentlemen* (W46 LAB).

Interpreters sometimes produce not just a tentative sentential adverb, or a 'gambit' Subject, but an actual predicate before the input predicate has appeared. Sometimes the predicate which is pre-empted is a 'pallid' verb (Mattern 1974, cited in Wilss 1978) as in the case of a presentative or existential whose meaning is virtually given in advance, e.g. for the 'ellipsed' verb in W-M5, or the first verb in this example, 'head', which is cued by the meaning of '**Leiter**' (leader):

M5β (may I just indicate that President O...)
früher 'Leiter der - 'Strafrechtsabteilung - in - 'München <u>war</u> bevor er 1983 -
earlier [leader of the penal law department - in - Munich   <u>was</u> [before he 1983

WA:that.@ - President   ODERsky   -   <u>used to</u> head.   -

Präs. des - Bayrischen [...]gerichts und dann 1988 Pr. - des Bundesg.[...] wurde
[Pres. ofthe - Bavarian [...] Court [V Ø[& then 1988 Pres. of the FederalCourt <u>became.</u>

WL:*and. he@ <u>was. also</u> the President. of. the. Bavarian- \High Court-*

Sometimes the meaning of the verb can be fully predicted from the higher clause, here the subordinate 'when... is asked to speak (supposed to make a speech)' (W-S2):

@mm wenn @ - **ein Räpräsentant eines Ge'richts ..... refe'rieren soll - dann-**
if/when -   a representative   of-a   court   make-speech supposed then
ist er wohl - 'schwerpunktmäßig @   darauf   angewiesen -
is he 'I-guess'   focally   thereon   advised
über   +   'Rechtsfragen ^L - und zumal- 'darüber zu <u>berichten</u>
about/over -   law questions -   and especially - there-about to report

WL: *then I think- he- @ has been@ ^L asked <u>to speak</u> principally about.....*

Less trivial verbal anticipations are common, however, and many verb or predicate anticipations are based on some form of presupposition. In the Würzburg corpus (see Table 5.5), presuppositions guide anticipated production of different types in

M2 ('Since NP PP V' >> 'NP is PP') and S4 ('under NP... >> there is NP'). The seemingly gratuitous NP expansions seen in the last Chapter as stalling devices are also based on a form of lexical presupposition (Fillmore 1985), simply generating general or context-based superordinate information about an NP: *subsidy fraud is a crime which...*; [rejoining the UN] is a task which..; talk on a topic focusing on...

6.1.1 Anticipation from a propositional attitude

A grammatical predicate may be an attributive phrase describing a propositional attitude—a belief or an evaluation—whose force may be signalled in advance by a clue. In WM-2, **vor allem** ('especially') marks the Speaker's attitude or evaluation of what follows. In this example the sense of the predicate 'of great interest' is probably anticipated from the PA 'above all' (the phrase 'is very important' is begun before **Interesse**):

> M2α: **ist es - vor allem auch für unsre \ausländischen 'Gäste -**
> is it - above all   also for our foreign   guests
> **von GROßem Inter'esse -   'WIE - die Er'fassung dieser...**
> of great   interest - how   the apprehending of these..
> WB: and.- its very important I think for our. FOReign guests -
> to t-to /KNOW - HOW

WB then completes the approximation with 'to know...'

6.1.2 Anticipation from pragmatic principles

Anticipation concerns not only final predicates, but also other sentence-final features, like negation, as in this example from W-M4 (W21-26/WA23-27), a stylistically marked preposed Object construction with negation cliticised to the final Verb complement:

> ('Professor Odersky is going to speak on this very topic....')
> **als Präsi'denten -   des 34.7 - deutschen 'Bundesgerichtshofs 36.3 - brauche**
> as President [Acc] ofthe   German   Federal Justice Court - need
> TA:.going to address precisely that /THEME35.4 - ᴿ he 36.9
>
> **ich Herrn - Professor Odersky 38.1 -   hier -   NICHT VORzustellen 40.1**
> I   Mr [Acc] Professor Odersky   here   not   introduce
>
> TA: - hardly 37.7 needs any introDUction 38.9 I think.@ for 40 as
> you know he's.the. President of the. Federal High Court

This example of anticipation provides an interesting test case for various (cognitive) pragmatic accounts. When she produces 'hardly needs any introduction', the interpreter has available, in terms of linguistic input, only a fronted Accusative phrase and the main verb 'I need'. We assume a 'greedy' Assembly process which uses all available linguistic information and strong cognitive assumptions: the 'President' phrase is referentially compatible with the salient 'Odersky'; it is marked as the Object of the Speaker's as yet unknown predicate, licensing the anticipatory logical hypothesis that Odersky is the Patient of something the Speaker 'needs' to do. Does the marked word order carry any further clue? A Gricean account might postulate flouting of the Maxim of Quantity (repetition of Odersky, already in focus from the previous sentence) or of Manner (marked fronted construction) as inference triggers, but it cannot explain the *choice* of inference. We can also assume the interpreter's speech-act competence (knowledge of social conventions and conditions on the felicity of speech-acts), and a script-based assumption: the interpreter knows from her agenda that the Moderator is now required to introduce Prof Odersky, and the previous sentence suggests that the act will be performed in this utterance. The RT account completes the picture: the fronted Object and 'given that' value of **als,** by virtue of the additional processing effort required, signal that a contextual effect is available if the premises are processed together in the deductive device. The **als** phrase is thus equivalent to a first premise 'given that [the Theme/Patient of the proposition] is Chief Justice'; the second premise is supplied from external knowledge: i.e. for 'Chief Justice', substitute 'in an exalted position whose incumbent must be known to all'. The deduction, that the moderator does *not* need to introduce him, is made and formulated in less than 2 seconds.

6.1.3 Long-range deductive anticipation

It is clear that at some points at least, the interpreter maintains some 'macro' or long-range representation of the developing discursive structure, and naturally makes deductions from the successive premises added to her own assumptions, as do the Addressees. In these examples of 'logical' (as distinct from 'thematic') anticipation an interpreter may (perhaps inadvertently!) voice the conclusion to an argument well in advance of the Speaker:

> In Taipei S11-13, the Speaker has explained that '*currently only 28 countries have relations with Taiwan, and of these only 25 are UN members, and there are 184 member states in the UN altogether, so these 25 States only make up a small proportion - one seventh - of the total ...*':

S14 (synchronized):
dangran zheige yao. juli -   dadao ...   SAN FEN ZHI ER duoshu - juedui zheige
of course this [is] distant (from) reaching [the] two-thirds   majority - absolute   d

TB:... only   account for - a   SEVENTH - of - of the UN   \members so - <u>it's not</u>

BIAOZHUN ne   - shi hai xiangcha - jiangjin yibai piao -   zhi duo +
criterion   p   still [by a margin of] - nearly a hundred votes - so-many

TB: <u>LIKELY that we will</u> be able to-   reach - a two-thirds @majority- vote

The Speaker does not conclude until S15: '...*so from this point of view we know
that this route via the UN General Assembly is honestly <u>not so easy/likely</u>*' (see
next example). In other words, TB overtly states a conclusion—not explicitly
stated by the *Speaker* until about 11 secs later—from premises laid out by the
Speaker over the past 30-40 seconds combined with assumptions from her own
frame knowledge:

Text premises and deductions	Premises supplied by TB	Conclusions
	UN General Assembly Resolutions can be revoked by a vote of members...	
[>>this] requires a 2/3 majority		
There are 184 UN Member States	All UN member states may vote	184 states could vote
States that recognise Taiwan = 25	States that recognise Taiwan would vote to revoke the Resolution	25 States could vote to revoke
States that recognise Taiwan = 1/7th of UN members	1/7th is less than 2/3rds	we=Taiwan will not get a 2/3 majority

Interpreters also sometimes autonomously explicate logical structure in the
discourse, reflecting monitoring of the status of successive propositions in terms
of the stage reached in the logical argument: the conclusion to the arguments for
and against applying through the General Assembly (T-S9-S14) is reached in S15
(added explicitation underlined):

T133/TB137-8
suoyi -   cong . zhei dian lai kan - women ye zhidao - jingyou. Lianheguo DAHUI
so -   from this point of view -   we also know - via[the] UN General Assembly

de zhei tiao lu ne shuo shizai 184 ye BUSHI name de 185 RONGYIDE   +
   this   route   say-honestly   also is not   so   easy
TB: 184 <u>so I conclude here that...</u>

By the time the discourse model is well-established, it is possible, in the face of indeterminate input structure, for an SI interpreter to confidently formulate an advance presupposition which turns out exactly to 'anticipate' the final predicate ('priority' in Chinese, literally: 'best-first'):

S23: (so I feel...) **yinggai shi yao** [should be[?need/if
yi- -chongfan.. yixie xiang shi-Guoji Huobi Jijin ...[B] **huozhe**[A] [................
[by - [rejoin - [some [like   Internat'l Monetary Fund - or...

TA: (...   therefore) ^we should seek
TB: (so -   I ~ FEEL)   +   that [B]we should. first start /by

[............] **Shijie Yinhang le - er ZHEI LEI de zuzhi ne - wei - youxian kaolü**
       the World Bank .... p such kind of organisation p - as - priority consideration

TA: RE-ENTRY - (to the International MONETARY.....
TB: becoming members of the IMF...

The above examples and discussion show various types of knowledge and inference which license the projections achieved by simultaneous interpreters. While in some cases they may be seen as presuppositions, implicatures or higher-order explicatures licensed by the immediate text or basic lexical information, others require logical representations based on long stretches of discourse, and deductions over these representations, additionally involving extralinguistic sources.

7 Contextual sources: summary

The phenomena we have seen so far confirm that, as has been shown in previous corpus studies (e.g. Seleskovitch 1975; Lederer 1981; Pochhacker 1994), simultaneous interpreters use both thematic and logical material, i.e. information not given in the text, including knowledge about the situation and the world, certain social conventions relevant to the event, and various additional attributes of the entities and relations being referred to by the Speaker. They also use deduction and inference from combined text and non-text information, including the logical structure of long segments of the discourse.

The additional extratextual sources provide them with a basis for making temporary approximations and generalisations about these entities and relations while the sentences in which they occur are still incomplete. This suggests that a small number of conceptual complexes—entities associated with certain properties and in certain relations (epr)—are highly accessible to the process of assembling propositional forms for production, so that the interpreter can, if necessary, safely produce relevant or at least uncontroversial assertions or qualifications about them when they are instantiated in text. Evidence from the spontaneous but relevant material in the interpreters' versions suggests that SI is better described in terms of these two processes than as a search for equivalents at the level of text units.

Some words and phrases produced by the interpreters could be explained as stock formulas retrieved from a mental phrasebook, but there are also many holistic and idiomatic renderings—corresponding to the traditional notion of 'free' translation—which pose a challenge to psycholinguistics in that they defy modelling in terms of semantic representations and 'other knowledge'. To account for them, we shall suggest an inventory of the concepts and procedures which must be available in the intermediate language of representation, extended to include a set of intentional primitives, probably rooted in affect and instincts; in other words, a language of thought (LOT) with a volitional dimension, comprising, as its vocabulary, the cognitive (conceptual and perceptually-based) stock of epr, with indexation for deixis and contrast, embeddable under attitudes and Intentional states (which can of course be attributable to others by meta-representation); and as its 'syntax', a set of inferential and deductive rules. (This is not to suggest that a language thus conceived, implying a uniform propositional format for all perceptual input, could account for all mental experience: to paraphrase Pascal, the affective dimension probably has its own rules.[7]) The basic vocabulary, or epr, can be illustrated in a hypothetical model of the contents of the interpreter's working memory at specific points in the discourse.

8 The discourse model: entities, properties and relations (epr)

We suggest that these processes cannot be efficiently supported by directly accessing an open-ended semantic or conceptual network, but instead require the establishment of a temporary, task-oriented perceptual-conceptual model holding tokens of the most current discourse referents, including entities, their properties and relations between them (epr), as sketched very tentatively in Figures 6.1 and 6.2. The models are highlighted and marked for fields and relations which are assumed to be active at Würzburg-M2/3 and S9/10, and Taipei S2 and S10.

Interpreters think more or less consciously about forthcoming assignments, so that even before a discourse begins, relevant entities, relations and properties (epr) from world and situation-specific knowledge, based on what is known about the Speaker, other participants and the subject-matter of the meeting from briefings, documentation or speculation, begin to be installed, albeit loosely and virtually at first, in a temporary, task-specific memory. As the Speaker's successive utterances introduce these and other new epr in various roles and relationships, they are strengthened in the discourse model to the point where any instance of such an epr in the discourse evokes its representation in the model. In this way, any meaning underdetermined in the fragment captured from the text, be it sense or reference, is enriched from the information in the discourse model to build propositional forms and attributed attitudes.

The left-hand part of each diagram represents what is most immediate in perceptual experience. It includes participants, including the Speaker and those with whom he interacts or identifies (Taipei), such as the audience and other Speakers, all of which are likely Subjects in the interactive parts of the discourse; possible Topics, such as 'the point' and 'the issue', which embed and index the left-hand, conceptual complex; deictic indices like 'here' and 'today'; and current modal values of attitude and intent (discussed below in Sections 9 ff.), shown in italics. (English words are used in the diagram merely for schematic convenience to stand in for concepts, attitudes, etc.)

The right-hand side represents conceptual and mostly 'core proposition' material, including salient entities in the subject matter, their contextually relevant attributes (not all shown), and currently salient relations, which are candidates for predicates. In the social and event-related discourse typical of Chairmen and Moderators, the left-hand side is typically foregrounded; as an invited Speaker moves on to address substantive issues, the focus of attention and mental activity shifts to the conceptual, on the right-hand side of our diagrams.

The distinction between percept-based data, and epr/assumptions derived from what Speakers say or other conceptual knowledge, is not absolute, since links are established in the text and suggested by Speakers ('cases which Dr Mennens and Dr Rump have described'; a connection between {we-Taiwan-political forces- 'everyone'} etc.). The right-hand side nevertheless contains only 'reported' assumptions evoked or invoked from linguistic input (what the Speakers say), and reinforced by extralinguistic assumptions in the interpreter's own conceptual base. In the event of a conflict, perceptually confirmed facts would be predicted to prevail.

The propositions of the previous discourse are whittled down selectively, and by natural memory decay, to the bare bones and tokens which form the permanent mental model, which is adjusted for current relevance as the event progresses. The putative models at different stages (Taipei S2 and S10, Würzburg M2/3 and S9/10) reflect shifts in emphasis and complexity as each discourse moves into a more substantive phase and new entities and relations are introduced. The model can be seen as a cognitive counterpart of descriptions of contexts offered in previous work (e.g. Pöchhacker's (1994) 'hypertext', situation and text)

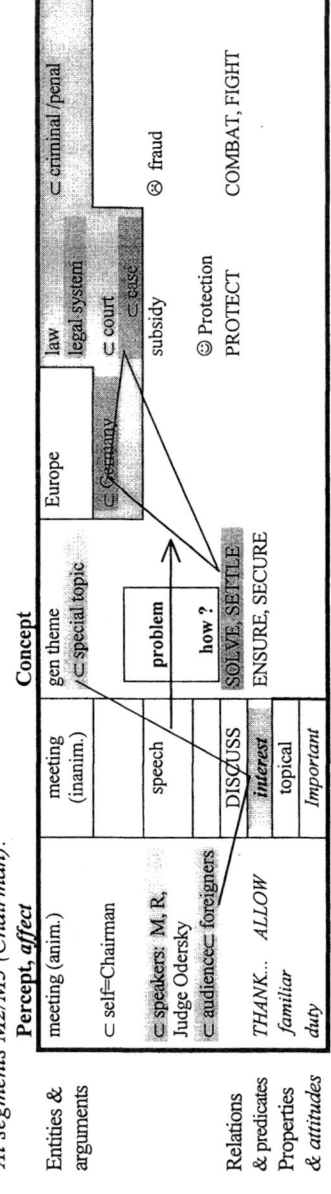

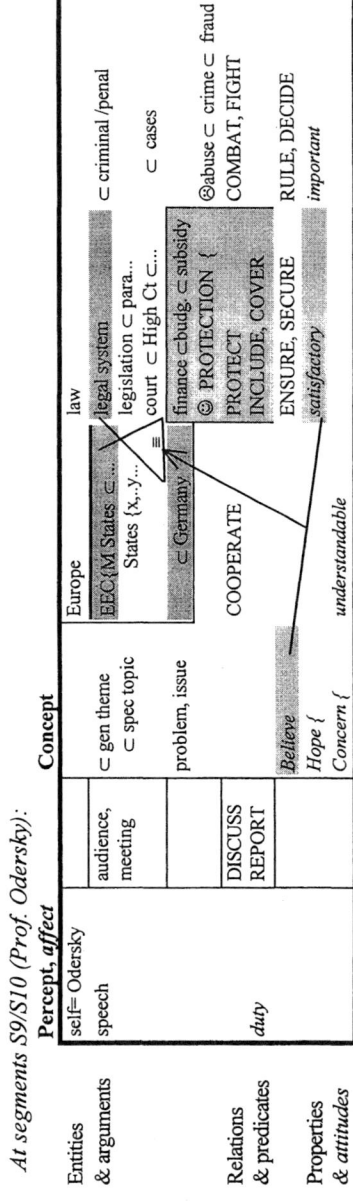

Figure 6.1 Discourse Models for SI: Würzburg

⊂ includes (subset)   ≡ is equivalent to   ☺⊗ desirability indexes (positive and negative)

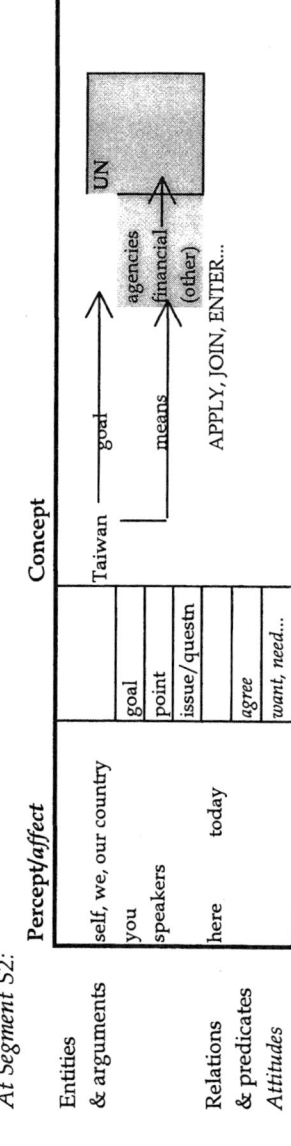

Figure 6.2 Discourse Models for SI: Taipei

in which the relative saliency or accessibility of inputs from these sources is dynamically constrained by principles of relevance and cognitive capacity.

The structuring of these epr in the discourse model presumably reflects (under illocution) both thematic saliency, or importance, and logical and set-membership relations. Our diagrams show only the most salient subsets. The biographical introduction in Würzburg M5 would introduce a sudden rush of relatively inaccessible subsets (Provincial Court, Criminal Law Department, etc).

The discourse model thus allows a simultaneous interpreter to produce a full Subject-Predicate clause before such a structure is available in the text, with the necessary elements and relations—a Subject, a Predicate, deictic relations, Tense, Aspect and so on, where necessary—being supplied, licensed or augmented by the information in the model. In general, the (re)presentation of the conference situation allows her to make simple statements about the meeting or its participants.

The conceptual structures are not bound to one linguistic form, but emerge in the discourse in different forms. Referents which recur frequently in the input, like **Subventionsbetrug** (subsidy fraud), **Finanzsystems** (financial system) or **chongfan Lianheguo** (return United Nations) are realised in a variety of output forms, suggesting that such entities are stably represented—i.e. highly accessible throughout the discourse—not in linguistic form, but as conceptual tokens which can be realised by the production system in whatever way is appropriate to the ongoing sentence. Tokens become established with a status in the discourse (e.g. topicality) and associated with likely clausemates: in the Taipei discourse, the phrase **[women] chongfan/hui dao/jiaru Lianheguo]** '(we) (to) rejoin(ing)/ return/ re-entry to the UN' occurs in one or two forms in the source text, usually as a bare V-O without either Tense/Finiteness or Subject. It is established not as a linguistic form but as a salient concept, and acquires two attributes *in this context,* which guide the choice of linguistic features necessary for its realisation each time it is evoked:

(1)   *discourse topicality*—by occurring repeatedly under an 'Aboutness' relation conferred by its initial status as discourse topic (in the title of the speech and the (English SL) introductory remarks) and its occurrence with 'about' prepositions (**duiyu...** in S2) or as Object of 'aboutness-marking' verbs like 'discuss' (in S1 and S4).

(2)   the *Goal case-role,* by default, of any action or desire predicate of which *we/Taiwan* is the Agent (overt or understood) as explicitly characterized in S3 as the 'goal' of desired action by *Taiwan/we.*

It may then be instantiated by a mention in the text, or inserted as considered appropriate to these two features, in various guises, e.g.

- as NP

  S4, S5: re-entry (IB: of Taiwan) into the United Nations/ need to re-enter...)

  S5: it is a task... / our goal of re-entering....

- as VP

  S3: how we should re-enter the United Nations / to re-enter the United N...

  S7: how we can... become a UN member again;

Through repeated instantiations, it also becomes associated with a Subject or class of subjects ('we/Taiwan') which can thus be confidently supplied in the absence of a text Subject (e.g. S5). It is inserted by interpreters as much as two minutes after its last mention in the text:

S10 (74 secs since last SL input): by making our way into the United Nations/

S16 (2 mins. since last SL input): to obtain membership in the United Nations / to re-enter the UN

Similarly, in Würzburg, the salient NPs are contextualized or evoked differently in each context to yield different forms for the same referents:

Input forms	WL	WA	WB
S5 Finanzsystem	financial interests	finances	financial system
S9 Finanzsystem	financial system	finances	financial resources
S9 Subventionen	subsidies	-	-
- (no instance in source)	financial interests	-	-
S9 ...deutschen Subventionssystems	...own interests	...state finances	budget

The left-hand side of the discourse model happens to correspond to what is most autonomously handled in interpretation, i.e. the raw material for the volitional and directive (or rhetorical) components of the discourse. This is natural, since what is most directly manifest is most sovereignly formulated.

9 Secondary pragmatic processing and communicative intent

Propositions are presented by Speakers in a certain order and marked with certain features to identify them as intended premises or conclusions, or for their intended relative or dependent relevance. A wide range of discourse features are used to mark propositional content for some form of directed Intentionality. Theories in this area are still tentative; in this Section we will explore how these ostensive features traverse the process of simultaneous interpretation between languages.

In the last two Sections we have tracked the fate of structures and propositional contents through the SI process in terms of the logical and thematic dimensions of meaning assembly. But this clearly does not exhaust the description of the Speaker's 'Message'. It is a generally accepted tenet of professional practice that an interpreter 'identifies with' the Speaker, and by convention, speaks in the first person on his behalf. Definitions of the ideal object of translation (the Message, or what is to be conveyed) often appeal to the notion of the Speaker's 'communicative intent'. How this is apprehended is not clear. IT writing reflects a belief in automatic, almost empathic perception and reproduction of the Speaker's intended meaning ('*vouloir-dire*') (Seleskovitch and Lederer 1986: 298). Authors in the IP tradition, in contrast, acknowledge the importance of style and impact, but define the Message in terms of information (Moser 1976: 135 ff.; Gile 1995: 125).

Neither of these positions are quite satisfactory. Firstly, communication, to perform its function of linking what are otherwise self-contained cognitive devices, as Relevance theory has it, must involve 'ostension', which signals both the intent to communicate and specific directions to relevance (Sperber and Wilson 1986/1995); in Gricean terms, it must be shaped by cooperative principles. Secondly, as authors like Austin (1955/1962) and Searle (1969) have demon-strated, speech utterances are acts which present meanings with illocutionary force. There is a close relationship between illocution, propositional attitudes, 'Intentional states' (modes of belief or desire that something is or should be the case), and communicative intent. Searle describes intentional states as intentional contents under psychological modes: Intentionality is 'that property of many mental states and events by which they are directed at or about or of objects and states of affairs in the world' (Searle 1983: 3; 12). Speech acts are the linguistic counterparts of Intentional states.

In identifying and modelling communicative intent we are therefore also concerned (to borrow Functionalist terms) with the persuasive or conative functions which embed information; in psychological terms, with volition as it interacts with cognition. Any plausible intermediate language of representation for real-life discourse must therefore have a means of capturing—and in translation, for assigning—the communicative features in discourse which express a Speaker's Intentionalities and attitudes.

As suggested earlier, we can represent these ideas in a universal utterance format in which a Speaker (S) expresses (a) predication(s) φ of some {epr} in some thematic arrangement (θ), under propositional attitude(s) (PA), and some illocution (IF), perhaps with some direction to processing (Dir) attached:

S [Dir [IF [PA*[φ* (θ {epr})]]

The features in speech which express attitude and intentionality, and which indicate the relative importance a Speaker attaches to an item, or direct the hearer to a context in which to process it—e.g. an assumption presented in the previous or next utterance, or evoked by another expression in the discourse—are those least adequately covered by standard grammatical theory, and most varied in their surface expression. These features include

1. *overt expressions of belief or desire* and their alleged derivatives (hope, intent, satisfaction etc), such as verbs of believing, hoping, etc., and attitudinal adverbs (*frankly, hopefully, fortunately*);
2. *expressions which imply such beliefs and desires,* such as factive and implicative verbs (*regret that, remember that*), and modal adverbs and auxiliaries;
3. *features which assign relative importance to propositions or their parts,* such as evaluative and evidential adverbs (*especially, most importantly, undoubtedly, probably*), discourse markers and connectives (*however, after all, anyway, since...*) and focusing and contrastive devices.

Attitude (we shall sometimes use PA as an abbreviation for the traditional term, 'propositional attitude') is commonly analysed in terms of two basic forces, Belief and Desire, of which expressions of modalities like necessity, possibility, purpose, assertions of veracity, etc. can be viewed for the purposes of this study as complex compounds.[8] These modalities do not stand in a one-to-one relationship to the features which express them in discourse.

The analytical difficulties in this area, and the need nonetheless for some kind of basic vocabulary of attitudes and modalities, can be demonstrated in a few examples from the corpus. The first does not involve the added complication of the speaker's own beliefs, but simply illustrates the perceived semantic kinship between 'attitudes' and 'modalities': in the translation, which seems viable, the word **yiyuan**, normally glossed 'intention', emerges as BELief ('consensus') + NECessity (T-S4):

T41-44:
zai... YIYUAN fangmian .. zheige chaoye .... yijing shi dadao yizhi de gongshi le
on   intention   side ...   govt & oppositn ... already *shi* reached unanimous consensus

A51-5:   have... all made a consensus... that re-entry ... is necessary
B46-50   have.. reached a consensus ...in (*sic*)..Taiwan's NEED to re-enter the UN

Attitudinal or evaluative adverbs are notoriously portable, and their scope is not always clear. In an example given earlier (W-M2α), WB can anticipate the evaluative predicate 'of great interest' from an adverb qualifying a left-branching PP: '[above all for our foreign guests [of great interest'. This shows how a shift in scope of such operators may not significantly distort the message, particularly when the correct focus can be restored by contrastive stress.

Another example of apparently 'free' translation, in which the linguistic form of the product is far removed from the input, is WB's version of WS3, which we used earlier to show how interpreters manage vague reference (WS3):

Das soll auch die Leitlinie -   für meinen - einführende n@ Worte hier sein...
That shall indeed the directing-line - for   my - introductory   words here   be

WB: and THAT's basically what I shall try and do / HERE

Various other features of translation can be identified, such as the dissolution and redistribution of lexical meaning: 'basically' conveys the generality in the meaning of **Leitlinie**. Other operations can be modelled in terms of a language of intermediate representation: a procedural or ostensive feature, perspective, is rendered by focalising and stressing THAT (is what...) (see Chapter 7); a volitional or attitudinal 'primitive', INTENT, is extracted from the modal **soll** and re-expressed in 'try and do'; while 'and' does the cohesive (procedural) work of the connective **auch**.

Two further examples will illustrate how far we can go toward analysing holistic translations with the apparatus taken on board so far:

(1)   T60   **wo xiang zui ZHUYAO de**   jiushi. jintian...
                  I think   most-important (Nominalized) thus is today...
       TA 64-5   there/fore. the ISSUE today...

Structural-semantic terms are adequate to describe part of the process: a single Noun (ISSUE) is found with semantic resemblance to '(the) most important (thing)' as a Subject for output. The 'null' or default context ($_A$most important$_N$ Ø) licenses translation by simply selecting a TL Noun *whose key attribute*, salient when the Noun is Definite, matches the attribute offered (ISSUE {+IMPortant...}); in another context the 'most-important' might have been a radish or a planet. The selective force of 'the' also covers the force of 'most' important. Analysis of the fate of **wo xiang** and **jiushi**, and of the source of 'therefore' in the translation, require prag-matic description: both appear to have scope over the utterance as such, one asserting belief, and one focusing; we can suggest that these effects are jointly achieved with (i) the connective 'therefore', (ii) rising intonation, and (iii) stress on ISSUE.

(2) W27-30   (Mr O. is well-known to you, he needs no introduction, but...)
               (als Strafrechtler) erlaube ich mir nur den Hinweis, daβ...
               as   penal jurist   allow   I   to me only the indication thereon , that...
     A32-3   *I'd just like to point out that...*
     L33-34   *perhaps I could just* indicate *however...*

Here concepts in speech-act theory seem useful. 'I allow myself.. ' implicates (in 'allow') that permission is required for an act, and explicates that this permission is taken. Since permission cannot felicitously be given and taken by the same person, and the Speaker carries out the act (indicating) in the same breath as asking permission, we interpret this by Gricean principles as a politeness function which 'hedges' the felicity of the act. Such hedges can be conventionally effected in English by mood[9], modals and discourse markers, viz. 'I would like', 'perhaps I could', 'however'.

Basic attitudes like Belief and Desire appear to be routinely expressed in spontaneous discourse in phrases like *I think*, or *I hope that...*, but such items may also be used by both Speakers and interpreters simply as fillers or attention-holders, or in a 'phatic' function at the opening of new utterances. A Speaker may also express degrees of confidence or emphasis in non-verbal ways: WL's *I think* at line 47 may well be a rendering of the tentative **@mm** prefacing the Speaker's modest opening ('@mm when - a representative of a court - is asked to speak...').

10 Processing instructions and procedural encoding

Contemporary theory recognises elements in discourse which function as 'directives', or instructions to a hearer on logical or thematic processing. There is a fine and somewhat fuzzy line between the expressions of attitude or modality directed at propositional contents, described above, and communicative or 'metadiscourse' devices which direct hearers' processing of discourse parts. Typically these are

(a) *discourse connectives*, like *after all, moreover, and, but, however, anyway, and so, given that..., assuming...,* which are more specialised in guiding co-processing (e.g. contrasting) of propositions and the assumptions contained in them; and

(b) *prosodic devices* like contrastive stress, which specialise in imposing perspective or contrasting at the clause-internal, phrase or word level, as well as expressing a range of attitudes. However, Blakemore (1987) suggests that prosody is a less reliable marker of scope (e.g. of focus).

Connectives and particles, in particular, have been analysed as guides to the (co)processing of propositions. Theories are currently being developed in pragmatics to account for those facets of discourse which do not directly encode propositional content.

Sweetser (1990) observes that many discourse connectives (and modals) function in two or three 'domains.' Adverbials like *however*, causatives (*because, since, therefore, though*) and conjunctions like *and, since, but* and *or*, may be used to relate propositions, not with their root logical or real-world values (e.g. *John came back because he loved her*) but in the epistemic domain, as arguments in a proof (*John loved her, because he came back*), or as speech acts, e.g. in *What are you doing tonight, because there's a good movie on*. Conjunctions, causal connectives, and modal adverbs may all display such functional polysemy (or pragmatic ambiguity) between root, epistemic and speech-act uses.

In the RT framework, Blakemore (1987) analysed some discourse connectives as 'constraints on relevance', i.e. pointers to the independent or associated relevance of the previous and/or current proposition. On this account, the connective *because* in *John loved her, because he came back* signals the dependent relevance of the two propositions; it is a form of conventional implicature which yields no extra information, but has as its sole function the guiding of the interpretation process. Another example is *After all*, which introduces a proposition (which it suggests is already accessible) that provides evidence for the truth of the previous one, e.g. *Tom has left. After all, his wife is not here* (1987: 82).

Dependent relevance makes meanings available by signalling an inferential connection, and so may also be indicated by a simple conjunction like *and*, or indeed merely by the adjacency of two propositions, as in *She's not happy, she's ecstatic.* Such relations can thus be found between segments under different propositional attitudes, or (in a dialogue) produced by different speakers.

Blakemore concluded that a range of linguistic elements and devices, including certain connectives, modals, word orders, intonational contours and parentheticals, might be viewed as encoding not contributions to the conceptual content of the propositions expressed, but rather constraints on relevance. In a 1993 paper, Wilson and Sperber developed this intuition that language encodes two types of meaning, and formulated it as a distinction between 'procedural' and 'conceptual' encoding.

In traditional linguistic accounts (Gricean and speech-act theory), utterances are said to encode (a) propositional or truth-conditional meaning, which is true or false of a state of affairs described, and (b) an illocutionary force corresponding to the 'speech-act' the utterance is intended to perform, the Speaker's attitude to the proposition, his evidence for it, the effect he intends the utterance to have, etc.

Relevance theory's answer to the issue of utterance meaning—'what was *said* (encoded) vs. what was *implied*'—is to classify all the assumptions communicated by an utterance into explicatures and implicatures. The basic determinate proposition which a hearer derives by enriching the decoded logical form of an utterance is called its 'explicature'. If Peter is unemployed and asks Mary *'Can you help'*, and Mary replies *'I can't'*, Peter can derive the explicature *Mary can't help me to find a job*. The extended representations of this proposition which may optionally be derived—embedding it under attitudes, speech-act descriptions, evidential indications and so on, such as *Mary says/believes/regrets she can't help me find a job*—are simply 'higher-order' explicatures. All other assumptions communicated in intentional acts of communication are implicatures, typically on a scale of strengths.

In this cognitive (RT) analysis of utterance comprehension, the products of linguistic decoding are input to an inferential phase which involves the construction and manipulation of conceptual representations. Accordingly, it is not surprising to find two basic types of information encoded in speech: representational and computational, or conceptual and procedural—i.e. material encoding (and evoking) conceptual representations, and directions on how to manipulate them (Wilson and Sperber 1993: 2).

Ordinary speech, in other words—and intuitively, oral discourse in particular—contains a large number of items and features which may be termed 'procedural' in that they do not themselves encode propositional content, but direct hearers or readers to contextual effects by indicating to hearers how they should 'take' propositions, contrast them, treat them as ironical, as evidence, as concessionary, etc., or by reducing the space in which to search for a hypothesis. In RT terms, procedurals are elements or features which direct hearers to the most relevant implicatures or higher-order explicatures: they form a large class, potentially including connectives, like *and, but, well, so,* or *after all* (German *ja, doch, immerhin*, French *certes, pourtant, donc*, Chinese *jiu, ye, cai*), demonstratives and pronouns, parentheticals, certain particles, mood indicators and pragmatic word order.

The implications of this analysis for processing models of comprehension are currently under study (e.g. see proposed formalism for 'processing instructions' in discourse in Luscher 1994 and Reboul & Moeschler 1998), and it is too early to attempt to integrate it fully into our model of SI. In particular, some elements may turn out to have both conceptual and procedural encoding functions. Our account therefore retains some traditional terminology, and in particular, does not always draw a sharp distinction between illocutionary force indicators, which contribute to higher-order explicatures, and procedurals which signal dependent relevance by constraining the search for the most relevant implicature.

All these features must obviously be addressed, reflecting as they do the volitional and communicative dimension of speech: propositional syntax and lexical semantics alone leave a substantial part of discourse unexplained except as variations to be attributed to stylistic preference or error. In modelling translation, and SI in particular, an account of pragmatic clues to inference sheds new light on the anticipatory hypotheses which make synchronicity possible, and explains many of the transformations and apparently sovereign production in the interpreter's versions.

A study of SI corpora suggests that the procedural and intentional dimensions of speech are processed somewhat differently than the propositional content itself. Hearers in any language can be assumed to be attuned to this 'packaging' of spoken discourse, and a good deal of directive material seems to be 'absorbed' by interpreters, instead of being reflected in corresponding structures in their output as if it had traversed the machinery of parsing and propositional enrichment.[10] On the other hand, the interpreters' output contains its own complement of such elements, which are increasingly fluent and sovereign as the discourse progresses.

Assuming that the ostensive-inferential nature of linguistic communication is universal, all speech will contain reflections of the Speaker's attitudes, and elements and devices to guide hearers to the intended meaning. However, since these must exploit linguistic resources, the method of encoding varies across languages. The next section illustrates some differences in procedural encoding in English, German and Chinese, and looks at how these features are transferred from SL to TL. On the basis of this and earlier sections, we then attempt to abstract out a universal LOT with conceptual, procedural and volitional elements.

10.1 Uses and distribution of modals and connectives: contrastive differences

The use and distribution of procedural and non-truth-conditional devices obviously varies between languages. Both German and Chinese appear to make more use than English of certain adverbs, which may also have purely logical 'root' meanings (*auch, noch, ja, schliesslich; ye, dou, you, cai..*), to cancel, modify or hedge presuppositions or otherwise guide the perception of relevance (in mental model jargon, significance) over segments of continuous discourse. Not surprisingly, such items tend to disappear in German-English or Chinese-English translation, since their closest equivalents in some uses would be parentheticals (Fillmore 1984), which may result in an undesirable loosening of the register (Pollard 1994).

Chinese and German both make frequent use of modal adverbs like (Gn.) **auch** or (Ch.) **ye,** placed before the verb (in IP), and of modal auxiliaries. English prefers adverbials, placed initially or parenthetically (marked off by 'comma-intonation'), e.g. ....*however..* , *...moreover...* early in the sentence. In particular, English makes far more use of intonational prosody to signal perspective and dependent relevance, or to hedge the felicity of a speech-act. Biq (1989) points out that while the Chinese 'logic-oriented' particles *ye, you, cai, jiu, dou* all operate on the three discourse planes (content, epistemic, and speech-act), the closest English equivalents *also, again, even, only, just, all* have not all developed a speech-act use (Biq 1989: 16).

German **auch** and **schon,** for example, are used in this text both in their ordinary 'content' senses ('also' and 'already' (W95, 109); cf. **bevor 35, und dann** 39), and in directive, epistemic or speech-act senses. In these functions such items may also occur sentence-internally to highlight or specify an element, as in W12 **vor allem auch für...;** W123 **und vor allen Dingen ...;** W48 **... zumal eines Revisionsgerichts...;** W55 **zumal darüber zu berichten, wie..;** W80 **vielleicht mehr von ...;** W121 **wenn auch nur...**

The same is true of Chinese **ye,** a widely used particle which functions

(1) in the content domain, like English *also*:

> *Daren shui jiao, xiaohai ye shui jiao*
> Adults sleep, children <u>also</u> sleep

(2) in the epistemic domain, to relate propositions in an argument:

> *Meiyou ren zai jia. Ni zai qiaomen ye meiyou yong.*
> There's no-one home; (<u>so</u>) it's no use knocking

or (3) at 'speech-act' level, to contrast an overt proposition with a presumed expectation (examples from Biq 1989):

> *Meiguo de xiaohai, shiji sui4 shi2 dou wufawutian, zhangdale ye jiu dongshi*
> American kids may be unruly in their teens, (<u>but</u>) once they grow up they (<u>do</u>) learn to behave

Ye may be used to hedge the felicity of a reminder, or a direction for co-processing, as in phrases in our sample like '*women ye (dou) zhidao* ', roughly equivalent to '(as) we (do) know (after all)' (see Table 6.3b, lines T104-5 and T133-8, T184).

The reason for treating all these features together is clear from Tables 6.3a and b, which summarise the fate of some overt indicators of this type in the corpus: not only are these expressions polysemous, making their interpretation entirely a function of context, but they also cluster together and appear to share functions, and a range of devices are found in the TL versions to render these different indicators in the source texts.

The distribution and position of procedurals, and particularly, of indicators of illocutionary force or communicative intent, probably varies not only between languages, but also between discourse types: in this Chinese argumentative-discursive text, they are usually clustered at the beginnings of utterances, after pauses; in the German text, which strives to be somewhat formal and contains fewer rhetorical 'lead' strings, they are inserted in different medial or final positions in the main sentence.

Table 6.3a Modal Verbs and Adverbs in SI : Würzburg (German - English)

Line	SL modal marker	Interpreter WL	Interpreter WA	Interpreter WB
10	soll	*8 is*...12 which we wish to...*	10-11 was to be	is*
49	soll	[fails to produce entire VP]	51 is asked to	51 is supposed to
51	wohl	*54 I think*	55 obviously	54 of course
62	Das soll auch	*65-67 that so much (by way of...*	[sentence omitted]	67 and that's basically what I shall try (and do)
89	deshalb auch...	*89 and* I hope that...*	89 and*...	89-90 and therefore I will..
111	und damit dürfte...	*113-122 this.. means that... are now...*	116/7-127 the point being to... and... this is...	121-125 is... therefore... I think...

* asterisks mark items which anticipate the SL modal marker

Interpreters make particularly free and sovereign use of 'cognitive prefix' phrases with verbs of thinking, saying, understanding, knowing (*I think.../ we all know... /we all understand...*, etc) or attitudinal adverbs; 'cooperative' directive or cohesive strings like '*I am now going to address.../my speech will be in two parts, firstly.../ so I conclude here that...*'); and connectives, especially interclausal conjunctions.

Sometimes, however, modal adverbs and particles which encode an attitude to a proposition are taken very seriously in interpretation—in this case, **zwar** off-setting an expectation set up by the previous clause:

Table 6.3b Modal Verbs and Adverbs in SI: Chinese 'ye'

Line	Procedural ye in input	Interpreter TA	Interpreter TB
T22-26	jiben shang you yi xie GONGSHI .. dan *ye* you xie butong de difang basically have some consensus ... but *ye* have some different points	their views. converge. somewhat - but there are some differences	\speakers have /reached a con\sensus - even though there are slight - differences
T48	NA- -dajia *ye* tongyang- renshi dao yi dian. well every one *ye* likewise - realise one thing	how/ever -	however - we all KNOW that
T66	na dangran - hen duo de jiangzhe ganggang *ye* dou tidao guo le... well of course - many speakers just now *ye* mentioned	many scholars - who spoke before me - mentioned	-
T87-8	*ye* jiushi shuo - women kan.... ye that is to say - we see if...	+ maybe we can ...	by going through the General ASSEMBLY perhaps its /possible...
T104-5	@m - danshi ne - women *ye* dou ZHIDAO ... but p - we *ye* all know -	-	we know that ...
T133-8	suoyi -cong . zhei dian lai kan - women *ye* zhidao so from this point of view see - we *ye* KNOW	as such	an-d - so- I con\clude here that -
T137-8	zhei tiaolu.. shuo shizai *ye* BUSHI name.. RONGYIDE this route p - say-honestly *ye* not so easy	... - it's not so EASY	it won't be EASY for us... '
T184	na wo ganggang *ye* tidao guo - women xianzai... well I just *ye* mentioned - we now	I feel...	as \mentioned
T197	Guoji-Fuxing Kaifa Yinhang. *ye* jiushi - women- tongchang suoshuo de. Shijie Yinhang.. International Reconstruction Development Bank *ye* that is - what we usually call World Bank...	...or the World Bank	...or the World Bank
T238	zhei *ye* shi zai wo de - lunwen de di LIU YE	- \which is on page \six	you will find that in - my PAPER .

* asterisks mark items which anticipate the SL modal marker

(Ladies and Gentlemen ...you are sitting in the finest auditorium we have to offer...)
der   zwar regelmässig genutzt wird - das ist. nicht - @ einfach nur ZIER
which indeed regularly   used   is -   that is not -   simply only decoration

```
TA:OFfer -                 131.5 which. HAS been used. very
regularly    +     .it is actually used and its not just there to
look pretty
```

As shown in Table 6.3a, the German modals and connectives in the text (**soll, wohl, auch, deshalb auch, und damit dürfte...**) are almost always reflected in either an equivalent verbal modal (*was to be, is supposed to...* or, if anticipated by a declarative, then compensated, e.g. WL10); or an attitudinal adverb (*obviously, of course, now, basically*); or an evidential embedding expression (*I think, I hope that, as you know*).

10.2 German-English

There is only one instance in the Würzburg source discourse of a conjunction used as a clausal connective (WS9, line W106: **und damit...**), but the German-English interpreters add generous amounts of interclausal connectivity of their own; '*and*' in particular does a lot of work (Table 6.4: underlined words have no overt source in input).

Table 6.4 Additional connectives supplied by interpreters - German-English

Segt	WL	WA	WB
M2	8 *as I have said*		9 *and that is...*
M2α	14 *and this is a point which...*	14 *and I think...*	13 *and its very important..*
M3			20 *and this is...*
M5	34 *...however*		
M5β	39 *and he was also...*		
S3			67 *and that's basically what...*
S4	75 *and (there are two main points of concern..)*		
S6	81 *and secondly...*		80 *and the other...*
S6			82-3 *and again this is...*
S7	89 *and I hope that...*	89 *and what I have to say...*	89 *and therefore..*
S8		96 *and its already been pointed out that...*	
S9		124 *and basically this is something that...*	

Many 'cohesive' insertions are generated autonomously by the interpreters from situational knowledge:

W6-7:   **da einer der Schwerpunkte... auf diesem Bereich.... liegen soll**
WL8-11   as one of the focal points ...   in this area ...   lie should
          which is as I have said one of the main points...

W18:   **Zu diesem Thema wird** (On this topic Professor Odersky will...)...
WA20   *now Professor....is going to speak*

W91-2:   **+ H Der europäische Subventionsbetrug...** (The European subsidy fraud...
WA92-3   *I'm going to address the fraudulent obtention of subsidies....*

or more gratuitously:

W15-17   'how [these cases]... by German penal law ... regulated'
B18-19   *how ... are in fact-@ treated in German law*

Focus and sentence perspective

Focus-marking devices vary between languages. German often uses word order, such as fronting, or immediate pre-verbal position plus contrastive definiteness. The focus is restored by the interpreter's use of devices such as an added adverb and/or special stress:

W18-20   **Zu diesem Thema wird - Herr Prof. Odersky - sprechen**
         On this   topic will -   Mr Pres. Odersky - speak:
L27   *... on precisely this topic*
A21-22   ...going to address precisely that /THEME

W6-7:   **da einer der \Schwerpunkte dieser Tagung... auf diesem BeREICH...**
         liegen soll
         as one of the focal points of this meeting ... in this area ...   lie should
A10-13: our symposium WAS to be devoted precisely to that
         SUBject

SL clause structure appears to be attended to only when perspective for relevance is affected. W-M2 (Appendix W1-3) begins with a 'Given that...' type of subordinate clause ('**Da...** 'Since...) which is produced by WA and WB as a new main clause assertion:

WA: 'One of the main points...'
WB '- and that is -@ one of... (finishing on rising intonation:) of this SEMi/nar'

both of which can accommodate a smooth 'causal' link to the next proposition. But WL has produced it as a final relative clause with sentence-closure intonation

> 'which is ... .in this sym\posium'.

Such a 'closed' sentence can tolerate only one more 'tacked-on' clause

> '- and @ this@ is a point which is. of- great. interest@ - to.our foreign guests'

so she has to start afresh, repeating herself with a lot of emphasis, to create the necessary link:

> I think @ that. it wi#be- especially - INTeresting - FOR our foreign guests to hear... '

Some passages show how interpreters may enhance the pragmatic profile of the text (perspective, contrast) at the expense of lexical distinctions, supporting the theory that oral translation, at least, is often more attuned to pragmatic properties, like contrast, than to precise semantic equivalence. In the parallel construction in WS5-6, the comparative **mehr** and intonational stress on **'andere** and **'Mitglied-staatsseiten** highlight these two as the contrast focus (non-synchronised extract):

> **Das Eine ist das 'Anliegen das ver'ständliche Anliegen der europaischen**
> the one   is the concern   the understandable concern of-the European
> **Ge'meinschaft nach- 'wirksamen straf rechtlichen Schutzzusicherung**
> Community for ... effective   penal-legal   protection-assurance
> **... ihre@s eigenen Finanzsystems**
> of-its(GEN) own   finance system

> WL: \firstly - there. is. the desire. - of the European Com\munity ....
> WB: @wwa-. the FIRST is the- quite. under STANDable - % % th- deSIRE.....

> **das 'Andere - vielleicht mehr von der 'Mitgliedstaatsseiten @ betonte**
> the other -   perhaps more from the   Member-State-side   stressed
> **Anliegen ist das-**
> concern is that

> WL: and SECondly - Member States \also- have- quite. leGITimate concerns. which
> THEY have emphasised@ - they wish to \ensure -
> WB: and the OTHer - which comes from member [...] and a/GAIN - this is
> something that they're particularly KEEN / on

The primary focus is interpreted as being on the Member States as contrasted with the European Community, neutralising distinctions among all the other, backgrounded elements: 'concern (need, desire)' 'understandable' and **von ... betonte** ('.... emphasize': 'be keen on'), which are distributed across both terms by (stressed) contrastive adverbs: WL \also- have- quite. *leGITimate concerns* and WB 'and   a/GAIN - this is something that... The rest is expansion for emphasis; stress and intonation are, as often in SI, slightly excessive, with another distinction, the hedge **vielleicht,** also being bleached out.

10.3 Chinese-English

Chinese **ye** mostly 'disappears' in translation, as expected; attempting to trace its effect on the prosodic contour is not reliable, in view of the general proliferation of ·prosodic effects in the TL versions, and non-native distortions, particularly in the case of TA.

In the Taipei discourse, conatives/phatics/connectives are particularly abundant in opening positions; their fate in TL is shown in Table 5.6. (Chapter 5). The interpreters add few such items of their own (TA line 59, 64; TB line 27)), and in fact show a clear tendency, increasing as the discourse unfolds, to pare down such material and in general use their own sovereign formulations quite autonomously.

Chinese uses a range of focusing devices, one of which employs the 'copula' *shi* (and negated *bushi*), 'the root meaning of which is that of the truth-value of a truth table in modern logic' (Cheng 1983: 95). *Shi* (and its combination with an emphatic discourse marker in *jiushi*) focusses on what follows, be it an NP, a verb or clause, but it also simply marks off scope (e.g. between Topic and Subject), and as such often simply acts as an overt bracket in the logical form of the utterance, disappearing in an English translation.

The concern to preserve focus can be seen in the Chinese-English interpreters' postponement of focussed preverbal Adjuncts which syntax alone would allow to precede the Verb in English, such as S4 **zai zheige yiyuan fangmian** ('from the point of view of intentions', S8 **yinwei Zhonggong** *ne* **zai Lianheguo - zai Anlihui limian** ('in the UN - in the Security Council'), or the preposition-verb phrase in S16 *jiushi* **jingyou Lianheguo tixi xia de zhuanmen jigou..** ('by going through specialized agencies of the UN system...'). Focus, like illocution, reinforces representations in the mental model, as seen in the length of time these focussed items can be held before production: for S4, about 17s until TA says 'that re-entry ... is necessary' and about 11s until TB's '(consensus) in Taiwan's need to..', both well beyond the average ear-voice spans recorded by early studies, and even the longest spans recorded by Goldman-Eisler (1972: 129) and Lederer (1981: 290, 298).

The combined operation of the pragmatic functions described in this Chapter is illustrated in Segments S8 and S9 from 'Würzburg' (Table 6.5), which contain some complex left-branching structures as well as some otherwise indeterminate input. Before applying the model to segments of discourse, we need to summarise the notation we will use in the tables for the theoretical apparatus which has been introduced in the course of the study in a first approximation to a language of thought (LOT) mediating interpretation.

11 A vocabulary of representation (and presentation[11])

The information which contributes to building representations falls into four broad classes (a key to symbols is provided with Table 6.5 and in the Appendices).

1. *Entities, properties and (binary) relations (epr)* introduced or evoked by both text and extra-textual (percepts and frame knowledge) inputs. Referents are contextualized for their relevant attributes, their roles in discourse (e.g. AGent, PATient, BENeficiary, INSTrument) and set-membership/boundedness. In principle, the mental model does not contain any unresolved referents or lexical attributes (such as the undirected arrows and question-marked features in the 'DRT' diagrams in Fig. 3.2 of Chapter 3).

   Epr may be potentiated by advance preparation or briefing, then *evoked* by text from knowledge. The significant property in terms of the mental model is familiarity, a psychological variable. Definiteness, where marked in input, functions as a processing instruction and is not represented; this is consistent with the RT proposal to consider pronouns as procedural items in propositional assembly. Italicised items in the 'Assembly' column represent projected or as yet unspecified epr, e.g. an unspecified relation r, or a projected predicate φ.

2. *Logical-semantic information* (see key to symbols) includes role-frames structuring epr as arguments, predicates and qualifications, and logical operators and indices over these, e.g. TENse, ASPect, FINite, 'some', 'most', $\sim$ negation, $\equiv$ equivalence, $\forall$, $\exists$, & etc. In this way a predicate salient in the discourse can be associated by default or strong probability with a Subject, e.g. the Speaker (or Speaker's identification class), or with an Object, based on probabilities established by a title or by repeated occurrence of these items in a particular role-frame. Logical relations and connectives are shown in symbols, e.g. $\Rightarrow$ 'results in' or 'entails'.

3. *Functions of illocution and attitude (IF and PA)*: Modalities expressing Speaker attitude, or evaluation, appear in small capitals: e.g. BEL (Belief), DES (Desire), in addition to some of their derivatives indicating eviden-

tiality/authority; possibility/probability; purpose, hope/necessity (e.g. think, feel, need, recognise that (x), intend (x), etc.; for instance BEL + DES (approximately, cf. Searle 1983) for 'hope and believe that' (as in **dürfte**); NEC, POSS for necessary, possible that; IMP(ortant), SATIS (factory) for the evaluations expressed in phrases like **vor allen Dingen**, and **befriedigend**. The model allows the necessary embeddings for other people's attitudes, attitudes about attitudes, etc.,[12] and may attach permanent indices of affect or attitude on certain items, which support assumed contrasts, as shown in the putative discourse model for Würzburg (Fig. 6.1): ☺ {protect, secure...}, ☻ {fraud, misuse...}.

4.   *Directives:* processing directions and clues to reference (definiteness); to relevance (focus devices, discourse connectives, referential and cohesive ties); or prosodic clues (e.g. a long pause, or expressive non-verbal sign, before a change of discourse topic). This category corresponds approximately to procedurals.

The tabular presentations of analysed segments (Table 6.5 and Appendices W1, W3, T2-A) display the following:

(1)   *Column 1 (left):* input and a word-for-word gloss, bracketed according to a basic GB-type syntax, under the lines of original discourse. The brackets reflect an incremental parsing standpoint: temporarily moot attachments are shown by a round bracket preceding any square bracket which cannot be unequivocally projected at that point, and constituents whose status is unclear are marked with a question-mark. Closing brackets have been simplified (reduced).

(2)   *Column 2:* 'Assembly', or semantic representation plus IF and PA: some symbolic notation, sometimes cumulative, of the assembly of representations from successive fragments and complementary sources, including projections licensed by the incoming structure, which are shown in italics (e.g. > *Obj*, 'Object expected downstream'), logical functions; abbreviated markers of propositional attitude, modality, or Intentionality (e.g. BELieve, DEsire, IMPortant, POssible, NECessary); and discourse markers and connectives (dm).

A key to abbreviations and symbolic notation is provided at the head of the tabular presentations. In the Chinese text, F> signals an imminent focus, e.g. by the

Table 6.5 Würzburg segments S8 and S9

Key to symbols and abbreviations

Input assembly and syntax: N: noun; V: Verb; d: determiner; M,F,N,G,D;S,P: gender, case and number inflections; P proposition ($P_{.1}$ previous, P_0 current, P_1 next); φ predicate; *Italics*:: unresolved; : resolved; pro: pro-form; # solecism; ? moot (attachment, scope, domain); > expect; >> infer; SMALL CAPS: intentionality; ⊂ includes; → access; DK, SK, FK discourse, situation, frame knowledge; ☺, ⊗ indices of affect. **Thematic roles:** subscript e.g. AGent, **Prosody/delivery:** - pause; + longer pause; CAPS stress; @ filled pause ('er'); \ rising, falling pitch. ESF: European subsidy fraud; FRG: Federal Republic of Germany.

	Input and syntax/gloss	Assembly	Interpreter WL	Interpreter WA	Interpreter WB
91	H Der europäische [CP[NPd? the A_N European_N	P_0 [Subj...] DK, pause →text	*will deal with BOTH. of. these.* *aspects.*	those. @ concepts and issues -	- my- divide my statement -
92	Subven'tionsbetrug -'wird - Nsubsidy fraud] Aux ?will/PASS	subsidy fraud → FK fraud, MM ⊗ ...> *?Ful/Passive Vφ*	+	I'm going.	into- two PARTS -
93	das ist [CP[NPPr that C Aux is	P_1 [CP *pro_Subj...*	*H*	to address.	h European-
94	hier in Ihrem Kreis [Adv here [PPin [NP your/her/their N circle]]	→ SK > φ	*European subsidy* @	fraudulent obtention	@ -
95	schon ge'sagt worden - Adv already [VP V said Aux been	>> *pro =P₀* P_1: P_0 has been said before	*-~fraud-* -	of subsidies. -	SUBsidy
96	in der Bundesrepublik 'Deutschland [PPin [NPd_DF the N Fed-Rep. Germany	P_0 Eur. subsidy fraud)_Subj... [in FRG.. > *Ful/Pass φ*	*as has been said. already* - *is* @ *a -*	IN Europe. and it's alREADY	fraud. - as alREADy been SAID@ -
97	durch den - @Pa@n [PPP through [NPd_A the - Pa#	P_0 THemeESF in FRG NST NP > *Ful/Pass Vφ*	@ @ / */crime-*	been pointed out. @ that -this is	in. this particular
98	in den siebziger 'Jahren' - CP[PPin [NP d₀ the A seventy years	P_0 THemeESF... INST NP.. past >> Pass >Vφ (P_1 THeme NP ...in1970s)	*which-*	something. that	semi/nar
99	eingefügten [P-V inserted...	(P_1 THeme NP inserted in 1970s)	*has been- en/shrined-*	+	+ s- @
100	Paragraphen N_A paragraph	P_0 ESF... NST [Art. inserted in 1970s] > Pass *Vφ*	- *in* -	+	- <R
101	zweihundertvierund'sechzig N two hundred four and sixty	... NST[Article 264 ...	*the- legal* *system of. the Federal*	% is @	R> /TREATed -

No.	German source text	Formal notation			
102	des Strafgesetzbuches - [NPdG ofthe NG penal code -	P_0 INST[of penal code > Pass$V\varphi$ →FK, DK: penal code ⊃law$_{AGent}$		REGulated in federal	in German law - in
103	gegen - Subven'tions betrug - [PPP against N subsidy-fraud]]] -	]?[...against subs. fraud] > Pass$V\varphi$ ⊚law against ⊛fraud : cancel	*by means of its insertion. in paragraph*	Germany BY⊚ the. penal	/article - two six
104	'MITerfaßt [vPP co-V covered]]]]	P_0 Φ_0 :THeme-ESF covered in FRG by..	*two sixfour - of.*	/code.there're. specific	\~FOUR - of @.
105	(S9) -		*the. H*	/paragraphs	
106	und damit - [CP& Pr-P therewith	{ P_{-1} $^{?domain}$ ⇒ >P_0 }	*German.*	that were. -	the criminal/CODE
107	dür- @ - # Aux migh-	. ?BEL + DES {P_{-1} ⇒ P_0 }	*penal*	introduced	+
108	das ist [CPd that [VP is	[CPProSubj...	*\code. +*	in the	+
109	'AUCH schon [PPalso[already	also > past φ > =said	*and - as has already*	penal code.	+
110	zum Ausdruck gekommen - [vP[PPto-the expression V come]]	>> pro =P_0 P_1: P_0 has been said before→ DK	*been said@*	in the. SEVen/ties	in /GERMany -
111	dürfte - might/should	: BEL + DES { P_0 {...	*during the course.*	+	and. has-s al\READy been said in. this /SEMinar
112	der - [IP[NPd? the	d	*of this- Sym/posium this-*	+	+
113	der 'Schutz. . - dN the protection	P_0 { P_1 [φ = protect	*therefore means.*	+	+
114	der des [NPd GP ofthe dG ofthe	r d	*that. the -protection.*	+	the. +
115	Finanzsystems - finan.cial systemG	: MM= PATient	*of the- financial*	+	proTECTion
116	des des Mißbrauchs - [NPdNS ofthe dNS ofthe abuseG	r : MM = ⊚ THREAT >> r = against, from	*/system@ -*	the point being	of @ -
117	der Subven' tionen - [NPd? the subsidies P -	r : subsidies ⊃ fin. system = PATIENT	*and. the. abuse- of. the. subsidies*	to -	th-e- of the fiNANcial
118	@der europäischen Ge'meinschaften - [d ofthe Europeano CommunitiesP	FK : r =granted by : P_1: protect x from y		@ pro/DECT - the European	resources of the European

Table 6.5 *Würzburg segments S8 and S9 (continued)*

119	**in unserem Land** [?v [PPin[NPoutDS country/*Land*]]	P_0 { P_1 ?[in Germany	*granted by the European*	community's finances for. bein.	Co/mmunity - is-
120	-		*Community*	mis/Used.	-
121	**in Kern -** [PPin core]	P_0 { P_1 ?[in core	+	from mis- being mis/Used	there-fore. +
122	**be'friedigend** [V [Adv satisfactorily	P_0 { ?{ SATIS { P_1	*are@ -*	+	+
123	**und vor allen Dingen** [and[PPabove all	& [IMP { P_0 { P_1	*now @m*	+	@
124	**in gleicher 'Weise** in sameDS way	>> P_0 : BEL{ SATIS{ $P_1 \equiv P_2$ > P_2 { φ_2 {i,j...}	+ *protected@*	and. @	dealt with -
125	**wie der Schutz** [Adv as [NPd the protection	φ_2 (i) = φ_1 (x) >> $\varphi_1 = \varphi_2 = \varphi$ protect	-	basically	I think satis
126	**der deutsch** [dFG ofthe German#	j = German....	*by means of@*	+	/FACtorily
127	**des deutschen Subventions systems -** dG ofthe GermanS subsidy systemG]	j ...subsidy system P_0 : φjEEC ≡ φj Germany	core. *legislation* -	this is something that @ is -	- and. dealt with @ -
128	**er.FASST sein** [VPcovered Aux be]	(in German law) P_0	*in. our legal system.* - *and.*	covered BY our penal	in .the /same /WAY -
129	+		*protection - of the*	code. in the SAME way -	as-@ the- -
130	**Die Rechtsprechung des B.gerichtshofs** [NP[NPthe jurisprudence ofthe Fed High Ct		*Community's financial interests*	AS it would be if it were to concern	budget of the. - GERMan @ -
131	**hat sich** [LP has *Refl*		*are equated - with the*	GERMAN. state	GOVern ment. is
132	**mit dem Tatbestand....** [PPwith the offence-material		*protection- of- Germ any's. own \interests.*	FInances - @ the- @	proTE Cted -

Chinese focusing word *(jiu)shi*; $>_{Obj}$ indicates that the next word is marked as the Object (e.g. by Chinese *ba* or *jiang*). Parsing steps and logical inference are not explicitly shown except at specific points. Contextualized epr is not shown except through the words of the transcript. The current discourse referents are as listed in the sketches of discourse models and their contents (Figs. 6.1 and 6.2). World and situation knowledge complete and enrich semantic representations into full propositional forms by filling slots in the selection frames (both argument positions and adjuncts, e.g. instruments, beneficiaries), or in establishing identities and relations which accelerate the deductive or inferential processes.

12 Microanalysis

Description of Würzburg input segments S8 and S9

At S8 the Speaker begins to read his prepared text (from **Der europä-ische...**), but immediately breaks off and continues *extempore*, producing a long and complex sentence. The first clause (S8) paraphrases the opening sentence of the text, stating the legislative situation; the second (S9) elaborates and evaluates its implications: a satisfactory situation in which equal protection is given to national and Community interests in German legislation. The two complex clauses are linked by **und damit** ('and thus'); each contains a parenthetical reminder of earlier references (**das ist schon [...] gesagt worden/zum Ausdruck gekommen**) and a long 'middle field' of adverbial and prepositional phrases separating the initial auxiliaries from the final verbs (by 15 and 20 seconds respectively). Table 6.5 sets out the source discourse and second-by-second versions (one row = approx 1s) by interpreters WL (on site), and WA and WB (mock session). The Assembly column shows approximately, but not exhaustively, what can be parsed from input, expected and inferred at each point. One source which is only occasionally shown, for example, is frame information which licenses expansions like '*European subsidy fraud ... is a crime...*'

Steps in encoding and production by the three interpreters are summarised below in Table 6.6, exemplifying most of the phenomena so far discussed:

(i)   syntactic expansions, not necessarily 'forced';
(ii) the finessing or postponement of an unresolved reference, the cataphor **das** (this/that);
(iii) the anticipation of the Main Verb and its Mood. (Although the auxiliary '**wird**' is ambiguous as to the Tense and Voice of the main predicate (Future, or Passive, or both), all three interpreters produce their anti-

cipated Main Verbs as a (past) passive. Clues are available from the written text—particularly if the false start **@Pa@n** is recognised as a fragment of the word '**Paragraphen**—and from context: *European subsidy fraud* is more likely to be the Theme of a passive construction than the Subject in any role of a future one, particularly at the beginning of the speech).

(iv)   enhancements and attachments licensed by frame knowledge in the mental model, such as '*which has been enshrined in the legal system of (...Germany)*';

(v)   some loss of content (WA Par. 264; WB: in the 1970s); and some semantic 'telescoping' by WL: '*by means of its insertion...*' merges two different propositions, making *crime* (i.e. *its*) the Theme of *insertion* instead of the 'Paragraph'.

Table 6.6 Segment W-S8: SI encoding steps

WL	WA	WB
Subject: *European subsidy fraud...*	**Discourse Topic:** I'm going to address. European subsidy fraud	**Subject:** European subsidy fraud...
Parenth. (ellipsis of Subject) *as has been said. already...*	**Postpone Subj. reference:** and it's alREADy been pointed out.@ that..	**Parenth. (ellipsis of Subject)** as alREADy been SAID@... [sic]
Expand Subject: *is @ a- a /crime which...*	**Expand Subj. (generic placeholder):** this is something that..	**Expand parenth:** ...in. this particular semi/nar
Main Verb (anticipated): *has been enshrined....*	**Main Verb (anticipated):** is regulated...	**Main Verb (anticipated):** is treated...
Locative PP (enhanced): *in the legal system of the Federal Republic of Germany*	**Locative PP:** in Federal Germany	**Locative PP (enhanced):** in German law
Merge: *by means of its insertion in paragraph twosixfour - of. the.German. penal \code.*	**Instrument PP:** BY@ the. penal /code.	**'Locative' PP:** in /article - two six \ ~FOUR- of @. the criminal /CODE .
	New existential sentence: there're specific /paragraphs...	**Expand PP:** in /GERMany
	Qualify (relative clause): that were. - introduced in the penal code.in the.SEVen/ties.	

S8 illustrates the paratactic effect of SI processing by the simplification and rationalisation of semantic structure, driven as much by efficiency in the mental model as by the constraining syntax of the sentence already begun. Once the SI interpreter has embarked on her own structure, as she must to handle a sentence like S8, she must generate certain constituents, for which she can draw only on the incoming text, her own discourse model with the information and inferences it licenses, and fundamental 'template' tolerances which allow the use, within limits, of conative and connective material. This pragmatic mediation and compensation (see next Chapter) are the necessary corollary for a faithful rendition when semantic structure is upset, as it is necessarily in translation (due to form-meaning asymmetries between language generally) and more so in interpretation (due to the additional forced structural asymmetry).

S9 is a resultative clause conjoined to S8: it begins with two connectives (a sentential conjunction **und**, and a resumptive preposition-pronoun compound **damit**), and in 'V2' (verb-second) position a fragment (**dür-**) of the modal **dürfte** (meaning roughly 'I daresay that') which is interrupted by a parenthetical insert:

und damit dür- @   **das ist 'AUCH schon zum Ausdruck gekommen - dürfte der -**
and with-that ModalAux#- - 'that has also been said already'   - ModalAux the

The 'middle field' from this Auxiliary to the final verb complex lasts 20.5 seconds, comprising a long complex Subject NP (about 10s):

der -'Schutz - der- des Finanzsystems - des des Mißbrauchs der Subven'tionen -
the protection -(of-)the of-the finance system of-the of-the abuse of-the   subsidies@der
europäischen Ge'meinschaften
of-the   European Communities

followed by adverbial and prepositional phrases, including a self-embedded quantifier phrase:

in unserem Land - in Kern - be'friedigend und vor allen Dingen in gleicher 'Weise - wie
in our country   -   in core - satisfactorily and above all (things) in same way   - as
der Schutz   der   deutsch   des deutschen   Subventionssystems - er.FASST sein
the protection of-the_FEMPL German of the German_NOMSING subsidy system   - covered be

The Subject NP is itself a string of Nouns connected by Genitive-case determiners which (as in S6) give little clue to their relations; meaning delivery is further obscured and delayed by repeated false starts and recastings of inflected determiners. The whole segment has the following structure_ (Conn = Connective(s); # = solecism or unclear relation; QP = quantifier phrase):

Conn - # (parenth.) Mod - Subj$_{NP}$[N#N#N N] - LP - PP - Adv & [PP[$_{QP}$PP -QP]]] - V Aux

In syntactic terms, these adverbials/PPs can be seen as adjoined to projections of IP (or VP), but the precise attachment of the second and third phrases, **in Kern** and **befriedigend**, and their relation to each other, is moot, and that of the first PP **in unserem Land** 'in our country' is ambiguous between NP and VP. The different semantic and pragmatic contributions of these items include locative specification, quantification (comparative), and expressions of attitude or evaluation:

$$_{PP} \text{ place - } _{PP} \text{ extent- } _{Adv} \text{ eval } \& \text{ } [_{PP} \text{ eval } [_{QP} \text{ } \textit{in the same way as } NP]]$$

As suggested earlier, then, it is necessary when discussing translation to go beyond structural-semantic description to try and capture a wider range of modal (attitude) and procedural features.

S9 can be represented as follows in terms of the features described above (semantic structure, with intentional marking added) in which r stands for 'indeterminate relation' and ? for 'uncertain attachment' (the main verb **erfassen** is glossed as 'cover', in the sense that legislation or a body of text 'covers' certain material):

> & BEL + DES ('one hopes that...')
> {{S8} ⇒:
> {$^?$ in Germany} {SATISfactor(il)y{$^?$ in core{**cover** {protection r abuse r subsidies r EEC}}}}
>   & {IMPortant(ly)
>   {≡ {**cover** {protection r abuse r subsidies r EEC, protection r Germ. fin. system}}}}

This approximation is adequate to our present purpose; strict logical notation would be extremely complex, not least because scope relations are not unambiguously determined. The underdetermined elements in this example include the scope or attachment of 'in Kern' ('in core'); the relations between the nouns, encoded indeterminately in Genitive case; and set-membership relations between the entities in the brackets. (Regarding Definiteness, the German article **der/die/das** mandatorily accompanies these singular nouns and therefore does not mark Definiteness by opposition with the indefinite or null article, as would English *the*).

The interplay between different types of information from input and the discourse model (see Fig. 6.1) in Assembly and production is illustrated in interpreter WA's version. In the following analysis, the first line below the input and gloss shows the information provided by each word; the second shows the assembled semantic and pragmatic representation, including some syntactic and lexical projections and the logical and pragmatic operators summarised at the beginning of this Section. The symbol > indicates the expectation or projection of an element. The proposition currently taking shape is glossed as P_0, that expressed in the previous clause (WS8) as P_{-1}. This extract is not fully synchronized: superscript ^{A} marks the start of each production burst.

WA lags behind the Speaker by a few seconds more than her colleagues, as she adds 'in the seventies' and 'in the penal code' at the end of S8, and ignores the parenthetical in S9. She realizes S9 in two clauses. The first is begun by combining Desire and ⇒ (Results in) to form 'the Purpose of P_{-1} ... , with ellipsis of the first term (representing the proposition in S8) licensed by the fact that it is still current in her Addressees' memory:

'the point Ø being...

The incoming Subject NP (**der Schutz des ...**) is perceived as a predicate with a selection frame, and realised as a non-finite VP to begin a first proposition, still unresolved in input, P_1: 'to protect the European Community's finances from being misused':

damit -	**dürfte**	**der Schutz des**
with/given *pro*	Modal: DES + BEL	Protect(ion) *projects three arguments:*
$P_{-1} \Rightarrow P$	DES + BEL {RESULT	{$_{IP}$ Ø [1$_{Subj}$] protect [2$_{Theme}$] (from ⊗ __)

Finanzsystems -		**des Miss^A brauchs....**
fills position 2 (Theme/Object arg)	*r*	abuse ⊗: *fills argument slot 3*

Select: PURPOSE   (of Ø = φ_{-1}) is {*pro* Protect finsyst$_{EurComm}$ from misuse}
Produce: ^{A}the point Ø being to - @ pro/DECT ....

The roles of the arguments of 'protection', underdetermined by the 'possessive' articles **des, des** ('of the'), are assigned from the mental model, in which 'financial system' is a Patient or Theme, a suitable object for 'protect', and 'abuse' is tagged as a danger. **Subventionen** ('subsidies') evokes a token stored as a subset of 'financial system', and so is merged with it:

der Subventionen	-	**der europäischen Ge'meinschaften^A**
subsidies ⊃ financial system	-	of the Eur. Communities: *attach to* 'financial system'

Produce: ^{A} the European community's finances for. bein. mis/USed.
(slip of the tongue, repair) from mis- being mis/USed

The next string delivers several 'middle field' phrases of indeterminate scope and attachment: the PPs 'in our country' and **in Kern** ('in core'), and two propositional attitudes, SATISfactory and IMPortant, the second qualifying a quantifying phrase 'in the same way'. WA uses **in Kern** as an evaluative sentential ('basically') prefacing a second clause:

in unserem Land in Kern befriedigend und vor allen Dingen in^A gleicher Weise
in our country   in core satisfactorily and most-of-all   in the same way

attachment moot   ?moot   PA: SATIS Conj PA: IMP   Quantifier: $\equiv \{i\_\_\ j\_\_\}$
                                                        $i = P_1 \{pro\ Protect\ finsyst_{EurComm} ....\};\ await\ j$

Select: new clause: P_0 [Connective [PA (Evaluation) SATIS ... [> *Subj*
Produce: ^{A} and.   @   basically

For her Subject, WA resumes her first placeholding proposition P_1 in the anaphor 'this,' (expanded: 'is something that'). The arguments of this new, higher proposition are thus states of affairs (objects of law) licensing anticipated production of the verb 'covered':

wie der Schutz der deutsch^A des deutschen Subventionssystems - ^{A} er.FASST sein 33.3
as the protection of the German of the German subsidy system   -   covered be

$= j:\ \equiv \{P_{-1}:\ protect\ finance/subsidies_{EurComm}\ \},\ \{P:\ protect\ finance/subsidies_{German}\ \}.$

Select: Subject of P_0: P_{-1} anaphor, expand with placeholder; Verb; then remaining adjuncts:
Produce: - ^{A}this is something that @ is - ^{A}covered BY
our penal code.34...

The final adjunct BY our penal code. is an inference product of 'in our country' of which some subsets relevant to this discourse are established in the model, with their default roles in the most recent discourse. 'Our country' = Germany:

Agent role: {Germany $\supset$ legal system (of Germany) $\supset$ penal code (of legal syst of G)}
Patient role: {Germany $\supset$ German government finance/budget/subsidy system}

The *immediate* context (mention in the last utterance) makes 'our penal code' the most salient subset of the Agent-indexed set.

The final quantification ('in the same way as') is distributed in language at a pure logical level which abstracts away from mentioning specific arguments and relations: the equating function is realised with the following adjustments:

(1)   deletion, for economy, in first (anaphoric) *it:* as it would be [$_V$ Ø])

(2) abstraction (perhaps from caution), reflected in the second (expletive) *it*; the 'hypothetical' mode (would be); and the general distributed predicate concern (aboutness):

Produce: ...in the SAME way 34.8 - AS it would be if it were to concern GERMAN. state FINances 38.7 -

The 'SATISfactory' feature is further expressed in a distributed stress pattern[13]: BY our penal code.- in the SAME way - AS ....- GERMAN ....

The other interpreters, WL and WB, also approach WS9 by producing a first, placeholding proposition, but they both retain 'protection' in nominal form as the Subject, leading to some ungainly formulation or repetition:

WL: *the protection of the financial system and the abuse of the subsidies granted by the European Community are now protected by means of core legislation in our legal system, and protection of the Community's financial interests are equated with the protection of Germany's own interests.*

WB: the protection of the financial resources of the European Community is therefore dealt with, I think, satisfactorily; and dealt with in the same way as the budget of the German government is protected.

To this extent, WA's more model-driven approach, less dependent on input constituent structure, is more successful.

The Speaker's belief in and desire for the thoroughness of these legislative arrangements is reflected with slight variations in the treatment of attitudinal and evaluative elements (**dürfte, befriedigend, in Kern**) and other items with indeterminate scope (**in unserem Land**, 'in our country'): WL enhances the Instrument/Agent adjuncts of P_1 'protected *by means of core legislation in our legal system*'; WA declares the Desire (purpose) of the legislation in her first clause ('*the point* being') and asserts its effectiveness, hedged with '*basically*', in her second, mentioning the Instrument neutrally ('by our penal code'); WB expresses the Speaker's Belief in the result, again hedged, in 'dealt with *I think satisfactorily*', but leaves its Agents or Instruments to the audience's inference.

This example illustrates how choices between vague or ambiguous readings may be biased by the demands of production; how in the absence of clear relations, a Noun (**Schutz**) evokes a frame which is filled from the available arguments, and the enriched result produced as a Verb phrase; and how the need to produce structure autonomously while a complex input sentence is in progress requires the interpreter to apply late-occurring quantifiers to her own ongoing output independently of the SL structure, with appropriate pro-forms or superordinates substituted to avoid tedious repetition of all the referents.

The analysis of these segments has revealed certain patterns in SI behaviour, in particular:

1. It is sometimes possible to find and produce an equivalent expression for an element which is in some way unresolved, such as a cataphor, e.g.'this has been said already'. More generally, certain items appearing for the first time cannot be indexed for context or for their relevant extensions and have very little except a logical or lexical entry from which to formulate. The barest items are numbers, which can hardly be associated.

2. It is sometimes necessary to produce a superordinate or generic expression, causing a temporary semantic dilution at word-level, or to approximate to or simplify a semantic relation, causing a loss or distortion at propositional level.

The net effect of these temporary approximations, mortgages on downstream meaning, superordinates, placeholders and pro-forms is a simplification or dilution of meaning which requires compensation. Chapter 7 describes how this is achieved.

Chapter 7 Judgment, Compensation and Coordination

1 Introduction

Up to this point we have been dealing with the processes which derive the Speaker's meaning in relevant contexts and organise it in a discourse model subserving the SI task. In the second part of Chapter 6 we discussed cues to the Speaker's ostension; in this chapter we develop the notion of secondary pragmatic processing, and move to the point where the interpreter recovers some autonomy, at the gate to production.

Sovereign speech production starts with conceptualisation. In interpretation, the 'Conceptualiser' in Levelt's model is replaced by the entire process of derivation of the Speaker's meaning, served by permanent and temporary memories. The interpreter becomes a Speaker at the point where her own speech-acts are formed. Since we are dealing with a task, coordination is required, and since speech is a form of action, it involves judgment and decisions.

In ordinary turn-taking conversation, the decisions involved in speaking concern the organisation of one's thoughts, preparing communicative intentions, and timing; deciding when to speak, when to think or listen, what and how much to say and how to say it. In SI, evaluation, coordination and decision for action are intimately related, and if it is possible to model them as distinct functions for reading, speaking or conversation, in SI they are forced together by the conditions of the task. At this point the technical and ordinary meanings of 'pragmatic' merge.

The centre of willed action and coordination has been modelled for cognitive functions in general, and speech behaviour in particular, as an Executive inside Working Memory (Baddeley 1986, Gathercole and Baddeley 1993), or as a Supervisory Attentional System dominating two lower levels of coordination among sub-systems (Shallice 1988). Connectionist theory stands out in postulating the absence of a central executive function (Rumelhart 1992: 70). In our model the functions of evaluation, coordination, and commands to production are combined in an Executive, the only component which receives all input (Fig. 3.1., Chapter

3). This is the link between the representational and coordinating dimensions of the SI task.

It is often pointed out that translation involves decisions, if only because of the mismatch between lexical fields. But ostension in discourse, its Speaker-to-Addressee dimension, also has to be largely recreated with every new re-expression of a Message, as is clear at the linguistic level from the non-correspondence across languages of illocutionary indicators, connectives, cohesive devices and other pragmatic markers (Fillmore 1984; Sweetser 1990). The process of inference and translation upsets the implicit-explicit balance as well as the informational content, but the opportunity for compensation remains in production, if judgment and coordination are associated in a component which receives representations and commands speech action.

Recalling how approximations and semantic simplifications are forced by the SI condition, we examine how interpreters recover pragmatic fidelity and compensate for dilutions and approximations by exploiting those expressive resources which do not rely on word order, such as prosody and local or relatively 'portable' items like adverbials and parentheticals.

Failure[1] in SI provides another window onto the process. Errors and breakdowns, or communicative failure, have been variously ascribed to language incompetence, gaps in extralinguistic knowledge or coordination problems (Gile 1995). An examination of failure and errors in our corpus will try to distinguish between these, and more specifically between the relative effects of text and presentation variables such as structure, conceptual input and ostensive guidance on interpreting performance.

A brief methodological caveat is necessary. It is hard to say when an omission is due to a judgment on relevance or to time pressure, or to part of the input having been missed, just as it is difficult to distinguish deliberate from instinctive or accidental behaviour due to the learning factor. The interpreters' prosody over the input string concerned is a guide. Listening and speaking together is possible, but those informative strings which are omitted generally coincide with fluent interpreter output: on this basis a tentative hypothesis is offered about hesitancy patterns as a window on SI processes.

2 Judgment

The use of judgment in SI is illustrated in the interpreters' treatment of implausible input. The interpreters are not visibly affected by occasional errors in the Speaker's discourse, as in T-S10, which is ungrammatical (see Table 7.1), or the solecisms (marked with a #) and fluffed case inflections of the second

Würzburg Speaker, which obscure grammatical relations between the NPs. Such phenomena are probably filtered out automatically as irrelevant at Assembly or even at the stimulus processing stage. Sometimes, however, well-formed strings deliver truth values which are judged implausible in the light of other knowledge, and rejected. There is at least one example in each corpus:

(i)   The surface meaning of W-S3, 'that is intended to (**soll**) be the main thrust of my introductory remarks', is interpreted as (WL) 'I have just finished my introduction' and (WB) '<u>that</u> [what I am supposed to do, talk about xyz] is what I shall try to do'.

(ii)   The primary, 'literal' reading of TS2 is:

> 'regarding our rejoining the UN, (among the) Speakers so far basically there is some consensus - as to method there is some consensus - but there are also some differences.'

suggesting that the Speakers also agree on the *method* for joining the United Nations, but differ on some other points. This conflicts with the presumption at S1 that the Speaker is here to discuss *different* methods of seeking Taiwan's return to the UN (i.e. via the UN's financial organisations). It is unlikely that he plans to discuss what is uncontroversial. It is more likely that there is consensus on the *goal* itself, with differences on tactics. Interpreter TB frankly prefers this interpretation, while TA tries to remain vague:

> TB: we know that the Speakers have reached a consensus, even though there are slight <u>differences in HOW we should re-enter</u> the UN.

> TA: their views converge <u>somewhat</u>, but <u>there are some differences</u> among their views.

In addition to executive judgments on plausibility (and, we suggest, upstream at the modelling stage), interpreters routinely simplify semantic structure pragmatically by merging like arguments. The treatment of Segment S10 of the Taipei corpus reflects this process, as well as providing an example of ungrammatical input (for the Chinese original, see Apps. T2 or T3 (pinyin), or T1 (Chinese character transcription):

Table 7.1 Taipei Segment S10

Syntax and input for assembly: d determiner; φ predicate; P_{-1}, P_0, P_1 propositions (previous,current,...); P/VP: preposition/verb phrase; >F, >Obj: focus, object markers; dm discourse marker; p particle; *Italics*: unresolved element; : resolved; {} scope; > expect; >> infer. ☺, ⊗ indices of affect; Dir: directive. ? moot syntactic attachment, semantic scope or pragmatic domain; ([uncertain constituent structure.
Thematic roles (subscript): THeme, AGent, INSTrument, PATH. SMALL CAPS: modal, intentionality, e.g. DES desire, POSS possibility.
Extratextual knowledge: → access; FK: frame (lexical and general/world) knowledge.
Shaded: previous and next utterances. UNGA: United Nations General Assembly.

	Input and syntax/gloss	*Assembly*	*Interpreter TA*	*Interpreter TB*
88	ye jiushi shuo 127 - $_{CP}$ so that's to say	Dir : P_0 elaborates on P_{-1}		Assembly of the UN 128
89	women sh.# kan shi bu shi [$_{IP}$we [$_{VP}$see [$_{CP}$whether-or-not [	P_0 look at [? Poss {... look at Poss >> = Des { Poss {...	√going to the General Assembly	instead of the
90	nenggou 129- @ jingyou zheige [$_{VP}$ able - [$_{P/VP}$via $_{NP}$ this...	P_0 we ?/DES {POSS { [via ....PATH	directly 129 +	Security Council
91	Lianhe- 130 - United Na...		+	+
92	k @ Lianheguo de Dahui ne 131 - United Nations Genl. Assembly p	?/DES {POSS { ... [$_{PATH}$UNGA... >.. VPφ	+	+
93	yong zhege yishi guize - 133 @ [$_{VP}$USE$_{NP}$ this rules of procedure	...POSS {[$_{INST}$rules [$_{PATH}$UNGA >.. *VPφ*	+	+ H 133 m a y
94	lai.- tuifan 134 - @ [$_{CP}$ to[$_{VP}$overturn	...POSS {we [$_{INST}$...[$_{PATH}$. [overturn >..Obj/THeme	+	b e - we
95	huozhe shi- - lai xiugai 136 - or else to amend	..POSS we{ [$_{INST}$[$_{PATH}$ ..[overturn or amend >Obj/THeme	135.5 by going through the General	~can - 136 use the-
96	zai yijiu-137 qiyi nian ([$_{NP}$) p[in 19 71 year	P_0 [....> ?$_{Obj/THeme}$$P_1$ [*Agent* [$_{Time}$1971...	Assembly perhaps its /possible 137.5	+
97	de shihou 138 - @m - time	P_0 [...[P_1 ...[$_{Time}$1971]...	+	H 138 rule of

#				
98	jingyou zheige di erqiwuba hao [? via this no. 2758 -number]	P_0 [...[P_1 ...[Time 1971 [PVP PATH /INST ...No. 2758...	H	- /order 139.5
99	@- jueyi²an - 142 jiang jiushi Resolution [PPObj> dm	[P_1...Resolution 2758, P_3 ....]	+ 142 to modify 143	- @parliamentary pro/cedures -
100	jiang wo- pai 143 chu @ Obj>[NPme/us [IP expel	[P_3 expel us(=Taiwan) ...]	- /or -	to- 143 make our way
101	Lianheguo 144 er rongna UN [and admit	?Obj /THeme [expel-from-UN Taiwan, admit..] Resolution] → FK Expel Taiwan ⊗ >> P_0 Overturn or amend {THeme Resolution	144 to over	- into the United
102	Zhonggong de zheige anzi - ChinCom de [this motion]	P_0: DES POSS {PATH UNGA {INST rules {Overturn or amend [[1971 expel Taiwan, admit PRC Motion ≡ Resolution]	ride. 145 - the Resolution two	Nations. 145 through the General
103	146 limian - + -inside]	discard	146 seven five	~Ass 146 em/bly
104			which -	+
105			excludes 148 -	to- revoke 149 the
106			Taiwan 150 - and	lution 150 - that admit
107			admits 151 -	ted - @ Mainland
108			\China 152 -	the UN in 1973

S10: So that is to say
  [_{IP}**we** [_{VP}see
    [_{CP}whether-or-not
      [_{VP}can -
        [_{P/VP}via _{NP}[the-@ United Na... United Nations General Assembly p
        [_{V/PP} use [_{NP}the-@ rules of procedure
        [_{CP} to[_{VP} **overturn** or else to amend
          ([_{NP}) _{PP}in 1971 year @time
          [_? via **this** no. 2758 -number **Resolution**
            [_{PP}*Obj marker* dm # [_{NP}me/us [_{IP} expel UN
            [and admit Communist China *de*
      [this Motion
      -inside

Table 7.1 shows hypothetical steps in the assembly of this utterance and how the interpreters formulate their sentences as meaning fragments become available. As in W-S8, arguments are merged using extralinguistic knowledge: neither TA and TB realise the *Resolution* as the instrument of the *Motion*, as in the semantic representation; both merge the two as the Object of 'overturn or amend' (to modify or to override / to revoke). This is only possible on the strength of encyclopaedic knowledge of the relationship between Motions and Resolutions, and greatly facilitates processing for both TA and TB, as it does for WL for the verb-final structure of W-S8. The interpreted versions are thus not *semantically* accurate on this point, but are *pragmatically* adequate insofar as the distinction between a Resolution and the Motion which adopts it is not relevant, or significant, in this context.

In the SI situation, Relevance has equal rights with the 'truth' of the semantic representation: communication being ostensive-inferential, all Speakers, including interpreters, also rely on their Addressees making appropriate inferences. SI discourse must be evaluated in this light: the goal is to convey the message to the hearers at the same level of relevance, i.e. requiring on their part no more effort for the derivation of the same contextual effects than is required of members of the audience who are listening to the Speaker directly.

An interpreter may decide to elaborate or embellish. Elaborations and additions may be cooperative, for instance in developing a reference which may not be as transparent to the TL Addressees as to the SL audience, such as 'the Tiananmen square incident' for 'eighty-nine' (§ 6.3); or may include gratuitous information, as in WM5β:

(in 1988) Präsident -   **des Bundesgerichtshofs wurde**
   .....   President -   of-the Federal High Court became

WL: *and. as. of. nineteen eighty eight. he has become. the- President #n Chief Justice. of the FEDeral High Court. of the Federal Republic of GERMany*

WB: *.in NINEteen ninety two. he became. President and Chief Justice of the Federal High Court of Justice in \ KARLsruhe*

Of course, in the event of an error (the one in the example below is probably due to mishearing), elaboration compounds it:

und Sie befinden sich im Augenblick hier sicherlich in dem SCHÖNsten
and you find   self at-the moment here certainly   in the   finest
Hörsaal - den wir zu bieten haben - der zwar regelmässig genutzt wird -
auditorium - which we to offer have - which$_{NOM}$ indeed regularly used is -
das ist. nicht @ einfach nur ZIER
that is not - simply only decoration

WB: *it is @ - not used very regularly - which I very much regret -*

Judgment is also necessary when there are timing consequences, as in the case of late modifications to the meaning of an utterance.

3 Late elements and afterthoughts

Individual judgment is involved in deciding whether to elaborate on certain items, or discard them under pressure of time. 'Late' features modifying elements in the main proposition often cannot be integrated on the fly; usually, if they are noticed and judged significant, new structure must be created.

Final constituents which radically alter the semantic value of the proposition are not found in the corpus. There are famous examples:

Der Graf von Hohenstaufen *fiel* **in der letzten Stunde der blutigen Schlacht**
The Count of Hohenstaufen 'fell'   in the final hour   of the bloody battle
zu Regensburg durch seine Tapferkeit *auf*
at Regensburg   by   his   bravery   'on'

('The Count of H. distinguished himself by his bravery in the final hour of the bloody battle of Regensburg': **fallen** = to fall, die; **auffallen** = to attract attention)

but this type of garden-path is extremely rare in normal cooperative discourse.[2] Examples in literature and legend are often due to 'accidental' local ambiguities

(Pritchett 1992), e.g. the transitive/intransitive options for the verb 'raced' in *the horse raced past the barn fell.*

However, there is undeniably a level at which a sentence corresponds to a proposition which, once posed, is only defeasible at some cost; so over such very long predicate-argument structures, when the limits of cruder tactics like waiting and stalling are reached, an interpreter must hedge. As we have seen, prefatory and conative items, or independent utterance-scope phrases, may be used in a kind of 'rhetorical recursion', and we have shown some examples where elements of more committal components—core predicate and argument elements—may also be ventured. But late-coming information may still thwart such techniques, as shown in Würzburg-S8 (reproduced here for convenience):

Der europäische Subven'tionsbetrug -'wird - das ist hier in Ihrem Kreis
The   European   subsidy fraud   - ?Fut/Pass- that is here in   your   circle
schon ge'sagt worden - in der Bundesrepublik 'Deutschland - durch 'den -@
already   said   been   - in the Federal Republic   Germany   - by/through the
Pa@n in den siebziger Jahren EINgefügten   Paragraphen zweihundertvierund
in the seventies   years   inserted   paragraph   twohundredfourand
'sechzig des Strafge'setzbuches - gegen - Subven'tionsbetrug - 'MITerfaßt
sixty of-the penal-law-book -   against - subsidy fraud -   also-covered

Up to **Strafgesetzbuches** (penal/criminal code) the sentence meaning is compatible with the assumption that Article 264 was inserted into German law specifically to deal with 'European' subsidy fraud. The final phrase **gegen Subventionsbetrug** (Article 264 ... 'against subsidy fraud') introduces a significant contrast, easily missed, with the more specific '*European* subsidy fraud'. The meaning which now emerges is that Article 264 covers 'subsidy fraud' (the target of the offence unspecified), and hence <u>*also* covers within its scope</u> (= **MIT-** in **MITerfaßt**) any case of 'European' subsidy fraud (targeting EEC subsidies, as opposed to German ones) which might fall within its jurisdiction. This amended meaning is retrievable only at the last three words, from the distinction between **europäische Subventionsbetrug**, the initial (subject) NP, and plain **Subventionsbetrug**, and the stressed prefix **MIT** on the final verb.

Even if this were noticed, a correction would be time-consuming. Predictably, therefore, the output versions are at least elliptical on this point; WL's version allows the implicature that European subsidy fraud is specifically referred to in the German legislation, although the distortion is not serious, being offset by the use of vague terms like '*enshrined*' and the omission of 'in the 1970s':

European subsidy @ - ~fraud- ... is@ a- - @/ crime- which- has been- en
/shrined- - in - the- legal \system of. the Federal Republic of Germany by
means of its insertion. in paragraph twosixfour - of. the.H German. penal \code.

WB's version also misses the distinction:

European- - SUBsidy fraud.- ... is - /TREATed - in German law - in
/ article - two six \ FOUR - of the criminal /CODE + in /GERMany

WA's version, in two separate clauses, neither suggests nor excludes the inference:

```
this is something. that     +     % is @ REGulated in federal
Germany BY@ the. penal /code. there're. specific /paragraphs
that were. - introduced in the penal code. in the. SEVen/ties
```

Late extensions to an utterance—after an interpreter has committed herself to a fluent version beyond a syntactic point of no return—may include features such as modification to the meaning or scope of a predicate, as in the above German examples; the unexpected Head of a long NP, especially a sentence-final Object, as in some Chinese sentences, and other relations which contradict, or cannot be easily reconciled with, the approximation already produced, or simply any significant afterthought to the utterance. Decisions to compensate or repair in such cases will depend on judgment and coordination (timing) factors. Table 7.2 lists 'afterthoughts' and late information in the utterances of the Taipei sample and their treatment by the interpreters. These elements comprise unexpected final Heads, postposed adjuncts or other 'late' material, i.e. coming after the interpreter has begun producing her main clause, and afterthought comments which reinforce or modulate the strength of an assertion.[3]

A rough redundancy hierarchy emerges from this data, from most to least valued information (see Table 7.2):

1. *Evaluatives* are rendered fully (TS2, TS21);
2. *Specifications* or *qualifications*, if caught in time, may be merged with or replace the first approximation (TS14, TS18, TS30);
3. *Metadiscoursal directives* like 'as I just said' or '...this everyone is familiar with' receive mixed treatment, possibly depending mainly on the time factor or their usefulness in stalling (TS17, TS27, TS29b, Würzburg).
4. *Repetitions*, simple reaffirmations (even whole sentences), and resumptive NP-suffixes are dropped (TS4, TS13, TS17), although they may be integrated or recovered if they contain a new attribute (TS1, TS3, TS18).

Table 7.2 'Late' meaning and afterthoughts (Taipei)
restricting, qualifying, evaluating, reinforcing, resumptive, reasserting, repeating, directing, specifying

Seg.	Utterance-final qualification or afterthought	Type	Interpreter TA	Interpreter TB
S1	.. discuss [NP[IP6 Taiwan return UN] _de_ N possibility]	+NP Head qualify-resump	dropped	fronted within NP (lag)
S2	..have N consensus but [I' also[VP3 have N differences]	VP restricting	adds new sentence	adds new clause
S3	..can reach [NP[we rejoin UN _de_ [d goal]]]]	+NP Head qualifying-resumptive	fronted within NP (long lag)	dropped, added in segment S5 (i.e. 35 seconds later)
S4	...[C1 [IP this [VP is[NP cannot³ deny [d fact] pfv	+IP reasserting	dropped	dropped (but intonational stress?)
S5	...[not-_shi_ say[VP just wish [VP then [V' can [instantly achieve	+CP rephrases, reinforces	adds new sentence (cleft back-focus)	dropped
S13	only...........only]	repeating	no repeat	no repeat
S14	nearly 100 votes _de_ many]	qualifying	adopts qual, drops number	error 'more than 100 votes'
S17	... I just said it pfv] }	reasserting	dropped	dropped
S18	but in....[VP not[V have [NP this Cl weapon]]]	add qualifying	dropped (Obj ellipsis)	integrated (lag), toned down
S21	...dm I think[IP thus[VP maybe[is quite...effective method	+CP evaluating	sentence	sentence + ...for us to..
S23	....vp as priority consideration	post-attribution	dropped	*dropped (partly anticipated)
S24	[CP but p [IP it also VP not _shi_ [wholly [V' not-have obstacles p	+CP restricting	confusion (see text)	new sentence, false start
S27	...this [everyone (is) familiar (with)	metadiscourse	dropped	dropped
S29a	..._de_ situation]	NP resumptive	dropped	dropped
S29b	...[IP if you all want to check -if	directions	dropped	same form (if...)
S30	...[IP especially _shi_ USA	adv specifying	particular replaces genrl	add as exemplification (for ex..)
S32	..._de_ [politic(al) consideration]]	resumptive	dropped	dropped
S33-9	*no afterthoughts or late qualifications*			

This suggests that propositional attitudes (1 and 2) rank high in the perception of useful information to be passed on, followed by cohesive devices (3), although these are also produced autonomously, as shown in previous Chapters.

4 Compensation

An interpreter does not have access to the Speaker's 'conceptualiser,' communicative intentions, or even his sentence plan. To form successive sentences fluently, she must approximate to projected meaning as she goes, by using generic terms and simple presuppositions, and in so doing inevitably introduces or loses layers of meaning. The perspective and emphasis of the input may also change unexpectedly in ways that cannot be corrected in the current output sentence, or 'late' items may modify or invalidate a proposition to which she is already committed. The nature of SI therefore requires constant on-line compensation: interpreters must augment and complete referents which have been approximated to, or meanings which have come too late for ideal integration. Some such meaning may have retroactive semantic scope (negation or quantification), some pragmatic; focus and emphasis continually have to be adjusted, and there may be late indications of illocution or propositional attitude, or pointers to relevance.

This process of approximation and compensation, which is visible in SI, has been overlooked in the literature. Lederer (1981) says that interpreters have to piece something together 'on a purely linguistic basis' while the sense is still unclear, but that once the idea is grasped, monitoring fades to superficial attention levels, after which formulation proceeds autonomously '*en roue libre*' ('freewheeling'). Moser's model (1976) issues a 'discard input' instruction when 'prediction is successful'.

Interpreters often compensate when an element has been anticipated by an approximate placeholder. WB anticipates the verb in WS9 with

...and. <u>dealt with</u> @ - in .the / same / WAY - as-@   .

then refreshes the verb with its fuller meaning in conclusion:

... the budget of the. -   GERMan @ -   GOVern ment. <u>is proTECted</u> -

SI may have a general flattening effect on the rhetorical structure of a speech due to the 'unpacking' of clauses, the merging of arguments, or the ignoring of rhetorical questions or stylistic repetition, and the telescoping of information.[4] Rhetorical effect is achieved by a range of devices, including word order, and more subtle manipulations of the logical and thematic pattern of meaning delivery.[5] A rhetorical or stylistic effect achieved in the input by means of word order can be retrieved in the output by the use of an adverb (reinforced by prosodic treatment) as in WM3-M4:

> **Zu diesem Thema wird Herr .... sprechen** 'On this theme Mr.... will speak... :
> *'...to talk to us on precisely this subject'; 'now Prof... is going to speak...'*

> **Als Präsidenten$_{ACC}$ des Bundesgerichtshofs brauche ich**
> As   President$_{ACC}$ of the Federal High Court need   I
> **Herrn$_{ACC}$ ..... hier nicht vorzustellen**
> Mr $_{ACC}$ ...   hier   not   to introduce
> *.... I hardly need to introduce him to you... he is...*

In both translation and interpretation, style and expressiveness achieved through word order or lexical choices may be redistributed and thus preserved for a text or discourse *overall*, but in SI this operation is constrained by simultaneity. In our model of SI processing, an interpreter makes use of the relatively elastic and distributed *scope* over the text of the conative and affective (or attitudinal, illocutionary) dimensions of Speaker meaning, as compared to that of (logical) semantic operators, which is usually limited to the sentence.

   Contrastive focus is an ostensive device which may be highlighted in this way. In WS5-7 (see Table 7.3) a parallel structure is taken to license the application of a qualification of the first term (which was not integrated in time), the '*understandable* concern' of x , to the second term: y '*also has legitimate* concerns'; similarly WB renders 'the second ... emphasised perhaps more by Member States' with 'and AGAIN this is something they're very keen on'.

   This suggests that these pragmatic values, reflected in **verständlich** ([Speaker sees as] understandable), **betont(e)** ([they] emphasised), **eigenen** (contrastive '[their]own') and **vielleicht** [hedge on Speaker's evaluation], strongly mark the intermediate representation, forming a class of features which are more easily maintained over the spans sometimes required for long sentences, and accordingly become dominant in shaping the output Message. When sentences are shorter (as in 'Taipei'), an interpreter may choose to use this span to organise two or three clauses on the basis of these pragmatic continuities.

   This latitude in SI may be constrained, or lead to dilution, only when rhetorical effects depend on precise local attachments of illocutions and attitudes to individual propositions, with frequent shifts and distinctions drawn at this level: this is the case in poetic and literary language, where aesthetic or emotive effects are achieved by combining word connotations, sounds or rhythm, often relying strongly on individual word choice, in contrast to the discursive genre typical of conference discourse.[6]

Table 7.3 Rhetorical compensation in SI

CAPS stress (pitch or volume); - pause; + longer pause; @ filled pause; % 'creaky' hesitation; ' / rising \ falling pitch; H intake of breath.

	Input speech	Interpreter WL	Interpreter WA	Interpreter WB
S5	das Eine ist	@m -	two main -	issues@ -in - the overall
	das 'Anliegen	under- the-	issues -	issue that
	das ver'ständliche Anliegen	@ main topic - of subsidy	@%	you're - re/FERRing -
	der europäischen Ge'meinschaft	\fraud - and there are TWO -	first of all - the approximation -	@wwa-. the FIRST is the-
	nach- 'wirksamen strafrechtllichen Schutzzusicherung	MAIN - points of con\cern \firstly H - there. is. the desire.-	the NEED @ for the European Community	quite. underSTAND able - % % th- deSIRE
	ihre - @- ihre @s eigenen Fi'nanzsystems	of the European Com \munity - to- @ have- effective. criminal	to have - efFECtive. @ legal protection -	of the European ComMUNity - to have @ -its own
S6	das 'Andere -	legal positions. to-	@ to protect its /FINances. for	finANcial system legally pro/TECted -
	vielleicht mehr	protect their own.-	in/stance -and @	and the OTHer -
	von der 'Mitglied staatsseiten betonte	H financial inter ests and SECondly - Member	the OTHer.	which comes from member
	Anliegen - ist	States - \also-	issue.	/STATES - and
	das- der-	have- quite. leGITi mate	that @ per/haps is a concern more for the member	a/GAIN - this is something that they're
	@Ver- der Ver'besserung -	concerns. which THEY have emphasised @-	/STATES - is. the.	particularly KEEN /on - which is-

Compensation is routinely performed at the encoding stage by restoring focus and perspective. In Chinese, emphasis and contrast may be expressed by repetition or a focusing device like *shi* (Cheng 1983) but they are typically rendered in English by cleft focus, or a suprasegmental feature like contrastive stress (TS5-TA):

(rejoining the UN)
shi xuyao - chang shijian de qu- - jingying chang shijian de qu- zuo jihua
F> *shi* [vp need long time   to   manage, long time   to make plan
TA: ....- how/ever - it is - a TASK that requires - \ long-term
PLAN.NING -

bu shi shuo. yi xiang QINGYUAN de - jiu keyi mashang   -   jiu cucheng de
F>not-*shi* say[vp just think wish   - then can instantly   - then accomplish
TA: and its- not \something - that can just be COMPLETED   -

The opening segments of Würzburg provide an illustration of production-based compensation (see Appendices W1-W4). At WM1, all three interpreters 'take the floor' with an emphatic 'THANK you' and highlight the title phrase 'SUBsidy fraud', which WA expands. All three flatten the structure of the second sentence by unpacking it into either a main, conjoined or relative clause, followed by conjoined segments, but add generous focus and emphasis (*INTeresting - FOR our foreign guests*, MAIN points, great \interest, /KNOW - HOW, *HOW CASes.*, CASES, \courts, LAW; precisely, really, in fact, *especially* etc.). WL adds *as I have said*, and *I think* in two places, and adds emphasis in expansions: *and @ this@ is a point which is....*

Another example, WS4 from the second Würzburg speech, shows how WL compensates for an early 'existential' approximation. WL handles the left-branching PP **unter dem grossen Feld, dass unter dem Generalthema erfasst ist** ('under the broad field which under the general theme covered is') with a simple presupposition, the statement *there is a very@ LARGE. RANGE of QUEStions*, postponing information about relations and hierarchies (**unter, General, erfasst**): at clause closure these residual meanings are attached conjunctively (*and there are two...*), given additional stress (*TWO MAIN*) and more explicit reference (*the main topic of subsidy fraud*), and linked to the now available **Anliegen** in *points of concern*.

However, here there is over-compensation. The assertion 'there is a very large range...' overstates the licensed presupposition. This is partly offset by the stress on *TWO MAIN*, but the effect is weakened since primary stress has already been used up in *very LARGE RANGE*: prosodic compensation can be overdone (further effect might have been achieved by the use of 'but' instead of 'and (..there are...').

An afterthought or late item may also lead an interpreter to overcompensate, as in the case of WA who elaborates and compensates more than her colleagues in several instances, to the point of missing WS3 while elaborating on an afterthought in WS2:

WS2-A:
wie Rechtsfragen DURCH die Gerichte[A] **bereits entschieden 'wurden -**
[cphow [ip[nplaw questionsp [ppby/through[npthe courts[already[vpdecided were]]]]]

WA:..................... - and the way in which.legal

ᴸoder welche *sich* Probleme sich da \ stellen[A] **28.7 -**
-[or[ip[npwhich f/p # [npproblems Refl there V pose

WA: ISSues are - are 27.5   + [A] are dealt with BY the
courts and the - deCISions that are taken BY the courts. and @ - the way
in which the cases. are \dealt with 34.9

Here WA spends 10 seconds on 5.7 seconds of input, and these three approximations apparently distract her from the incoming material, '**Das soll auch die Leitlinie... hier sein'**, 'that shall be the main theme of my introductory words here', which is not rendered. No critical meaning is lost in the main corpus from such initiatives (here only a secondary 'metadiscoursal' comment is sacrificed), but in tight conditions there will be serious knock-on effects (cf. Gile 1995, 1997), as shown below for the dense recited written text in TS29-39.

In another example, where some emphasis is added late in the utterance (from the supplementary Würzburg corpus), WA again elaborates almost over-conscientiously, perhaps expecting to have to compensate after anticipating the main verb (last lines, underlined):

in Europa entsteht ein geWALtiger WIRTSCHAFTSRAUM +   mit über 320 Millionen
in Europe   arises   a   mighty   economic-space +   with over 320 million

WA: a.- tremendously large European area's emerging.IN Europe with. three

Einwohnern der durch die \Einbeziehung. der EFTA Staaten +   und dem für die Ende
inhabitants which$_N$ through the incorporation of-the EFTA-states +   and the$_O$ for the end

hundred and twenty million inhabitants -   and - this - extends

dieses Jahrzehnts anstehenden Beitritt Polens 221 +   Ungarns und der Tschekoslowakei 224
of-this decade   imminent accession of-Poland   + of-Hungary and of-the Czechoslovakia

also to the EFTA countries 219.5 -   221 and -the -it is planned.that it will

+   **noch beträchtlich - erweitert werden wird**
              still(more) considerably - extended be(pass) will

be enlarged to encompass Hungary - Czechoslovakia and Poland - by the end of
this century and hence this region will become much larger

The general tendency of translators and interpreters to explicate and add cohesion is visible in the compensatory emphasis given to discourse-structuring features: in W-S6 (Table 7.3.) 'firstly' and 'secondly' are either stressed (WL, WB) or expanded (WA), and, as discussed above, the contrast in the parallel structure is almost over-exploited, particularly by WL and WB.

Compensation is a function of the relatively autonomous production system, which we have modelled as being governed by the Executive. In SI, where the pace and pattern of input are imposed, the further a process is from input, the more autonomous it is. Semantic structure may be streamlined in the representational process, as a natural economic property of the mental model (e.g. in the merging of *Motion and Resolution*, or *subsidies* and *financial system*); compensation is initiated in the Executive by commands to production to select focus, perspective, and referents, to insert adverbs or phrases which hedge, evaluate, attenuate or direct, or to modulate articulation. The relatively high autonomy an interpreter exercises in speech production in professional SI is confirmed by the 'additional' cohesive and directive packaging elements found in the output, and not least, in articulation, by the rich prosodic contour of the interpreters' versions.

Compensation in SI is limited to relatively local devices. According to Clark and Clark (1977):

> '[speaking is] a task using the tools of language, including certain partial ready-made or conventional solutions (e.g. turn-taking devices), and entailing strategic choices at three levels: discoursal (the organisation of the flow of information in the whole discourse), tactical (the design of sentences), and local (constituent assembly)' (1977: 226)

Such 'partial ready-made or conventional solutions' are used by interpreters as autonomous ostensive material, which can be seen as the equivalent in monologue of turn-taking or turn-holding devices in conversation. In SI, the cooperative speaker-interpreter is limited to local, and to some extent 'tactical' (word order) devices, to restore the discoursal balance, i.e. the 'organisation of the flow of information.' The heavy prosodic profile in SI generally (in addition to its use to restore specific contrast and focus) partly reflects the attempt to project meaning about dependent relevance back to past propositions, in compensation for the forced hesitancy of speaking 'blind'. A good deal of post-editing and shaping of the product to the listeners can be done through prosody and articulation, which is the last and most sovereign stage of all.[7] It is not surprising to find that these SI protocols are very richly modulated, since this is the last chance, as it were, for the interpreter to shape the Message after the distortions due to the processes of inference, anticipation, re-ordering and reformulating in another language.[8]

As further incoming meaning modifies the representations in working memory, compensation can be initiated at various points in the production system (see Fig. 3.1, page 63):

(1)   in the *Microplanner*, through choices of emphasis and focus for the next output string, realised by selecting full or reduced reference, and limited word-order choices. The instructions for the required adjustments are passed on for encoding.

(2)   *Grammatical encoding* receives instructions such as 'encode phrase as instrumental: postpose'; or 'encode as non-finite complement';

(3)   *Phonological encoding* applies prosodic effects; and lastly,

(4)   the *Articulator* is instructed to vary voice modulation or speed ('throwaway lines', etc).

The encoding system would thus sometimes be instructed to start a new clause, which might entail 'find Subject' or 'expand Subject', as in '(*subsidy fraud*)...*is a crime*...', '*(re-entering the UN)...is a task*...' etc.; or to insert phrases like *I think* or *as I have said*, perhaps directly from a 'phrasebook' of common ready-made expressions including both these simple conatives and directives, and formulas like '*ladies and gentlemen*'. According to Levelt (1989) adults, through experience, build up a stock of conversational tools, such as turn-taking devices, as well as stock-in-trade opinions; and indeed whole messages may be stored in and retrieved from long-term memory. The generation and insertion of phrases like '*they wish to ensure*...' suggests the richness of the frame structures which can be accessed by the production system. Such a TL-indexed frame and lexical base is much richer in a native (A) than an acquired (B) language, and such insertions are generally fewer in the versions of non-native speakers (TA and FA); but they also seem to be correlated with 'situatedness', being more abundant in live (WL) than mock-session interpretation (WA and WB).

From the production standpoint, then, the SI processing cycle can be seen as a combination of three types of operation:

1. Normal production of contextually-appropriate chunks (for output) delivered by the comprehension system, subject to judgment, with a lag of upwards of 2-3 seconds;

2. Independent generation of structures or placeholders like superordinates or generics, null quantifiers and vague pro-forms, etc. (not to be confused with 'anticipation' which is usually the expression of a spontaneous inference);

3. Compensatory qualification or emphasis, by adjustments to reference and perspective, insertions, parentheticals, repairs etc. for late meaning, and voice modulation.

5 Pragmatic fidelity

Compensation is by no means necessary for all the structural and semantic gambits forced by the SI condition. As we saw, in WM2-3, for example, all three interpreters abandon the Main/Subordinate clause structure—hence potentially losing whatever balance of emphasis or dependency might have been encoded in the hypotaxis—and produce the content of the subordinate '**Da**... (Since...)' as a Main or Relative clause:

Da einer der Schwerpunkte dieser 'Tagung auf diesem Be'REICH des Subventionsbetruges liegen soll...
'Since one of the focal points of this meeting is supposed to be in this area of subsidy fraud...'

WL: *...which is ... one of the main points which we wish to deal with in this symposium*
WA: one of the main points of our symposium was to be devoted precisely to that subject
WB: ...and that is one of the important points of this seminar

But the hypotactic subordination as such does not have to be restored for pragmatic fidelity, since it does not encode a logical link but merely points to dependent relevance, which is adequately done in English by simply joining two clauses with extra intonation and a focusing adverb (WAS to be devoted precisely to that SUBject..). The passage continues:

ist es [...] von großem Inter'esse 'WIE die Er'fassung dieser 'Fälle [...] vom deutschen Strafrecht ge\regelt ist'
it is of particular interest to our foreign guests how such cases as [...] are dealt with in German criminal law

Again, the semantic presumption in using 'this' for the cataphor ('it is of particular interest [...] how...) is pragmatically quite safe:

WL: *and this is a point which is of great interest to our foreign guests - I think that it will be especially interesting for our foreign guests to hear how such cases as...*

WA: and I think that this is of great interest to our foreign guests: they 'd really like to know how such cases as...

When the delayed Subject appears as the complement 'how..', WL and WA reverse the perspective in a new Clause (WA avoids repetition with a creative paraphrase 'they(*'d)really like to know..); but compensation is unnecessary, since 'how such cases...' etc. can pass as a subset or specification of the interpreters' gambit referent 'this' (= subsidy fraud).

Shifts in perspective and semantic relations in SI often result from simplification or advance approximations which are not fully restored or compensated for, but in many cases the distinction is not significant when inference as well as semantic meaning are taken into account, i.e. if the semantic value of an item or relation is correctly identified for its significance in the current domain. Connecting two propositions by means of a relative clause, a conjunction, or simple juxtaposition by making one into a new clause, may perfectly well perform the same function as an SL device whose root meaning is causative or conditional. As

Blakemore (1987) and Sweetser (1990) have shown, the contents of the propositions, or other context, often rule out the root meaning of a connective and select a pragmatic function (an epistemic or speech-act relation). The reverse also applies—a pragmatic relation emerges between propositions which appear syntactically to be merely coordinate—which explains the cohesive insertions found in SI. The same criterion of significance can be applied to mergings of entities like *Motion* and *Resolution* in Taipei S-10) or 'crime' and 'article' (in Würzburg S8).

Pragmatic fidelity does not require production of the same semantic structure, since firstly, what is explicit in one language is implicit in another; and secondly, well-signalled inferential connections, which may be produced in ways that are less dependent on syntactic structure, are as valid in communicating meaning to the target audience as are explicatures: psycholinguistics experiments show that subjects recalling the content of an oral discourse cannot distinguish between what was explicitly stated and what they had inferred (Garnham 1987).

In summary, syntactic recasting and semantic streamlining do not necessarily create distortions of meaning. If they do, and are perceived and judged significant in the pragmatic context of the communication, they can be offset by secondary pragmatic processing, either in the form of relevance judgments on the representations, resulting in some elimination or elaboration, or at some stage within the production system, by re-ordering to adjust perspective, or the manipulation of reference (microplanning); lexical choice (retrieval); phonological effects like contrastive stress (encoding); or modulation of relative voice speed and volume, etc. (articulation).

Production is the most autonomous part of the SI cycle, being driven

(i)   conceptually, by non-linguistic representations;

(ii) structurally, to a large extent by the interpreter's own immediately preceding output; some temporary dilution may result from the experienced interpreter's tendency to favour 'open grammar' (Seleskovitch and Lederer 1989), or words and structures with the broadest possible subcategorisation and selection frames.

(iii) pragmatically, by cues in input as well as by autonomous and ready-made ostensive and 'cooperative' devices.

In our model, pragmatic decisions to discard, summarise, elaborate or compensate are taken in the Executive, which receives all input (including instinctive and affective promptings), assesses the Speaker's intentions, and commands the production system. The Executive's 'knowledge base' consists of these inputs; its 'rule-base' for the interpretation task consists of the interpreter's internalised norms and sense of responsibility, weighed against her motivation.

6 Coordination and attention in SI

It has been argued, from assumptions about attention and the basic cognitive architecture, that such operations as SI, or even thinking while listening, involve rapid switching between modules or channels. In previous chapters, we questioned the impression of SI as a constant switching of attention and balancing of efforts which emerges from IP accounts.[9] Certainly, given the peculiar conditions of speech production in SI a model of upstream processes, and of coordination, is necessary to explain errors and the pattern of delivery. We have located the centre of coordination in SI schematically between the representational and production systems.

That there is some degree of parallel processing between perceptual and central processes is undeniable—we have thoughts while listening to people speak; in SI we have Pinter's results (1969, cited in Gile 1995) to show that performance in this regard can be improved by training. Modularity of peripheral systems suggests that input parsing is automatic, but may be probed at some cost, while speech planning and encoding, which involve conscious action, require some attention (this is necessary to explain why competent native speakers produce ill-formed sentences). Our hypothesis is that in SI, as in any coordinated task, attention is naturally centred *by default* on coordination between input and output, with a bias toward the action-oriented functions (judgment on inputs, and production of fluent and clear speech), but may be partially diverted—to cope with the contingencies and opportunities of a changing environment—either to probing one of the (successively fading) levels of input representation, or to meeting special challenges of formulation.

In the present hypothesis, attention in SI is centred by default on a pragmatic rather than any syntactic-semantic dimension. Interesting indirect evidence of this is provided by the fact that interpreters occasionally absent-mindedly interpret into the same language (e.g. English to English) for several minutes without noticing. Although unfortunately no data is available, we can report from experience that the product is a paraphrase of the original, sounding just like the interpreter's usual output, with the same autonomous stresses, pauses, hesitations, etc., suggesting that attention is centred on some work independent of any cross-linguistic syntactic-semantic conversion process.

Attention is therefore *switched and directed* only when called by special demands on listening or formulating. The former, especially, may be many and frequent, especially when adapting to a new unfamiliar Speaker, or in any number of difficult conditions (noise, speed, accents etc.); but successful performance will not allow excessive attention to either, on pain of a lapse on the other side. We may also suppose that, as a speech or lecture (or any coherent discourse, such as a dialogue) develops, less and less special probing of input will be needed to obtain full and consistent representations for formulation.[10]

6.1 Hesitancy and delivery patterns

The interpreter's output is the only direct source of evidence for theories about coordination in SI. Production patterns were explored in early studies, but no direct correlation could be found between pausing in the two streams. IT writers stress that SI production differs from sovereign speech chiefly due to the interfering effect of the SL, requiring a constant additional effort of resistance (Lederer 1981: 317). To our knowledge, no attempt has yet been made to describe fluency patterns in an SI corpus in terms of a model of SI processing, and certainly only a general hypothesis can be advanced in the present state of research.

Studies of speech production suggest a hierarchy in what is attended to by speakers, in which meaning imposes its will on structure, and prosody and rhythm dominate all. Cutler (1987) reports (citing Cutler and Isard 1980) that 'in practice semantic[11] factors tend to override syntactic factors in determining which words receive accent [...]' (1987: 28). Prosody and rhythm are particularly powerful in shaping speech: 'the speaker can be shown to be monitoring prosody and adjusting it with the listener's comprehension in mind.' Darwin (1975, cited by Cutler p. 35) found that in shadowing, a task with very little autonomy at all, prosodic continuity overrides semantic continuity. Finally, regularity of *rhythm* has an obvious role in facilitating speech production: imposing regular rhythm on one's speech is hearer-friendly.[12]

Several distinct articulatory phenomena are found in these short samples, including

(a)   silent and filled pauses of varying length;
(b)   vowel lengthening (drawl) and final consonant stopping (clipping) or schwa-suffixing;
(c)   stress, loudness and pitch variations;
(d)   the use of lexical items as verbal fillers;
(e)   various solecisms and boggle effects.

Each Speaker and interpreter has his/her own repertoire of phonetic effects and variations in pitch. The speech string can be analysed in terms of the following:

1.   *Fluent strings.* A string uttered with no break or modulation can be assumed to have been encoded or retrieved as a single chunk ('freewheeling'). Such strings are relatively rare, or short, in SI, since

they allow no insertion or adjustment. Some strings seem relatively fluent, or 'free', but monitoring of input is often disguised by natural-sounding modulation and articulatory and phonetic effects (drawls, etc. see below). When input is relatively formal and controlled (e.g. Würzburg), pauses are shorter and more numerous in the interpreter's output than in the Speaker's; the reverse may be found for highly impromptu input, as for instance in our rejected sample (Appendix B)

2. *Silent pauses* reflect highly directed, sometimes exclusive attention to input, or for special formulation or retrieval (or, more rarely, controlled 'ideal' breaks as in sovereign delivery, for instance at constituent or discourse boundaries),

3. *Filled pauses and syllable-lengthening* can be seen as a reflex akin to turn-holding in normal speech (as if to hold the hearer's attention while planning). They are more likely to reflect brief attention to planning or retrieval than directed listening, without sacrificing balanced attention.

4. *Uncorrected speech errors*, like slips of the tongue and omissions, reveal a lapse in self-monitoring due to a distraction from centred attention.

5. *Minor 'rhythmic' articulatory modulations* such as syllable 'clipping', beats or semi-pauses (shown as a word-final stop in the transcripts), and some pitch and stress contouring, may help to combine listening with speaking and self-monitoring by organising the two auditory inputs rhythmically in a kind of counterpoint. Prosodic modulation may also be used to disguise input-related hesitations.

In general, professional SI delivery differs from sovereign speech in its combination of careful or deliberate articulation, abundant pitch, stress, and other modulations, and occasional sudden changes of speed unrelated to content.

We may speculate that the above features correspond to three levels of attention to input:

(1)   (near-) exclusive concentration (probing) or formulation (searching);
(2)   normal listening, or
(3)   relaxed or switched-off attention.[13]

The hypothesis that strings produced with no modulation or pausing whatsoever reflect reduced attention to input is supported by several examples in the last (recited) part of the Taipei corpus, in which the informative density is such that inattention easily leads to missed input. The few unbroken strings in the interpreters' output over this passage almost all coincide with source material which is omitted or inaccurate in their subsequent output: in TS-31, TA misses

Table 7.4 Fluency and attention in SI

Hesitancy feature	Attention to input	...to formulation
long silent pause	high	-
short pausing	normal listening	routine planning
filled pause	normal listening	routine planning
mixed: short & filled pauses & voice effects	normal listening	routine planning
long filled pause (cf. turn holder) (@-@-)	relaxed or off	planning/searching
fluent unmodulated string	relaxed or off	off

'draft a name-list' ('has made a ruling that...'), apparently suppressed by the unmodulated 'merely derives from the approach taken by the United States'; while TB misses 'agree to refuse' while producing 'developing countries instead of the Third World for example the United States'. In S32, TB misses 'extreme socialist regimes' coinciding with 'based on technical reasons but basically it's because...' Other omissions (e.g. in S34 and 35) also coincide with exclusive attention to output. The German-English interpreters, who are more experienced, produce some short unmodulated bursts, but these hardly if ever coincide with new or difficult source material.

The significance of ear-voice span (EVS) is in some doubt if we assume that the representations and presentations which reach the Executive do not distinguish between elements of meaning integrated at the different stages, from the semantic form delivered by the input, through the contribution from the mental model, to inferences about the Speaker's attitude and intent from any other source. In fact, our own analysis and previous studies (Lederer 1981) showed a wide variety in the time of sojourn of different elements. A word may appear to pass from input to output, being slotted into a different structure, within less than a second:

T-S3 (line 37):
chongfan Lianheguo de 66 - zheige mubiao 67   +
rejoin   UN]   *de*   this   goal]

TA: -   we can 66   +   67 ob\tain. the \goal. of 68 re-\entry.

S15 (138):
Dahui de zhei tiao lu ne - shuo shizai 184 ye *bushi* name de 185 *rongyide* +
GenAss]] *de* d cl route]] [cp say-honestly [IPalso[AP not F>*shi* [AP so easy]]]]

TB: an-d 183   -   %   so- I con\clude185 here that - it won't be EASY for us

However, interpreters also regularly build satisfactory sentences which integrate text meaning over up to 12 seconds (plus other input) and produce them while more speech is coming in (e.g. Würzburg S8-S9); and there are several examples of input material which is reflected in output up to 2 minutes downstream. Against this background it seems otiose to speculate whether a given element comes from a specific expression in input (e.g. a Chinese Topic emerging 2 minutes after its last mention in the text, as described in § 6.8), or from a conceptual representation in short or medium-term memory. However, there is evidence that words in recent input do influence production, both from 'interference' and from examples such as WS6, where the intervening appearance of **'Anliegen'** (concern) clearly contributes to the choice of the word 'concern' slotted into the rendition of the previous phrase ('two *complexes* emerge'):

insbesondere zwei Komplexe her'auskristallisieren - das Eine ist das **'Anliegen**
in particular   two   complexes   out-crystallize - the one is   the concern

there is a very@ 9.2 LARGE. RANGE of QUEStions @m - under-   the-

das ver'ständliche Anliegen der europäischen Ge'meinschaft 16.7 -
the understandable concern   of-the European   Community -

main topic - of subsidy \fraud - and there are TWO 16.9 - MAIN - points of
con\cern

7 Executive and secondary pragmatic processing

It remains to be seen what a pragmatic model predicts about coordination and the limitations on SI. We have defined the Executive as an interface where cognition meets communication, and assigned to it (in the SI task) secondary pragmatic processing of the Message and overall task coordination. Firstly, the Executive must deal in material which is expressible in production as propositions with attitudes and illocution. As we have seen, this combines meaning from different sources, so we can assume that it no longer distinguishes between what was originally decoded and what was inferred, i.e. that it deals in IF {PA {epr}} with a scale of implicatures of different strengths. As the component which integrates all input and feedback, and decides how and what to produce, the Executive can be described as a kind of secondary pragmatic Assembler located downstream of the primary Assembly of propositional forms from linguistic rules and the mental model.

Some consensus is emerging in pragmatics on the notion that semantic and pragmatic processes are 'interdigitated' in utterance processing (Turner 1997: 167). As illustrated by our examples in Chapter 6, the output of linguistic decoding requires considerable 'filling-in' by pragmatic processes (Carston 1995: 240) to become propositional and evaluable for truth and falsity; then, as a result of further pragmatic processing, implicatures are generated in the standard way (Turner 1997: 167). We can expand the definition of secondary pragmatic processing of *extended discourse* to include the derivation of meaning from multiple propositions, both implicature, guided by procedurals like connectives, and further higher-order explicatures, guided by various clues to illocution/ attitude, or to intended interpretive uses (metaphor or irony). In practice this phase of processing can be said to yield meaning from the multi-propositional text or 'discourse-level', with maximum input from other cognitive sources (situational bias, Speaker's body language, cognitive prejudice from strong beliefs about the Speaker's intentions, etc.) and to distil an impression of the Speaker's overall and local intentionality, which for translation/interpreting purposes may license the insertion of 'neutral padding' or conative material of a particular flavour (persuasive, diffident, etc.) at apparently random points.

For SI, the first phase of meaning derivation may often be curtailed: partially resolved material may be translated without first being disambiguated or reference assigned. The second phase, in contrast, may be extended: in a task involving production and hence ostension, secondary pragmatic processing for comprehension extends, as it were, into the interpreter's re-ostensive preparation of the TL discourse for the Addressee; she has to take into account her own ongoing utterance in framing each next sentence, as well as reflecting the adjustments of emphasis, etc., discovered from the input.

7.1 Cognitive management and difficulty in SI

From a cognitive modelling point of view, secondary pragmatic processing takes whole propositions as input, so that any doubt arising at this stage as to reference or semantic ambiguity will require expensive and possibly disruptive backtracking ('re-analysis'). Once propositional forms have been assembled, any residual indeterminacy can only be resolved by special consultation of invoked knowledge, or less accessible implicatures and contextual effects, to make bridging inferences. Unresolved words can be translated; but it is much easier to translate from concepts, which allow a far wider choice of confident formulations. In any case, even if the uncomprehending transfer of structures and lexical items were viable for a while, the mental model would begin to show serious gaps and no longer offer support when an inference base was needed, for example for features to be mandatorily encoded in TL. *Maintaining* a coherent mental model might indeed be viewed as a significant central processing effort in SI, i.e. the permanent component of 'inferential load'.

Difficulty is predicted when these processes are hampered. At the primary assembly stage, the mental model may be challenged by a concentration of new or unassociable referents, or the lack of a conceptual base in long term memory to support the input. Comprehension, and therefore production (if honest) are then forced to draw on the uncontextualised products of the Parser-Assembler.

The Executive is responsible for higher-order inferencing (evaluation and selection), and for production decisions: timing, and decisions to discard, elaborate, or compensate on-line. Difficulty at this level is predicted when the input is poor in local ostensive guidance to illocution and dependent relevance, in the form of conatives, connectives, intonational contour, and so on. When the mental model does not deliver a coherent picture in which intentionalities are associated with propositions, the Executive must resort to other sources of propositional material, i.e. unenriched words and structures direct from the parser, and other, 'floating' clues to intentionality (Speaker gestures, or the interpreter's assumptions about the Speaker).

Since the SI condition favours a maximally incremental, opportunistic process of assembling meaning, we may suppose that it involves more frequent internal reanalysis than ordinary comprehension. Two levels of corrective processes can be hypothesised (at a more central level than 'reanalysis' as it is conventionally understood, as a syntactic parsing problem): a constructive process, which revises logical and thematic structures in the mental model; and an evaluative process, which assesses plausibility and communicative significance, taking intentionality into account, in the Executive.

Since the former precedes the latter, we can surmise that logical or thematic reanalysis—a revision of the truth-conditional proposition itself—is more troublesome, at the production stage, than the need for (secondary) pragmatic adjustments; but that indeterminacy of communicative intent, due to a lack of guidance on how to take the propositions together, or on their relationship to the Speaker, the Addressee and the immediate situation (as when a prepared text is read out expressionlessly) is ultimately more troublesome than logical or thematic indeterminacy.

The challenge of SI is sometimes seen as a balance between short-term memory capacity and the need to wait for 'more context.' This blurs a significant distinction between two types of 'context'. Short-term memory depends on the familiarity of incoming logical structures and thematic material (referents), and on the integrating performance of the mental model. This is one type of context, contributing to the clarity of the conceptual representation. However, language forms are treacherous as guides to logical and pragmatic structure:

(1)   *No fish will come near the monitoring buoy*

... without its every move being recorded by the underwater camera.

(2)   *For the many colourful species which inhabit the reef*
        ... the long winter has begun
        ... live in a perfect symbiosis

(3)   *As the marine biologist manoeuvres the underwater camera*
        ... the turtle follows, peering at the lens
        ... a thought suddenly occurs to him
        ... so the ornithologist trains his binoculars

These examples from a television documentary, with other possible continuations, are not typical of conference discourse, and help to explain why interpreters require the script of recorded commentaries for interpretation. But when dependency is uncertain because of logical scope, as in (1) above; or homonymy, as in in (2) ('for') and (3) ('as'); or pragmatic ambiguity (between a real, epistemic or speech-act relation), as in example (4) from Sweetser (1990), an illocutionary context is necessary:

(4) *John must go to all the department parties*
        ... because he's agreed to be bartender
        ... because he's always out on those nights

Difficulty is predicted in SI when both types of 'context' are required simultaneously, as for an utterance like (5) at the beginning of a meeting:

(5)*This may be the IGCRN's last CUG session ...*
        ... but I'll be damned if it's the last time we all drink together
        ... unless we can fix something up next year

where invocation, or memory retrieval would be necessary to get thematic support for referents like 'IGCRN' and 'CUG' (= Closed User Group), while the 'logical' or pragmatic relation remains in suspense with the ambiguity of 'may'. In most ordinary discourse, context is always available for one or the other dimension, usually from clues to illocution, and the Executive can produce hedging material. In recited written discourse, on the other hand, new referents may coincide with logical and pragmatic dependency, as in this construction with the quantifier **cai** (cf. German **erst**) (synchronised extract from the Taipei corpus, T-S35, App. T3):

'The US Congress once refused to allocate funds for a World Bank replenishment of until Governor Macnamara [to a Congressional Committee submitted a statement promising [in the short term not to grant loans to Vietnam and only then **(cai)** release(d the funds)'

Meiguo Guohui. ceng. yi du jujue. 360 pizhun   bojiao. 361 Shijie Yinhang.
[NPUS Congress [IP *past*   once [VPrefused [V·permit [V·allocate [NPWorld Bank

xinzengzi 362- xinzengzi. an 363 - H   zhi dao- 364 - Shijie Yinhang zongcai 365 -
recapitalisation   recapitalisation motion - [PP right [until - [CP [IP[NPWorld Bank Chief -

TA: once refused   - to \allocate funds - 364 for the /new - ~funding -
TB: ....

@m -   Maina.   -   mala 367 -   @m- 368xiang ZHONGYUAN - xiaozu weiyuanhui
            Macna   mara   -   [P/VPto House of Represves.- group-committee

TA: ~scheme of the - World 367 \Bank - until the   /new -   \Governor
TB: the World- 368@m \President .of the World. /Bank   +

-   tichu 370 shuotie +   chengNUO -   zai duanqi NEI 372 -   bu ZAI -
- [VPsubmit[NPstatement [VPVpromise ([IP[PPat short period -within] -   [not again

TA: of the World Bank - MannaMAra 371 - pre\sented - a back\grounder -
TB: recent/ly 371-   - promised372   +

daikuan Yuenan 373 zhiHOU - HH cai   -   jiedong 374   +
loan Vietnam]   -after] - [IP then-only [VPunfreeze ø]

TA: statement 373 -   to -   the - representative \house - of the
\Congress - that's when the fund - was not frozen - by - th United States)
TB: +   +   H to- 375   +
H \stop - providing loans to the. Vietnam. 378 in order to appease the United- States

The form of the construction is 'X refused to VP$_1$ until (**yizhi dao**) [after-Y-did-W] and only then (**cai**) V$_2$-ed' (where VP$_1 \approx$ V$_2$). The terminal sequence '...**zhihou cai jiedong** (...- afterwards, and only then unfroze Ø') encodes the retroactive logical dependency overtly, but is not syntactically mandatory. TB may have expected it and remained in suspense, but the intervening material is complex, with embedded syntax and a good deal of new content, and she loses a lot of it in her late summary: 'the President of the World Bank recently promised to stop providing loans to Vietnam to appease the United States'. TA, for her part (not an English native speaker) does not find the expressive resources to render the logic retroactively *in extremis* ('that's when the fund was not frozen').

8 Failure in SI

In the SI literature, errors and failure have either been played down (IT theory) or attributed in general terms to capacity overload (Gile 1995: 80 ff.). We shall not be concerned here with slips of the tongue and other speech errors common to SI and normal speech (although the causes may be different), but only with significant losses or distortions of the Speaker's meaning as it appears from listening to the tapes. We shall attempt to distinguish failure originating in the primary assembly of the basic proposition (due to missed semantic or syntactic information) from failure in a subsequent process, in the organisation of propositions relative to each other or their embedding under speech-acts or attitudes, whether due to a failure of pragmatic competence or to coordination problems or information overload. We can also distinguish between major breakdowns, or compound failures (which can no doubt be triggered by any obstacle, from noise to a gap in knowledge), and 'routine' losses of information or qualification.

8.1 Problems in primary assembly

In SI, secondary or incidental qualification and other information are often lost. However, some elements may resurface 20 or 30s downstream, while others which could have been inserted within echoic memory span are omitted. Examples of lost secondary qualification include in WM1 **diesen aktuellen Überblick** 'this *up-to-date* overview': WB 'that view', WA `that clear view'`; in WM5 (WA, WL) **'als Strafrechtler'...** *as a criminal lawyer* (allow me simply to...); in TS28-TB '*which is on page six* (of my paper)'; in TS29 (TA, TB) 'politicisation of the World Bank and IMF differs from that of *most* other international organisations'. In almost every case these items are entities or properties which are

(a)   'brand-new' or not inferrable (Prince 1979) from the current model, presented simultaneously with other new epr; *and/or*

(b)   presented in marked or unusual constructions (e.g. the fronted phrase 'as a criminal lawyer I...').

We may infer that both special retrieval of concepts from outside the MM, and processing unusual syntax, are semi-peripheral operations which compete for limited resources.

   Numbers, names and dates are classic examples of items difficult to associate into the mental model, and are notoriously vulnerable to error or omission. Omissions in Würzburg include 'in the 1970s' (WS-8-WL, WB), 'Paragraph 264' (WS8-WA), and most strikingly, most of the dates and titles in the Moderator's biographical introduction of the invited Speaker (Würzburg segment M4β). Here there is no structural complexity, but a sudden influx of brand-new referents, particularly for WA and WB, in the 'mock' event, who attempt to retrieve the information from documents (rustling noises), but are only partially successful, and the rate of informational input is too fast and concentrated for recovery or repair. WL, in the live situation, performs better. There is a similar rate of loss (half of the placenames, and the title of the event) in the introduction to the Chinese taped interview with Fang Lizhi—also a simulation, for which only minimal background knowledge was available, and no documentation.

Numbers, in particular, are likely to be lost in SI if not retrieved within 3-4s. If information cannot be represented in time, there is no conceptual basis for formulation, which must then fall back on primary semantic-syntactic sources, including untreated names. Our data seems compatible with this, as shown in Table 7.5:

Table 7.5 SI interpreters' accuracy in rendering numerical data (German-English corpus) with EVS to correct, incorrect or approximate recovery

line	Input (Würzburg)	WL	WA	WB
36	1983	ok 2.5-3s	missed	missed
39	1988	ok 2.5-3s	missed	about 4s, wrong
101	Paragraph 264	ok 3.5s	glossed over	3s, consulted
	Input (Taipei)		TA	TB
96	in 1971		dropped	wrong (1973) 20s
98	Resolution 2758		'the Resolution' 10s	ok 8s
108	28 countries		wrong (27) 4s	ok 2.7
110	of which only 25		ok 2.8s	ok 3s
116	184 Member States		ok 2.8s	ok 1.1
121	these 25 countries		ok 4s	ok 2.2
124	equals 1/7th		'less than 1/7th' 5.5	ok 3.8
131	nearly 100 votes		anticipated by an approximation	'more than 100' 2s

These results must be seen in the light of certain other variables, particularly familiarity and predictability:

(a)   smaller numbers are probably much easier to remember, and have some identity or *gestalt*, so we have ignored single-digit numbers.

(b)   numbers meaningfully integrated in a logical structure, like a clear calculation, are probably easier to remember (e.g. in Taipei S11-14).

(c)   numbers related to frame knowledge are more accessible, e.g. '12 (now 15) European Member States', or the population of Europe (320 million).

(d)   memory for numbers can be supplanted by finding documentation (Paragraph 264: WB), or supported by making a note, as possibly in the case of TA for 'Resolution 2758'

The mental model hypothesis also makes certain predictions about processing effort and difficulty in SI. If our hypothesis is correct, then, given full linguistic comprehension, the effort of rendering different parts of the input will depend not so much on their length or constituent structure as on the nature of representation in the model. Thus a phrase like **na dajia ye tongyang renshi dao yidian jiushi...** ('well everyone likewise also realises one thing which is...') is a trivial matter to represent, and perhaps is almost 'presented', reappearing as the simple directive 'However,...'; while a single word like the German anaphor **da** may give rise to a clause like *'in taking these decisions'*. Similarly, since a mental model merely instantiates a single thematic representation for different token referents, the difficulty of handling complex referents (e.g. complex NPs, proper names) will depend on their familiarity, not on their linguistic structure. The mental model hypothesis predicts that both newness and indeterminate reference may hamper SI, however simple the input structure. This is suggested by the mild boggle effects, and an error, at the introduction of the new referent **Anliegen**[14] in Würzburg S6 (% indicates creaky voice quality, hardly found elsewhere in these two subjects):

...zwei Komplexe her'auskristallisieren 48.5   -   das Eine ist das 'Anliegen
two   complexes   out   crystallize   the one is the concern
WA: it has emerged. 48.2 that there are TWO MAIN –ISSues 50.5
WB: -   @TWO 47.5   - speCIFic issues-@ 49 - IN - the OVERall ISSue that

das ver'ständliche Anliegen der europäischen Ge'meinschaft 53.7 -
the understandable concern of the European   Community
WA: -   @%   first of all 53 -   the *approximation –
WB: you're - re/FERRing 51.7   - @wwa-.   the FIRST is the- 54.4

WA: +   the NEED 56.5 @   for the European Community
WB: quite.   under STANDable 55.7 -   %   %   th- deSIRE

WA's production of 'approximation' is rather mysterious; she may have misheard **Anliegen** as **Annähern**, in which case this is certainly an instance of direct lexical translation, since 'approximation' makes no sense in any conceivable context.

9 Processing breakdown and compound errors

IT researchers do not entertain the possibility of serious errors or breakdown in professional interpretation, claiming that failure in SI is due either to inadequate mastery of the languages, or of SI technique (which should involve responding to *sens* instead of structure). Lederer does however give an example in which a significant omission appears to be linked to the 'watershed' model of fluent production following a *'déclic'*:

Ferner beabsichtigen wir dem Verwaltungsrat gelegentlich der Sitzung
further we intend   [to the$_{DAT}$ Board of Directors [on the occasion of the meeting
Interpreter: *D'autre part nous avons -   l'intention -*
                                        Besides this we have   .   the intention

am achtundzwanzigsten März in Basel - je einen Prototyp -
on the twenty-eighth   March in Basel - [each one$_{ACC}$ prototype
                           le vingt-huit -_____ - mars à -
                           (on) the twenty-eighth   March in

mit jeder der beiden Varianten der Inneneinrichtung -   vorzuführen.
with each of the two versions of the internal furnishings [to present
...Bâââle   à l'occasion de la   reunion   du comite   de
    Basel   [on the occasion of the   meeting   of the Board of

direction de montrer chacun des prototypes aux directeurs généraux
Directors [to show each of the prototypes to the Directors (from Lederer 1981: 116 ff.)

Lederer claims that the unit of *sens*, which clinches comprehension of the meaning of the utterance and allows prediction of the verb **vorzuführen** (to present), crystallizes at **Prototyp**. Evidence for this is given in the loss of what follows '**mit jeder der beiden Varianten der Inneneinrichtung**', 'with each of the two versions of the internal furnishings', attributed to the relaxation of monitoring once an idea of the sense was grasped. Significantly, although Lederer does not provide detailed prosodic transcription (pausing and modulation), this lost string appears to coincide with fluent unmodulated 'freewheeling' production by the interpreter.

The IP tradition has not produced corpus studies, but Gile has presented a 70-second sample containing numerous errors as an introduction to his limited-capacity theory of SI processing. Two examples are analysed here to illustrate the difference between failures in which SI coordination or technique are defeated at the level of primary assembly, perhaps by the embedded syntax and concentrated new reference of recited input, and those attributable to a weakness in pragmatic competence. The first is taken from our written corpus; for the second, we propose a pragmatic analysis of Gile's sample (Gile 1995).

9.1 Failure in SI from recited written text

Even in professional SI, serious breakdowns may occur when concentrated written text is read as it stands with no warning or documentary support, as in TS29-38. TB's difficulties over the first part of this passage are analysed here by way of illustration. The extract is glossed phrase by phrase for easier reading (for a labelled word-for-word gloss, see Appendix T3).

S29 (*recited from a text not supplied to the interpreters*):

Shijie Yin 298 hang - he Guoji zu- Guoji Huobi Jijin 299- liangge jinrong 300 zuzhi
The World Bank   - and the I M F   - (these) two financial orgnanisations'

TB: .... World 300 /Bank

de ZHENGZHIhua 301 - yu Lianheguo -   tixi xia 303 -   qita daduoshu 304 -
   politicisation - (compared) to [under the UN system   the other most of

TB: - and. the I M/F 301   -   h-have become -   highly po\litical 304

zhuanmen jigou   zhengzhihua   - you qi. genben - 306 bu tong. zhi chu +
specialised agencies' politicisation -   has some basic differences

TB: + H   as 305 compared. to the   -   H 306 other insti\tu 307

S30: H zhe liangge jinrong 308 zuzhi zhengzhihua de 309 FANYONG ne - BUSHI. 310
     these two financial organisations' politicisation   scope/demain - is not

TB: tions the - political- isation of the \other institu - tions 310

   di   san   shijie 311 -   er shi. yikaifa 312 guojia   -   TEbie shi Meiguo +
(the) Third   World   - but   (the) developed nations - especially *shi* [NPUSA

TB: there is - a difference 311   +   H   because these 314 institutions
-

S31: Meiguo juece 315 jieceng- niyou yi 316 fen mingdan   +
     US decision-makers   -   drew up a   list

TB: -   @-   315 app/ly-   - to- de\veloped countries instead of 317 the

JIN keneng jujue 318 - tongyi- lie zai   mingdan 319 shang - guojia de - 320
do (their) best (to) refuse - (to) agree/approve [countries on the list]   (getting)

TB: Third World for example the United \States   +   H

<zheige> DUOBIAN DAIKUAN SHENQING 321 +   qi zhong -   you Yuenan 323 -
fp   multilateral loan applications   among them there is Vietnam

TB: H   the United /States 322 -   can agree. to -

   Guba 324   -   Geruinada -   he Nijialagua   326 deng guo   +
   Cuba   -   Granada   -   and Nicaragua   [such countries]

TB: multi lateral-   \loans 325 including -   Vietnam Cuba and-

---

S32: Meiguo fandui daikuan de liyou 328 -   biaomian shang shi JISHUXING de
     (The) US oppose loans (the) reason -   on the surface is technical

TB: Nicar~ 327 agua H   +   H 328 the- US has -   \opPOSed

+ shiji shang 330 ne. ze shi. jiyu 331 YANWU.   zhexie   guojia   332 JIJIN
         in reality   however it's based on (their) detest (ation of) [these countries
extreme

TB: to- oans 330 by these - \countries 331 - based on technical reasons but 332 basically...

TB feels the need to elaborate and rephrase S29 ('the- H other insti\tutions - the-political- isation of the \other institutions'), but S30 begins with a complex abstract nominalisation (**FANYONG**: 'scope' of the politicisation; a nominalised unaccusative), at which a long silent pause suggests she is probing comprehension resources. By the time 'apply to' is found, the Subject NP has apparently decayed in memory to its determiner 'these institutions' (instead of 'the politicisation of these institutions'), yielding 'these institutions apply to...' The Theme is then output fluently in a single burst:

'..de\veloped countries instead of 317 the Third World for example the United 318 \States'

i.e. with no pause, and significantly, no modulation, suggesting that attention to input is suspended (see Table 7.4 above). TB misses the next main verb '*refuse* (to agree)', capturing only 'agree', which was coming in during her first modulation/ slowing at \States. A very long pause ensues, but the unprocessed input has now built up to include the complex and new NP Subject 'US decision-making authorities', the serial Main Verbs 'draft a list and do their utmost to refuse', a Verb complement which contradicts its higher Verb ('to refuse...to agree'), and an Object NP with double embedding: [name-list-on [countries' [multilateral loan applications]]]. Furthermore, all the referents are new in the discourse.

TB takes 'agree' as the Main Verb: 'United States agrees..', forcing self-contradictory correction at S32 (**Meiguo fandui** ... 'the US opposes...').

The lack of a stable mental model base appears to lead to increasing forced switching of attention away from the point of balance, alternately to input-probing and production, leading to cumulative losses (cf. Gile's 'knock-on' effects, Chapter 2). In the case of TA, working into an acquired language, the pressure is felt on the production side: she pares her formulation down to a concise minimum, but the quality and clarity of the English falls sharply.

This example suffices to illustrate the problems which begin to accumulate when there is (1) no time to build up conceptual and referential support in a model; and (2) virtually no pragmatic marking, or rhetorical 'lubricating' material, in the input.

9.2 Pragmatic failure

Gile (1995: 81-4) introduces his Effort models with a starkly realistic view of fidelity in SI, observing that 'examples of professional SI with a high rate of error, not attributable to adverse environmental conditions [...] are not rare' and that 'errors often occur on strings with no visible difficulty of [...] terminology, line of reasoning or syntactic complexity.' Gile advances an explanation in terms of the difficulty of coordinating various efforts (see Chapter 2), and gives the following example of a passage with numerous errors (1995: 83) in which he sees the incomplete sentences and recasting as the knock-on effects of processing capacity conflicts. We take up his example to illustrate the role of pragmatic competence in SI, particularly the need to recognise elliptical cues to logical/pragmatic scope (from Gile 1995: 82-3; he does not supply a synchronised transcript).

> Speaker:
> Before I dissertate on some of my ideas, first of all Bob Kearney says to me he says 'I would much rather you have said your piece before lunch so we could have a good laugh and enjoy our lunch' And I took that as a compliment and then I wanted to answer Cliff's request about now that we found this tremendous resource what are we going to do with it and how we gonna utilise it? I purposely did not go back to my room and outline what I was going to say, because if I did I would probably say a lot of things that weren't really on my mind and I would try to tailor it after the context of this meeting .... etc (from Gile 1995: 82-3).
>
> Interpreter: *Avant de commenter certaines de mes idées, surtout en ce que / mon ami a dit 'j'espère que tu auras fini ton discours avant le petit déjeuner afin que nous ayons un bon déjeuner par la suite'. J'ai pris cela comme un compliment et et j'ai voulu répondre à la question de Cliff sur la façon de trouver ces ressources comment nous allons les utiliser. A dessein, je ne suis pas retourné / je ne suis pas revenu sur ce que j'ai dit auparavant... etc.*

Gile identifies 11 errors in the space of 70 seconds. He notes a big difference between his own and other authors' data, which contain 'several error-less 70s segments'; but reports finding the same levels of error for this passage in 'ten other professionals in analogous conditions'. This finding by Gile suggests either that SI is very unreliable, or that discourse with a high 'pragmatic index' is sensitive to removal from the live event.[15]

The sample is in a North American dialect which is rather elliptic as to markers of speech-act structure, but near-native speakers familiar with this dialect should close the gaps with inference. Certainly in French more overt marking of speech-act structure is required. The cause of breakdowns and errors seems to lie in a failure to capture and/or render pragmatic meaning at this level (and some simple defects in lexical comprehension, e.g. later in the extract: 'I find it intriguing: ..*me surprend un peu*'). Gile rules out the (rather sweeping) objection that the interpreter is 'incompetent,' on the grounds (also rather sweeping), that she 'enjoys a good reputation.' The possibility remains, after all, that she performs well on all but this particular style of discourse.

The following pragmatic analysis may appear complex, but we believe it reflects normal English native or near-native inferential abilities (>> means 'infer'; the necessary bridging inferences are underlined):

'Before I dissertate on some of my ideas first of all Bob Kearney says to me he says....

Interpreter: *Avant de commenter certaines de mes idées, surtout en ce que... mon ami a dit*
'Before discussing some of my ideas especially in so far as...my friend said'

The following inferences should be possible, given a familiarity with this usage:

1. We can infer from the Tense of *Bob Kearney <u>says</u>* that what follows does not stand in a causal or temporal relation to the *Before* clause, but signals the introduction of relevant context:

   'Before discussing my ideas.... [>> <u>I wish</u> first of all <u>to convey the relevant background information that</u> Bob Kearney said...

   French requires more overt marking of such 'speech-act' use, as reflected in the *puisque/parce que* distinction (Sweetser 1990: 82): this might be realised here by something like *sachez que..., laissez-moi vous dire...*

2. The interpreter apparently does not catch Bob Kearney's name, and so substitutes a contextualised hypernym *mon ami*; this is hardly an error if it is clear to listeners deictically; and if friendliness may stand in for politeness.[16]

---

he says 'I would much rather you have [sic] said your piece before lunch so we could have a good laugh and enjoy our lunch'   And I took that as a compliment

---

Interpreter: '... '*j'espère que tu auras fini ton discours avant le petit déjeuner afin que nous ayons un bon déjeuner par la suite'. J'ai pris cela comme un compliment"*
'"I hope you'll have finished your speech before breakfast so that we can then have a good lunch" I took that as a compliment'

In this passage, the humorous effect depends on retrieving the following implicatures:

1. *said your piece*: connotes 'get it over with' >> <u>relief</u>
2. *so we could have a good laugh* >>
                     (a) my (Speaker's) views are laughable
                     (b) (secondary) I (Speaker) should be offended
3. *and enjoy our lunch* >>(a) >> relief
                     (b) >> (secondary) Speech creates tense expectation
4. *and I took that as a compliment*: responds to (cancels) implicature 2 (b), assuming audience also has in mind 3 (a), which is stronger (two implicatures of 'relief')
'Petit déjeuner'(breakfast) is an unexplained slip.

And then I wanted to answer Cliff's request...

Interpreter: *et et j'ai voulu répondre à la question de Cliff*
             'and I wanted to answer Cliff's question'

1. *And then*: the speech-act domain (governing pragmatic as opposed to logical relations between propositions) is still valid by default for interpreting connectives: 'then' is a speech-act use and indicates a second preamble to the speech. *'Et'* is inadequate to introduce a new context; *'et puis'* would work better, as English 'and then', for encoding what is a sequence in mental processes.
2. Cliff: new participant   >> thematic change
                           >> current structure is series of prefatory remarks
>> *and then* → *second context in which I want you to process my views*

...(request) about now that we found this tremendous resource what are we going to do with it and how we gonna utilise it?

Interpreter: *sur la façon de trouver ces ressources comment nous allons les utiliser*
             'about how to find these resources how we're going to use them'

1. *Request about now that...*: relaxed colloquial device encoding reported speech; again, this requires more structure in French, for instance *la demande de Cliff qui voulait savoir...*
2. Situation knowledge seems to play a part here. If the interpreter was not present when Cliff made his request, she does not yet have the presupposition (*'we have found a resource'*) nor the referent of *we*, etc., and must rely on the bare input form. This may have come too fast for literal translation, forcing what is probably an interpretation of the 'cognitive prejudice' type,

based on a prototype concept of people's intentions towards 'resources' (i.e. finding them): hence the error *about how to find these resources...

> I purposely did not go back to my room and outline what I was going to say, because if I did I would probably say a lot of things that weren't really on my mind and I would try to tailor it after the context of this meeting ... etc.

Interpreter: *A dessein, je ne suis pas retourné / je ne suis pas revenu sur ce que j'ai dit auparavant... etc.*
                'Purposely, I did not go back ...(restart) I did not go back on what I said before....'

The words *what I was going to say* bring us back to the macrostructure 'introduction to discourse', and we can infer that this a third prefatory remark. But the interpreter seems to be following input too literally (and possibly too closely; the synchronised transcript is not available), and missing evidence of pragmatic dependencies. No context evoked by '*I [...] did not go back to my room...*' yields relevance by itself—relevance is achieved at the earliest after processing this together with '*and outline what I was going to say*', revealing the scope of '*purposely*'. (As such the sentence carries some rhetorical narrative 'suspense' effect, always a challenge for SI). The significance of *purposely* becomes even more explicit in the next few clauses:

I purposely did not ... outline what I was going to say
                (a) >> you may expect a loose format (no outline)
if I did I would probably say a lot of things that weren't really on my mind
                (b) >> I decided to be spontaneous, spontaneous is better

A translator with the whole text available might achieve pragmatic fidelity effectively with something like *j'ai résisté à la tentation de faire un plan...* or *j'ai fait exprès de ne pas rédiger un discours...* In SI the whole text is not available, but cues are usually there to warn that the minimal context needed may extend over several words or phrases. A single word like Lederer's '*Furthermore*' may sometimes allow a self-contained, 'context-free' rendition, but not an item like *purposely* whose intentional scope can only be discovered here by co-processing at least two propositions for dependent relevance. At first sight, *A dessein* looks like a safe gambit which could prefix any downstream proposition, but it won't work: apparently it will not happily coexist with a negative, still less govern conjoined propositions (? and * signify 'poor' and 'bad' forms according to standard notation in linguistics):

?A dessein je ne suis pas retourné dans ma chambre... *et (je n'ai pas) fait un plan....

Predictably, therefore, the interpreter is 'garden-pathed' by trying to process *purposely* independently or with the irrelevant (as such) *I did not go back to my room.* She restarts with *je ne suis pas revenu sur ce que j'ai dit auparavant...*, which bears no relation to propositions encoded in input, suggesting that the task priority of saying something relevant (in the Executive) has overriden the stalled process of meaning assembly.[17]

It is suggested, then, that breakdown here stems initially from the failure to wait for a minimal relevant unit as the basis for formulation—the appropriate compromise in SI between the single word, for which it is risky to formulate without context, and a longer stretch of discourse. The interpreter appears to miss a pragmatic dimension which is significant in this informal, communicative speech style, and in fact, throughout this discoursal introduction, seems to be attuned to a form of processing more suited to the transfer of information than to interactive communication.

9.3 Causes of failure in SI

In our own main corpus, significant errors are virtually confined to hard data like numbers, names and dates. Most of the propositions absorbed or not passed on are reminders, emphatic conatives, or 'resumptive' and directive signposts. Actual breakdown and loss of content has been shown above in two cases: (1) highly structured (written text) input, relying on complex coding of meaning (words and structure carry all the meaning) and (2) 'unstructured' input relying on sophisticated inference.

The problems encountered in TS29-39 are predicted if we assume that two levels of representation are drawn on, the lower or linguistically-based one requiring more of the 'non-sharable' attention required by more peripheral systems. In composing a written text (as in T-S29-39), a writer need make no allowance for the time taken by the reader to install new referents and work out their relevant extensions, or the number of passes he has to make to assemble a representation (he can re-read it at leisure), and so can make free use of the coding possibilities in language. But when such text is received linearly on line, processing is limited by the power of the parser in applying grammatical and lexical knowledge, unrelieved and unguided by the ostensive features which normally help to find supporting contexts in comfortable time. The lack of contextual support for the new referents forces a reliance on the bare semantic-syntactic representation, but the embedded structures are too long and complex to handle without this conceptual support from the mental model. Theoretically, data which cannot be associated into the mental model at all (such as numbers and names), or not in time for formulation before phonological memory decay, might be better retrieved by reducing the EVS (Seleskovitch and Lederer 1989: 152 ff.) But this makes the interpreter vulnerable to structural asymmetries and interference, and the loss of connectivity over multiple propositions, as seen in the problems encountered by (usually inexperienced) interpreters who follow the input too closely. As pointed out in the literature, numbers can be retrieved more effectively with the help of an external memory support, in the form of a notepad, which again illustrates the need for temporary representations to support mental tasks.

Speech of the type in Gile's sample lies at the other, 'oral' extreme of the 'oral-literate continuum' (Shlesinger 1989), where a whole implicit macro-structure at the speech-act level has to be inferred and modelled, particularly when it needs to be encoded in the target language. But unlike the first example, where performance is limited by peripheral computational power, here it depends on making the correct secondary inferences, which in turn depends on familiarity with the type of discourse or pragmatic dialect.

10 Summary

In this Chapter we have observed how SI forces approximations and simplifications of propositional structure, and is vulnerable to afterthoughts and modifications which come late in each utterance. We have also confirmed the observations in the literature (Lederer 1981, Gile 1995 etc.) that SI is vulnerable as regards numbers and proper names, but we generalise this problem to all items which are difficult to associate into the mental model, predicting difficulty at any sudden influx of new referents.

Several features of the interpreters' production can be viewed as compensating for or restoring perspective and rhetorical impact. This justifies the hypothesis of a function which receives all inputs, coordinates the task and directs production accordingly, making decisions based on both the content of the discourse and timing. The data does not justify the view that capacity constraints are necessarily severe in SI, with peripheral and central processes competing for resources and attention, except in certain conditions which are typically present in the recitation of written text. The distinctive characteristics of such input are its complex embedded structures, high density of new referents, and the absence of pragmatic markers of illocution and attitude. The rest of the corpus tends to disconfirm the hypothesis that syntactic embedding in itself (if normal to the language concerned) is an obstacle, since elsewhere complex sentences are handled adequately using the various cues and sources described in previous Chapters, which also confirmed the value to SI of pragmatic marking. An effect of the second factor, new referents, is suggested by individual observations in the corpus, and by the generally poor performance with proper names and numbers. This suggests that complex structure only becomes troublesome in combination with one of the other two factors: a concentration of new referents, or a poverty of markers of pragmatic values.

Steps in SI meaning assembly are shown in Figure 7.6., a simplified diagram highlighting the pragmatic dimension in the model as presented in Chapter 3. Values in italics or round brackets represent virtual information which is sourced but not yet fully integrated into the representation at each stage: deictic values in situation knowledge; potential epr structures, with some intonational or word-order clues to their relative importance, in the Assembler; some clues to illocution, and some deictic indexing, in the Mental Model; and in the Executive, possibly some additional clues to the Speaker's (S) intentionality from his non-verbal behaviour.

Plain face indicates the level of representation which is resolved at various stages: in the Assembler, constituent structure and some lexical information; in the Mental Model, contextualised {epr} embedded under integrated deictic and attitudinal values; and in the Executive, the sequence of propositions attributed to the Speaker under attitude and illocution, structured according to dependent relevance, with their background presuppositions and implicatures in a scale of strengths—these latter are not necessarily produced explicitly, but guide the final resolution of all values which must be reached in the Executive, if necessary based on additional judgments, for production. The structure and form of the output utterance is then further defined by the interpreter's previous speech (and, of course, by her TL retrieval and encoding performance).

The main efforts are hypothesised to arise

- for maintaining coherence in the Mental model;
- when additional knowledge must be invoked, or background implicatures probed, to make thematic, logical or pragmatic sense;
- when linguistic Assembly must be probed, in the event of indeterminacy due to inadequate or delayed contextualisation (Mental Model) and/or intentionality (Executive).

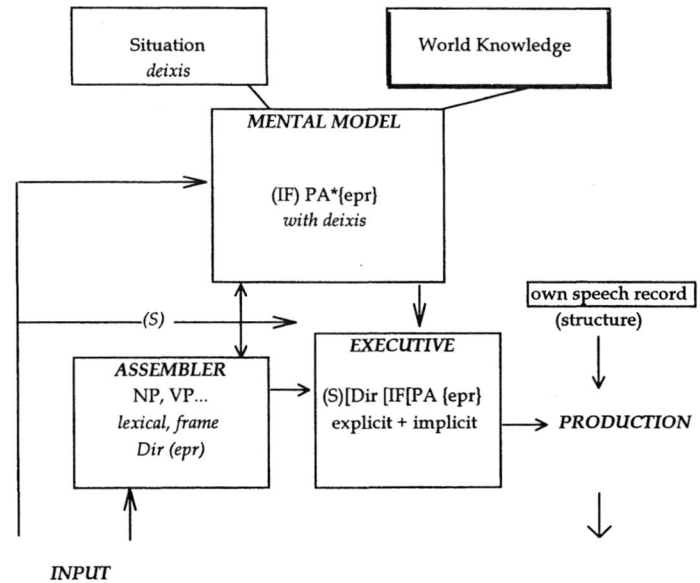

Figure 7.6 Pragmatic Assembly in SI

Chapter 8 Summary and Conclusions

What can a cognitive-pragmatic analysis of simultaneous interpretation contribute to our understanding of translation, language, or the mind? Speech communication involves interaction between three dimensions: the communicators' intentions, their representations of the world, and the tool of language. Simultaneous interpretation brings the processing of intentions, content and language together in a type of cognitive activity probably not seen before this century. To describe it we are forced to look at these dimensions interacting. Mental representation is the best metaphor we currently have for a medium to accommodate all three and provide a way out of the impasse in which language is seen as encoding information, intentionality is assumed to be impenetrable (and at best, conveyed automatically in translation), and the operations of the mind are modelled, for want of something better, on those of its artefacts (information processing systems).

An activity like SI, though apparently complex, can be investigated through its products. But before description can be developed into explanation, more theory is needed about the three-way interaction between intentionality, representation and language. The research effort has naturally consisted in trying to zero in on SI from base disciplines in which we have strong theories, from linguistic descriptions of the product or cognitive models of the process, and where intentionality is concerned, from strong intuitions about some function of natural empathy. The challenge lies in combining these elements. Pragmatics forms a natural bridge between cognitive psychology and linguistics in studying how we exploit each other's mental abilities and resources for language communication. A cognitive-pragmatic analysis begins where cognitive modelling and linguistic description leave off. It is also radically psychological, recognising aspects of the world, intentionalities, and meaning in language only through evidence of their mental representations.

On the assumption that speech in context is used to convey information-with-intentionality, the cognitive-pragmatic approach can aim to construct an account of SI from its products, but formulated in terms of a theory of intermediate representations. In this concluding chapter, we summarise the procedure adopted to investigate SI, our inferences about meaning assembly and production, and the cognitive arrangements they suggest; and discuss their implications for current models.

Starting from a skeleton model of speech processing and some assumptions in cognitive science, we set out to fill the gap between decoding and re-encoding with an account of semantic and pragmatic processes, and then, with the help of data on failures and breakdowns in SI, proposed a configuration of ordinary cognitive functions compatible with this particular type of utterance processing.

Existing psycholinguistic models were adopted for peripheral operations like word recognition and articulation (on which in any case our data cannot enlighten us), assuming some demarcation between these and the core of speech processing in which there is cognitive involvement. We then compared input and output, and tried to describe their relationship, allowing ourselves to be carried along by successive failures of correlation to whatever 'level' of description turned out to be necessary to make generalisations. First, a thorough if perhaps disingenuous search for some regular input-output correlation in terms of constituent structure illustrated the problems facing an account of SI as a rapid linguistic restructuring operation which might be generalised and taught in terms of on-line strategies. When no significant degree of matching was found between constituents or lexical items, an inventory of TL discourse phenomena were assembled and their origins investigated. This pointed to different sources of meaning and communicative intentions contributing to the interpreter's version, and when timing was taken into account, revealed the sojourn in memory of these meaningful elements. We searched contemporary cognitive linguistics for a conceptual apparatus to accommodate the processes suggested by these findings, and found congenial accounts in Relevance theory, frame semantics, mental models theory and some post-Fodorian ideas about modularity, which together offered a basis for relating discourse features to a model of cognitive function in communication.

The most interesting aspect of professional SI to an outside observer is its fluent synchronicity, which suggests that simultaneous interpreters are not bound by a sequential logical structure dictated by word order. As sentences have barely begun to unfold interpreters often produce an expression with sentence scope: a connective, a phrase of saying or believing, a parenthetical reference to previous discourse, or a phrase reflecting a modality or propositional attitude; or even begin substantial propositions. Since these productions are often not translations of anything in the incoming utterance, and on the principle that there is no articulate speech without meaning, we looked for their sources.

Comparison of the synchronised versions showed that the content of the last utterance is by no means the only source of ongoing production. Interpreters rely on a wide range of extratextual information and pragmatic cues: knowledge or inference about the audience, about social conventions and standard conference arrangements, and general knowledge about history and society, are all seen to contribute. That there is more to translation than transcoding language forms has long been accepted; but to say that translators and interpreters 'use external knowledge' is not enough. Linguistic analysis shows that the text itself contains abundant information: the word order, prosody, connectives, lexical choices and anaphora of spontaneous speech contain numerous clues supporting the anticipation and rhetorical presentation that contribute to SI fluency. Secondly, and conversely, the existence of these pragmatic potentialities in speech, to which we can assume that natives or near-natives are sensitive, may also account for an interpreter's delaying, hedging or paraphrasing over what looks like straightforward vocabulary and grammar. In short, a pragmatic account is substituted for one in which the interpreter's constraints are explained in terms of logic, and her liberties in terms of style.

Sources for formulation may be roughly classified as follows:

(i)   *Thematic:* lexical choices reflect the evocation of wider structures, as predicted by frame theory; more conceptual information is involved than is available from basic lexical entries, and is used to expand lexical items by mentioning their known attributes.

(ii)   *Logical:* recent salient relations between propositions are maintained in extended logical structures, such as the protasis portion of a conditional, a context set up by the Head of a Topic chain, or premises awaiting a conclusion. Simultaneous interpreters maintain logical macrostructures (premises and conclusions, contrasts etc.) over 30s or more, allowing them to produce appropriate discourse markers, and to explicate these relations.

(iii) *Pragmatic:* interpreters use and express both implicatures and explicatures of the source discourse.

The ready accessibility of this contextual and inferrable information to simultaneous interpreters on line suggests that the interpreter assembles and maintains a complex mental model representing these features. This hypothesis is supported by the finding that several different TL words are generated in the discourse for the same SL referent, and by the use of superordinates; and by the finding, corroborating earlier studies, that SI is vulnerable to elements which cannot be quickly associated to an existing model, such as unpredictable new incidental qualifications, numerals and place names.

Secondly, SI on-line 'strategies' can be described in terms of different forms of natural inference followed by production from the representations inferred. SI literature usually distinguishes syntactic (or 'lexical') anticipation, based on the prediction of a structure, a collocation or a formula, from 'extralinguistic' anticipation. But the predictive power of surface forms alone is weak. In this corpus at least three different kinds of cues were found to license anticipation: social convention, propositional attitude, and logical deduction (shown in a conclusion voiced before the Speaker). *Saucissonnage,* or the pre-emptive segmentation of input dependent on downstream elements into self-contained units, was found to rely largely on the production of simple existential presuppositions. 'Stalling' often makes use of frame knowledge to expand items by referring to some of their known attributes, or else relies on cues to the Speaker's intentionality to insert connectives, or phatic and conative phrases.

In SI, interpreters draw on these cues to begin formulation rather than waiting for constituents required to form a parallel TL sentence. To optimise the assembly of viable meanings on line, SI processing appears opportunistic where necessary, following a Principle of (Pragmatic) Incrementality:

SI Principle of (Pragmatic) Incrementality

To produce speech before an utterance is complete, a simultaneous interpreter may draw either on a contextualised mental model, or on a logical or propositional form, which are more or less enriched stages of representation of a recent utterance. Different types of meaning (logical, thematic and pragmatic) may come in any order, and pragmatic or prosodic features relevant to the interpretation of a string can inform formulation before parts of its semantic representation.

The incremental assembly of meaning was tracked for parts of the corpus, including complex left-branching sentences, and represented in terms of a symbolic notation, which is used experimentally in the tabular transcripts. The main primitives used in this notation include projected syntactic and semantic structures (subcategorisation and selection frames), thematic roles, logical operators, and intentional states.

The evidence suggests that syntactic structure (involving long-range *syntactic* dependencies) does not of itself constitute an obstacle to SI. No significant decrement in performance or delivery was noted in connection with long or syntactically complex sentences, and the few Speakers' ungrammaticalities were ignored or circumvented. Over the longer sentences of the German source discourse, all three interpreters routinely generate and pursue their own sentence structure, using content from all sources as described above, and largely disregard the input structure except insofar as it delivers meaning. The mechanism by which formulation can be started in the absence of full propositions is summarised in a Placeholding Principle:

SI Placeholding Principle

In SI, incomplete or partly unresolved logical forms can be used for formulation as 'placeholders': provisional approximations standing in for referents, relations, or attitudes and illocutions which have not yet been adequately contextualised or resolved. These devices may include:

(i)   existential quantifiers and pro-forms (e.g. *this, something, what*) as place-holders for referents;

(ii)   existential presuppositions, presentative constructions or Aboutness functions (e.g. *(there) is a..; I'd like to discuss...; as far as... is concerned*), as place-holders for attributes and relations;

(iii) declaratives and assertions, as placeholders pending the clarification of modality.

Output structure is provisionally generated or expanded from something confidently evoked from input: logical (recursive expansions with dummy variables and connections), thematic (expansion of attributes, superordinates) or pragmatic (expressions of illocution and attitude).

Semi-enriched fragments, or partial propositional forms with phonologically-represented placeholders—such as a sentence with one or two unknown content words, as may occur in a technical conference—can thus, if necessary, be used to formulate output by default. (Where necessary, one may make do with 'Jabber-wocky'-level comprehension: even a bare phonetic form may go through to production slotted into a syntactic position in a sentence, without first being disambiguated as a name or an acronym, or even identified as a word in a particular language).

No processing unit which might be tracked from input to output can therefore be viably defined for SI in terms of syntactic or semantic chunks. Interpreters appear to be sensitive to the possible pragmatic values of relations marked on the surface of sentences as conditional, causative, interrogative, and so on, favouring delaying as far as possible to allow holistic or paraphrase processing. The Chinese-English interpreters, who were dealing with shorter, marked-off clauses, were often able to avail themselves of this option.

There is much debate in SI literature over the significance of the typology of the source and production languages. Comparing corpora in different language pairs, the differences observed in transformation patterns appear to some extent to be an artefact of the syntactic units of measurement: the Chinese clause is shorter than the German, while the Topic chain, a series of clauses sharing a Topic/Subject, may be longer than the German sentence. The German sentences in the corpus are 12s long on average, compared to 5.8s for the Chinese sentences. The German-English interpreters routinely begin their own sentence structures while the input sentence is unfolding. Chinese clauses, defined as a Subject or Topic (initial adjunct) plus a Verb phrase (or Comment) are significantly shorter, so that the Chinese interpreters more often have a whole clausal proposition available before formulating; but they frequently rearrange even those orders compatible with English.

The same kinds of sources for assembly were shown in both corpora, and all interpreters insert their own conative and parenthetical material, expand lexical items, re-order, paraphrase, and produce immediate holistic renditions which are difficult to analyse with any linguistic apparatus. But comparison of the two corpora showed an apparent equalising or centering of register and cohesive texture, as noted by Shlesinger (1989): in the German discourse, which is somewhat more formal, the interpreters supply connectives generously, and phrases like *I think* and *I hope that* are commonly used to express modalities marked on the German verb or in pragmatic particles *(soll, dürfte; auch, wohl)*; whereas the more abundant directive and rhetorical material in the Chinese corpus also receives sovereign treatment by the interpreters, but in the sense of being somewhat reduced.

What does SI suggest about intermediate representation in linguistic tasks? No-one has yet suggested how, in the passage from SL to TL required for translation, linguistic representations indexed to concepts might support parsing with compositional semantic assembly and integration with other knowledge. Instead, we have suggested that to be able to handle fast, abundant and unfamiliar material, SI must involve highly organised non-linguistic intermediate representations, maintained and revised over the medium term (for the duration of the task), constructed from a resident stock of semantic and pragmatic primitives with which to model input from many unfamiliar Speakers.

A mental model adapted to a specific task can be expected to maximise its task-specific efficiency. This principle would not favour language-specific forms as the format for intermediate manipulation (since there is no reliable one-to-one match between codons in different languages), but rather, we suggest, a conceptual-intentional language with a vocabulary of '{epr}': entities, their attributes, and relations between them evoked from its own stock of concepts, percepts, and representations of intentionality, as analogues of those denoted and connoted by a Speaker in a discourse. L1 and L2 expressions and structures would be indexed to this intermediate language. The engine for this mental model can be described simply as the human deductive device, using elimination rules (Sperber and Wilson 1986/1995: 83 ff.) and pattern-matching.

Pressure for efficiency in the mental model also explains the tendency observed in SI toward rationalisation and simplification of semantic structure, in which logical structures as well as thematic entities (for instance, pragmatically equivalent arguments in different clauses) are merged. This and other aspects of efficiency in intelligent comprehension can be summarised as follows:

Principle of Efficiency for an SI Mental Model

A mental model for SI is sensitive to context and relevance. It may represent vague epr (with more or less attribution) but not ambiguous or unresolved sense or reference. It integrates input logical forms with their associated current referents, generates their presuppositions and derives primary implicatures. It represents the results as concisely and efficiently as possible, eliminates redundancy and fuses input epr. The currency of referents in the model fades unless strengthened by repeated reference.

The pressure for incremental production leads to some erosion of semantic content by the natural simplification process of intermediate modelling, as described above; but it also disturbs the focal scale or perspective (the 'figure-ground' relationship) of the discourse, inasmuch as presuppositions may also become overt assertions: entities simply introduced by definite reference may be highlighted in presentative (existential) statements, or material introduced in a non-restrictive relative may by foregrounded by assertion in a Main Clause. In structural terms, there is a paratactic effect: an interpreter may build up the informational structure of a complex sentence by stating the presuppositions or propositional content of embedded material, or postponing marking clause-to-clause semantic dependency or pragmatic features such as illocutionary force. For a normally structured (semi-rehearsed) input discourse, this tendency results in a larger number of clauses in output, notably matrix and relative clauses, and increased use of anaphora for linking these clauses.

Potential dilution or distortion can also arise from the loose use of attitude and illocution markers like *I think* or *obviously*, which sometimes drift between clauses or are spontaneously generated with indeterminate scope, suggesting a distinct process of attachment into the representation (driven by more global inter-pretation in the Executive).

The approximations due to placeholding, merging, and the dismantling of hypotactic constructions, which may mark perspective, lead to some dilution of meaning or impact at the lexical and propositional level. However, these tendencies do not usually result in major distortion in terms of the overall communication, since much of the lost meaning is restored through pragmatic compensation at the production stage. Meaning which is expressed in input lexically and by word order may be restored in output by local devices which can be more easily applied in SI, like adverbials, modals, parentheticals and especially, prosodic colouring. Focus and perspective are largely restored in this way to make up for the paratactic effect on structure. This compensatory behaviour, centred on the relatively autonomous production system, can be summarised in a

SI Pragmatic Compensation Principle

The principle of efficiency in representation for understanding, and the need to approximate on line in SI, lead to a primary flattening and paratactic effect on the discourse. In successful SI, attention is focused by default on an Executive function which coordinates all cognitive, instinctive and task-normative inputs and compensates in the production stage for losses and shifts of perspective due to the nature of the task, or on the basis of judgments of relevance. The interpreter thus reclaims a degree of autonomy at this stage, assuming responsi-bility for the reconstruction of the pragmatic and ostensive dimension of the discourse in production, using local devices in the target language appropriate to the linear dependency of the SI process.

Since sentence-level framing of informational structure (e.g. by the deliberate choice of word order) is difficult in SI conditions, simultaneous interpreters make more use of local linguistic devices, and particularly any means of making more explicit any relations or references which may have been backgrounded or could not be fully rendered 'on the fly', such as prosody (stress, intonation), modals/adverbials, parentheticals, versatile connectives like *and*, 'equating' constructions ('*x* is a *y*'), and anaphora.

We can hypothesise that there are central processes which specialise in representing (MM), others in deducing, others in assembling (Assembler) or deciding (Executive), but that they share a common language of intermediate representation. This is also made necessary by the need in SI to derive and recreate the ostensive or communicative dimension of discourse. This task is illustrated in the different ways used in languages to express modality and attitude and to direct hearers to relevance: for example, both Chinese and German favour modal adverbs for expressing connectivity and attitudes, while English uses more prosody and parentheticals. In German, focus or perspective are often expressed in pragmatic variants on word order; in Chinese, by a range of devices including specific markers, or by contrast or elimination through ellipsis, repetition or topicalisation. English prefers stress and attitudinal or evaluative adverbs. To be recreated in production, this dimension must also therefore be represented, or at least 'presented': no definitive conclusion is possible on whether all such intentionality is propositional, and our model allows for some such meaning to pass directly as 'presentations', or affect, to the Executive. The idea is that one level of language, involving mainly those conative, attitudinal or evidential expressions which fall 'outside' the scope of sentence structure, may be triggered directly by affect without transiting propositional representation.

SI researchers have attributed *errors or failures* variously to linguistic competence, a lack of extralinguistic knowledge, or co-ordination problems. Failure, defined as a loss of intended meaning, was seen in our data on incidental qualifications, particularly when presented in original and unpredictable modifiers, and in numerals and proper names. Analysis of more serious or compound failure suggested an interesting relationship between syntactic, semantic and pragmatic processing: SI seems vulnerable to complex sentence structure only in the presence of a sudden influx of new or unfamiliar referents, or the absence of illocutionary marking. It is suggested that these two conditions respectively delay conceptualisation (in the mental model), and overall executive judgments on relevance and the Speaker's intentionality, forcing a temporary reliance on the assembly of uncontextualised input.

Compound failure was seen for dense, recited written text, which combines the three factors mentioned; but the responses to separate challenges on each factor (reference, structure, illocution) elsewhere in the corpus did not suggest a significant effect of any of them individually. This confirms the widely-held view among interpreters that SI is not suited to recited written text.

SI clearly demonstrates the need for pragmatic input in the primary assembly of basic, truth-conditional propositions, since certain features not marked in the SL need to be inferred for their mandatory marking in the target language, e.g. the Tense, Number and Boundedness required for English from Chinese. The frames evoked, intersecting with context, allow such inferences to be introduced into the model as set-membership representations and deictic indices which are then applied when these features are not marked on the current utterance.

A secondary level of pragmatic competence necessary for good SI was illustrated. Examples of pragmatic failure showed that additional implicatures must sometimes be inferred to build a model of the speech-act structure of an input discourse, which may be quite elliptical in terms of surface forms. Ultimately, for adequate representation and communication, a discourse may lack many things, but not illocutionary indicators and ostensive guidance. This was illustrated by the marked difference in performance from semi-rehearsed spontaneous text and recited written text (tested in the Chinese corpus). For the prepared but spontaneously delivered portion of the discourse, interpretation was clear and acceptably fluent, with some minor errors and omissions (incidental qualifications and numerals), while the recited continuation on the same topic, which combined a high density of new and unfamiliar referents, long-distance structural dependencies, and an almost total absence of directive or rhetorical packaging, posed major problems for SI, leading to virtual breakdown over some segments.

The study concentrated on developing a general process model from the corpus at hand, and was not designed to test or control for certain variables considered to be important in the literature, such as discourse-type, Speaker, language, and the interpreter's motivation or choice. The model provides the modular flexibility to accommodate changes in these parameters. Discourse type and subject variables are reflected in variations on routing and contributions from different components. Variations in the clarity of Speakers (whether phonetic or pragmatic), the interpreter's readiness, the depth of her conceptual assimilation on-line, or the voluntary effort she puts into packaging the message for her Addressees, can be expressed in terms of peripheral efforts, or of activity in the MM (conceptual cohesion) and/or Executive (secondary pragmatic processing, overall intentionality assessment, 'communicative management').

Reflecting the importance of situational awareness, in the German-English corpus, for which mock and live conditions were contrasted, differences between the versions of the interpreter at the event and those in the simulation were clearly visible in delivery, compensatory behaviour (more at the live event), familiarity and comfort in recovering referents, and confidence in making insertions.

In summary, while simultaneous interpretation appears to be technically constrained at certain points by the condition of simultaneity, by input characteristics like information density and ostensive packaging, and by the specific flexibilities of each language, these factors may be offset by *cognitive mobilisation* (the quality and coherence of the knowledge and awareness base for representation), and *pragmatic competence* for both comprehension and production. This potential emerges more clearly if we look beyond a narrowly cognitive, 'information'-based paradigm to recognise the volitional dimension which necessarily pervades all communication, and thus discern the realisations of both content and *vouloir-dire* in Speakers' and interpreters' discourse.

Implications for cognitive modelling

The model assumes limitations on cognitive performance based on psycho-linguistic findings, but allows that standard cognitive functions might be flexible enough to allow some configuration for specific tasks. The mental tools and resources traditionally postulated for language processing are, basically, input and output decoding and encoding devices, and memory or memories subdivided in various ways as suggested by different kinds of data from different disciplines. The subdivision we favour provides for a conceptual working memory, a deductive device (or inference engine) supported by pattern-matching, and an arrangement of linguistic knowledge which allows for cross-linguistic associations to be built up over time at the lexical level.

To summarise the cognitive architecture proposed: decoded fragments are combined with top-down information from the MM to partial or complete propositional forms; the resolved parts are represented in a conceptual language in the MM and integrated with implicatures derived by Relevance principles (so that the contribution of decoding and inference are merged). Higher-level explicatures are derived with the contribution of intentions and attitudes inferred from various sources. All these propositions and attitudes are available to an Executive which prepares their formulation, subject to additional clues, judgments and input from the interpreter's own self-monitored speech. Less resolved fragments are also briefly available from the Assembler to be translated and slotted in to output formulations ('shallow lexical processing'), but we suggest that in the best SI, formulation is fully grounded in the MM. Both sovereign formulation and partial translation draw on TL lexical stores, including long-term learned correspondences.

We suggested that the focus of *attention* in SI in normal conditions is on this secondary pragmatic assembly in the Executive, with some accessory attention to production. This Executive combines pragmatic assembly and judgment, coordinates the overall task, and directs the production system to infuse ostension and communicative features into the product, including compensation for losses and 'signal weakening' in the interpretation; in short, recreating the ostension to accompany the content.

The idea of a distinct conceptual *working memory* (MM) is based on the assumption, on grounds of efficiency, that we preferentially assemble and keep available the mental resources appropriate to an ongoing task. On the same argument, working memory should favour the most efficient storage format for immediate translation, i.e. a non-language-specific one (indeed, it seems that all linguistic activity involving cognition must pass through this stage). That format must be readable by all central processes, and by the output encoders; we have tried to describe an intermediate language which would meet these constraints. On the same principle, we may suppose that a subset of our lexicon is preferentially activated for a specific linguistic activity (cf. Gile's Gravity Model).

Lastly, we assume that we learn to adapt these mental resources to variations in the task. Some discussion of this last point is necessary, since the account presented so far has been pitched to cover SI tasks involving maximal inference and/or pragmatic reformulation. It is clear that for some interpreters in some task conditions, the *bilingual lexicon* may play an overwhelming role, while less constructive activity is required in the mental model. Professionals undoubtedly build up and refine a huge 'phrasebook', which may contain entire formulas (Levelt 1989), refined by habits of inter- and intra-linguistic association and selective suppression. An experienced staff interpreter in an international organisation, for example[1], where phraseology is relatively standardised and her basic MM is valid from one meeting and Speaker to the next, may draw systematically on such ready-made elements, and very little complex inferencing or sovereign formulation may be necessary.

In a corpus, these ready-made sequences, and the syntactic environment they generate, are probably not distinguishable from spontaneously assembled structure. This does not mean that meaning assembly and executive supervision are not there; simply that comprehension is facilitated by rich top-down support from the mental model, which contains certain well-established representations indexed to formulas: formulation fully exploits the phrasebook if it contributes to efficiency. The model is meant to account for the whole process, not just the parts which are accessible to conscious introspection by a practitioner; as researchers, we will find interpretive and constructive processes to be pervasive in speeches which interpreters felt to be quite straightforward.

The model is modular in the sense of allowing interaction between distinct processes, with some alternative routings and configurations, and some limitations on sequence; some feedback is allowed, but some forms of reanalysis or backtracking are costly. It is emphatically *not* 'modular' in the sense, quite persistent in the literature but apparently resting solely on a literal (mis)-interpretation of modularist doctrine in cognitive psychology, that the SI task can be broken down into sub-*tasks*. As Gerver suggested (seeing beyond the restrictive conditions of his own experiments to the reality of practice) 'at high task load, attention becomes almost unitary' (1976: 193). This is not a matter for SI theorising, but of the solidity of inferences which can be drawn in cognitive science. The basic principle of modularity is independent of the further question, to be explored by extended research, of what the modules really are. A cognitive function which draws on many specialised modules located in different parts of the brain can itself be at least 'interestingly' modular in the Fodorian sense. For instance, a metafunction that translates visual perception, episodic memories, and the propositional output from incoming discourse into a single central representational format, allowing integrated processing, might be interrupted, or slowed, by backtracking to check the details of these inputs (looking again, replaying auditory memory or remembering harder). Similarly, the finding that certain types of operations are disrupted by local lesions does not allow the inference that they correspond to subtasks which compete for attentional resources. Still less justified, particularly for training purposes, is the idea that a task like SI can be analysed into component tasks like 'listening' and 'speaking': these activities, done separately or in alternation, whether in experimental or spontaneous (e.g. conversational) contexts, are governed by different, sovereign goals, and consequently, *ab initio,* configure mental resources quite differently.

In regard to the *management of cognitive resources* in SI, Relevance theory and the Fodorian account of modularity suggest a refinement of the tripartite theory of efforts proposed by Gile (1995, 1997). Efforts for listening and production should only be significant, and possibly disruptive, when they demand special probing away from the centre, as in the case of difficult syntactic computation, phonological replay or conceptual/lexical retrieval. Our own analysis, and the notion of effort in Relevance Theory, suggest that the 'central' component of cognitive load in SI should be seen not as a 'memory' effort due to retaining language forms for processing, but as inferential effort needed to retrieve the contexts which yield relevant meaning, which can be assumed to increase

(i)   in proportion to the newness of epr (from the interpreter's point of view) which may require 'invocation' from encyclopaedic knowledge and/or integration into the MM, and

(ii)   in *inverse* proportion to pragmatic (ostensive) guidance provided by the Speaker, which makes contexts available in comfortable time for processing.

The fact that literary and poetic texts are unsuited to SI can also be explained in terms of relevance, and the time factor: in these uses, high cognitive benefits may be promised in exchange for greater inferential efforts involving several steps, which rely on the hearer's (and therefore interpreter's) having time to find multiple and complex contexts to develop inferences and negotiate the subtle gradations of weak implicature associated with such material.

Even if this proposed model of SI is debatable on many points, it is hoped that the introduction of pragmatic theory into SI research will contribute, firstly, to resolve a theoretical and methodological bottleneck: the question of how we can constrain the knowledge/contextual base used by the interpreter in a way that allows a workable model of meaning assembly. This possibility is opened up by the originality of the radical psychological approach, adopted notably by RT, in which meaning in communication is sought neither in the language itself (as in conventional semantics), nor in the world (which leaves 'context' too open-ended), but in the speaker/hearer's representations based on these sources.

Relevance Theory claims, essentially arguing from current theories of evolutionary psychology, that human comprehension is governed by the search for optimal Relevance, defined as optimal cognitive effects (new information, meaning) against minimal effort. In adopting his role, a Speaker declares an offer of cognitive effects to be derived from his speech. The motivated interpreter is conscientious (has thought about the task in advance and collected information) and attentive. In her mind there is already a virtual structure of expectations (strong assumptions) about the Speaker's reference base and intentions. As the speech unfolds, her decoders spontaneously deliver to her awareness not only logical and propositional forms, but also give access, essentially through content words, to a spreading web of associations which update and sharply structure this universe of potential context (the better prepared she is, the smoother the merge). As the first sentence of the speech unfolds, this potential is suddenly constrained towards the *relevant* contexts for deriving the intended meaning far more tightly than hitherto, by a powerful and precise tool—language—i.e. by *further* phono-syntactic-semantic aspects of the arrangement of the speech string. In case of residual indeterminacy, a sovereign listener simply continues to seek more context to the extent of his own interests, while an interpreter has a prior obligation: as a priority, pending a complete and explicit rendition, she must supply at least the raw material from which the end user can process his product, which may be only a bare semantic representation or phonosyntactic arrangement—a blueprint delivered to the TT listeners in the hope that they will find the contextual resources necessary to derive relevant effects—or a hint to the discourse structure derived from some non-propositional clue. On this account, interpretation that does not syntactically resemble the input is not due to some effort spent *re*phrasing or *re*formulating, but to the best formulation in TL of the (most relevant) meaning derived from the utterance as constrained, in the context then available.

The reality of the communication processes in translation deviates from idealised utterance comprehension or production models in two ways. Firstly, the traditional (Gricean) assumption in pragmatics about the 'cooperative' nature of communication was too strong, and has recently been revised (Sperber and Wilson 1995; Attardo 1997): Speakers may be more or less cooperative or capable, and their presentation may be more or less comfortable to interpret; interpreters may be more or less competent; and Addressees may be more or less aware. Secondly, translation allows the transfer of some partially decoded or understood material (as shown in our diagram by arrows leading directly from the Assembler to the Executive without transiting the mental model). In practice, interpretation will contain a mixture of more or less processed material, the proportion probably being closely correlated with quality.

Future research

Traditionally, SI research has been aimed explicitly at improving training and the quality of professional performance and practice, while only tentatively claiming to make an original contribution to cognitive science. Empirical studies have focused on investigating the effect of different variables on SI performance, such as language pair, rate of delivery, content, the interpreter's competence, and environmental factors.

Data involving production and a second language may appear less than ideal for research in descriptive (language-internal) linguistics. But in a wider cognitive science perspective, the unique conditions of SI (simultaneity, the change of language, and the task pressure for production quality) provide a unique window on the extent to which cognitive-linguistic functions can be configured to share resources. As a tool in the study of discourse comprehension, SI provides a unique and rich database of externally-paced, on-line paraphrase illustrating how formulation may proceed from minimal pragmatic and semantic elements rather than complete propositional or syntactic units.

In terms of peripheral processes, a closer examination of fluency and hesitancy patterns in the light of assumptions about SI processing may reveal that, at a very fine-grained level, listening and speaking are not *strictly* simultaneous but that rhythm and voice modulation hold the key to coordination between the two streams.

In terms of the search for the most significant variables in SI, we have argued that hypotheses about effort, attention or difficulty in SI need to be based on more complete models of intermediate representation, encompassing the pragmatic dimension. In methodological terms, physiological indicators are unlikely to yield precise data giving insights into the correlation between SI operations and effort. A more promising avenue for future research might lie in the careful manipulation of variables such as

- the type of text or discourse (but without constructing texts);
- the Speaker (accent and grammar), and
- the degree of support available to the interpreter from context, background knowledge, and intentionality marking in the discourse.

The use of external knowledge in comprehension is not in doubt, but a detailed account of its role can only be developed through corpus-based studies. Some of the key factors in SI processing proposed here might be explored by comparative studies of the performance effects of variables which can be manipulated without seriously disturbing the naturalness of input discourse. Specifically, we have predicted that (given professional competence, preparation and motivation) marked syntactic structure alone does not obstruct SI; that substance may be lost over high concentrations of new referents or qualifications; and that failure or breakdown will ensue when these two phenomena coincide in a passage, or when there is little or no pragmatic guidance in the form of connectives, intonation, and so on. Experiments could be mounted to test these predictions: the effect of the newness or familiarity of referents could be tested by introducing additional examples, qualification and proper nouns into real-life discourses; or by suggesting to a Speaker that his audience is keen on factual content. Varying the amount of secondary qualification and information, or of redundancy and/or delivery rate, might also illustrate interpreters' prioritisation patterns. It might also be instructive to see how interpreters respond to explicit requests, either for a very 'full' rendition, or conversely, for 'intelligent gisting', over a specific segment of discourse.

Other factors which deserve to be explored in contrastive empirical studies include cohesive texture (an important dimension of ostensive guidance); the presence or absence of Addressees; the effect of the interpreter's knowledge about her Addressees; the general effect of proxemics as a probable key factor in distinguishing the practice of SI from other modes, like court and community interpreting; and the specific problems associated with culture-bound discourses.

More generally, corpus studies are needed in a wider range of languages and discourse types; but the interplay between pragmatics and language form, as well as situation, mandates a thorough knowledge in the researcher of the languages involved, as well as a comprehensive picture of the situation of any discourse which is analysed.

Training and the changing SI environment

The IT school has developed what is probably still the most widely accepted interpreter training doctrine, and a recent survey of SI user expectations has confirmed the importance of situationality and communicative context, which have constantly been stressed by this school and other interpreter-researchers (Kurz 1994). The present study has focused on the importance of extratextual knowledge and clues to intentionality in SI, corresponding approximately to the variables of situation and Speaker. Contemporary SI practice is faced with new realities:

- increasing technicality and specialisation of the subject-matter, while some users in these conference genres state a preference for intelligent 'gisting' over verbatim completeness (Kurz 1994; Mackintosh 1994).
- fast and/or recited discourse, with increasing numbers of people enfranchised to public speaking, and longer lists of Speakers on each working day; and last but not least,
- newly emerging conference languages, with their differing background cultures.

Sentence structure-based strategies do not offer a response to these challenges; a more promising approach lies in recognising the importance of background and documentary information, and the ability to handle it (i.e. to organise an adequate mental model for each task), and the ability to adapt to a wide range of different Speakers, that is, to recognise individually and culturally variant expressions of intentionality.

There is no suggestion that the technicalities of pragmatic theory should be introduced into the SI training classroom. The impatient SI trainee will learn to wait for more context, and the assumption that a mental model is being constructed is safe enough that the cautious can be encouraged to 'say something' in the face of indeterminate input structure, in the assurance that they will naturally find the knowledge on which to base it: it would be perverse to teach the nature of presupposition, or Gricean maxims, for application on-line.

But the critical aspects of SI can be usefully illustrated through variety. In view of current trends in the practice of interpretation, the discourses used for training should reflect a wide range of Speakers, discourse types, and situations, particularly in the finishing stages, so that students may naturally become aware of the value of extratextual and background information, and develop a sensitivity to the intentional cues (and non-standard speech patterns) of different Speakers.

In the preface to this book we declared two ambitions: to redress the balance in research on interpreting by reinjecting some linguistics, and to introduce SI as a new and fertile source of data in the study of language use. If we have been successful, translatologists who have read this far, notably IT theorists, will acknowledge that linguistics is no longer what it was in the fifties and sixties and now offers a range of concepts and tools with which to capture aspects of language relevant to its professional users. The rejection of conventional linguistics in translation research has sometimes been justified rather glibly by the objection that 'everything depends on context'. Paradoxically, perhaps, this investigation into the pragmatics of SI, while confirming this principle, has shown how discourse itself constructs contexts, and that, in a real sense, there is more to 'bottom-up' processing than may sometimes be thought.

Elsewhere in SI research, linguistics had largely been sidelined for reasons which suggest a different kind of impatience: to solve the puzzle, or find the algorithm, by quantifying, classifying and decomposing into subtasks, assigning to modules, locating them in the brain, computing energy use, and calculating quality. But if it ignores the details of speech in communication, thus consigning to black boxes processes which are critical to our understanding, this superficially 'scientific' approach is condemned to remain no less speculative. If interpretation involves even a fraction of the conceptualisation, selective retrieval of context, and inference that this study suggests, then there is likely to be significantly more to the leap from MT (machine translation) and ST (speech translation, currently focused on recognising queries and responding) to simulating the exchange of ideas than what even the most spectacular advances in cognitive modelling and technology can resolve. But this remains to be seen, and this view is no doubt swayed by emotional factors. Besides, our own hypothesis of meaning assembly in SI is also presented in a symbolic formalism (in the tabular Appendices)—which is hereby submitted, for what it is worth, as a contribution to the cognitive modelling project. This researcher is more enthusiastic about what SI can teach us about human psychology for its own sake, through a better understanding of the relationship between thought and language.

Appendices

Appendix A   Parsing theory

Parsing theory has generally tried to reflect a direct relationship between the grammar and the parser, i.e. to show how sentences are parsed for comprehension or production by the application of a reader/hearer's linguistic competence in his native language, defined as a set of grammatical rules, and a lexicon of words and phrases which together can generate well-formed sentences in that language. The general description of the lexicon, the grammar and their interplay as applied to parsing research has been supplied by the dominant Chomskyan paradigm, from the phrase structure analysis and transformations of Syntactic Structures (Chomsky 1957) and Aspects of the Theory of Syntax (1965) through the refinements of Government and Binding Theory (Chomsky 1981, 1986), the Principles and Parameters approach and the latest version, Minimalism, which has yet to be implemented in parsing theory.

Sentence processing research has concentrated on deducing the mechanisms of the 'human parser' from experimental observation of responses to certain manipulated sentences. Processing breakdowns on over-complex constructions, or difficulties with 'garden-path' sentences like *the horse raced past the barn fell,* which force backtracking and reanalysis, are explained on different hypotheses about how rules of grammar or other parsing principles are applied to build up a representation of sentence structure. The difficulty lies in the application of modularity to language as it is classically conceived, in terms of distinct levels of phonology, lexical morphology, syntax and semantics, in which the knowledge base for the last, semantics, is not clearly distinct from general knowledge about the world. Modularity for language was understood by some to mandate a serial process in which representations are built at each level then passed on without feedback or interaction (e.g. Kimball 1973); these 'garden-path' models assume that memory limitations only allow one representation for an input string to be held at any one time, and predict a slowing of processing, or trouble ('boggle' effects) due to necessary re-analysis when a contrary sense emerges. Other researchers, observing that some syntactically ambiguous sentences are processed without trouble or delay, claim that alternative representations are computed in parallel, but — in recognition of the processing economy argument — allow various restrictions, for instance that semantic or pragmatic implausibility, the frequency of certain constructions in the language, or other factors rapidly eliminate all but one representation (Crain and Steedman 1985, Taraban and McLelland 1988, Tanenhaus, Carlson and Trueswell 1989, Gibson 1991). Parallel processing theories claim that the parser interacts with post-syntactic systems (semantics) when choosing which analysis to favour, and hence make more allowance for interplay with other levels of linguistic analysis — a more attractive hypothesis for an activity like SI, which depends on the on-line incremental integration of meaning from different sources.

Most recently, models of human parsing have evolved in two ways. Firstly, with increasingly ingenious experimentation and sophisticated analysis, the weight of evidence has shifted to favour a model of parallel, partly interactive models in which different types of information contribute to comprehension incrementally on-line. Secondly, advanced computer techniques and the streamlining of Chomskyan theory in its later versions have led to new attempts to implement the grammar in syntactic parsing, although these models recognise that semantic and contextual and discourse factors are at least as important as syntax. Gibson (1991), for example (who also provides an excellent review of the field) proposes an algorithm based on processing loads associated with various properties of sentences to account for most of the sentence-level phenomena so far reported: three of the properties are based on GB theory, and one principle (of phrase attachment) reflects the 'parsing strategies' tradition, but he concludes in recognising a number of other processing costs or weights, still to be defined, associated with non-syntactic or 'message-level' factors, i.e. 'lexical, semantic, pragmatic and contextual properties of linguistic structure'.

Another weakness inherent in the Chomskyan model of language in accounting for the course of comprehension over extended real discourse lies in its focus on core predicate-argument structure, neglecting items like connectives, epistemic and evaluative items, cohesive relations in discourse or the joint processing of multiple propositions, and in general, syntactically optional constituents like adjuncts and adverbials, which may carry significant epistemic and attitudinal cues. These are the most frequently occurring constituents in ordinary discourse, but traditionally the most neglected in the study of grammar (Jackendoff 1972: 47). 'Attachment' options for adjuncts may be moot in syntactic terms and depend entirely on pragmatic factors. Recently, two leading exponents of neo-serial parsing theory, L. Frazier and C. Clifton, have addressed the parsing of adjuncts and 'secondary' constituents in a 'construal' hypothesis which postulates two different types of constructions in discourse, primary and non-primary phrases (Frazier and Clifton 1996). Again, a broad and open-ended concession is inevitable: 'non-primary' phrases, it is suggested, are parsed not on the basis of structural relations (by Attachment), but are 'associated' and interpreted using an array of Principles: their precise operation is not further specified except to say that they include 'LF (logical form) and discourse principles [...] Gricean interpretive principles, an A Priori Plausibility Principle (Crain and Steedman 1985), a Referentiality Principle and 'focus and perhaps discourse salience', which perhaps 'determine the preferred host for predications of non-primary phrases' (ibid.).

Finally, some models based on recent Chomskyan theory, such as Head-driven licensing parsers (HDLPs) and Theta-attachment parsers (Johnson 1989;

Abney 1989; Pritchett 1988, 1992), appear to fail the cross-linguistic test in being too dependent on subcategorisation by phrase heads or θ-role assignment by the main verb, thus wrongly predicting delay in Head-last languages like German (Bader and Lasser 1994). Again, their critics stress the need for a principle of incremental comprehension 'to maximise the interpretation and comprehension of the sentence at each stage of processing (i.e. as each lexical item is encountered)' (Crocker 1994: 250).

More generally, parsing models have not integrated the contributions to on-line comprehension of aspects like word-meaning, referentiality and definiteness, presupposition and assertion, topicality and focus: in short, those dimensions of language in use which involve knowledge beyond the sentence or the text. Most sentence processing research is therefore difficult to apply to the study of SI because of this traditionally restrictive definition of the 'linguistic' dimension which it may legitimately address, and the relative lack of cross-linguistic validation (attempts to verify the leading parsing models for other languages than English have been perfunctory). Last but not least, even if an encapsulated pure syntactic parser exists, its operations would have to be so fast as to make a serial model of sentence processing empirically indistinguishable from the fine-grained interactive account we have adopted[1].

---

[1] i.e. Altman and Steedman 1988. Thanks to Steve Nicolle for making this point in an email discussion about parsing accounts compatible with Relevance Theory.

Appendix B   Sample of conference discourse unsuited to analysis

Stressed words are underlined, foreign words are in italics; p : discourse particle or marker (cf. 'so, well, that is'); **zheige** ('this') is often used in this way and is therefore glossed as '(this-)erm'.

('Mr Chairman..')
'a women de pinglun ren, a jiaoshou] gewei gechangde zheige zhuchiren baogaoren
er our commentators,   er Pr ofessor   all sessions'   erm   Chairmen rapporteurs

gen zheige..aa pinglunren haiyou women zaichangde gewei aa faxue de xianjin name
and erm ... er commentators and   us   here-present   all er   jurist   seniors p

gewei.. aa b.u.s.h.i tongren tamen gewei zheige aa xiansheng nushi name jin tian wo
everyone er not   colleagues they   all   erm er gentlemen ladies   p   today I

baogao zheige timu ne shi woguo fanjing sunhai peishang yi bushang a fazhi
speak on this-erm topic p is our nat'lenvironmt damage compensation & indemnity legal system

qianghua name cong gonghai zeren baoxian name zheiyang de yige zhidu lai
strengthen p from public nuisance liability insurance p this-kind   of a system to

zuo wei aa qianghua woguo a youguan gonghai huoshi fanjing sunhai de a zheige
treat as er strengthen my-country er [concerning public nuisance or environment damage er [this-er

peichang buchang zhidu de aaa yizhong a zheige fangfa he huoshi huxiang
[compensation indemnification system er a kind of a erm method and or   reciprocal

peichang huo cong jiu yao shuo jiuji zheige guandao.Jintian women zheige *aspect*
compensate or [from we should say emergency erm channel Today   we this-erm *aspect*

***environmental hazard compensation* zheige *system* jiushi shuo women jintian zheige**
environmental hazard compensation   this-erm *system* that's to say we   today this-erm

zhuti ne name YINGwen ta shiyong zheige *environmental* danshi women de zhongwen
topic p, well ENGLISH it uses this-erm *environmental* but   our   Chinese

ne women jiao zuo zheige YATAIDE zheige GONGHAI zhei liangge zhijian ne name
p   we   call it this-erm ASIA-PACIFIC erm *GONGHAi* these-two-between p,   p

feichang nan zheige lai - QUFEN. name suoyi ne wo zheige zheizhong wenzhang de
extremely hard erm to ... DISTINGUISH p   so p   I   erm   this-kind   paper

cai de shi GUANGYI.   he.jiushishuo zai yingwen fangmian jiushishuo fanjing de zhei
usedis BROAD-DEFINED and that is tosay in English   aspect   that is to say environmental this

zhong aaa zheige weixian fengxian aa zheizhong sunhai de KENENG de yige JIUJI
kind of errr this-erm   danger risk   er this kind of [damage POSSIBILITY-of an EMERGENCY

de zheige fangfa aa JIUJI ZHIDU.   **name women zhongwen ne name   shi   yatai a**
erm method er EMERGENCY SYSTEM - p   we   Chinese-(language) p - p is Asia-Pacific er

gonghai shi zheige a   aa aa *public nuisance* **a zheiyangde yige name** QIANZHE **ne**
gonghai is   erm er er err er *public nuisance* er this kind of   a..   well the FORMER p

zheige fanwei bijiao DA **zhe yingwen de zheige zheige mincheng bijiao** DA   **name**
erm   scope   is   LARGer er English   this-erm erm   term [is] LARGER (broader) p

zhongwen de zheige mingcheng a a keneng bijiao xiao.name suoyi wo jiu zhezhong
Chinese   this-erm   term   er er perhaps   narrower   p   so   I about this-kind of

HUANYIJU HUA SHUO zai women de zheige YINGWEN LIMIAN NE **name ta zhu**YAO **de**
in other words   in   our   this-erm   IN ENGLISH p p   it MAINLY

keneng ye shi zheizhong a   GONGHAI WEIZHU   yinwei zheige zheige fanjing
perhaps actually is this-kind of er MAINLY PUBLIC NUISANCE because the-erm the-erm environt

dangran baokuo gonghai   gen ziran baoy.u.   name   jintian women de zhuti.. etc.
of course includes public nuisance and nature conserv#ation -well today   our   topic is.. etc.

Interpreter (extract) : The topic is how to consolidate erm and to multiply erm the channels erm, for redress, erm for relief, compensation and indemnity in the case of public nuisances in this country, now erm we have called erm the Symposium [...] on the ENVIRONMENTAL HAZARD but erm in Chinese the word i- that we use is *gonghai* which means public nuisance or public hazard so a these terms are not exactly totally - erm congruent they don't cover exactly the same field so I'm going to talk in a very BROAD sense I'm going to talk about er the whole range of systems to obtain relief so erm *gonghai* which is defined as translated as public nuisance is not quite as wide as environmental HAZARD it seems so I've sort of made a trade-off between the two in other words most of the cases being discussed in fact in spite of the English title are public nuisances in the Chinese sense and the whole issue is how to provide indemnity and compensation for that kind of eh m ehh public HAZARD although of course environmental covers err a number of natural disasters so as in fact erm whatever term I use I will be covering systems of relief and compensation for....etc.

Appendix W1 'Würzburg' SI in a live conference situation: input and interpreter WL (analytic transcript)

Input syntax: N: noun; PN: proper noun; V: Verb; M,F,N,G,D,S,P: gender, case and number inflections; d: determiner; D demonstrative; *pro:* pro-form; # solecism; *Assembly:* representations for formulation combining input semantics and other cognitive and pragmatic sources. P_{-1}, P_0, P_1 propositions (previous, current,...) *Italics:* unresolved element; : resolved; i,j,k arguments; r relation; {} scope; φ predicate; $\Leftarrow$ results from; $\Rightarrow$ results in; > expect; >> infer. *Thematic roles:* THeme, AGent, PATient, EXPmcr, INSTrument, BENeficiary. SMALL CAPS: modal, intentionality; ? moot syntactic attachment, semantic scope or pragmatic domain; SA speech act. *Extratextual knowledge:* → access; SK situation knowledge; DK discourse knowledge; FK frame knowledge; MM mental model; ☺, ☻ indices of affect; ⊂ includes; ESF: European subsidy fraud; FRG: Fed. Republic of Germany.

0		German: input, syntax and English gloss	Assembly	Interpreter: WL output
1	M1	Vielen 'Dank 0 ø [NP much_A thanks	P_0 SA [i_ Thank j_ - (for k_)] SA : i = Speaker j, k → SK, DK	
2		Herr Doktor - @'Rump 1.2 Mr Dr - Rump	j : Rump → SK, DK: Rump =last Speaker	
3		für diesen - AKtuellen 2.2 - 'Überblick 3.1 [PPfor [NPd_A this - topical_A - overview	k : d this → DK, SK : = Rump's speech	2 THANK 2.4 you very much indeed -
4		zu dem 4.2 - Spe'zialthema [PPon [NPd_D the - special THeme	k + ... about special theme →SK, DK	Doctor Rump for having given@ us this. 5
5		des - Subven-'tionsbe'truges 7.2 NPd_G ofthe - subsidy fraud _G	SK, DK : subsidy fraud = special theme N r, N : r = identity	UP-to-date@ 5.8 overview - of. the.@ 7.2
6	M2	H Da einer der 'Schwerpunkte 9.3 - [CPsince [NPone_N d_GP ofthe focal-points	P_1 '$\Leftarrow P_0$ [Subj one-of main points >> given that P_0, then P_1	specific. - topic. of @ 8.6 SUBsidy 9.6 -
7		dieser -'Tagung 10.5 - [NPd of this-meeting_G	meeting →SK : 'symposium' →SK symposium themes	ffraud- 10.6
8		auf diesem - Be'REICH 12.3 [IPpron [NPd_D this - area	SK >> this area = sub. fraud FK : main points r area >> r : be in/on	- which isas I have said. 12.4
9		des - Subventionsbetruges 13.9 NPd_G ofthe - subsidy fraud_G	: this area = sub fraud P_i; a focus of the meeting be on subsidy fraud	one. of- the - 13.8
10		liegen soll 14.5 [VPV lie Modal should]	INTENT { P_1 }	main@
11	Mα	+ H ist es 15.6 - [CP is it-	cleft > $P_0 P_1$	points@ 15.2
12		vor allem auch [IP[AdvP above all also	P_1 [P_0 [IMP { 'also { ....}	which we-wish to deal with 16.8
13		für unsre 'ausländischen 'Gäste 17.9 - [PPfor [NPOUR_F foreign_N guests_P -	P_1 [P_0 [IMP { 'also { Ben foreign guests	- 17.5 in this. symposium 18.1

		German	Analysis	English
14		von GROßem Inter'esse 19.3 - [PP of greatD interest -	P1: [P0 SubJ {Interest IMP { Benforeign guests... }}]	- H and @ 19.2 this@ 20.5
15	M2 αβ	'WIE - die Er'fassung dieser 'Fälle 21.5 - [CPhow - NPd the apprehending dG ofthese casesP	P0 [how THeme[P2 Treat THemed cases...] d >> ? DK { cases in speeches M,R}	is a point which is -
16		die Herr Doktor Menenz und Herr Dr 'Rump 23.4 - ge'schildert haben 24.3 [CPC that [IP [NP PN Dr Men.N & Dr. RumpN [VPdepicted Aux have]	d : DK {cases in speeches M,R} WL: = some Europ. sub. fraud (ESF) cases P1 : THeme[Treat some ESF cases]	of- great. interest@ 22.5 - to. our foreign guests 24.4
17		H vom DEUTSCHen - Strafrecht 26.3 - [PPdp of/by-the GermanO - penal law] geIregelt ist 27.3 settled Aux is]	P0 how AGent German law Treat THeme someESF cases (Regulate ≡ Treat, deal with) P1 : [P0 Interest IMP { Benforeign guests...}}]	H I think @ 25.2 that @ it wi#be- especially 27 -
18	M3	+ Zu diesem Thema 29.2 - wird - [CP[PPON [NPdD this topic] Aux ?Fut/Pass	Fut/Pass V [SubJ __ , About P0]	INTeresting 27.9 -FOR our for eign guests to hear H 29.4 -
19		Herr Professor Doktor - O'dersky 31.7 - [[NPMr Professor Doctor - Odersky	: Subj SK = next speaker >> Fut >> Prof. Odersky will speak about P0	how CASes. 30.3 such as those outlined by @
20		'sprechen 32.5 speak	: Prof. Odersky will speak about P0	Juergen@ 32.4 Rump@ 33 -
21	M4	H als Präsi'denten [CPC ?as/when/if [NPPresident ?PI/ACC	SK (doc) > = Odersky is Pres...] Marked word-order: >> P0 [[THeme Odersky]	are- \deals with at the level. 34.4 - of
22		des 34.5 - deutschen 'Bundesgerichtshofs 36 [dG ofthe - German G Federal Court G	SK (doc) : P1 [Odersky is President of....] FK: 'President of ... ' : famous	th e. German@ \courts. 36.4
23		brauche ich V need PronN I	P0 [NEC V [AGent I THemeOdersky] SK, FK: 'I' [DUTY: Introduce	H
24		Herrn - Professor Odersky 37.7 - [NP PN Mr A - Prof. Odersky]	FK: Introd{AGent, PATient, BENef} Felic- itous only if most BENef don't know PATient	we have invited Professor Doctor 38 +
25		hier - NICHT here - not	here: SK: PAT's fame, BENef's knowledge Introduce (duty) NEC ; (logic) not NEC	H Odersky 39.7 - to
26		VORzustellen 39.98 to introduce	(introduce)	come and speak
27	M5 α	H als - Strafrechter 41.7 erlaube [CP ([NPCas/if - penal juristN allowFPS	P1 [? is jurist] ; (marked order): P0 SA[I SubJ allow BENef , ?jurist];	to us. on precisely this topic. 41.3 -I don't need to
28		ich mir [IP [NPPronN I [I' PronD myself	P0 [I SubJ allow BENef I >> P2 >> politeness	introduce
29		'nur 42.7 - [v only -	: politeness { SA {	him he-
30		den 'Hinweis [NPdA the indication]	P2 SA Indicate THeme P3	is - 43.the- Presidentand the

#		Text	Notation	Gloss
31		darauf 43.7 _PP_PrP thereon	P_3 [[Odersky	Chief @-
32		H daß Herr Presi'dent O'dersky 46 - [_CP_ C that [_IP_[_NP_Mr_N_ Pr es Odersky	P_3 [[Odersky	44.5 Judge of the Federal High \Court 46.1
33		früher 46.8 [_I'_ formerly	P_3 pastTense [[Odersky → SK (doc)	H - perhaps
34		'Leiter der - 'Strafrechtsabteilung 48.8 in - 'München war 50.8 [_VP_[_NP_N head d_G_ ofthe - Criminal Law Dept [_PPin_ - Munich [was	P_3 pastTense [[Odersky = N r PN FK: Head (x, y ; y = group, institution) PN = institution	I could-just- 48.1 indicate however - that. 49.6 Professor- Odersky
35	M5β	bevor e# [_CP_C before [_IP_ [_NP_ he	P_4 [past, then [[Odersky → SK (doc)	H was-
36		neunzehnhundert - 'dreiundachtzig 52.6 - Adv nineteen - eighty three	past [point time > change : became	51.3 the- Head. of. 52.5 the.
37		Präsident. [_NP_President_N_		Criminal. Law Department in.
38		des 54-Bayrischen Obersten Landesgerichts 55.4 [d_G_ ofthe - Bavarian_O_ Highest_G_ Province Court_G_	PN → FK, SK doc: P_4: 1983 Od became Pres of...	Munich 54.3H @ before. @ 55.4
39		und dann- neunzehnhundert achtundachtzig 57.5 & and [then - [nineteen eighty eight	& P_5 [past, then [point time [> change: became	nineteen eighty- three 56.5 - and. he@
40		Präsident - des Bundesgerichtshofs wurde 59.5 [_NP_President_N_ - [d_G_ ofthe Federal Court_G_ became]	DK: now {Od =President of Fed High Ct} P_5: Aspect completive	was. 58 also the President. of. the. Bavarian- 59.7
41		pause between speakers 4.5s		\High Court- 60.8 and.as. of. nineteen eighty eight he has become. 62.7 the-
42				President #n Chief Justice. of. the FEDeral High Court. 64.5 of the Federal Republic of
43		64 Vielen Dank [_CP_[_NP_much_A_ thanks	[i, THANK j _ (for k _)] SA: i = speaker; DK: j = Chairman	GERMany 66.5
44		Herr 'Vorsitzender 0.0 [_NP_Mr Chairman	j: Chairman	+
45		meine sehr verehrten Damen 1.4 - [_NP_ my _F/P_ [very honoured_P_ ladies_P_ -	j₂ vocative	0.0 H THANK you very much @Chairman. 1.7
46		meine 'Herren 2.6 [my _F/P_ gentlemen_P_]	j₃ vocative SK: j₄ colleagues	ladies. and. gentlemen 3.
47	S1	+ @mm wenn 5 @ - ein Räpräsentant eines Ge'richts. 7.4/0 [_CP_ ?when/if - [_IP_ [_NPd_ a _N_ representative _N_ d_G_ of-a/one _G_ court _G_	P_0 [P_1 hypoth. + indef. DK: _Subj_ [a repres...] ⊂ self	+ colleagues 5.9 +

#	§	German	Analysis	English
48		zumal eines Revis'ionsgerichts 9.4 [NPin-particlr [NPdG an appeal court G	DK: ⊂ self: > self as Appeal Ct judge / SK, FK: P_0 About speech/subject matter	H 8.2 I think@ @ when@- 9.6 H
49		@ refe'rieren soll 11 - [VP V make-speech Modal supposed]	P_1 INTENT/DUTY { self {about speech hypoth concept = present reality (rhetor.)	the-@ 10.5 representative.
50	S2	dann- ist - C then is -	P_0 present reality: I speak (now)	of a- 12.1
51		er wohl - [IP [NP heN [Modal Adv I-guess -	EVID (Subj I	a \court particularly
52		13.2 'schwerpunktmäßig @ [Adv focally	EVID (Subj {About [speech ⊂ main points]	a representative of@ 14.9 @-
53		darauf angewiesen 16.4 - [PP Pr-P thereon] advised	EVID { DUTY (Subj self > / INTENT { now { self {speak about...	15.7 a High Court- 16.4
54	S2α	über 17.7 - @ 'Rechtsfragen 19.1 - [PPabout/over - law questionsP -	...about subject-matter : legal issues	then I think- he- @ 18.8 has been@ 19.2
55		und zumal 20.3 - [& in particular	→ FK: law ⊂	asked to speak
56		'darüber zu berichten 21.6 [PPPr-P there-about [VP to report	(report ≡speak) ...about pro >P_2	principally about. 21.5
57		wie Rechtsfragen [CPhow [IP [NP law questionsP	P_2 how law issues THeme?	questions. of the.
58		DURCH 22.9 die Gerichte [PPby/through[NPd the courts P]	courts AGent/Path / FK: AGent courts decide THeme law issues	\law 22.8 -
59		bereits entschieden 'wurden 24.8 - [already[VPdecided were/have been] -	: Past completive { decided	and in particular 24.1 -
60		oder welche sich Probleme 26.5 [& or [IP[NPwhich FP#/ReflPass [NPproblems P	& ? √/√ P_3 indef problems #	he-@ H 25.7 -is asked.
61		sich da \stellen 27.3 - Refl/Pass Adv there pose	arise in {P_1, P_2} vague →FK	to talk on- 28.3
62	S3	# Das 28.7 soll [CP[NPPr that [shall/should	INTENT { $P_{-1?-n}$	decisions.already
63		auch [IP also	(Dir, link)	taken. by
64		die Leitlinie 29.9 - [NPd theN directing line -	FK: x Leitlinie of y : y expands x / >> P_{-n} = x (past, summary) >> of y	courts. 29.3 and the
65		für meinen - einführende n@ 32.2 Worte [PPfor [NPmy MS- introductory# words P	?Deixis: 'my opening words'(?past=x/fut=y) / DK: (?plans to speak later) fut=y	difficulties which the courts. 31.5 experienced. in taking these decisions 32.6 that-@ -
66		'hier 'sein 33.6 here [VP be]	SK ? here = now	so much. @ -

#	Sp.			
67	S4	In Ihrer 35.1/0.0 Tagung hat [CP [PPin [NP your-/their-/her meeting [Aux has	P_0 past [→SK, DK P_{-n} [	35.2/0.0 by way of intro
68		sich bereits her'ausgestellt 2.6 - [PNPReflPr [v-already [VP V emerged]]]] -	$P_0 >> P_1$ known from DK	DUCtion 1.6 + / I think
69		daß sich #Fe# unter dem 'großen Feld 5.8 [CPC that [P[NPRefl #fie# [r[PPunder[NPD the largeD field	P_1 [... [DK: MM subj.-matter structure: subject-matter is broad (top level ⊂ .....)	during the course- of this / seminar- 5.1 it- has@
70		das unter dem Generalthema 7.3 - er'faßt ist 8.4 [CPthat [IP [PPunder [NPD the general-THeme]] - [VPsubsumed is] -	DK: 'general theme' (WL→ subsidy fraud ⊂.....)	become. quite \clear 7.3 - / that. there is a very@
71		insbesondere zwei Komplexe 10.3 her'auskristallisieren 11.8 - [r especially [NPtwo issue-groupsp [vp Vout -crystallize] -	DK general theme ⊂ 1, 2 / P_1: Dir: highlight 2 issues >> $issue_1, issue_2$	9.2 LARGE RANGE of / QUEStions
72	S5	das Eine ist [CP[NPd the oneN is	P_0 [$issue_1 = P_1$	@m 12.1 -
73		das 'Anliegen 13.5 ?that([NPdNthe concern (s)	$P_1 →$ FK	under- 13.1 the-
74		das ver'ständliche Anliegen 14.6 ? that[NPdN the understandable concern(s)	P_1: SYMP {? EXPmcr DES {... P_2	@ 14 main topic - of subsidy
75		der europäischen Ge'meinschaft 16.7 - [NPd ofthe European o Community]]] -	P_1: {EC {DES{... P_2	\fraud 16 - and there are / TWO 16.9 -
76		nach- 'wirksamen strafrechtlichen Schutzzusicherung [PP after-/for- [NPeffective D penal-legal o protection-assurance	P_2: (?AGent) [INSTpenal law [effective [secure > [.... THeme	MAIN 17.7 - points of con\ / cern \firstly 18.9 H - there. is. / the desire. 20.2 -
77		ihre 20.3 - @- ihre @s 22.3 eigenen Fi'nanzsystems 23.4 + [NPd#her/your -her/your#G[own ofinance system G	P_2: THeme[EC finance system → FK / P_2: [INSTpenal law[effective [secure[THemeEC finances	of the European Com\munity / 21.2 - to- @ have- 22.5 / effective. criminal / legal
78		+	P_0: $issue_2$ ...	
79	S6	das 'Andere 24.8 - ?that [CP[NPd the other -	ATTENua { Contrast ? { P_1 [... $issue_2$ ...]	positions. to- 24.9
80		vielleicht mehr 25.7 [CP [PPperhaps [more		protect their own. 26 -
81		von der 'Mitgliedstaatsseiten 27.4 betonte [PP from/by dDFthe member-states-sideO [A stressed	P_1: Contrast ? {M-StatesAGent BEL/DES {IMP [...issue2...]	H financial interests 27.6 / and SECondy 28.5 - Member

No.		German	Analysis	English
82		**Anliegen 29.3** - ist concern - [$_{VP}$ is	P_0 concern$_2$ = (concern →FK, DK= {EXPer- ?BEL/DES- THeme}	*States - \also- 30*
83		das- 30.6 der- [$_{NP}$Pr *that*- [$_{NP}$d$_2$ *(of)the*	P_0 concern$_2$ =	*have- quite. leGITi mate*
84		@Ver- der Ver'besserung 32.8 - # - [$_{NP}$d *(of)the improvement* -	→FK: ☺ >> DES P_2 Subj >> M-States >> P_2 [Mem-States DES {improve ...	*concerns. 31.5 which THEY have emphasised @-*
85		@ der der Zusammenarbeit 34.7 [$_{NP}$ d$_2$ *the the cooperation*	P_2 [M-States DES { improve cooperation...	*33.1 they wish to ensure 34.1 -*
86		in der Kriminalitätsbe'kämpfung 36.4 - [$_{PP}$in d$_{DF}$ *the criminality-combatting*] -	(→ FK) P_2: [M-States DES {improve coop. fight crime }]	*\that. they can imPROVE cooperation - 36.5*
87	S7	meine kurzen 'Worte 38.2 - [$_{CP}$[$_{NP}$MY $_{F/P}$ *short*$_P$ words$_{Sp}$] -	P_0 [... γ>> this speech ...] → DK	*in the area 37.2 -of the fight against@ 38.8*
88		@ gliedern sich[$_{IP}$[$_{NP}$ are-articulated	→ FK structure, component parts →divide, assemble	*/crime 39.3 -*
89		deshalb 40.2 auch in diese beiden \Teile 41.1 [, *hence also* [$_{PP}$in d these$_{F/P}$ two$_P$ parts]	P_0: INTENT {this speech ⊂ these two parts these two → DK: issue/concern$_{1, 2}$	*and@ I@ 40.5 \hope. that*
90		+		*my@ 41.8 - brief presentation*
91	S8	H 42.7 Der europäische 44.4 [$_{CP}$[$_{NP}$d, *the European*$_N$	P_0 [Subj...] DK, pause →text	*will deal with BOTH. 43.9 of. these. \aspects.44. 6*
92		Subven'tionsbetrug 45.9 - 'wird - *subsidy fraud*] C Aux - ?*will/Pass*	subsidy fraud → FK fraud , MM ☺ ...>?Fut/Pass Vφ	+
93		das ist [$_{CP}$[$_{NP}$Pr *that is*	P_1 [$_{CP}$ pro$_{Subj}$...	H
94		hier in Ihrem Kreis [*here* [$_{PP}$in [$_{NP}$*your/her/their* $_D$ circle	→ SK > φ	*46.2 European subsidy 47.9 @*
95		schon ge'sagt worden 48.8 - *already/indeed* [$_{VP}$said Aux been -	>> pro =P_0 P_1: P_0 has been said before → DK	*- -fraud- 48.3 - as has*
96		in der Bundesrepublik 'Deutschland 51 [$_{PP}$in [$_{NP}$d$_{DF}$ *the Federal-Republic Germany*]]	P_0 Eur. sub fraud 'ESF')$_{Subj}$... [in FRG.. > Fut/Pass φ	*been said. al ready 49.9 - is* @ a -
97		durch 51.8/0.0 den - @Pa@n [$_{PP}$through [$_{NP}$d$_A$ *the* - Pa#	P_0 THeme ESF in FRG INST NP >Fut/Pass Vφ	@ @ *51.8/0.0 /crime- 0.7*
98		in den siebziger 1.6 Jahren' [$_{CP}$[$_{IN}$ d$_0$ *the seventy years*$_{Sp}$] -	P_0 THeme ESF.. INST NP.. past >> Pass >Vφ (P_1 THeme NP ...in1970s)	*which- -*
99		eingefügten 2.7 P-V inserted$_0$	(P_1 THeme NP inserted in 1970s)	*has been- 2.1 en /shrined- 2.7*

#		Text	Notation	Translation
100		**Paragraphen** paragraph_A	P_0 ESF... _INST_[Article... inserted in 1970s] > Pass $V\varphi$	- in -
101		**zweihundertvierund'sechzig 4.5** - two hundred four and sixty	... _INST_[Article 264 ...	the- 4.2 legal \system 4.6 of. the Federal Republic of Germany
102		**des Strafgesetzbuches 5.8** - [_NPD_ ofthe penal code_G	P_0 _INST_[of penal code > Pass V → FK, DK: penal code ⊃ law_Agent	
103		**gegen - Subven'tions betrug 7.6** - [_PP_against subsidy-fraud -	]?[...against subs. fraud] > Pass$V\varphi$ ⊕law against ⊕fraud: cancel	by means of its insertion. in paragraph
104		**'MITerfaßt 9.1** [_VP_ co-covered]	P_0 Φ_0: _THeme_ESF covered in FRG by _INST_[....	two sixfour 8.5 - of. the. 9.7 H
105		-		
106	§9	**und damit 10** - [_CP_& and Pr-P there-with	{ P_{-1} ?domain ⇒ >P_0 }	German.
107		**dür-@ 11.1** - Modal Aux # migh--	?BEL + DES {P_{-1} ⇒ P_0}	penal \code. 11.5 +
108		**das ist** [_CP_ d that is	[_CP_pro_{Subj}....	+
109		**'AUCH schon** [_IP_ also [already/indeed	also > past φ > =said	
110		**zum Ausdruck gekommen 12.6** - [_VP_[_PP_ to expression come]-	>> pro =P_0 P_1: P_0 has been said before → DK	and 12.5 - as has already been said@13.6
111		**dürfte** - Modal Aux might/should	: BEL + DES { P_0 {...	during the course.
112		**der 14.6** - [_IP_[_NPD_ the_? -	d	of this-\Sym/posium 15.5 this-16.5
113		**der 'Schutz 16.3** - d_N the protection -	P_0 { P_1 [φ = protect	
114		**der des** [_NPD_ GP ofthe d_G ofthe	r d	therefore means.
115		**Finanzsystems 18.1** - finan.cial system_G -	: MM= PATIENT	that. 17.5 the -protection.
116		**des des Mißbrauchs** [_NPD_NS ofthe d_NS ofthe abuse_G	r : MM = ⊛ THREAT >> r = against, from	of the- 18.8 financial
117		**der Subven' tionen 20.5** - [_NPD_? the subsidies _GP -	r : subsidies ⊃ fin. system = PATIENT	\system@ 20.7 -
118		**@der europäischen Ge'meinschaften 22.6** - [d ofthe European _O Communities_P	FK: r =granted by: P_1: protect x from y	and the. 21.3 abuse- of. the. 23 subsidies
119		**in unserem Land 24.3** [?_V_[_PP_ in [_NP_our _DS_ country/province]]	P_0 { P_1 ?[in Germany	granted by the European
120		-		Community 24.8

121	in Kern 26.1 - [$_{PP}$in core]	P_0 { P_1 ?[in core	+
122	be'friedigend [$_{V'}$ [satisfactory$_{adv}$	P_0 { ?{ SATIS { P_1	are@ 26.4 -
123	und vor allen Dingen 27.9 [& and [$_{PP}$ above all	& [IMP { P_0 { P_1	now @m 28
124	in gleicher 'Weise 29.7 [$_{PP}$in same$_{DS}$ way	>> P_0: BEL { SATIS { $P_1 \equiv P_2$ > P_2 { φ_2 {i,j...}	+ protected@ 29.7
125	wie der Schutz [$_{Adv}$ as/how [$_{NP}$d the protection	φ_2 (i) = φ_1 (x) >> $\varphi_1 = \varphi_2 = \varphi$ protect	-
126	der deutsch 30.4 [d$_{FG}$ ofthe German$_H$	j = German....	by means of@ 31
127	des deutschen Subventionssystems 32.3 - d$_G$ ofthe German$_{GS}$ subsidy system$_{GS}$] -	j ...subsidy system P_0: φjEEC = φj Gny	core. legislation 32.1 -
128	er.FASST sein 33.3 [$_{VP}$covered be]	(in German law) P_0	in. our legal system. 33.6 - and.
129	+		protection 34.7 - of the
130	St0 Die Rechtsprechung des Bundesgerichtshofs [$_{IP}$the$_N$ jurisprudence d$_G$ ofthe Fed. High Ct$_G$		Community's financial interests
131	hat sich [$_{IP}$ hasRefl		are equated 37.1 - with the
132	mit dem Tatbestand [$_{PP}$with d the$_D$ offence-material		protection-of- Germany's.
133	wenn auch nur in - einzelnen. Beziehungen [$_{CP}$ though[$_{IP}$vP yet only[$_{PP}$in individual aspects		own \interests. 39.7
134	befassen müssen [V concern Aux must]		
135	Die Probleme -- [$_{NP}$d the problems...		

Appendix W2 'Würzburg' SI in a live conference situation: input and interpreter WL (synchronised transcript)

Source discourse is in bold, word-for word English gloss in regular face, and the synchronised interpreter's version, in italics.

Syntax: some case, number or gender marking is shown in subscripts on the gloss, e.g. ACC accusative; FEMPL, NOMSING etc.

Pauses: - short + longer; Filled pause: @ ('ah', 'er(m)'). In the English text, - marks syllable-lengthening; e.g. the-; a final . (full stop) indicates a 'clipped' syllable ending (short extra beat); ## solecisms (or phonetically unclear); H audible intake of breath.

Pitch: rising: ' or / precedes syllable; falling: \ precedes syllable. Stressed syllables are shown in CAPitals.

[Moderator]

Vielen 'Dank Herr Doktor - @'Rump 1.2 für diesen - AKtuellen 2.2 'Überblick 3.1 + zu dem 4.2 -
Many thanks Mr Doctor - Rump for this - topical overview - to the -
.... *THANK 2.4 you very much indeed - Doctor Rump for having given@*

Spe'zialthema des- Subven-'tionsbe'truges 7.2 + H Da einer der \Schwerpunkte 9.3 - dieser - 'Tagung 10.5 -
special theme of subsidy fraud Since one of-the focal-points - of-this meeting -
us this. 5 UP-to-date@ 5.8 overview- of. the.@ 7.2 specific.- topic. of @ 8.6 SUB sidy 9.6 @ /fraud- 10.6 -

auf diesem - Be'REICH 12.3 des - Subventionsbetruges. 13.9 liegen soll 14.5 + H ist es 15.6 - vor allem auch für
on this area of-the - subsidy fraud - lie should is it - above all also for
which is. as I have said. 12.4 one. of- the - 13.8 main@ points@ 15.2 which we- wish to deal with 16.8

unsre \ausländischen 'Gäste 17.9 - von GROßem Inter'esse 19.3 - 'WIE - die Er'fassung dieser 'Fälle 21.5 -
our foreign guests - of great interest - how- the apprehending of these cases -
- in this. symposium 18.1 - H and @ 19.2 this@ 20.5 is a point which is. of

die Herr Doktor Menenz und Herr Doktor 'Rump 23.4 - ge'schildert haben 24.3 - H vom DEUTSCHen - Strafrecht 26.3
that Mr Doctor Menenz and Mr Doctor Rump depicted have from/by-the German penal law
great. interest@ 22.5 - our foreign guests 24.4 H I think @ 25.2 that. it wi#be-

- ge.regelt ist 27.3   +   Zu diesem Thema 29.2 - wird -   Herr Professor Doktor -   O'dersky 31.7 -
- regulated is   To this topic will   Mr Professor Doctor -   Odersky -
especially 27 - INTeresting 27.9 - FOR our foreign guests to 'hear H 29.4 -   how CASes. 30.3 such as those outlined by @

'sprechen 32.5 -   H als Präsi'denten   des 34.5 - deutschen 'Bundesgerichtshofs 36 - brauche ich Herrn - Professor
speak   as President_ACC ofthe   - German Federal Justice Court-   need I Mr_ACC Professor
Jürgen@ 32.4 'Rump@ 33 -are- \dealt with at the level 34.4 - of the @ German@ - \courts. 36.4   H we have invited

Odersky 37.7 -   hier -   NICHT VORzustellen 39.8 H   als   Strafrechtler 41.7 erlaube ich
Odersky -   here -   not introduce   as   penal jurist allow I
Professor Doctor 38   +   H Odersky 39.5 - to come and speak to us. on precisely this topic. 41.3 -   I don't need to

mir 'nur 42.7 - den 'Hinweis darauf 43.7   H   daß Herr Presi'dent   O'dersky 46 - früher 46.8 'Leiter der -
to-me only - the indication thereon   that Mr President   Odersky - earlier leader of-the -
introduce him. he- is- 43 the- President and the Chief @- 44.5 Judge of the Federal High \Court 46.1 H-   perhaps I could-

'Strafrechtsabteilung 48.8 - in - 'München war 50.8 bevor er# neunzehnhundert - 'dreiundachtzig 52.6 -   Präsident.
penal law department - in - in Munich was   before he nineteenhundred threeandeighty -   President
just- 48.1 indicate however - that. 49.6 Professor- Odersky H   was- 51.3 the-   Head. of. 52.5 the.Criminal.LawDepartment

des 54 -Bayrischen Obersten Landesgerichts 55.4 und dann - neunzehnhundert achtundachtzig 57.5 Präsident - des
of-the Bavarian Highest Province Court -   and then -   nineteenhundred eightandeighty   President of-the
in.Munich 54.3 H @ before @ 55.4 nineteen eighty-   three 56.5 -   and. he@ was. 58 also the

Bundesgerichtshofs wurde 59.5 ....pause between speakers: 4.5 s.........
Federal High Court became.
President. of. the. Bavarian- 59.7 \High Court- 60.8 and. as. of. nineteen eighty eight.he has become. 62.7 the-President #n
Chief Justice. of the FEDeral High Court.64.5 of the Federal Republic of

[Odersky]

Vielen Dank Herr 'Vorsitzender (0.0) meine sehr verehrten Damen 1.4 - meine 'Herren 2.6 + @mm wenn 5 @ - ein
Many thanks Mr Chairman   my very honoured ladies -   my gentlemen   if/when -   a
GERMany   0.0 H THANK you very much @Chairman. 1.7 - ladies. and. gentlemen 3   + colleagues 5.9

Räpräsentant eines Ge'richts 7.4 zumal eines Revis'ionsgerichts 9.4 @   refe'rieren soll 11 -
representative   of-a   court   especially of-a   appeal court   make-speech supposed
+   H   8.2 I think@ @ when@-   9.6 H the-@ 10.5 representative.

dann- ist er wohl -   13.2 'schwerpunktmäßig @   darauf   angewiesen 16.4 - über 17.7 +   'Rechtsfragen 19.1 -
then   is he 'I-guess'   focally   thereon   advised   about/over   law questions -
of-a-   12.1 a \court particularly a representative of@14.9   @- 15.7 a High Court- 16.4 then I think- 16.4 he- @ 18.8 has been@ 19.2

und zumal- 20.3 'darüber zu berichten 21.6 wie Rechtsfragen DURCH 22.9 die Gerichte bereits entschieden 'wurden 24.8 -
and especially -   thereabout to report   how law questions through/by   the courts   already   decided   were
asked to speak principally about.   21.5 questions of the. \law 22.8   - and in particular 24.1 -

oder welche sich Probleme 26.5 sich da \stellen 27.3 -   #Das 28.7 soll auch   die   Leitlinie 29.9 -   für meinen   - für my -
or which #unacc problems   unacc there pose   That   shall/should also   the   directing-line   - for my -
he-@ H   25.7   -is   asked.   to talk.. on-   28.3 decisions. already taken. by courts. 29.3 and the difficulties which the

- einführende   n@   32.2 Worte   'hier   'sein 33.6   +   In Ihrer 35.2/0.0 Tagung hat sich bereits
introductory   words   here   be   In your   meeting has unacc already
courts.31.5 experienced in taking these decisions 32.6 that-   @   - so much@-   35.2/0.0 by way of introDUCtion 1.6

her'ausgestellt 2.6 -   daß   sich #Fe#   unter dem 'großen Feld 5.8 das unter dem Generalthema 7.3 -
emerged -   that   unacc #   under the large   field that under the   general theme -
+   I think during the course-   5.1 it-   has@   become.   quite   \clear 7.3 -

er'faßt ist 8.4 -   insbesondere zwei Komplexe 10.3 her'auskristallisieren 11.8 -   das Eine ist das 'Anliegen 13.5 das
subsumed is -   in particular two complexes   out-crystallize -   the one is the concern   the
that. there is a   very@   9.2   LARGE.   RANGE   of   QUEStions   @m 12.1 -   under- 13.1   the-

ver'ständliche Anliegen 14.6 der europäischen Ge'meinschaft 16.7 -   nach-   'wirksamen   strafrechtlichen
understandable concern   of-the European   Community -   towards(for) -   effective   penal-legal
14 main topic -   of subsidy   \fraud 16   - and   there are TWO 16.9 -   MAIN 17.7 -   points of con\cern \firstly18.9 -

Schutzzusicherung   ihrer 20.3   - @   @   ihre   @s   22.3   eigenen Fi'nanzsystems 23.4   +
protection-assurance   of-her/its/their -   it   S(GEN)   own   finance system
H there. is.the desire. 20.2 - of the European Com\munity 21.2 - to- @ have- 22.5 effective. criminal legal

das 'Andere 24.8 -   vielleicht mehr 25.7 von der 'Mitgliedstaatsseiten 27.4   @   betonte   Anliegen 29.3   ist das-
the other -   perhaps more   from the   Member-State-side   stressed   concern -   is that/the
positions. to- 24.9   protect their own. 26 - H   financial   interests 27.6 and SECondly 28.5 -Member States -\also-30 have-

30.6 der-   @Ver-   der   Ver'besserung 32.8   @   der   der   Zusammenarbeit   34.7 in   der Kriminalitäts-
(of-)the   imp-   of-the   improvement   (of)the   (of)the   cooperation   in   the   crime-
quite. leGITimate concerns.31.5 which THEY have emphasised@- 33.1 they wish to \ensure 34.1 -   that.   they can   imPROVE

be'kämpfung 36.4 - meine kurzen 'Worte 38.2 -   @   gliedern sich deshalb 40.2 auch in diese beiden \Teile 41.1
combatting   my   short   words   articulate unacc   hence   also   in these two   parts
cooperation   36.5 - in the area 37.8 - of the fight against@ 38.8 \crime39.3 -   and@   I@ 40.5   \hope. that

+   H   42.7   Der   europäische 44.4   Subven'tions betrug 45.9 -
          The   European   subsidy   fraud -
my @ 41.8 - brief presentation will deal with BOTH. 43.9 of these. \aspects.44.6   +

'wird -   das ist hier in Ihrem Kreis schon ge'sagt w orden 48.8 -   - in der Bundesrepublik 'Deutschland 51 -
is/PASS -   that is here in   your circle   already   said   been   in the Federal Republic   Germany -
H 46.2   European   subsidy   47.9 @   - ~fraud- 48.3 - as has been said.   already 49.9   - is@   a- -   @

durch 51.8/0.0 den - @Pa@n in den siebziger 1.6 Jahren EINgefügten 2.7 Paragraphen zweihundertvierund'sechzig 4.5
by/through   the   #   in the seventies years   inserted   paragraph   twohundredfourandsixty
@ 51.8/0.0 /crime- 0.7 which-   has been- 2.1 en /shrined- 2.7 in -   the- 4.2 legal \system 4.6

des Strafge'setzbuches 5.8 -   gegen -   Subven'tionsbetrug 7.6 -   'MITerfaßt 9. -
of-the penal-law-book -   against -   subsidy   fraud -   also-covered
of. the Federal Republic of Germany   by means of   its insertion. in paragraph twosixfour 8.5 -   of.

und damit 10 dür-@   11.1 das ist 'AUCH schon zum Ausdruck gekommen 12.6 -
and with-that mi-#   that is also   already to   expression   come
the. 9.7 H German. penal \code. 11.5   +   and 12.5 -   as has already been

dürfte   der 14.6 -   der -   'Schutz 16.3 -   der-   des   Finanzsystems 18.1 -
might   the   the   protection -   (of-)the   of-the   finance system
said@ 13.6 during the course.of this- Sym/posium 15.5   this- 16.5 therefore means. that. 17.5 the- protection. of.

des des Mißbrauchs der Subven'tionen 20.5 -   @der europäischen Ge'meinschaften 22.6-   in unserem Land 24.3 -
of-the of-the abuse   of-the subsidies -   of-the European Communities -   in our country
the- 18.8 financial /s y s tem@ 20.7 -   and. the. 21.3 a\buse-   of. the. 23 subsidies granted by the Euro

in Kern 26.1 -   be'friedigend und vor allen Dingen 27.9 in   gleicher 'Weise 29.7 -
in core -   satisfactorily and above all (things)   in   same way -
-   are@ 26.4   now   @m 28   +   protected@ 29.7 -
pean Community 24.8

wie der Schutz der deutsch 30.4 des deutschen Subventionssystems 32.3 - er.FASST sein 33.3
as the protection of-theFEMPL German of the GermanNOMSING subsidy system covered be
by means of@ 31 core. legislation 32.1 - in. our legal system. 33.6 - and.

protection 34.7 - of the Community's financial interests - are equated 37.1 - with the protection-of-
Germany's. own \interests. 39.7

Appendix W3 'Würzburg' SI in mock session: input and interpreters WA and WB (analytic transcript)

Input syntax: N: noun; PN: proper noun; V: Verb; M,F,N,G,D,S,P: gender, case and number inflections; d: determiner; D demonstrative; *pro:* pro-form; # solecism; Assembly: representations for formulation combining semantics and other cognitive and pragmatic sources. P.1, P0, P1 propositions (previous, current,...) *Italics:* unresolved element; : resolved; i,j,k arguments; r relation; {} scope; φ predicate; ⇐ results from; ⇒ results in; > expect; >> infer. *Thematic roles:* THeme, AGent, PATient, EXPrncr, INSTrument, BENeficiary. SMALL CAPS: modal, intentionality; ? moot syntactic attachment; semantic scope or pragmatic domain; SA speech act. *Extratextual knowledge:* → access; SK situation knowledge; DK discourse knowledge; FK frame knowledge; MM mental model; ☺, ☻ indices of affect; ⊂ includes. ESF: European subsidy fraud; FRG: Fed. Rep of Germany.

	German input, syntax and English gloss	Assembly	Interpreter WA	Interpreter WB
1	M1: Vielen 'Dank 0 ø [NP much_A thanks	P0 SA [i_ Thank j _ (for k_)] SA : i = Speaker j , k → SK, DK		
2	Herr Doktor - @'Rump Mr Dr - Rump	j : Rump → SK, DK : = last Speaker		
3	für diesen - AKtuellen 2.2 - 'Überblick 3 [PPfor [NPd_A this - topical_A - overview	k : d this → DK, SK : = Rump's speech	THANK you 3 -	2.7 THANK you Doctor. RUMP@
4	zu dem 4.2 - Spe'zialthema [PPon [NPd_D the - special theme	k+... about special theme →SK, DK	Doctor@ /RUMPF.4.7 for GIVing us that@	+
5	des 5.6 - Subven-'tionsbe'truges 7.2 NPd_G ofthe - subsidy fraud_G	SK, DK : subsidy fraud = special theme >> N r N : r = identity	- clear 6.9 - OVERview 7.7 on.	for- that. VIEW 7 - of @ -
6	M2: H Da einer der \Schwerpunkte 9.4 - [CPsince [NPoneN d_GP ofthe focal-points	P1 ?⇐ P0 [Subi one-of main points >> given that P0, then P1	the specific TOPIC. 9 of fraudulent	the view of @ 9.6
7	dieser -'Tagung 10.6 - [NPd of this -meeting_G	meeting →SK : 'symposium' →SK symposium themes	obtention. of	s- FRAUD. 10.7 -
8	auf diesem - Be'REICH 12.6 [PPon [NPd_D this - area	SK >> this area = sub. fraud FK: main points r area >> φ: be in/on	SUBsidies 11.1 h - one of the 12.1	in SUBsi/ dies 11.9 -
9	des - Subventionsbetruges [NPd_G ofthe - subsidy fraud_G	: this area = subsidy fraud P1: one focus is on subsidy fraud	M MAIN points 14	P and that is-@ 14
10	liegen soll 14.7 [VP V lie Modal should]	INTENT {P1}	of our symposium 15.2 - WAS	one of-@ 15.4
11	M2α: + H ist es - [CP is it -	cleft > P0 P1	to be	the important
12	vor allem auch [IP [AdvP above all also	P1 [P0 [IMP {'also {....}	devoted 16.4 -	points 16.6 -

#				
13	für unsre 'ausländischen 'Gäste 18 - [$_{NP}$our$_F$ foreign$_P$ guests$_P$	P_1 [P_0 [IMP {²also { $_{Ben}$foreign guests}	precisely to that SUBJect 18.1 -	of this SEMi/nar 18.1 - and.-
14	von GROßem Inter'esse 19.5 - [$_{PP}$ of great$_D$ interest -	P_1 : [$P_{0\,Subj}$ {Interest IMP {$_{Ben}$foreign guests... }}]	and I think. that 19.6 this is of	its 19.2 very important 19.9
15	M2αβ: 'WIE 20.3 - die Er'fassung dieser 'Fälle 21.7 - [[$_{CP}$how - [$_{NP}$d the N apprehending d$_G$ ofthese cases$_P$ -	P_0 [how $_{THeme}$[P_2 Treat $_{THeme}$d cases...] d >> ?DK { cases in speeches M,R}	great interest. 20.5 to our foreign GUESTS. they	I think for our. FOReign guests 21.4 -
16	die Herr Doktor Menenz und Herr Doktor 'Rump - ge'schildert haben 24.5 [$_{CP}$C that [$_{LP}$ [$_{NP}$PN Dr Men.$_N$ & Dr. Rump$_N$ [$_{VP}$depicted Aux have]	d : DK {cases in speeches M,R} = some Eur. subsidy fraud (ESF) cases P_1 : $_{THeme}$[Treat ^{some} ESF cases]	REALLY like to know 22.5 + H 25 HOW	to rea- 22.3 - t-to /KNOW 23.3 - HOW 24.5
17	H vom DEUTSCHen - Strafrecht - [$_{PP}$d$_D$ of/by-the German$_O$ - penal law] gelregelt ist 27.4 settled Aux is]	P_0 how $_{AGent}$ German law Treat $_{THeme}$ ^{some} ESF cases (Regulate = Treat) P_1 : [P_0Interest IMP {$_{Ben}$foreign guests...}}	such cases - 26.2 AS presented. by. Doctor Mennen n	CASES 26.7 - @. which Dr Rump
18	M3: + Zu diesemThema 29.3 wird - [$_{CP}$P$_0$n [$_{NP}$d$_D$ this topic] Aux ?Ful/Pass	Ful/Pass V [$_{Subi}$ __, About P_0]	Doctor Rumpf. 28.5 - are regulated under German cri minal LAW 30.9 -	has reFERRed to 28.8 - are in fact- @
19	Herr Professor Doktor 31.1 - O'dersky 31.9 - [[$_{NP}$Mr Professor Doctor - Odersky]	: Subj SK = next speaker >> Fut >> Prof. Odersky will speak about P_0	now. @	TREATED in Ger man LAW31.7 -
20	'sprechen 32.7 speak	: Prof. Odersky will speak about P_0	Professor	and
21	M4 : H als Präsi'denten [$_{CP}$C ?as/when/if [$_{NP}$President ?P/ACC	SK (doc) > = Odersky is Pres...] Marked word-order : >> P_0 [[$_{THeme}$ Odersky]	Doctor ODERtsky's 33.5 going	THIS is. an ISSUE. 33.6
22	des 34.7 - deutschen 'Bundesgerichtshofs [d$_G$ ofthe - German$_G$ Federal Court$_G$	SK (doc) : P_1 [Odersky is President of...] FK: 'President of...' : famous	to address precisely that /THEME 35.4 - $^{<R}$	that 34 - $^{<R?}$ Doctor Walter ODERsky will speak / to 36.6
23	36.3 brauche ich V need Pron$_N$ I	P_0 [NEC V {$_{AGen}$ Speakr$_{THeme}$ Odersky} SK, FK: Speakr's DUTY : Introduce	he 36.9 - hardly	-
24	Herrn - Professor Odersky 38.1 - [$_{NP}$ PN Mr$_A$ - Prof. Odersky]	FK: Introduce {AGent, PATient, BENef} Felicitous only if most BENef don't know PATient (Odersky)	37.7 needs any	he's President and Chief Justice

#				
25	hier - NICHT here - not	here →SK: PATient's fame, BENef's knowledge >> Introduce (duty) NEC (logic) not NEC	intro	of the Federal
26	VORzustellen 40.1 to introduce	(introduce)	DUCtion 38.9 I think. @for 40 as	High Court of /JUStice. 39.8 I hardly need
27	M5α: H als - Strafrechtler erlaube [CP[NPS/if] - penal jurist_N allow_FPS	P₁ [? is jurist] P₀ SA [I_Subj allow _BENef ↪ ijurist] ; marked order	you know he's. the. 41.5	to introDUCE him TO you 42 -
28	ich mir [IP [NP Pron_N] I [I' Pron_D myself	P₀ [I_Subj allow _BENef I : maxim flouted >> politeness { P₂	President of the. Federal	as-
29	'nur 43 - [I' Adv only -	: politeness { SA {	High	a.
30	den 'Hinweis [NP_A the indication]	P₂ SA Indicate_THeme P₃	Court of	criminal
31	darauf 44.3 PP Pr-P thereon		JUS/tice 44 -	LAWyer 44.3 -
32	M5β: H daß Herr Präsident O'dersky 46.4 - [CP C that [IP[NP M_N Pr es Odersky	P₃ [[Odersky	- I'd just like to point OUT	I'd simply like @ to.
33	früher [I' formerly	P₃ pastTense [[Odersky → biodata	that. 47.2 @ -	/SAY 47
34	'Leiter der - 'Straf rechtsabteilung 49.3 in - 'München war [[VP[NP N head d_G ofthe - Criminal Law Dept [PP in - Munich [was	P₃ pastTense [[Odersky = N r PN FK: Head (x, y ; y = group, institution) ; PN = institution	President ODERsky 48.8 - used to head. 51 -	+ P that @- Doc tor Walter ODER Sky 50.4 - used
35	bevor e# [CP C before [IP [NP he	P₄ [past, then [[Odersky →biodata	the-	to be 51.8 - @
36	neunzehnhundert - 'dreiundachtzig 53.3 - [Adv nineteen - eighty three	past [point time > change : became	@ CRIMINAL 52.3 - @ @	the-@ 53.4 -
37	Präsident. [NP President_N		LAW 54.3	@m +
38	des - Bayrischen Obersten Landesgerichts 56.3 [[d_G ofthe - Bavarian_O Highest_G Province Court_G	PN → FK, SK biodata : P₄ : 1983 Od became Pres of...	+	@m
39	und dann - neunzehnhundertachtundachtzig & and [then - [nineteen eighty eight	& P₅ [past, then [point time [> change : became	the 57 Federal. Supreme Court	-MAIN @ 56.8 - crim inal /JUDGe.57.8-
40	Präsident 59.1 - des Bundesgerichtshofs wurde 60.4 [NP President_N - [d_G ofthe Federal Court_G became]	DK: now {Od =President of Fed High Ct} P₅ : Aspect completive	in- @ BaVARia. in MUNich 60.2 -	IN@ - the. Highest Court 59.8 -

41	*pause between speakers: 4.5 secs*		before becoming President. of the. -	in \BaVARia. 60.9 and he-. in NINEteen ninety two he be came. 62.6 President
42			High Court of JUStice 63.5 + ^{R>}	and Chief Jus tice of the Fed eral High Court
43	**S1: Vielen Dank 65.1/0** [CP [NPmuchA thanks	[i_ THANK j_ (for k_)] SA : i = speaker ; DK : j = Chairman		in \KARLsruhe 0.6
44	**Herr 'Vorsitzender** [NPMr Chairman	j₁ : Chairman		-
45	**meine sehr verehrten Damen 2.2 -** [NP my F/P [very honouredP ladies P -	j₂ vocative	THANK you 1.1 very much /Chairman 2.1	THANK 1.2 you very much indeed- @
46	**meine 'Herren 3.6 +** [my rF/P gentlemen P]	j₃ vocative SK: j₄ colleagues	- ladies and /gentlemen 3.4	/CHAIRman 2.8 ladies and /GENTlemen 3.7
47	**S2:@mm wenn 6@ - ein Räpräsentant eines Ge'richts.** [CP ?when/if - [IPi,NPd a N representative N dG of-a/one G court G	P₀ [P₁ hypoth. + indef. DK : subj [a repres...] ⊂ self	+	+
48	**zumal eines Revis'ionsgerichts 10.7** [NPin-particlr [NPdG an appeal court G	DK : ⊂ self: as Appeal Court judge SK, FK: P₀ *About speech/subject matter >> ? law c⊂ourts ⊂ cases...*	when 10 - somebody. -	WHEN. 8 - a.-
49	**@ refe'rieren soll 12.2 -** [VP V make-speech *Modal* supposed]	P₁ INTENT/DUTY {self {about speech hypoth = present reality (rhetoric)	who represents a /court. 12.3	a - /COURT 11.9 -
50	**S2α: dann- ist -** C then is -	P₀ present reality : I speak (now)	particularly a court of	is supposed
51	**er wohl 14.3** [IPNP heN [*Modal Adv* I-guess -	EVID (subj I	apPEAL.13.8 is asked.	to talk about 14 -
52	**'schwerpunktmäßig @** [*Adv* focally	EVID (subj {About [speech ⊂ main points]	to give a SPEECH 15.5	this ISS/UE 15.3

#	German	Logical / semantic	+	English (i)	English (ii)
53	**darauf angewiesen 17.6 -** [pp Pr-P thereon] advised -	EVID { DUTY (Subj self > INTENT { now { self {speak about...	+		+ then
54	**über - @ 'Rechtsfragen 20.6 -** [pp about/over - law questions_P -	...about *subject-matter* : legal issues	+		of course- 18.5 +
55	**und zumal-** [& in particular	→ FK : law ⊂			+
56	**'darüber 22.9 zu berichten** [pp Pr-P there-about [vp to report	(report ≡ speak) ...about *pro* >P_2		obviously- 21.7 he- is going	he HAS-
57	**wie Rechtsfragen**[cp how [ip [np law questions_P	P_2 how law issues THeme?		to talk	MAINly. 22.1 -
58	**DURCH 24.1 die Gerichte** [pp by/through[np d the courts _P]]	courts AGent/Path → FK: AGent courts *decide* THeme law issues >> φ		about.legal - /Issues 24.4 -	to- -
59	**bereits entschieden 'wurden 26.1 -** [already[vp decided *were/have been*] -	: Past completive { φ decided	+	and the way in which. legal +	discuss-@ 24.4
60	**oder welche sich Probleme** [& or [np[np which _FP_#/_Refl/Pass_[np problems _P	& ? √/∨ P_3 *indef* problems #	+	ISSues are - are 27.5	- legal ISSues 25.7 -
61	**sich da 'stellen 28.7 -** _Refl/Pass_ Adv there pose	arise in {P_1 P_2} *vague* → FK	+	are dealt with B	and HOW legal iss ues have been 27.5 -
62	**S3: # Das soll** [cp [np Pr that [shall/should	INTENT {$P_{-1?-n}$		the courts 30.4	H@ n- TREATED. 29.4 by. /COURTS 30.8
63	**auch** [p also	(Dir, link)	+	and the - decisions that	+
64	**die Leitlinie 31.3 -** [np d the_N directing line -	FK : x Leitlinie of *y* : *y* expands x >> P_{-n} = x (past, summary) >> of *y*	+	are taken BY the courts.	+
65	**für meinen - einführende- n@ Worte** [pp for [np my _MS_ introductory_# words _P	*?Deixis* : 'my opening words' (*?past=x/ fut=y*) DK : (*?plans to speak later*) >> *fut =y*		and @ 33.1 - the way in which the cases. are \dealt with 34.9 -	and @. how. - they go about 34.1 -
66	**'hier 'sein 35.1** here [vp be]	SK ? here = now	+		+
67	**S4: In Ihrer Tagung 37 hat** [cp [pp in [np *your/their/her* meeting [Aux has	P_0 past [→SK, DK P_-n [	+		\TREATing these cases 35.4 - — and THAT's basica lly what I shall try and do /HERE 37.7 -

68	sich bereits her'ausgestellt 39 - IP[NPReflPr [V'already [VP V emerged]	$P_0 \gg P_1$ known from DK	in. the. - symPOSium	y-
69	daß sich #Fe# unter dem 'großen Feld 42 [CPC that [IP[NPRefl #fie# [I'[PPunder[NPDP the largeD field	P_1 [... [DK : MM subject-matter structure : subject-matter is broad (top level ⊂ .....)	so /far40.4	/Y_OUR- 40 - m\MEEting 41.2 +
70	das unter dem General thema 43.6 - er'faßt ist 45 - [CPthat [IP[NPunder [NPDP the general-theme]] - [VPsubsumed is] -	DK : 'general theme' (WL→ subsidy fraud ⊂.....)	+	h-has @ alREADy 45.1 -
71	insbesondere zwei Komplexe her'auskristallisieren 48.5 - [I' especially [NPtwo issue-groupsP [VP V out - crystallize] -	DK general theme ⊂ 1 , 2 / P_1: Dir : highlight 2 issues $\gg$ $issue_1$, $issue_2$	it has emerged. 48.2 that there are	disCUSSed@ 46.2 + @TWO 47.5 - speCIFic
72	S5: das Eine ist [CP[NPd the oneN C is	P_0 [$issue_1$ = P_1	TWO MAIN 49.4 -	issues@ 49 - IN - the OVERall ISSue that
73	das 'Anliegen ?that([NPdN the concern (s)	$P_1 \to$ FK	ISSues 50.5 -	ISSue that
74	das ver'ständliche Anliegen [? that([NPd N the understandable concern(s)	P_1 : SYMPath {? EXPmor DESire {... P_2	@%	you're - re/FERRing 51.7 -
75	der europäischen Ge'meinschaft 53.7 - [NPdG ofthe European o Community]]] -	P_1 : {EC {DES{... P_2	first of all 53 - the approximation	@wwa- the FIRST is the- 54.4
76	nach- 'wirksamen strafrechtllichen Schutzzusicherung [PP after-/for- [NPeffective D penal-legal o protection-assurance	P_2 : (?AGent) [INSTpenal law [effective [secure > [.... THeme	- the NEED 56.5 @ for the European Community	quite. under STANDable 55.7 - % % th- deSIRE
77	ihre 57.9 - @- ihre @s eigenen Fi'nanzsystems 60.6 [NPd,her/your - her/your,G [own o finance system G	P_2 : THeme[EC finance system $\to$ FK / P_2 : [INSTpenal law [effective [secure [THemeEC finances	to have 58.8 - effective.@ legal protection 61.1 -	of the European ComMUNity 59.5 - to have @ 60.5 -its own
78	+			finANcial system
79	S6: das 'Andere 62.1 - ?that [CP[NPd the other -	P_0 : $issue_2$ ...	@ to protect its /FINances. for	legally pro/TEC ted 63.1 -

#	German	Structure	English (col 1)	English (col 2)
80	vielleicht mehr 64.6 [CP [IP perhaps [more	ATTENua {Contrast ? {P_1 [... issue $_2$ ...]	in/stance 63.8 - and @	and the OTHer 64.3 -
81	von der 'Mitgliedstaatsseiten betonte [PP off/from/by $d_{DP}$the member-states-side$_O$ [A stressed	P_1 : Contrast ? {M-States$_{AGent}$BEL/DES {IMP [...issue$_2$...]	the OTHer.	which comes from member
82	Anliegen 66.5 - ist concern - [VP is	P_0 concern $_2$ = (concern →FK, DK = {EXPer - ?BEL/DES- THeme}	issue. 66.3	/STATES 66.5 - and
83	das- 67.7 der- [NP Pr that- [NP d? (of)the	P_0 concern $_2$ =	that @ per/haps is a concern more for the member	a/GAIN 67.6 - this is something that they're
84	@Ver- der Ver'besserung 70.1 - # - [NP d (of)the improvement -	→FK: : ☺ >> DES / P_2 Subj >> Member-States >> P_2 [Member-States DES {improve..	/STATES 69.2 - is. the.	particularly KEEN /onn 69.9 - which is-
85	@ der der Zusammenarbeit [NP d?² the the cooperation	P_2 [Member-States DES {improve cooperation...	need 71.5 -	- that- 72.1 - there should
86	in der Kriminalitätsbe'kämpfung 73.8 - [PP in d_DF the criminality-combatting] -	(→ FK) / P_2 : [Mem-States DES { improve coop. fight crime }]	to imPROVe. 73.4 -	be 73.1 - a- better
87	S7: meine kurzen 'Worte 75.6 - [[CP[NP my F/P short$_P$ words$_P$] -	P_0 [...?>> this speech ...] → DK	cooperation in combatting.	cooperATion 74.8 in - the fight
88	@ gliedern sich [IP[NP are-articulated	→ FK structure, component parts → divide, assemble	CRIME 76 -	AGAINST 76.4 -
89	deshalb auch in diese beiden \Teile 78.6 [I·hence also [PP in d these$_{F/P}$ two$_P$ parts]	P_0 : INTENT{speech ⊂ these two parts these two → DK : issue/concern₁, ₂	and what I have. to say -	criminALity 77.3 - and-
90	+		fits 79.1 - under BOTH of	therefore-@79.2 I will make@m 80.3
91	S8: H Der europäische [CP[NP d? the European$_N$	P_0 [subj:...] DK, pause → supplied text	those.. @ concepts and	- my-. divide my statement -
92	Subven'tionsbetrug 82.5 - 'wird 83 - subsidy fraud] C Aux - ?will/Pass	subsidy fraud → FK fraud, MM ☺ ...> ?Fut/Pass Vφ	Issues 82.1 - I'm going.	into- 82.3 two PARTS 83 -

#				
93	**das ist** [CP[NPPr that is	P_1 [CP pro_{Subj}...	to address.	H European-
94	**hier in Ihrem Kreis** [PPin [NPyour/her/their]D circle	→ SK > φ	fraudulent obtention	@ -
95	**schon ge'sagt worden 85.4 -** already/indeed [VPsaid Aux been -	>> pro =P_0 / P_1: P_0 has been said before → DK	of SUBsidies.86 -	SUBsidy
96	**in der Bundesrepublik 'Deutschland 87.7** [NPdDF the Federal-Republic Germany]]	P_0 Eur. sub fraud 'ESF')Subj... [in FRG.. > Fut/Pass φ	IN Europe. 86.7 and it's alREADy	fraud. 86.1 -- as alREADy been SAID@ 87.4 -
97	**durch den 88.7 - @Pa@n** [PPthrough [NPdA the - Pa#	P_0 THeme ESF in FRG INST NP > Fut/Pass Vφ	been pointed out. @ that 88.8 - this is	in. this particular
98	**in den siebziger Jahren'** [CP[PPin [NP d0 the seventy yearsP] -	P_0 THeme ESF..INST NP... past >> Pass >Vφ / (P_1 THeme NP ...in 1970s)	something. that 90.8	semi/nar 89.4
99	**eingefügten** P-V insertedO	(P_1 THeme NP inserted in 1970s)	+	+ / s- @
100	**Paragraphen 92** paragraphA	P_0 ESF... INST[Article... inserted in 1970s] > Pass Vφ	+	- / <R
101	**zweihundertvierund'sechzig** two hundred four and sixty	... INST[Article 264 ...	% is 92.9 @	R> /TREATed 93 -
102	**des Strafgesetzbuches 94.4 -** [NPdG ofthe penal codeG -	P_0 INST[of penal code > Pass V φ / → FK, DK : penal code ⊃ law_AGent	REGulated 93.7 in federal	in German law 94 - in
103	**gegen - Subven'tions betrug 96.3 -** [PPagainst subsidy-fraud] -	]?[...against subs. fraud] > Pass Vφ / @law against @fraud : cancel	Germany BY@ 95.1 the. penal	/article 95 - two six
104	**'MITerfaßt 97.6** [VP co- covered]	P_0 $Φ_0$: THeme ESF covered in FRG by INST[....	/code.96.6 there' re. specific	\~FOUR 96.7. - of @.
105	-		/paragraphs	
106	**S9: und damit 96.7 -** [CP& and Pr-P there-with -	{P_{-1} ?domain ⇒ >P_0 }	that were. 98.7 -	the criminal /CODE 98.9
107	**dür- @ - Modal Aux # migh- -**	?BEL + DES {P_{-1} ⇒ P_0 }	introduced	+
108	**das ist** [CPd that is	[CPpro_{Subj}...	in the	+

#				
109	'AUCH schon [IP also [already/indeed	also > past φ > =said	penal code.	+
110	zum Ausdruck gekommen 99.4 - [VP[PP to expression come] -	>> pro =P_0 P_1: P_0 has been said before → DK	in the. SEVen/ties 101.1	in /GERMany 101.3 -
111	dürfte 102.8 - Modal Aux might/should	: BEL + DES { P_0 {...	+	and. has-s al\READy
112	der - [IP[NPd₇ the₇	d	+	been said in. this /SEMinar 103.8
113	der 'Schutz 105..2 - d_N the protection	P_0 { P_1 [φ = protect	+	+
114	der des [NPd GP ofthe d_G ofthe	$r\ d$	+	the. 106.3 +
115	Finanzsystems 107.3 - finan.cial system_G -	: MM= PATIENT	+	proTECTion 107.6
116	des des Mißbrauchs - [NPd_NS ofthe d_NS ofthe abuse_G	r : MM = ⊗ THREAT >> r = against, from	the point being	of @ -
117	der Subven' tionen109.5 - [NPd₇ the subsidies GP	r : subsidies ⊃ fin. system = PATIENT	to 109.6 -	th-e- 109.7 of the fiNANcial
118	@der europäischen Ge'meinschaften 111.5 - [d ofthe European o Communities_P	FK : r =granted by : P_1: protect x from y	@ pro/DECT 111.2 - the European	resources of the European
119	in unserem Land 113.5 [?_V [PP in [NPOUR DS country/province]]	P_0 { P_1 ?[in Germany	community's fin ances for.bein.	Co/mmunity 113.2 - is-
120	-		mis/Used. 114.3	-
121	in Kern115.2 - [PPin core]	P_0 { P_1 ?[in core	from mis- being mis/Used 115.6	there-fore. 115.6 +
122	be'friedigend [V' [satisfactory/adv	P_0 { ?{ SATIS { P_1	+	+
123	und vor allen Dingen [& and [PP above all	& [IMP { P_0 { P_1	+	@
124	in gleicher 'Weise 118.5 [PPin same_DS way	>> P_0 : BEL { SATIS { P_1 = P_2 > P_2 { φ_2 {i,j...}	and. 117.2 @	dealt with 117.9 -
125	wie der Schutz [Adv as/how [NPd the protection	φ_2 (i) = φ_1(x) >> φ_1 = φ_2 = φ protect	basically 118.4	I think satis
126	der deutsch [d_FG ofthe German_#	j = German....	+	/FACtorily 119.5
127	des deutschen Subventionssystems 121.6 - d_G ofthe German_GS subsidy system_GS -	j ...subsidy system P_0: φjEEC ≡ φj Germany	this is something that @121.2 is -	- and. dealt with @ 121.1 -

		(in German law) P₀	
128	er.FASST sein122.7 [$_{VP}$covered be]	122.1 covered BY our penal	in.the /same /WAY 122.4 -
129	SI0: +	code.123.2 in the SAME way 123.9 -	as-@ the- 124 -
130	Die Rechtsprechung des Bundesgerichtshofs [$_{IP}$[$_{NP}$the$_N$ jurisprudence d$_G$ ofthe Fed. High Ct$_G$	AS it would be if it were to concern	budget of the. 124.9 - GERMan 125.8 @ -
131	hat sich 126.2 [$_{IP}$ has Refl	GERMAN. state	GOVern ment. is
132	mit dem Tatbestand 128.4 [$_{PP}$ with d the$_O$ offence-material	FINances 127.7 - the- @	proTE Cted 127.4 -
133	wenn auch nur in 129.6 - einzelnen. Beziehungen 130.7 [$_{CP}$ though[$_{IP}$ yet only[$_{VP}$in individual aspects	/COURTS @ 130.7 +	@ the. -e 129.5 +
134	befassen müssen132 [V concern Aux must]	HAVE handed down	highest @ 131.5 -
135	Die Probleme 133.6... [$_{NP}$d the problems...	a numberof /ver dicts @ 133.6 -	federal COURT 132.7 @ has had to DEAL with
136		not very many but some -	cases of this kind. 134.9 <R ....R>
137		\IN this @ /field 135.9	

Appendix W4 'Würzburg' Interpreters' versions transcribed as fluent text

Interpreter WL ('live')

(MODERATOR) Thank you very much indeed, Doctor Rump, for having given us this up-to-date overview of the specific topic of subsidy fraud, which is, as I have said, one of the main points which we wish to deal with in this symposium; and this is a point which is of great interest to our foreign guests - I think that it will be especially interesting for our foreign guests to hear how cases such as those outlined by Jürgen Rump are dealt with at the level of the German courts.

We have invited Professor Doctor Odersky to come and speak to us on precisely this topic. I don't need to introduce him: he is the President and the Chief Judge of the Federal High Court. Perhaps I could just indicate, however, that Professor Odersky was the Head of the Criminal Law Department in Munich before1983, and he was also the President of the Bavarian High Court; and as of 1988 he has become the President and Chief Justice of the Federal High Court of the Federal Republic of Germany.

(ODERSKY) Thank you very much Chairman. Ladies and gentlemen, colleagues -

I think when the representative of a court, particularly a representative of a High Court ... then I think he has been asked to speak principally about questions of the law, and in particular, he is asked to talk on decisions already taken by courts, and the difficulties which the courts experienced in taking these decisions. That so much by way of introduction.

I think during the course of this seminar it has become quite clear that there is a very large range of questions under the main topic of subsidy fraud, and there are two main points of concern: firstly there is the desire of the European Community to have effective criminal legal positions to protect their own financial interests; and secondly, Member States also have quite legitimate concerns, which they have emphasised - they wish to ensure that they can improve cooperation in the area of the fight against crime; and I hope that my brief presentation will deal with both of these aspects.

European subsidy fraud, as has been said already, is a crime which has been enshrined in the legal system of the Federal Republic of Germany by means of its insertion in paragraph 264 of the German penal code; and, as has already been said during the course of this Symposium, this therefore means that the protection of the financial system and the abuse of the subsidies granted by the European Community are now protected by means of core legislation in our legal system, and protection of the Community's financial interests are equated with the protection of Germany's own interests.

Interpreter WA (mock session)

(MODERATOR) Thank you, Doctor Rumpf, for giving us that clear overview on the specific topic of fraudulent obtention of subsidies. One of the main points of our symposium was to be devoted precisely to that subject, and I think that this is of great interest to our foreign guests: they 'd really like to know how such cases as presented by Doctor Mennen and Doctor Rumpf are regulated under German criminal law. Now Professor Doctor Odertsky's going to address precisely that theme - he hardly needs any introduction, I think, for as you know, he's the President of the Federal High Court of Justice. I'd just like to point out that President Odersky used to head the criminal law... the Federal Supreme Court in Bavaria, in Munich, before becoming President of the High Court of *Justice*.

(ODERSKY) Thank you very much, Chairman. Ladies and gentlemen -

When somebody who represents a court, particularly a court of appeal, is asked to give a speech, obviously he is going to talk about legal issues, and the way in which legal issues are dealt with by the courts, and the decisions that are taken by the courts, and the way in which the cases are dealt with.

In the symposium so far it has emerged that there are two main issues: first of all, the approximation - the need for the European Community to have effective legal protection, to protect its finances, for instance; and the other issue - that perhaps is a concern more for the Member States - is the need to improve co-operation in combatting crime; and what I have to say fits under both of those concepts and issues.

I'm going to address fraudulent obtention of subsidies in Europe; and it's already been pointed out that this is something that is regulated in Federal Germany by the penal code. There are specific paragraphs that were introduced in the penal code in the seventies, the point being to prodect the European Community's finances from being misused; and basically, this is something that is covered by our penal code in the same way as it would be if it were to concern German state finances.

Interpreter WB (mock session)

(*MODERATOR*) Thank you, Doctor Rump, for that view of fraud in subsidies - and that is one of the important points of this seminar - and it's very important, I think, for our foreign guests to know how the cases which Dr Rump has referred to are in fact treated in German law; and this is an issue that Doctor Walter Odersky will speak to.

He' s President and Chief Justice of the Federal High Court of Justice: I hardly need to introduce him to you. As a criminal lawyer, I'd simply like to say that Doctor Walter Odersky used to be the main criminal judge in the Highest Court in Bavaria, and he - in nineteen ninety-two - he became President and Chief Justice of the Federal High Court of Justice in Karlsruhe

(*ODERSKY*) Thank you very much indeed, Chairman. Ladies and gentlemen -

When a representative of a court is supposed to talk about this issue, then of course he has mainly to discuss legal issues, and how legal issues have been treated by courts, and how they go about treating these cases ; and that's basically what I shall try and do here.

Your meeting has already discussed two specific issues in the overall issue that you're referring ... the first is the quite understandable desire of the European Community to have its own financial system legally protected ; and the other , which comes from Member States - and again, this is something that they're particularly keen on - which is that there should be better cooperation in the fight against criminality; and therefore I will divide my statement into two parts.

European subsidy fraud - as has already been said in this particular seminar - is treated in German law in article two six four of the criminal code in Germany; and, as has already been said in this seminar, the protection of the financial resources of the European Community is therefore dealt with, I think, satisfactorily; and dealt with in the same way as the budget of the German government is protected.

The highest federal court has had to deal with cases of this kind....

Appendix T1 'Taipei' Chinese source discourse

Prosody is not marked except for ⓐ (filled pause).

S1:
ⓐ謝謝主持人ⓐ各位好. 我今天ⓐ是一要跟各位談談ⓐ就是要以我國加入ⓐ
聯合國金融組織這個層面呢來跟各位談談我國重返聯合國的這個可能性.

S2:
我想各位從剛剛的幾位來自國内外的講者ⓐ的這演講當中就可以發現呢, 他
們個個ⓐ講者呢他們對于我們重返聯合國呢, ⓐ基本上有些共識. ⓐ在做法
上有些共識. ⓐ但也有些不同的地方.

S3:
ⓐ那今天呢, 我特別要跟各位強調的就是我們如何透過參加ⓐ聯合國的這個
金融組織ⓐ能夠達到我們ⓐ重返聯合國的這個目標.

S4:
我想, 如果講到這個重返聯合國呢, 在這個意願方面, 我想這個朝野啊, 以
我想是一定是達到一致的共識了. 就是ⓐ不可ⓐ不可ⓐ不可否認的一個事實

S5:
那大家也同樣認識到一點就是, 在當前的這國際形勢之下呢, 重返聯合國是
需要長時間的去經營ⓐ, 長時間的去做計劃, 不是説一廂情願的, 就可以馬
上就促成的.

S6:
我想最主要的就是, 今天我們用一個什么樣的方式能夠最有效的回到聯合國

S7:
那當然很多的講者剛剛也都提到過了. 我們重返聯合國呢, 要是要透過這種
ⓐ經由安理會來決定的這個路途的話是相當困難的.

S8:
爲什么, 因爲中共呢在安理會里面是有否決權的.

S9:
所以, 當然我們今天, 要以要能夠重返聯合國的話呢, 必須能夠繞過安理會
這個途徑, 能夠把我們的這個申請案呢, 看是不是能夠把它轉到這個聯合國
的大會上面.

S10:
ⓐ也就是説，我們是看是不是能夠ⓐ經由這個聯合ⓐ聯合國的大會呢，用這個議事規則ⓐ來推翻ⓐ或者是來修改在1971年的時候，ⓐ經由這個第2758號ⓐ決議案將就是將我排除ⓐ聯合國而容納中共的這個案子里面．

S11:
ⓐ但是呢，我們也都知道，現在跟我國有外交關系的國家呢，只有28個國家，而其中，只有25個國家呢是聯合國的會員會員國．

S12:
那我們都知道，在聯合國呢，ⓐ這個總共有184個會員國，

S13:
那這就代表，ⓐ跟我們有邦交的這些ⓐⓐ25個聯合國會員國呢，其實只不過是占了總數的七分之一弱而已．

S14:
ⓐ當然這個要距離達到這個三分之二ⓐ多數ⓐ決的這個標準呢，是還相差將近一百票之多．

S15:
對從這點來看，我們也知道，經由聯合國大會的這條路呢，説實在也不是那么的容易的．

S16:
那另外一條可能走的路是什么呢就是經由聯合國體系下的專門機構，ⓐ從這個方面也許我們可以找到另外一個可能性．

S17:
ⓐ爲什么呢？因爲我們知道在在聯合國，在安理會里面呢中共有否決權，我剛剛説過了．

S18:
可是呢在聯合國的專門機構里面呢，確没有這項武器．

S19:
ⓐ現在在聯合國的體系之下現在總共有18個政府間的ⓐ組織，ⓐ這種專門專門機關ⓐ，ⓐ還有三個銀行組織型的這種專門機關，

S20:
那我覺得我們現在最能夠掌握的一個實力就是我們在經貿上面的實力．

S21:

那我覺得我們應該用這種實力然后很是很謹慎的去選擇一個 @ 一個組織。然后呢作爲我們重返聯合國的一個跳板。@ 那我想呢，這樣子可能是一個比較比較有效的一種方法，

S22:

那我剛剛也提到過，我們現在最能夠 @ 應用的一個武器呢，就是我們龐大的這個貿易實力，還有我們的財經的實力。

S23:

所以我覺得，應該是要以重返 @ 一些象是國際貨幣基金啊，或者是 @ 國際復興開發銀行，也就是我們通常所説的世界銀行了。而這一類的組織呢，爲優先考慮。

S24:

但是我還要再强調的一點就是這條路呢并不是那么容易走的。它是障礙比較少，就是比較能夠成功 @，就是成功的機率比較大，但是呢，它也不是完全是這個完全是沒有沒有沒有障礙的。

S25:

那我呆會兒就是要我强調要跟各位强調它的這個最主要的障礙是在什么地方。@ 我想它最主要的障礙就是説這些這些組織他們現在已經有一種 @ 政治化的的一種現象。

S26:

那各位在你們的手中 @ 我想都有我這持這次爲大會所 @ 寫的這個論文。

S27:

我跳過前面的 @ 因就是介紹 @ 聯合國以及我國 @ 加入聯合國，@ 參與聯合國跟退出聯合國的這個歷史的部分，@ 這大家都很熟悉了。

S28:

我直接跟各位談談 @ 就是聯合國這些專門機構他們的這個政治化的情況。@ 這也是在我的論文的第 6 頁，如果各位要參考的話。

S29:

世界銀行和國際組國際貨幣基金兩個金融組織的政治化，與聯合國體系下其它大多數專門機構政治化有其根本不同之處.

S30:
這兩個金融組織政治化的泛用呢，不是第三世界．而是已開發國家，特別是
美國．

S31:
美國決策階層擬有一份名單，盡可能拒絶同意列在名單上國家的這個多邊貸
款申請，其中有越南、古巴、格瑞那達和尼加拉瓜等國．

S32:
美國反對貸款的理由表面上是技術性的，實際上呢則是基于厭惡這些國家激
進社會主義的政權和仇視美國態度的政治考慮．

S33:
已開發國家曾經指控，第三世界國家常以所謂「人爲的多數」，@强行在其
它專門機構的議程上，加列與該組織毫無任何關聯的政治性議題，

S34:
但聯合國在國際貨幣基金和世界銀行中，對敵視美國的國家，拒絶予以貸款
的政治立場，同樣受到第三世界國家的指責．

S35:
美國國會曾一度拒絶批準撥交世界銀行新增資新增資案，直到世界銀行總裁
@麥納瑪拉@向衆院小組委員會提出説帖，承諾在短期内不再貸款越南之后
才解凍．

S36:
美國財政部經調查證實，維護美國利益具有重要功能的武器之一，乃是財政
力量．

S37:
美國爲變更多@爲變更國際多邊銀行這種「實務與程序」政策的這個特殊目
標，就是以運用財政方式而成功的．

S38:
這項財政方式的運作，有時全部成功，有時僅能部分達到目的．

S39:
美國行等當局行政當局和立法部門都了解，布列頓森林會議成立國際貨幣基
金和世界銀行兩個金融組織的目的，是促使全球經濟自由化，并對美國產品
和資本市場開放，符合美國一般利益．

Appendix T2-A Taipei: Romanised transcript with gloss and analysis, interpreters TA, TB

Input/syntax: N noun; PN proper noun; V Verb; A adjective; CP complementiser phrase; VP verb phrase; NP noun phrase; T Topic; C Comment; d determiner; sm subordination marker; *pro* pro-form; # solecism; p particle; pfv perfective; ([non-predictable constituent structure; - pause; + long pause; @, fp filled pause ('er'); dm discourse marker/connective; cl classifier; >F focusing device; >Obj Object marker. *Assembly:* representations for formulation combining input semantics and other cognitive and pragmatic sources: P_{-1}, P_0, P_1 propositions (previous, current,...) *Italics:* unresolved element; : resolved; i,j,k arguments; r relation; {} scope; φ predicate; ⇒ ⇐ results in/from; > expect; >> infer; ? unclear syntactic attachment, semantic scope or pragmatic domain; SA speech act; qualif. qualification. ☺, ⊗ affective values. *Thematic roles:* THeme, AGent, INSTrument, PATH, SOUrce, GOAL.... SMALL CAPS: modal/attitudinal, e.g. POSSIBILITY, DES Desire, EVIDENTIAL. *Extratextual knowledge:* → access;SK, DK, FK: situation, discourse, frame knowledge; MM: mental model; ⊂ includes; ⊃ is included in. *Topical (most salient) propositions:* P_{TRU} '(we/Taiwan)(want)$_{Goal}$[Taiwan rejoin UN]'; P_{JUF} '$_{PATH/INSTrument}$Taiwan join UN financial bodies'

	Chinese input, syntax and gloss	Assembly	Interpreter TA	Interpreter TB
1	S1: @ xiexie zhuchi ren 25 thank you Chairman	SA formula +	25 Thank you Mr	25 Thank you very much Mr
2	+ @ -m 26 - gewei hao - you all hallo +	polite formula + SK time: TL polite formula	Chairman 26	Chairman/ 26.5 - H
3	wo - jintian 28- @shi - y- 29 [IP I today [VP*shi*>F	P_0 ? I today... (SK >> P_0 about speech)	good afternoon. 28.5 ladies	+
4	yao. gen gewei 30 tan tan @ intend [V[PPwith you all discuss	INTENT [with POLITE you-all [discuss	and gent.men. 30 - l	H ladies and 30 gentle/men -
5	jiushi yi 31 woguo - jiaru 32 - dm ([IP[PP by/Obj> [my country [VPjoin	?$_{sm/Obj}$ (*THeme*) P_1 my country join... DK, SK >> = Taiwan	been invited - to	today/ - I will be 32 talking
6	@Lianheguo jinrong zuzhi 34 - UN financial organisations.	?$_{sm/Obj}$ (*THemeF*)P_1 Taiwan join UN fin. org. = P_{JUF} FK : UN ⊂ UN finorgs (UF) **TA**: expand FK 'theme'	talk 33 - on - a topic 34 -	to you about 33 - H
7	de zheige cengmian~ ne 35 - de [this aspect p	P_0 discuss [*THeme*?] from P_{JUF} pt-of-view **TB** : Object/THeme P_{JUF}	focusing	H Taiwan's 35
8	lai gen gewei 36 tan tan - to[PPwith you all discuss	(*repeat*) INTENT [with POLITE you-all [discuss	- on 36 -	- lentry into UN's
9	woguo chongfan 37 Lianheguo de - ([NP[P6 Taiwan return UN] *de*	THeme [P_{TRU} Taiwan return UN]	+	financial 37

#	Chinese transliteration / gloss	Notation		
10	38 zheige kenengxing\ this possibility]	P_0: INTENT {discuss [POSS P_{TRU} through P_{IUF}]	Chinese Tai\pei's -	insti\tutions 38
11	+	TA : Object/Theme [mixed P_{TRU}/P_{IUF}] / TB repair INTENT {discuss [POSS P_{TRU} through P_{IUF}]	re-entry 39	+
12	S2: H wo xiang - gewei. 40 [CP I think [LP1 you-all	P_0 BEL { P_1 you	to 40 -	40 |
13	cong - gang gang de ji wei 41 [PP from[NP]just-now [several cl	? source[just now.... [> φ →SK,DK	international financial	will be looking at the possibility
14	- lai zi. guoneiwai [come from country-in-out	? source[just now[source home and abroad NP [> φ NP → SK	organisations 42	of the ROC's 42 -
15	de JIANGZHE 43 - @- de [speakers	source previous speakers [> φ	+	re-entry into the - UN 44 from
16	- de zhe yanjiang dangzhong de d [speeches within]	source ....speeches > 'cognitive' φ	+	this point of ~view 45
17	jiu keyi faxian ne - 46 dm vp can realize p	P_1 : Poss realise EVID P_{+1}	+	- from the
18	tamen gege - @47 [CP2 [LP2 they every	P_0	46 speakers from home and abroad 47	\speeches that we have heard 47
19	jiangzhe ne tamen 48 speaker p they	P_0 subj Speakers	- who	so \f a~ r- 48
20	duiyu women chongfan 49 [PP2 as-to [LP3 we rejoin	P_0 Speakers [About..>P_1 [> φ	spoke before me 49	- we /k n o w H 49
21	Lianheguo ne - @m- - United Nations] p	P_1 [Taiwan return UN] = 'P_{TRU}'→MM	-	- that. the \speak50ers -
22	jiben shang you yi xie 51 gongshi [VP]basically have some consensus	P_0: Speakrs [About P_{TRU} {qualif1 {qualif2 φ	have shared with us 51 -	+ H
23	- @ zai 52 zuofa shang [VP2 approach-wise	P_0 + {qualif1b { $φ_2$> Contrast qualif1	their \v i e w s 52 -	-
24	you xie 53 gongshi - [V there-is some consensus	$φ_2$: {repeat qualif2 $φ_1$ > Contrast qualif1b	+	/reached 53 -
25	@- 54 dan ye you xie but [I also[VP3 V there-is some	But : Contrast focus : {some agreement/...}	on- Chinese Taipei's	a c o n \s e n
26	butong de difang 55 + different de points]	:.../some disagreement}	re-entry. 55 to international	sus - 55 even though

#				
27	S3: @ - na jin tian ne 56 - [CP1 dm today p	>> P_0 > about speech	.financial orgnis/ations 56 -	there are 56 \slight -
28	wo- 57 tebie- [IP ([NP I especially	P_0 IMPortant	their views.	differences 57
29	yao gen gewei 58 qiangdiao de - want [with you all stress de -	P_0 IMP {P_1	converge. some58 what -	+
30	jiushi . women 59 - ru-he- [dmshi >F[CP[we [CP2 how	P_1 we(=Taiwan) POSS [INST/PATH.... [φ	but there are some -differences.	in \HOW 59 we should re-enter
31	- tou 60 guo - [IP2 [vp through	P_1 POSS [we [PATH.... [φ	among their \views 60 -	the UN 60 - but
32	canjia 61 - [IP3 [∅] join	P_1 POSS [we[PATHP_2... [φ	today I'd \like 61 to stress	to/day 61 - I'm going
33	@Lianheguo de. 62 [NPUN de	P_2 [we join UN's...	~more -	to \emph a s i62z e
34	zheige jinrong zuzhi 63 - d financial organisations]	...financial organisations] = P_{JUF}	- on 63 +	+
35	@ nenggou 64 dadao - women- 65 vp can reach {[NP[IP4 we	P_1 POSS [we PATH P_{JUF} POSS [φ reach GOAL....	+ how 65	H 64
36	@- chongfan Lianheguo 66 de - rejoin UN] de	...GOAL = P_{TRU}	- we can 66	H the-
37	zheige mubiao 67 + d goal]	(: = Goal)	+ 67 ob\tain. the \goal.	re- 67 entry-
38	S4: 68 wo xiang - [r I think	P_0 EVID {	of 68 re-\entry. into	of- 68 Taiwan into the United
39	ruguo jiang dao 69 zheige {[CPif [IP1 vp address [NPd	P_0 {About ... { >P_1	the United	Nations 69 -
40	chongfan Lianheguo 70 ne - rejoining UN] . p }	P_0 {About ... P_{TRU} { >P_1	\Nations - 70 by -	V I A - the financial
41	zai zheige yiyuan fangmian 71 - [r {[IP2 [PP on [NPd intention side	P_1 ?Subj INTENT { >>Subj →DK = Taiwan	r#- \entering 71 -	institutions of 71 the
42	wo xiang zheige chaoye 72 @ -yi- [cl think fp [IP[NPgovt -&-oppositn # al	EVID P_1 : =Subj Govt & opposition ... > [φ >> gov&opp/public ⊃ Taiwan	to - the 72 - inter	U N -
43	wo xiang shi yijing shi [cl think [vp shi² >F/V is already shi	EVID P_1 [past {gov&opposition/public.... [> φ }	national fin\ancial 73	H -

#	Chinese / gloss	Formal notation	English (1)	English (2)
44	dadao yizhi de 74 gongshi le - / [reached unanimous consensus pfv	P₁ : perfective {gov&opp{About INTENT [P_TRU ... / agreed	organisations first 74 / +	H I \ think / that - @m
45	zhe shi - @-buke 76 @ buke / [pₜthis is - ([NPcannot cannot	P₂ : IMPOSS [... [P₁	+ / politicians 77	75 Govern/ment.- and / private 76 sectors have
46	#b - buke fouren de / cannot deny de	P₂ : IMPOSS [deny [P₁ / >> EVID [P₁	- with\in the / Govern	\already 77 reached / a
47	yige 78 shishi + [d cl fact]	+ EVID [P₁	ment/ 79	consensus 78 +
48	S5: NA- 80 dajia ye tongyang- - / cₚwell[ₚ₁ everyone dm [vₚ likewise	Dir : new premise { P₀ / everyone → DK = Taiwan ⊂ govt&opp ⊂ Speakers	+	- 80 in- H
49	81 renshi dao yi dian. jiu shi 82 / recognise one thing dm shi>F	P₀ +EVID (=All BEL) { P₁	and. 81 from the / opposition	+ / Taiwan's 82 need
50	+ zai 83 dangqian de / [cₚ[ₚ₂[ₚₚ in present de	> P₁ [in....→SK? φ	\party - 83 have all.	to re-enter 83 the U/N
51	zhe 84 guoji qingshi zhi xia ne - / d international conditions -under] p	>P₁ [in ....→SK : world ⊂ UN ⊂ China/Taiwan ... φ	made - / a consensus - 85	- h o w e v e r - / we all know 85
52	85 chongfan Lianheguo 86 - / [ᵣ [NPrejoin UN	P₁ ⁿ [...P_TRU...	that - 86 reentry. / to	that - / under the 86 current.
53	shi xuyao 87 - / [vₚ₂shi>F [vₚ need	P₁ ⁿ [...P_TRU... [φ{NEC / >>reach GOAL P_TRU [φ{NEC... TB >>+ Subj Tense	the United 87	international 87 -
54	chang shijian de qu- 88 - / [long time de [go	φ₁ long-time ...	Nations - is. 88	situation/ 88 -
55	jingying @ chang shijian de / manage, [long time de	φ₂ + long-time...	necessary - / how/ever -	we will 89 need -to-
56	qu- 90 zuo jihua - bu shi shuo / [go make plan - [cₚnot-shi say>F	P₁...] / Not [P₂...	it is 90 - a \task 91 / that	- 91 plan/
57	yi xiang qingyuan 92 de - / [vₚjust think wishing p	P₃ {φ₁, φ₂} / φ₁ : DES (P_TRU >>Goal) ...	requires -	- and
58	jiu keyi mashang 93 - / [vₚthen [v-can [instantly	⇒ φ₂ POSS ...	\long-term / \planning 93 -	~w o r k 93 - / for a
59	jiu cucheng de 94 - / then accomplish] p	not P₂ [just{DES TRU ⇒Reach TRU }]	and its -not / \something - that 95	long time. 94 in / order to achieve

#				
60	S6: wo xiang zui zhuyao de 96 [CPI think ([NPmost essential de	BEL { +IMP {... P_0	- that can just be completed 96	95 our goal of re-entering the UN\ -
61	jiushi. jintian 97- women yong yige dm shi>F today - [IP we[VPP use d	P_0 now [we use	+ by 98 -	I think 97 most importantly 98
62	shenmeyang de fangshi - what-kind de method	... which method	our - own wish 99	H +
63	99 nenggou zui youxiaode 100 - [VP can [most effectively	best method >> ⇒ Reach Goal	+	H
64	hui dao Lianheguo 101 - return to UN -	P_{TRU} = (Reach) Goal	there/fore - the 101 issue	+ H101 - we
65	S7: na dangran - hen duo de jiangzhe [cpdm of course -[IP[NPmany speakers	New premise : EVID {P_0	today - is how	need to lknow how we
66	ganggang ye dou 103 tidao guo le - [VPjust now also p mentioned pfv	P_0 Dir / Evid : many Speakers said [P_1	can we 103 +	can 103 - most \efficiently
67	104 women - chongfan T[cp[IPwe - return	P_1 [→ P_{TRU}	re	- become a UN mem
68	Lianheguo ne 106 - yaoshi United Nations p [cp4 if	P_1 [¹if/givenP_2 [GOAL TRU {...	\enter the United 106 Nations -	ber algain 106
69	yao touguo zheizhong - [IP[vpwant [P/vpthrough such	P_1 [²if/givenP_2 [GOAL TRU, PATH···	through the 107 most. efficient	+
70	@ jingyou 108 Anlihui - PPby/via ([NP([VPSec.Council	P_1 [²if/givenP_2 [GOAL TRU, PATH {Sec Council...	\way 108 -	H if
71	lai 109 - jueding Aux to - V decide	PATH {... decides} Sec Council→FK : votes on TRU	?man# scholars	we / were.109 /to -
72	de zhege lutu de hua de this path] -if]	{...=PATH}	+ 110 who spoke before	+
73	shi xiangdang kunnan de 111 - shi [APvery difficult] de]	P_1 : [P_2 is very difficult]	me - mentioned 111 -	H
74	S8: weishenme - 112 yinwei- - [cpWhy? - because	Dir P_0 : Why (P_1) ?	that it's very \difficult	follow the /path.- 112 of having the -
75	Zhonggong ne zai Anlihui limian China Com p ([VP[PPin Sec. Council] in → FK...	China → FK : China oppose TRU Sec Council → FK...	to re-enter. - th- United	@m the Selcuri 113

76	shi you foujuequan de 114 - *shi*>F have veto right p	veto → FK = block >> China block TRU in Sec Council >> block [PATH Sec Council]	Nations 114 - by 115	ty Council +
77	S9: suoy-. 115 dangran women [CP1SO of course [IPwe	[P-1 + >>] ⇒ EVID P_0 [we...	+	@ vote - for us
78	jintian 116 - today ([T [CP2[IP øIVP *if/want*	P_0 [*if/given* P_1 [we INTENT now... [>P_2	obtaining	Vfirst 116 - we know that 117 -
79	nenggou chongfan Lianheguo de hua able rejoin UN -if	P_1 [..we INTENT..] → = P_{TRU} *redundant, discard*	support - from the 117 Security \Council 118	it would be very difficult be cause we know that
80	118 - bixu nenggou RAOguo 119 - C[IP must able [bypass	P_2 [NEC [bypass...(FK = not PATH.... direct PATH >...)	- as Mainland \Chi-na 119	118 - H@ Mainland China
81	Anlihui - zheige tujing - ([SecCouncil d this route]	P_2 [NEC φ {direct PATH >....[not PATHSec Ccl	+	has VETO RIGHT 120 - IN. the
82	121 nenggou- ba women de able *ba >Obj* [our	P_2 [NEC φ [7THeme our... [PATH ...	commands. vetoing	Security Council
83	zhege shenqing'an 123 ne - d application] p -	AGenWe, 7ThemeOur application = we Apply [x Apply to y for z] >> φ apply	power 123 -	H +
84	kan shi bu shi nenggou 124 ba ta see [CP whether [IP [able *ba* F> it	see if Poss >> = Try [Apply toPATH...not PATH....	within the Security 124	H so 124 - we -
85	zhuan dao. zhege Lianheguo de [divert [PPto fp ([NP [UN	...{direct PATH >...[to UN's	\Council - therefore	need to see -
86	DAhui 125 shangmian - Gen.Assembly] -on	P : try [apply [PATH direct to Assembly not Sec Council	it is nec 125 essary to	if we. 125 can.
87	S10: @-		bypass the Security Coun	apply.126
88	ye jiushi shuo 127 - [CPdm so that's-to-say>F	Dir : P_0 elaborates on P-1	cil - by 127	through the General Asslemblyof the UN
89	women sh.# kan shi bu shi [IP we [VP see [CPyes-or-no >F	P_0 look at [? Poss {... look at Poss >> = Des { Poss {...	\going to the General Assembly	128 instead of the
90	nenggou 129 - @ jingyou zheige [VPable - [PVPvia [NPd	P_0 we ?/DES {Poss { [via ...PATH	directly 129 +	Security Coun cil
91	Lianhe- 130 - United Na....		+	+
92	k@Lianheguo de Dahui ne 131 - United Nations Gen Assembly p	?/DES {Poss { ... [PATHUNGA... >.. VPφ	+	+

#	Transliteration / gloss	Formal notation	Tier A	Tier B
93	yong zhege yishi guize - 133 @ [VP PUSE NP fp rules of procedure	...POSS {[INST rules [PATH UNGA >.. [Overturn >..Obj/THeme VPφ	+	+ H 133 m a y / we
94	lai. - tuifan 134 - @ [CPL VP to overturn	...POSS {we [INST...[PATH.. [Overturn >..Obj/THeme	+	b e - we
95	huozhe shi- - lai xiugai 136 - or else shi to amend	..POSS we{ [INST[PATH..[Overturn or Amend >Obj/THeme	135.5 by going through the General	~can - 136 use the-
96	zai yijiu- 137 qiyi nian ([NP] PP in nineteen seventy-one year	P_0 [.... > ?Obj/THeme P_1 [Agent [Time 1971]...	Assembly perhaps its /possible 137.5	+
97	de shihou 138 - @m- - time	P_0 [...[P_1 ...[Time 1971]...	+	H 138 rule of
98	jingyou zheige di erqiwuba hao [? via this no. 2758 - number	P_0 [...[P_1 [Time 1971 [PVP PATH/INST ...No. 2758...	H	/order 139.5
99	@141 - jueyi'an - 142 jiang jiushi Resolution [PP Obj > dm shi	[P_1...Resolution 2758, P_3...	+ 142 to modify 143	@parliamentary pro/cedures -
100	jiang wo- pai 143 chu @ Obj> me/us V [expel	[P_3 ,Expel us(=Taiwan) ...]	- /or -	to- 143 make our way
101	Lianheguo 144 er rongna UN and admit	?Obj /THeme [Expel-from-UNTaiwan, admit.. [Resolutn] →FK Expel Taiwan ⊗ >> P_0 Overturn {THeme Resoln	144 to over	into the United
102	Zhonggong de zheige anzi - ChinCom] de this motion]	P_0: DES POSS {PATH UNGA [INST rules{Overturn.. [[1971 expel Taiwan, admit PRC Motion ≡ Resolution]	ride. 145 - the Resolution two	Nations. 145 through the General
103	146 limian - + -inside]	discard	146 seven five eight -	~Ass146em/bly
104	SI1: @m147 danshi ne - women ye [CP but p ≻F - we also/dm	Contrast : But {	which -	+
105	dou zhidao 148- xianzai gen all/dm know - [CP now[(P)[NP]][VP LP with	EVID {P_1 [now	excludes 148 -	to- revoke 149 the Reso
106	woguo 150 you waijiao guanxi our-country have dipl relations	dipl. relations→FK >> EVID {P_1 [now...countries	Taiwan 150 - and	lution 150 - that admitted -
107	de guojia ne 151 - de country(s) p ≻F		admits 151 - \China 152 -	@Mainland China in to the UN in nineteen 152 seventy three

(continued in Appendix T2-B)

Appendix T2-B Taipei Segments 11-28: Input with gloss, interpreters TA, TB

Input and syntax: N noun; PN proper noun; V Verb; A adjective; d determiner; *pro* pro-form; sm subordination marker; p particle; pfv perfective; ([uncertain constituent structure; dm discourse marker/connective; T Topic; C comment ; cl classifier; >F focusing device; >Obj Object marker. *Delivery:* - pause; + long pause; @, fp filled pause; # solecism; H intake of breath. CAPS: stress; / rising intonation; \ falling intonation; ~ modulation; % 'creaky' hesitation.

		Chinese input, syntax and gloss	Interpreter TA	Interpreter TB
104.	S11	@m - 147 danshi ne - women ye [cpbut p >F - we also/dm	which -	+
105.		dou zhidao 148 - xianzai gen all/dm know T[cpnow[(ip)([np)[vp [pp with	excludes 148 -	to- revoke 149 the Reso
106.		woguo 150 you waijiao guanxi our-country have diplomatic relations	Taiwan 150 - and	lution 150 - that admit
107.		de guojia ne 151 - *de* countrie(s)] p >F	admits 151 -	ted - @ Mainland China into the UN
108.		zhi you- - 152 ershibage guojia - C[vponly (there)are 28 cl] countries	\China 152 - 153 right	in nineteen 152 seventy three we know
109.		153 er - qizhong 154 - and T[ipof those	now we \only have diplomatic \ties	that 153 - presently -
110.		zhi you- ershiwu 155 ge [vponly (there) are [np[25 cl	154 with twenty seven 155	only twenty EIGHT countries 155 have
111.		guojia ne - shi Lianheguo de countries p - [are UN *de*	countries 156 -	diplomatic 156 ties with
112.		huiyuan 157 - huiyuanguo - members - member countries]	out of which -	us - 157 and only ~twenty f ive
113.	S12	na women dou zhidao - [cpdm we all/dm know	only twenty-five - 158are members.	of them are UN me-. 158 UN members -
114.		zai Lianhe 159 guo ne @- T[ip[pp at UN p -	to the United 159 \Nations	we know that.
115.		160 zhege zonggong fp [ı· altogether	+	160 at the UN/ -
116.		you yibaibashisige - [vp(there) are a hundred and eighty-four	+	there are one
117.		huiyuanguo 162 member countries]	161 we also understand	hundred 162 and eighty
118	S13	na zhe jiu daibiao 163 - [cpdm ('so') this dm means	- that there are one hundred 163 n	\four mem ber163 nations.
119		@m - gen women you bangjiao de - [ip ([np([vp[ppwith us have relations *de*	\eighty four - mem ber 164 nations	alto\gether 164 -
120		165 zheixie- @ @m these	- in United \Nations 166	H
121		166 ershiwuge Lianheguo twenty-five United Nations	+	H
122		huiyuanguo ne 167.5 - qishi zhi - member-ctries p] - [cp actually [iponly	+	H 167.5 /so - the twenty
123		buguo shi zhan le 169 zongshu de - merely *shi* >[ap[vpcomprise p total number	169 these twenty-five	five - 169 UN \members -

124		qifenzhiyi 170 RUO er yi on-seventh] weak] -is all]	/countries 170 - which	that have diplomatic ties
125		+	maintain - diplo	171 with us -
126	S14	@ dangran zheige yao. [CPof course [IPthis [VP *Aux*	matic ties 172 with Tai	only account for -
127		juli - dadao 173 zheige [N/VPdistance(from) - reach [NPd this/fp	/wan - only count	a seventh 173 - of -
128		san fen zhi er @ - duo174 shu - two-thirds - majority -	for less than one 174 seven -	of the UN 174 \members so
129		@ - 175 juedui zheige biaozhun ne absolute d/fp criterion p	of the 175 - member.	it's not likely that we 176 will
130		- shi hai 177 xiangcha [F>*shi* IP [VP still lack	- nations - 177 of the	be able to- 177 reach -
131		- jiangjin yibai piao - nearly one hundred votes	UN -	a two-thirds 178 % majority vote.
132		zhi duo 179 - -so-many]	you know we are. a \long	we 179 need more than.
133	S15	suoyi - CP so	/way 180 -	a 180 hundred votes in
134		cong. zhei dian lai kan 181 - [IPfrom this point of view to look	from. obtaining. 181	our f a v o u r 181
135		women ye zhidao - jingyou. 182 [I' we[I' also/dm [VPknow [CP[IP ([NP[PP via	majority. support.	+
136		Lianheguo Dahui [NP UN General Assmbly]	from .the 183	an-d 183 -
137		de zhei tiao lu ne - shuo shizai 184 *de* d this cl route p] [CPsay-honestly	U N +	% /so-
138		ye bushi name de 185 rongyi de [IPalso/dm [APnot F>*shi* [AP so easy]	185 as such -	I con\clude 185 here that -
139		+	it's not so-	it won't be easy 186 for -
140	S16	name lingwai yi tiao. 187 T[CPdm[IP[NPanother[d cl ([NP[VP	easy -	us to -
141		keneng zou de lu ne. shi shenme ne 188 possible go *de* route] p> C [*shi* what? p]	187 to obtain -	re-\enter the UN/ - \through 188 -
142		- jiushi- jingyou Lianheguo tixi 189 C[VPdm*shi*>[IP[V/PPvia [NP[PPUN-system	membership in th United Nations.189	the General Ass/embly 189
143		xia de zhuanmen jigou 190 -under] *de* specialised agencies]	by going through the Gen 190	+ H
144		+ @ cong zheige - [V/PPfrom/via this	eral As\sembly - the other	another 191 - al\ternative-
145		fangmian 192 yexu. women keyi side [IP maybe we [VP can	proach -	is 192 to
146		zhaodao lingwai yige193 kenengxing find [NPanother d possibility]	193 that we can	- \try 193 to re-enter
147	S17	- @ weishenme 194 ne - T[CP why p ?	~consider 194 - is by	the UN through 194 specialised
148		yinwei women zhidao zai 195 - C[because [IP we know[IP[PP at	going through	\agencies. of the U/N 195

149		zai Lianheguo - zai Anlihui limian　ne at　UN　　　- [PP at Sec Council -in] p	+	+
150		Zhonggong　you 197　foujuequan - [IP[NPChiCom [VPhas　　　veto right	specialised 197	H we know that 197 -　\in
151		wo gang gang shuoguo le 198 - {[I just　　said (it) *pfv*] }	organis/a 198 tions　-	the Security /Council -
152	S18	keshi~ ne -　　　zai 199 - Lianheguo [CPbut　p　- [IP[PPat　[NPUnied Nations	under umbr/ella. of the U\N 199	Mainland /China 199 has. a
153		de zhuanmen jigou 200 \ limian ne - *de* specialised agencies]　　-in] p	+	right- - a /veto 200 right
154		que 201　　　-　　　meiyou - [IPhowever/p　- [ø [VP not[have	+	+
155		zhei xiang 202 wuqi - [NPthis　cl　　weapon]	China 202 - comm ands voting	-　yet 202 - y @--
156	S19	@m-　204 xianzai - [IP now	power - in the Secur ity Coun	@　204 Mainland China
157		zai -　Lianheguo 205 de - [PP at　[Unied Nations *de*	cil but not 205　- in the other.	does not have this adVANtage
158		tixi　zhi xia 206 - [system -under] p	specialised 206　-	in the specialised 206 agencies
159		xianzai zonggong you 207 - now [VP altogether [(there)are	agencies 207	-　of 207 the UN under the
160		shibage 208 - zhengfu jian de 209- [NP eighteen　intergovernmental.	+	UN 208 /system - H there are
161		@- -　210 zuzhi @ organisations	there are eighteen 210 - inter	eighteen -　inter govern210ment.
162		zhezhong zhuanmen 211 - [this kind　specialised	governmental 211 -	al organisa 211 tions
163		zhuanmen jiguan - 212 @ - specialised agency	specialised 212 -	H -　@ special ised 212
164		hai you -　213 san　ge - and (there)are [NPthree cl	organisations or agencies. under	agencies 213 -
165		yinhang 214 zuzhi - x- xingde 215 - ([APbank organisation -　type *de*	the　214 umbrella - of - UN　215 -	a_ - nd. 214 there# three -
166		zheizhong zhuanmen jiguan 216 - such　[NPspecialised agencies]	there are \also 216 -	H　　　　H
167	S20	H + NA　　- wo juede - dm (well /so) - [CP I　feel	three -　BANK -	\bank　-　@
168		women xianzai 218 - [IP ([NP) [IPwe.　now	TYPE 218 -	organisations 218
169		zui nenggou. zhangwo de yige shili. ([IP(NP[VP most able command *de* d power	organisations 219 -	+
170		jiu　shi　women 220 F>dm [VPis ([NP) we	under	and I think 220 -
171		zai. jingmao shangmian de shili 221 - [PP at economy-trade -on] *de*　power]	the UN	the most concrete -
172		na wo juede 222 - women yinggai -# [CPdm I feel　- [IP we　[VP should	+	@　strength that -

173		yong zheizhong shili 223 - [PV/Puse this cl power	+	w % 223 % - we
174		ranhou 224- hen sh- hen jinshen de 225 [IP then [VP very # very carefully	+ I feel 225 # ess	have is our - economic 225 -
175		- qu xuanze yige 226 - [V' go choose [d one cl	ential +	and. financial \strength 226 -
176		@m - yige 227 zuzhi - - an organisation	+	so we mu- we must
177		ranhou ne 228 - [IP then p	that we 228 - make the	build. 228 - on this strength.
178		zuo wei women 229 - chongfan [VPtreat[NP] as [NP[IPwe [VPrejoin	most ~use. of our 229 economic and	and scrup 229 ulously -
179	. ..	Lianheguo de yige tiaoban - United Nations de a springboard]	tray strength	~designate
180	S21	@ 231 na wo xiang ne 232 - [CP dm (so) I think p	+ and seek. 232	231- as- a-
181		zheyangzi -keneng shi yige bijiao- 233 [IPthus [VPmaybe [is [NPd cl quite	entry - to- 233 -	financial insti \tution which would 233 serve
182		bijiao you xiao 234 de quite effective de	a specialised trade	as a spring board - 234 for
183		yizhong fangfa 235 - a kind cl (of) method]	or economic	our \entry into the 235 UN
184	S22	na wo ganggang ye tidao guo 236 [CPdm I just dm mentioned	organisation - 236 \first -	I think this will be a more 236
185		- women xianzai - zui nenggou 237- [IP we now - [NP[CP most able	I feel 237 this.	efficient H - H
186		@- yingyong 238 de yigewuqi ne - use] de d weapon] p	will be. one of the most. efficient	way 238 - for
187		jiushi 239 women pangda de dm shi F> [NPwe [huge de	approaches 239 -	us to re-enter the
188		zheige - maoyi 240 shili - d this/fp trade power]	as I \mentioned 240 -	U N 240 H -
189		hai you women de caijin de shili 241 and-also [NP our finance power]	we have +	our greatest ad VAN 241
190		+	.	tage is our economic 242 -
191	S23	H suoyi wo juede- 243 - [CP so I think	tremendous +	and financial strength
192		yinggai shi yao yi- 244 - [IP[VP should shi F> Aux [P/VPby/Obj>	trade 244 -	- 244 so-
193		chongfan- @m yixie xiang shi- [CPrejoin [NPsome [like F>shi	strength - and econom	I ~feel 245
194		Guoji Huobi 246 Jijin a~ - International Monetary Fund	ic ~power 246 -	+
195		huozhe shi 247 - or shi F>	therefore we should seek	that we should. 247 first
196		@m Guoji- 248 - Fuxing Kaifa International Reconstructn Development	re-entry 248 - to the Inter	start /by 248 - becoming

197		Yinhang. ye jiushi 249 - Bank [cpdm/also dm *shi*	national Monetary Fund. -	members of 249 the-
198		women- tongchang 250 suoshuo de ([cpwe usually p say] *de*	250 /or -	- I M /F 250
199		Shijie Yinhang le 251 - World Bank] pfv	the 251 - \World	- 251 or the
200		er zhei lei de zuzhi ne 252 - p this kind of] organisation] p	Bank	World /Bank - 252 and
201		wei - youxian 253 kaolü - [vp be/as [np priority consideration	+	\similar - 253 organis\ations
202	S24	danshi wo hai yao zai [cpbut I still must again	+	+
203		qiangdiao de yidian 255 jiu shi - stress one point dm *shi* F >	+	however I must
204		zhei tiao lu ne 256 - bing bu shi [ipthis cl route p - [vpnot-at-all is	+	also \stress 256 -
205		name rongyi zoude 257 - ta shi [v· so easy (to) go - [ipit is	again 257 - I'd like	that this. 257 is not an easy
206		zhang'ai 258 - bijiao shao [c/apT obstacles - C comparatively few]	stress. that -	path 258 - /either.
207		+ 259 jiushi ([ip dm F>*shi*	the road - to- -	there are less 259 /ob
208		bijiao - # nenggou cheng 260 gong @ [vprelatively can succeed	260 I M F- 261	stacles - 260 that's
209		jiushi chenggong de jilü 261 bijiao da [ipdm *shi* [apsuccess rate relatively big]	~or	to /say - the
210		danshi ne. 262 ta ye bu shi wanquan [cpbut p [ipit[also[vpnot-*shi*[v·wholly	/World /Bank	chances for success. are 262 ~higher
211		sh #263- zhege- wanquan shi meiyou sh# fp [v·wholly[v· *shi*[v·not-have	- will \not be	- how 263 \ever
212		meiyou- 264 meiyou zhang'ai de - not-have not-have obstacles p]	as 264\smooth	+ H
213	S25	na wo daihuir 265 jiushi yao - w- [cpdm I [soon dm *shi* > Aux	- as - someone -	it is not - 265 this path
214		qiangdiao - gen gewei qiangdiao 266 [stress - [v·with you all stress -	had 266 expected - there	is not. 266 obstacle
215		tade zhege 267 zui zhuyao de zhang'ai. [ip[np its fp most major obstacle	are less hurdles -	free - and
216		shi zai shenme 268 difang @ - [vp*shi* [pp at which place	on this road 268 - than	I must stress 268 - I will stress
217		wo xiang ta zui zhuyao de zhang'ai [cpI think[ip[npit most major 269 obstacle	the road to the Uni 269 ted	the -b -obs 269 tacles
218		jiushi shuo zheixie-270 - zheixie [cpdm*shi* say F> [ip[np these - these	\Nations. H perhaps I will -	\la/ter - 270
219		zuzhi 271 - tamen xianzai yijing you organisns - they [now [vpalready have	271 say a few words more.	+ H I think
220		yizhong 272 -@ zhengzhihua de 273- [npa kind-of - politicisation] *de*	about 272 the HURDLES - on the road 273 -	the 272 main obstacle is that these 273 -

221		de yizhong xianxiang 274 - *de* d cl phenomenon]	to these - econ 274 omic	- organis/a
222	S26	na gewei - 275 zai - w- nimen dm (well) [IPyou all [PP in your	organi/sations - H 275 one of	tions - have become.
223		de. shou zhong - @ 276 wo xiang hands -in] - I think	the hurdles is 276 - the -	highly political 276 - in ~nature
224		dou 277 you wo zhei #- zhei ci wei - [VPall/dm have [NP[IPI [this - this time for	politiga- ciSAtion 277 - of these	+ H and I'm 278
225		dahui - suo#xie de zhege lun279 wen. meeting that wrote]this/fp paper]]	- two - agencies 279 -	sure that +
226	S27	wo - tiaoguo 280 qianmian de - [CP[IPI [VPskip past [NP[PPfront de	I'm sure you have obtained	you have 280 - my-
227		@ 281 ying- jiushi jieshao- # [CP that is ([NP[IP [VP present	the handouts 281- that I provid	paper 281 - in your -
228		@282 Lianheguo - yiji woguo 283 - [NPUnited Nations - and [IPour-country	ed - 282 to the /organiser	conference packet - so I will.
229		@jiaru Lianheguo284@- canyu [VPjoin United Nations - participate	+ in be	skip a few /pages 284
230		Lianheguo gen tuichu Lianheguo de UN and withdraw UN] *de*	ginning 285 of the /paper - I	+ H
231		zheige 286 lishi de bufen @ - d/fp history] *de* part]	elab 286 orated. on the	and 286 -
232		zhe dajia dou287 hen shouxi le [CPthis[IPeveryone dm/all [APvery familiar pfv]	~history. 287 of.	I'm going to skip the
233	S28	wo zhi 288 jie - [CP[IPI [VPdirectly	-	@m- 288 - H -
234		gen gewei tan tan 289 + with you-all [V'V address	289 my country's -	his- the
235		@ 290 jiushi Lianheguo zheixie dm*shi* [NP UN [NPthese	m e m b e r	descrip 290 tion of @m -
236		zhuanmen 291 jigou- tamen de special. agencies [their -	s h i p 291 -in the UN. - and. 292	@ the 291 historical
237		zheige zhengzhihua de 293 - d/fp [politicisation *de*	withdrawal from the UN 293 -	+ 293 @m-
238		qingkuang - @ zhei ye shi situation] - [IP this[VP dm/also[VPis	and I'd-	- I'm going to
239		zai wo de 295 - lunwen de di liu ye - [PPat [my - paper *de* [sixth page]	295 talk about -	skip the 295 portion describing.
240		ruguo gewei yao cankao 296 de hua [CPif[IPyou all [VPwant Vcheck] -if]	the. politiciz 296ation	the- @ history. of. 296 the Republic
241		+	of these.agencies 297 -\which	of China in the UN 297 - you will find
242	S29		is on page 298 \six	that in - my 298 paper.
243			+	if you need to
244			World	refer to it 299 -

Appendix T3 Taipei: Recited discourse (S29-39) and interpreters TA, TB (synchronised transcript)

Delivery: - short pause; + longer pause; @, @m filled pause ('er', 'ah', 'erm'); final . short extra beat (clipped syllable);_, *the-* (attached dash): drawl (lengthened syllable); / \ ~ rising,/falling/modulated intonation (precedes syllable) ;CAPITALS: stress; # solecism, unclear phonation; H intake of breath; % creaky voice quality; <R ....R> audible rustling (interpreters consulting documents in booth)

S29: Shijie Yin 298 hang - he Guoji zu- Guoji Huobi Jijin 299- liangge jinrong 300 zuzhi de ZHENGZHIhua 301 - yu
[CP[IP[NP World Bank - and int'nl org-# I M F - two cl finance organisations *de* [politicisation] - [PP compare

TA: is on page 298 \six - and -
TB: my 298 PAPER . if you need to REFER to it 299 World Bank World 300/Bank - and. the IM/F 301 -

Lianheguo - tixi xia 303 - qita daduoshu 304 - zhuanmen jigou zhengzhihua - you qi. genben - 306 bu tong. zhi chu +
[NP UN - system -under -[other [majority - [specialised [agencies[politicisation] - [VP have[NP its[basically - different points]

TA: \I M /F 303 - are under - a trend. 304 - of. - politi 305 cis\ation + the politicis\ation of 307\these
TB: h-have become - highly political 304 + H as 305 compared. to the - H 306 other institu307tions

S30: H H zhe liangge jinrong 308 zuzhi zhengzhihua de 309 FANYONG ne - BUSHI. 310 di san shijie 311 -
[CP[IP[NP these [two cl [finance orgnisations [politicisation *de* [impact/scope]] p - [IP[VP not-*shi* Third World -

TA: two agencies. is different 308 - from. that. of the \other agencies in 310\nature - the
TB: the- political- isation of the \other institutions - 310 there is - a difference 311

er shi. yikaifa 312 guojia - TEbie shi Meiguo +
[IP but[VP *shi*[NP developed nations - [PP especially *shi* [NP USA

TA: pan politicis\ation 312 - of these two \agencies +
TB + H because these 314 institutions -

S31: Meiguo juece 315 jieceng - niyou yi 316 fen mingdan + **JIN keneng jujue 318 - tongyi -**
[CP[IP[NP USA [decision level - VPdraft [NP d one cl name-list ([IP ø[VPutmost possible[V'refuse - [V'agree

TA: \merely derives from　　　316 the approach taken by the United States - not the　318 th-ird world \coun
TB: @-　　315 appl/ly- - to- developed countries instead of the Third World for example the United 318 \States +

lie zai mingdan 319 shang - guojia de -　320 <zheige> DUOBIAN DAIKUAN SHENQING 321 + **qi zhong -**
([NP[V list[PPon [name-list -on]]] - countrie(s)]] de - fp multilateral loan application]] [IP[PPthese-among -

TA: tries　-　319 H the- decision \making 320　　　　　auth\orities -　of. the. 322 United
TB: +　　　H　　　　　H　　　　　　　+　　　　th United /States 322 - can

you Yuen_an 323 -　Guba 324 -　Geruinada -　he Nijialagua　326 deng guo +
[VP(there)is [NP Vietnam　Cuba -　Granada -　and Nicaragua　[such countries]

TA:\States - 323 has /made. a. \ruling 324 that - they should try to 325- go against - the. application.
TB: agree. to -　multi lateral-　lloans 325 including -　Vietnam Cuba and-

S32: Meiguo fandui daikuan de liyou 328 -　biaomian shang shi JISHUXING de 329 + **shiji shang 330 ne.**
T([CP[IP [USA oppose loans [de Nreason]]] - [VP[PPon surface] is technical [IP[PPin reality p

TA: for \fund ing 327 - for examp# by countries such as Viet\nam Cuba 329 and Nica\ragua - and the United
TB: Nicar~ 327 agua H + H 328 the-　US has -　lopPOSed to-　loans 330 by these

ze shi. jiyu 331 YANWU. zhexie guojia 332 JIJIN shehuizhuyi de zhengquan -　he. choushi 334
[r.however F>shi [NPbased on [VP detest [NP these countries ([NPthese [NP[extreme socialist de regime] and [VPabhor

TA: States has-　331 technico#-\reasons -　but in FACT -　the United States
TB: -　lcountries 331 - based on technical reasons but 332 basically it's because 333 - the United States does n- is n- 334

Meiguo taidu de - zhengzhi 335 kaolü   +
USA ([) attitude]] -[politic(al) consideration]

TA: is   antago\nistic   335 - to/wards - the-
TB: -   does not 335 -   /like the anilmosity of

S33: H yikaifa guojia 337 cengjing zhikong   +   **H 338 di san shijie guojia -   339 chang yi   -   suowei. 340**
[CP[NP developed nations [VP AdvPast Tense V accused   [NP Third World Nations [CP often [P/VPby/as - [NPas-called

TA: m - socia\listic 337 approach of these \countries 338- and they# \attitude towards 339 th United ~States H -
TB: these countries 337towards the United. \States 338 - developed countries have /said -   that third world

RENWEI de duoSHU   -   **#a QIANGxing**   -   **zai 342 qita. zhuanmen   jigou de 343 YICHENG shang**
artificial majority   -   # vp forcibly   -   [PP at   other special.   agencies de   agenda -on]

TA: developed \countries - sometimes 341 accused - the developing nations or third world countries 343   +
TB: countries v e r y ~o f t e n 341 H   +   343 try to get their ~way

+   **H jialie. yu gai 345 zuzhi - HAO WU RENHE guan 346 lian de - zhengzhixing yiti 347**   +
vp V add on[NP[PPwith such organstns - [not-slightest] connection de - political points]]]

TA: +   of 345   +   stipulating 346   +   political agenda 348
TB: - in 344 - specialised 345 /agencies -   w i t h-   their overwhelming \presence -

S34 :   H dan Lianheguo [SIC] - 349 zai- Guoji Huobi Jijin 350 - he Shijie Yinhang 351 zhong -
[CPbut [IP[NPUN ('s)   -   [VP[PPat International Monetary Fund - and World Bank   -in] -

TA: that has nothing - to do with. 349 the.   +   \agencies   +
TB: very often   pushing -   irrelevant -   issues into   the i\tineraries

dui 352 dishi. MEIguo de guojia - jujue yuyi DAIKUAN 354 de - zhengzhi lichang 355 -
[PPtowards[NP[VPhostile-to USA *de* nations] - [VPrefuse provide loans] *de* - political position]] -

TA: 352 however + the UN. 353 and the ~IMF 354 - are re\fusing
TB: 352 of these special ised intis# instutions % + as for. the political

TONGYANG - shou 357 dao di san shijie guojia de. zhizhe 358 +
[VP likewise - [V'received [NP Third World countries *de* censure]]

TA: to fund. - those 357\countries that are an\tagonous towards United 358 /States - had been
TB: stance TAKen. 357 by the United \Na/tions - 358 /in - H reFUSing

S35: H 359 Meiguo Guohui. ceng. yi du jujue. 360 pizhun bojiao. 361 Shijie Yinhang. xinzengzi 362 -
[CP[IP[NPUS Congress [IP *past* once [VPrefused [VPpermit [V'allocate [NPWorld Bank capitalisation

TA: under 359\criticism - from third 360 world \countries - the US Congress - once
TB: to 359 provid- to provide \loans to certain \countries. this has also received a lot of criticism - 362\from.

xinzengzi. an 363 - H zhi dao- 364 - Shijie Yinhang zongcai 365 - @m - Maina. - mala 367 -
capitalisation motion - [PP right [until - [CP [IPNPWorld Bank Chief - Macna mara

TA: refused - to \allocate funds -364 for the /new - ~funding -~scheme of the - World 367
TB: third world countries + + the world-

@m- 368 xiang ZHONGYUAN - xiaozu weiyuanhui - tichu 370 shuotie + chengNUO - zai duanqi
[PVP to House of Reprsentves. - small-group committee - [VPsubmit[NPstatement [VPVpromise ([IP[PPat short period

TA:\Bank - until the /new - \Gover nor of the World Bank - MannaMAra 371 - pre\sented
TB: 368@m \Ppresident .of the World. /Bank + recent/ly 371- - prom

NEI 372 - bu ZAI - daikuan Yuenan 373 zhiHOU - H H cai - jiedong 374 +
-within] - [not again - loan Vietnam] -after] - [IP Q then-only - [VP unfreeze ø]

TA: - a back\grounder - statement 373 - to - the - representative \house -
TB: ised 372 + H to- 375 +

S36: Meiguo Caizhengbu. jing 376 diaocha zhengshi 377 + weihu Meiguo liyi 378 -
[CP[IP[NP US Finance Dept. [PVP thru/conduct survey [VP prove [CP[IP([NP[CP PRO protect US interest -

TA: of the \Congress 376 - that's when 377 the fund - providing loans to the. Vietnam. 378
TB: + H \stop 377 -

juyou zhongyao gongneng de 379 - wuqi zhi yi 380 - nai shi - caizheng liliang 381 +
[VP possess [essential function de - weapon] -one-of]]] - [r:actually F>shi [NP finance power]]]

TA: - by 379 - th United States 380 - 381 the United States 382 -
TB: in order to appease the United- States \recently + +

S37: Meiguo- - wei. bian383geng - duo@- wei biangeng guoji duobian yinhang 385 - zheizhong SHI 386WU.
[CP[IP[NP USA[PVP - for modify - mult# - for modify international multilateral bank - [this cl (['practical

TA: under stands - 383 that - a very im\portant power 384 to secure political\interest - is by \holding to. 386
TB: + H the United 383 /States - H H384 + +

yu CHENGXU 387 - zhengce - de zhege teshu 388 mubiao - JIU shi 389 - yi yunyong . 390 CAIZHENG FANGSHI -
and program' policy [de d special aim [VP F> just shi [PVP by implement financial method

TA: economic \strength - while reaching 388 - these specific ~goals 390 - of. \changing - the.
TB: +

S38-39: 391 er chenggong de + H zhe xiang caizheng fangshi 393 de yunzuo - .youshí 394 quanbu chenggong -

[CP[IP[?NP this [? cl/P finance method *de* operate [VP sometimes [completely succeed
so succeeded *de*]

TA: 391 rules of the- - w-wi YMF or \World Bank - is - \using 394 - fi\nancial -
TB: H + H392 ha_s 394 exerted its - H

youshí jin neng - bufen 396 - dadao mudi + [S39] Meiguo 398 xingdeng dangju - xingZHENG dangju 399 -

[VPsometimes only [able - [part [VP ttain goal]] [CP[IP[NP US # # authorities - administrative authorities

TA: manip- @- manoeuvering - sometimes - the- 397 financial ma\noeuvering is eff~ec/tive - sometimes. it can 399only
TB: @ political 396 /clout H H in its- @ operations in -@m financial institutions. 399

he lifa bumen - dou liaojie 400 + Buliedun 401 - Senlin huiyi. chengli 402 de - Guob#ji Huobi Jijin 403 - he Shijie

[and legislve organs - [VPall/dm understand [CP[IP[NPBretton - Woods meeting founded *de* - [N I# IMF and [World

TA: reach. \partial effect H 400 the executive. and legislative \branches of the United States will under 403 s~tand -
TB: under the UN 400 - the United States 401 - au~thorities + ackno\w403ledge

Yinhang 404 - liangge jinrong zuzhi de mudi + shi - 406 cushi quanqiu jingji ziyouhua - 408 bing dui

Bank [two finance organisns *de* [goal [VP*shi* [CP[IP[VP promote ([NPglobal economy liberalise - [IP *con*/[VPpas-to

TA: the- 404 I M. F and - ~World Bank - fou- 406 founded - as a result of ~Bretton Woods. 408 Agreement -
TB: + + 405 the- - objective of the World Bank. and the I MF. is to promote 408 -

Meiguo chanpin - 409 he. ziben shichang. kaifang 410 - fuhe Meiguo 411 yiban liyi 412 +

US product - and capital market opening - [VPcorrespond-to [NPUS general interest]

TA: were- to- pro\mote - 410financialliberalisation. and - the. \opening - of goods. 412 and services \sector413
  - by # United States 414
TB: global - economic globaliSA/tion 410 - and - to promote 411 - \open \markets to meet- 413 US ~needs

Notes to Chapters

Notes to Chapters

Chapter 1   Introduction

1. 'Speakers' and 'Addressees' with initial capitals are used to distinguish sovereign communicators from secondary receivers and speakers like translators and interpreters.
2. Danish, Dutch, English, Finnish, French, German, Greek, Italian, Portuguese, Spanish, Swedish. Some language pairs (e.g. Portuguese-Finnish, Greek-Dutch) must be handled through a single or even a double relay (Speaker → Interpreter → Interpreter (→ Interpreter) →Addressees) because of the scarcity of competent interpreters.
3. thematic: from the original Greek sense of *thema* as the 'setting', we use this term to denote the set of significant entities and their attributes concerned by the discourse, as opposed to logical relations (see also Glossary).
4. AIIC: Association Internationale d'Interprètes de Conférence (International Association of Conference Interpreters), founded in Paris in 1953 and now based in Geneva. The Association currently has about 2300 members in 65 countries.
5. In *Relevance* (1986/1995), Sperber and Wilson adopt the convention of a female Speaker and a male Hearer. Since most conference interpreters are women, and most conference participants are men, we will use the feminine pronoun for the interpreter and the masculine for both Speakers and Addressees.
6. AI researchers trying to develop speech-to-speech translation systems have identified the recognition of the Speaker's intentions as a key problem alongside the perceptual and parsing challenges of fast, noisy, ill-formed or elliptical input (Kitano 1993:6-7).
7. We shall use 'translation' and 'translator' generically where applicable, but in professional usage, these terms distinguish the written activity or product from to of (oral) interpretation, performed by an interpreter. (The term 'code-switching' is not appropriate in a pragmatic theory, which addresses both code and inference-based processes.)
8. Gile has suggested (p.c.) that these are not 'real' retroactive pointers but that they simply mark the end of the 'meaningful part of the sentence'. However, in our own analysis we understand 'meaning' in the broadest sense, to include any indication which may elsewhere be described as metadiscoursal, ritualistic, or marking values like politeness.
9. In Marr's computational theory of vision, perception is a multi-layered process. The different layers have filters of different gradation, which makes perception at each of them approximative. At the primal sketch stage, light intensities and edges are distinguished and '*gestalt*-like principles of good continuation, similarity and so on are used to group tokens together so as to identify global patterns of organisation' (P. Wenderoth). The '2.5D' sketch assigns parts of the image to objects and surfaces in the world and specifies their orientations and distances, for which (in addition to the primal sketch) it draws on cues to size, depth and object boundaries provided by stereopsis, motion, texture, shape-from-shading, shape-from-motion etc. This stage makes use of non-accidental properties of the image—that is, it assumes that things that are very

similar would not be alongside each other by chance, and so groups them (adapted from webpage material by Prof. Peter Wenderoth of Macquarie University, Australia, with his permission).
10. For example, if in a cinema someone has just thrown a bottle at the screen, understanding the cry *'He did it!'* does not require previous discourse (Johnson-Laird 1983: 390).

Chapter 2   SI Research

1. The relative marginalisation of non-English-language writing in recent decades may also have lessened the impact of SI research in linguistics. Most pioneering work on interpretation has appeared in French, and to a lesser extent, German, and Slavic languages.
2. In the last ten years, the dividing line has been blurred somewhat, and interpretation research has been integrated with translation studies into academic programmes in several universities, beyond the already established vocational courses.
3. This refers to the American Structuralist school in linguistics, not European structuralism.
4. See Gile (1990).
5. NATO Symposium on Language Interpretation and Communication, Venice 1977 (Gerver and Sinaiko 1978).
6. Pauses in the input speech were mostly shorter than one second in Goldman-Eisler's corpus, one to two seconds in length in Barik's; in Gerver's own corpus, only 13% of all pauses were longer than 1 second, and only 4% were longer than 2 seconds.
7. To refute this theory even more conclusively, Lederer (1981: 240) offered the transcription of an extract where, far from alternating with the Speaker's articulation, the interpreter speaks simultaneously with the Speaker most of the time, and every other possible pattern of simultaneity and alternation is also represented.
8. An impression of the 'lag' or EVS in SI as reflected in our corpus can be obtained from Appendix T2-B, in which macro-'segments' are marked in input and output.
9. Both the word and the syllable raise problems as units for comparing passage lengths, or speech and articulation rates, not only because of probable inter-language variations in the definition of these units (e.g. due to different patterns of compounding, agglutination and cliticisation), or in syllable-to-word ratio, but more fundamentally because, as Gerver points out, 'syllables as phonological units do not necessarily correspond with morphemic or semantic units, and it is surely meaning rather than sound that we are concerned with in discussing translation' (1976: 174).
10. Barik's 'errors' include omissions ('inaccurate/incomplete' and 'gist-preserving') and 'additions' consisting of either the addition of adverbial qualifiers, e.g. *deeply* rooted (A1), 'elaborations' (*aware and conscious of what is just and fair*) (A2), or 'relationship additions' (e.g. *because...*) and those which 'serve to give closure to the sentence but do not add anything substantial to it.' Errors were subdivided as

> E1: awkward translation of lexical item causing mild semantic error;
> E2: lexical item: gross semantic error due to confusion with homonym, of reference or other translation error;
> E3: mild phrasing change (gist-preserving: 'generally acceptable within context of SI');
> E4: substantial phrasing change but only slight change of emphasis;
> E5: gross departure from meaning; bluff or 'fib'; wrong proposition (e.g. question for statement), meaningless output, opposite meaning etc. (summarised from Barik 1975: 275-9).

11. 80% of interpreters work with one earphone slightly off the ear in order to be able to monitor the sound of their own voice. Lambert also found (1989: 14) that interpreters make significantly fewer errors when listening through one ear than both simultaneously.

12. 'General Abstract Memory' (GAM) in the terminology of Massaro (1975, 1978) and Moser (1976, 1978).

13. All translations of quotations are my own.

14. ESIT: Ecole supérieure d'interprètes et de traducteurs (Université de la Sorbonne, Paris III).

15. D. Seleskovitch, one of the founding generation of the modern interpreting profession, played an important rule in establishing the first professional interpretation service for the European Communities.

16. *'Sens*[...] does not appear to the reader as the result of semantic elements assembled successively piece by piece: rather, the awareness of meaning (*sens*) comes as all the relevant features are perceived simultaneously'

17. Errors due to what we may term 'cognitive prejudice' are reported by Lederer and in other SI literature. Lederer gives an example (1981: 92-3) in which the string **'nun ist unsre RIC-Wagenschuld bereits auf 125 Millionen Schillinge im Jahr angewachsen'** ('our RIC wagon debt has already risen to 125 schillings per year') is rendered as 'we would have preferred the UIC wagon' The interpreter may not have heard of 'RIC', a clearing house through which railways pay for the use of each other's stock. The known referent 'UIC' suppresses perception of the unknown 'RIC', and an entire proposition is fabricated with what is known about 'the UIC wagon,' while the rest of the sentence, which is audible but inconsistent, is suppressed or discarded.

   Garden-pathing due to probabilistic expectations (e.g. of formulaic strings) has been demonstrated by Chernov (1992), who mounted an SI experiment on discourse which included 10 unexpected strings of the following type:

   '...we are trying to transform subsistence economies into modern societies with modern industry and modern agriculture. Very often we are told that Rome was not built in a *dale, that it was a built on seven hills*'

   Chernov obtained an error or omission rate of 76.5% (from 80 analysable responses): after the unexpected turn, most interpreters either rendered the wrong 'prompted prediction' (37.5%), or gave no translation of the string at all (38.75%).

18. The very general, all-embracing terms of the theory of action underlying ATT may be partly responsible for its rather unconstrained, open-ended character: *'Handeln kann aufgefasst werden als situations-, kontext- und institutions-abhängiges, regelbezogenes normen-, wert- oder ziel-orientiertes, systemhaft eingebettetes, wenigstens partiell ablaufkontrolliertes oder teilbewusstes motiviertes Verhalten eines personalen oder kollektiven Akteurs, das diesem als von ihm durch-geführt zugeschrieben wird'* (Lenk 1978: 345, cited in Pöchhacker 1994).

19. AIIC (the International Association of Conference Interpreters) classifies its members according to their language combination. An AIIC member must be a native speaker-comprehender of at least one language, and have near-native active (B) or passive (C) competence in one or more acquired languages. AIIC's Committee of Admissions and Language Classification (CACL) defines the language competence required of interpreters as follows:

   A: the interpreter's mother tongue (or another language strictly equivalent to a mother tongue), into which he interprets from all his other working languages, generally in the two modes of interpretation, simultaneous and consecutive. Members shall have at least one A language, but may have several.

   B: (one or more) language(s) into which the interpreter works from one or more of his other languages and which, although not a mother tongue, is a language of which he has perfect com-mand. Some interpreters work into B languages in only one of the two modes of interpretation.

   C: one or more (optional) 'passive languages': languages of which the interpreter has a complete understanding and from which he interprets (AIIC 1993).

Examples of professional language combinations: A English, B German, C Italian; A Russian, A English; A German, C French, Italian, English, Spanish and Portuguese; A Mandarin, B Cantonese and English, C Fujianese.

20. Anderson (1979) found little significance for either visibility (video vs. audiotape) or prior information about the discourse, but no extensive corpus-based study of these factors has yet been undertaken.

21. One methodological reservation can be made regarding the role of prior knowledge in Lederer's analysis, especially in view of her own emphasis on the importance of this variable. Half of the corpus was produced in real conference conditions; interpreters then completed the corpus in the laboratory to yield two complete interpreted protocols of the discussion. With respect to the evaluation of passages, we are not always told which of the extracts used to demonstrate points in the text are 'live' or 'reconstructed' versions. At the time of the live event, these professional interpreters would probably have remained in the booth to listen for at least part of each half-hour 'off-mike', making it difficult to accept versions produced in the laboratory a few days later as first-pass efforts.

22. SSLMIT: Scuola Superiore di Lingue Moderne per Interpreti e Traduttori, at the Università degli Studi di Trieste.

23. With regard to memory, the IT account is not entirely consistent. Two memories are proposed: immediate (auditory, echoic) memory holds 'only 7-8 words', which disappear after being integrated into cognitive memory (Seleskovitch and Lederer 1986: 275), whereas 'the display [of meaning] in immediate memory proves that *sens* is acquired as an immediate synthesis, not a stepwise process of assembly' (Lederer 1981: 144). But the operation of these memories is said to overlap; meaning from words, for instance, is derived at more than one stage.

24. The link from representation to production is also somewhat underspecified: on the one hand, enunciation proceeds from cognitive memory, but production is sometimes described as a direct path from semantic traits to articulation (*la phonation est commandée par les traits sémantiques*); evidence is claimed from 'floating semes', a term used for a type of cross-language interference, exemplified in errors like '*dessins (m)...remises (f)* (drawings ... handed over) in which the feminine feature ('*sème*') in the German noun **Zeichnungen** (f., = drawings) leaks into the French output (marked on the adjective).

25. This view is strongly stated in the 'toolmakers' paradigm: in this metaphor, individuals live in separate environments, but don't know what other environments are like, nor even that they are different from each other; they have no common language, but send each other blueprints of tools, and are surprised when their tools are returned with incomprehensible modifications. This implies that speakers may have incorrect conceptions of what their addressees know, or of what 'everybody' knows, and that communication 'probably misfires more often than we realise'. (Green 1989; Reddy 1979, cited in Green 1989: 11).

26. The current consensus is that good interpretation depends on the interpreter's competence, various aspects of her working conditions, and features of the input texts themselves. A conference interpreter's competence can be said to comprise three elements (Setton 1994):

1) Linguistic competence, including pragmatic competence, both 'pragmalinguistic' and 'sociopragmatic' as distinguished by Leech (1983), or in Fillmore's terms, both the 'small facts' about the conventionalised meanings of individual expressions (like '*Why don't we..*'; or the different values of German *schon* and English *already*); and the 'large facts' of politeness, register etc. (Hara 1988; Kondo 1988).

2) General knowledge providing a sufficient base on which to build the 'local' and specialised knowledge needed to understand and speak convincingly in the various fields covered in each successive conference, given advance notice and documentation;

3) Skills in handling information. In consecutive interpretation, the basic specialised skill is a technique for using notes to support the accurate rendition of discourse lasting several minutes.

27. SI users probably tolerate occasional silences of up to about 8-10 seconds, depending on the general rhythm of the discourse. Our interpreters' fluency is acceptable in this respect: the main corpus contains only two or three pauses reaching 6-7 secs, all located at clause boundaries (at WA110; TA91, 201).

28. The Beijing School of Interpretation and Translation (BSIT), successor to the original UN-sponsored programme at Beijing Foreign Studies University (BFSU).

29. In the following extract three verbs are 'anticipated': the first (*make available*) is said to be possible based on 'a cognitive memory [...] of the previous discussion', the third (*organise*) on 'semantic prediction' of the verb from its direct object (in my transcription, $_{ACC}$ and $_{OBL}$ indicate Accusative and unspecified 'Oblique' (indirect Object) Case inflections respectively). I do not think the translation of both streams into English obscures the point at issue:

[context (previous sentence): *unfortunately the [specially equipped] protoypes will be delivered too late for a presentation to the press to have any impact...so...*

Spkr: ' we would be very glad if the French Railways [one$_{ACC}$ of their own prototypes
Interpr.:   it would   be particularly desirable for

with [*these special fittings*] [make available could (....so that...)
the French Railways to <u>make available</u> one of these [*specially fitted*] prototypes ....

....

The Swiss Railways have[us $_{OBL}$ offered, [this press conference, which [by sales reps
The Swiss Railways— have offered to <u>help us to organise</u> this

in the G. company suggested been had, <u>jointly with us to conduct.</u>
press conference which was suggested by...etc.

The second supplied verb (<u>*help us to*</u> organise), which anticipates the meaning of 'jointly', is attributed to a third type of knowledge: it is known from previous discourse that the press conference is seen as an initiative of the organisation as a whole (not only of the Swiss Railways). The distinction proposed is not between anticipation based on long or short-term knowledge, but between the linguistically-based prediction of forms, and the (other-knowledge-based) anticipation of meaning (*sens*) (1981: 255).

A more striking example of anticipation than the above (of the Verb on the basis of a direct object) again from Lederer's corpus, is the production of a verb and its Object before the appearance of either an input verb or any arguments (only adverbial and prepositional adjuncts):

(Context: *discussion among railway administrations who have commissioned a consortium to design a European railcar, which they are then committed to buy.*
Problem currently under discussion: *if one or more railway administrations starts asking for the drawings of the protoype in order to be able to start ordering rolling stock ahead of the planned release time, the event might lose its public relations value to the manufacturers*)

..if the consortium were to say, let us just suppose they said, we are [in view of this extension
Int 1:   and if the consortium said, at least let us suppose that they said
Int 2:   and if— the group- of manufacturers should then say

Spkr: of the request*] not prepared [IP in advance, [i.e.] before the time at which we had
Int 1:   we do not   agree to @
Int 2:   the - this is just a hypothesis - that it was not ready - to provide these

Spkr: promised to, [the drawings to hand over, then today's discussion is pointless ...
Int 1: give out the drawings earlier than planned
Int 2:   drawings before the time at which they had promised....
(* i.e. request for the drawings) (Lederer 1981: 262 ff.)

30. Probably not more than twenty or thirty of the world's languages are regularly used in conference interpretation.
31. It has been maintained at different times (but not, to my knowledge, by interpreters) that SI from German, and (later) from Japanese, must be impossible because of the structure of these languages.
32. Gile (1992) claims that Japanese offers processing relief at frequent intervals due to a higher frequency of predictable sentence endings (sentence-final politeness and obligatory closure forms) which are not found in European languages. Gile found that 46% of sentence-endings in his Japanese texts were predictable over at least 5 syllables: at average EVS and Speaker delivery, this corresponds to predictable strings of 1-3 secs in length at the end of nearly half the sentences in these Japanese discourses (ibid.: 202). None (0%) were found in 12 French and 10 English texts. German was somewhere between these extremes: six grammatically predictable sentence-endings were found, comprising 12% of sentences in six speeches; all were VP complexes of 5 syllables or less. However, no evidence of resulting facilitation is offered, either in time/processing load terms, or contrastively between languages.
33. e.g. the French, English and German educational systems; or the different anatomical and physiological descriptions underlying Chinese and Western medicine.
34. This claim is made (according to Keenan) notably by Katz (1978).
35. The situation would be far worse with some languages, like Javanese, in which whole areas of the vocabulary are reserved for use in certain kinship-relation contexts.
36. Seleskovitch claims that 'intentionality' does not concern the translator, inasmuch as she does not translate 'there's a draught' as 'close the window,' even when this is clearly the intended message, because it goes beyond the *sens* of the utterance. The role and fate of the implicit often appears to be an embarrassment to translation theorists, and writers like Seleskovitch are at pains to avoid misunderstanding: translation 'should stop short of exegesis or hermeneutics [..;] a translator often takes the implicit into account to gain a better idea of the *sens*, but translation reflects only the latter.' (Seleskovitch and Lederer 1986: 269-271)
37. Implicatures can hardly be transferred with exactly the same strengths in translation: for instance, the following translation into French, favoured by Seleskovitch, significantly strengthens the implicature of an *unfavourable* political climate (in the Europe of the 1930s):

... es wurde möglich, losgelöst von der politischen Landschaft, die Zusammenarbeit der Partner und den Stromaustausch überregional and grenzüberschreitend zu sichern
(it became possible [for national electricity grids in Europe] to 'work together' and transmit power across regional and national borders 'freed/disengaged from' the political landscape)

'la collaboration des réseaux ... n'était pas affecté par le climat politique qui régnait alors'

Chapter 3   An Outline Model for SI

1. Lichtheim's diagram (1885), based on Wernicke's empirical findings on dyslexic and aphasic impairments, pictured stages for input, 'auditory word-representations' and a 'centre where concepts are elaborated'.
2. The connectionist account sees the representation of general semantic knowledge as distributed through the brain by domains, but it seems to be compatible with Fillmorean frame theory:

   'each memory unit or 'engram' is realised as a pattern of activation distributed over many coding elements, forming an 'auto-associated' functional unit. Activation of a subset of such a network recruits the remainder so that the whole composite pattern comes to be retrieved as a unit [...] when one reads [...] 'the man lifted the piano' one's knowledge of pianos as heavy objects becomes salient [...]; in contrast, reading 'the man tuned the piano' appears to prime a different subset of piano attributes (Funnell and Allport 1987: 393-5).

3. Or in the machine, but here we will be concerned with human processing.
4. This term is used to denote *parole* (i.e. language products, although technically this includes written text) in order to distinguish it from *langue* (the linguistic resources that may be used to produce *parole*).
5. A more complex example encountered in the author's recent SI experience was the genetics term *restriction fragment length polymorphisms*, in a presentation addressed to a non-specialist audience. This probably requires something like *polymorphismes dûs aux (variations dans les) longueurs des fragments de restriction*, 'polymorphisms due to variations in the length of fragments of restriction'. In any event, inserting the attributive particle *de* throughout will not do, since French *de* is not as semantically neutral as juxtaposition is within the English NP.
6. Fodor points out that if you gently push your eyeball, instead of moving it in the normal way by an act of will, you get apparent motion, although you know what you are doing. Further evidence is provided by the Müller-Lyre illusion: subjects who have measured the two arrows insist that one *still looks* longer than the other (Fodor 1983: 63-67). The application of the principle to language is of course not so straightforward.
7. This is the Chomskyan sense of 'logical form'. In *Relevance*, the term designates a structured arrangement of concepts (see Glossary).
8. Fabbro et al. (1991), for example, used a dichotic listening task (two different texts) to study hemispheric specialisation in interpreters, but appeared to equate this genuine dual-task condition with SI in the surprising statement that 'listening simultaneously to two different speeches, in regard to both their *respective content* and their linguistic codes, is however, a usual task for simultaneous interpreters' (Fabbro et al. 1991: 12; my emphasis).
9. The original diagram includes touch, a channel not normally open in standard conference interpreting conditions.
10. According to a story told in the profession, this phenomenon was experienced directly by interpreters on one occasion when a Japanese delegate began reading from a *katakana* phonetic transcript of an English translation of his speech.
11. English is the language most affected, but other world languages, like Chinese, show wide dialectal variations, even at leadership level, which pose a major challenge to interpreters (Kratochvil 1968: 145; Setton 1993);
12. For comfort to listeners, and because of the SI lag, interpreters also often verbalise turn-changes in a debate by saying 'Chairman' or e.g. 'Delegate of Canada' at each change of Speaker.
13. Conditions stipulated in ISO (International Standards Organisation) standards 2603 and 4043 for conference interpretation booths, required by Art. 8 of the standard AIIC contract.
14. See also Ch.2, note 19. Of course, the ideal situation of native active and passive proficiency in both SL and TL obtains only in the case of 'perfect bilinguals'. In Europe, practice favours the

recruitment of native Speakers of the TL language, but this is hardly ever possible with, for example, Chinese-English or Arabic-English. The question of whether interpreters should work from an A to a B language has always been controversial (see e.g. Seleskovitch and Lederer 1989: 135).

15. Shadowing: repeating speech exactly immediately as it is heard.

16. We use the term 'information' to encompass any and all sources which may contribute to the interpretation of an utterance or discourse, including word order, morphology and other grammatical features of words and sentences, prosody and intonation, perceptual and conceptual knowledge, and indeed any perception or assumption, text-based or not, which contributes to interpretation.

17. Evidence of the existence of a component with prioritising and task coordination functions is also provided by disorders such as 'dysexecutive syndrome', typified in the symptom of perseveration observed in some frontal-lobe-impaired patients, in which the control of action is captured at a low level by a single powerful schema that continues to inhibit all other schemata; conversely, effective behaviour is characterised by the ability to accept override from superordinate schemas (Shallice 1988).

18. A recent AIIC survey reported that many users of SI services prefer 'intelligent gisting' to an informationally complete rendition (Mackintosh 1994, Kurz 1994). In informationally dense and fast discourse, prioritising may be necessary. Sometimes, users explicitly ask interpreters to 'just summarise'.

19. 'The interpreter shall be morally responsible for the integrity of his or her work and shall not bow to any pressure in performing it' (AIIC General Conditions of Work, Article 2).

20. An example is given by Herbulot (1990) of the translation into French of an English text instructing yachters on how to lay a course using equipment not used in France, including special instrument and charts comprising a compass-rose. The English source text begins with instructions in the use of the instruments. Herbulot's French translation begins with the course-laying instructions adapted for users equipped only with an ordinary ruler and protractor, before describing certain specialised instruments which can be obtained if desired.

21. A rather trivial, but ill-understood corollary of this is that speech performance ('fluency') in a language, native or learned, depends not only on mastery of its grammar and vocabulary but also on what one tries to express.

22. There are a few individuals who appear to produce speech indistinguishable from native production in two languages on all levels, but close analysis would probably reveal differing degrees of cross-linguistic influence.

Chapter 4   Research Issues, Corpus and Methodology

1. 'The only actual phenomenon we are engaged in elucidating is the total speech act in the total speech situation.' (Austin 1955/1962, Lecture XII).

2. More precisely, by which the source discourse becomes the output discourse.

3. It was not possible, for reasons of space, to reproduce the entire corpus in this volume. The remaining interlinear synchronised transcripts (for Würzburg interpreters WA and WB, and Taipei interpreters TA and TB for segments S1-28) may be obtained from the author.

4. Semi-rehearsed speech is probably the most common register in international conference practice, lying between spontaneous dialogue, as in the negotiations in Lederer's (1981) corpus, and speech recited from text, which is also quite common. Conference discourse typically belongs to the discursive or argumentative genre; it is rarely primarily descriptive or narrative.

5. Recordings of the Würzburg conference were graciously supplied by Sylvia Kalina of the University of Heidelberg, also a professional conference interpreter and researcher into SI, who

obtained permission for their use in research. Copyright for the content of the extracts belongs in the last instance to the organisers of the Symposium.

6. The author.
7. Due to a technical error, the last part of Segment S9 was not captured on the multi-track recording of the mock session, but only 10s were lost and the back-up tapes ensured that no significant timing problem resulted. The possible distortion over this passage due to timing from single-track recording only is estimated at 0.2-0.3 seconds.
8. The sample for analysis, chosen for its high impromptu content, ends here: the next segment (not analysed) begins with the next sentence of the supplied text (**Die Rechtsprechung**...), which was also paraphrased, though less so. For the remainder of his presentation, the Speaker alternates between extracts from the paper, paraphrase or elaboration, and unscripted accounts of cases.
9. In other words, as it turned out they were given three different versions of the theme of the presentation.
10. Intonation foci are realised with rising pitch in German. Pitch is flatter in English, with numerous crisp word-final phonetic effects not clearly distinguishable from short filled pauses. In Chinese, pitch is phonological (tones are not shown in the transcription), so contrast is achieved by other means.
11. Modern (GB) theory views German surface word order as the result of three types of movement: extraposition, topicalisation and scrambling. Extraposition, which moves embedded clauses down beyond the non-finite verb, is obligatory for finite clauses, and preferred for non-finite clauses:

> er hat   behauptet, PRO viel Geld zu verdienen
> he *past-Aux* asserted,   much money to earn
> 'he claimed he earned a lot of money'

'Scrambling' generates permutations in the order of arguments and adjuncts in the middle field, adjoining elements either to the Verb phrase (VP), or the 'inflected phrase' or main proposition (IP). Adjunction to an adjective phrase has also been termed 'scrambling' (Grewendorf and Sternefeld 1990: 9-16):

> [$_{NP}$Der [$_{AP}$ seiner Studien [$_{AP}$[$_{NP}$ in höchstem Masse] [$_A$.t$_i$überdrüssige]]] Student
> The   of-his studies   in highest measure   fed-up   student

12. One approach to the analysis of Chinese deals with the apparent presence of more than one sentence-initial nominal phrase by distinguishing Topic and Subject (although 'identical Topic-subject' and 'double-subject' constructions are also identified), suggesting a new typological category of 'Topic-prominent' languages (Li and Thompson 1981: 85-100). Topic in this sense includes sentence-initial expressions deemed to have 'sentential scope', beyond the Y- and L-dislocation phenomena traditionally recognised, and is seen as a feature incorporating crucial discoursal and information-structure functions. Some Chinese grammarians do not distinguish between Topic and Subject; thus Chao allows time, place and condition to occur in the 'Main Subject' (Chao 1968: 69-73, 100). See also Glossary.
13. The construction '**yi** [NP,IP...] **wei** [NP]' may also prepose a nominal or propositional Object (cf. Taipei corpus S1, S23).
14. To clarify the criterion of simplicity, Peirce cites Galileo (translator's name not given): 'it is the simpler Hypothesis, in the sense of the more facile and natural, the one that instinct suggests, that must be preferred; for the reason that, unless man have a natural bent in accordance with nature's, he has no chance of understanding nature at all.'

Chapter 5   Strategies and Structures

1. Setton (1993) highlights some typological and cultural specificities of Chinese public discourse, suggesting that they may pose a problem in conjunction with other factors, like text written-ness—not (as inferred by Lonsdale (1998: 97)) that they require certain 'structural strategies' as defined here. Admittedly, though, I had not developed the cognitive-pragmatic approach at that time, and my use of the term 'syntacrobatics' does leave the text open to that interpretation.
2. French does not normally have this kind of pitch stress on individual words; this is an African dialect.
3. For instance, W-M2α (W15-17) 'how ....[by German law [regulated is'; or TW61-2 (Wh *in situ*): **women yong shenmeyang de fangshi** [we use [what-kind of method [to...).
4. A Definite NP is identified by Strawson as the most basic type of 'presupposition trigger' (Levinson 1983: 181) presupposing simply the existence of the entity.
5. ROC: Republic of China (on Taiwan).
6. Chinese Noun determiners include classifiers (measure words), but these are very short.
7. NP-Headedness is sometimes claimed to be a problem for SI from English (basic Head-final NP) into French (basic Head-initial NP), but very complex elliptical Noun Phrases are common only in formal and technical discourse.
8. This refers to true questions, not the Chinese free-variable uses of '*wh*-words' as e.g. *shei* in *shei ye keyi,* 'anyone will do'.
9. 'Clauses' include all the root, subordinate, relative, and complement clauses which are connected up to form sentences. Conjoined clauses are counted as separate sentences.

Chapter 6   The Pragmatics of Interpretation

1. There are clear differences between WL and WA/WB in overall prolixity and fluency: WL talks 27.6% more, and 27.4% faster than her colleagues in the simulation (both separate and average values for WA and WB). Although WL is by far the least experienced of the three, her tone is more lively and authoritative, although audibly more tense. She finds and produces an early verb faster than the other two, makes more daring simplifications, adds more conative material more confidently and appropriately, and is more explicit, perhaps because she has a far better model, having being directly involved in the event since the previous day.
2. '*obtention*' is a Gallicism, intruding from the interpreter's first acquired language (French) into her native language (English) while she is interpreting from her second acquired language (German).
3. This countability influences the interpretation compositionally: 'the courts have addressed the case material, but only some aspects' is rendered as (WA) '*handed down verdicts - not very many but some*' perhaps a more significant, representational effect of a 'floating seme' than the feminine marker example given by Lederer (Ch.2, note 24).
4. The 'reflexive' pro-form *sich* is used here not as a reflexive but as the marker of an unaccusative verb. The first '**sich**' in this string is a (ungrammatical) speech error (premature articulation).
5. In fact the whole speech (10 mins. approx.) itself is intended to amount to 'introductory remarks' by each of the five panel members.
6. Or, expressed in another formalism, as a 'mental space' having been 'built' by such a verb (Fauconnier 1985).
7. '*le coeur a ses raisons, que la raison ne connaît point*'. Damasio (1994) reclaims cognitive status for emotions, on the grounds that rational decision making depends on the biasing of representations by 'somatic marking', and revises Pascal: 'the organism has some reasons that reason must utilise' (1994: 164-201).

8. The Belief/Desire analysis is not fine-grained enough to distinguish, for instance, between *sad that, annoyed that* and *sorry that*, all of which would be analyzed as Bel (*p*) & Des (~*p*) (Searle 1983: 36).

9. 'Mood' is used here in the traditional, not the Hallidayan sense.

10. This is more apparent in the Taipei text, where such items are more pervasive; but it may be that the relatively inexperienced Taipei interpreters have not yet learned to pass on this dimension, receiving them as interpreters *qua* addressees, and so absorbing them like the scope-marking connectives *shi* and *ne*, instead of passing them on as interpreters *qua* messengers.

11. According to Searle, remembering and prior intention are mediated by representation, while visual perception and action employ *presentation* (a sub-class of representations) (1983: 97). We might therefore assign a fifth class of features which contribute to interpretation, including non-verbal signs and perhaps some conatives, as direct reflections of volition, to this medium.

12. In conference SI, the Speaker's attitudes, illocutions etc., are conventionally formulated as the interpreter's own (first person singular).

13. Readers familiar with this British dialect can appreciate this effect by reading the interpreter's version aloud.

Chapter 7   Judgment, Compensation and Coordination

1. 'Failure' is more appropriate where communication is concerned, 'error' for rule-governed values like well-formedness or basic semantic equivalence. 'Failure' is therefore used here as a comprehensive term.

2. They are even rarer in informal registers, which are characterised by 'leaking', or extraposition of arguments and adjuncts below the verb (see e.g. Hawkins 1988).

3. Utterance-scope items like evidential or attitudinal adverbs may also occur finally, either as afterthoughts (in SVO languages like English which prefer to place them early), e.g. *You shouldn't try to do it all in one go, frankly/I'd say*; or *He got to the station before any of us arrived, obviously*; or standardly in some languages, as in the case of the polite and attenuative forms described by Gile (1992) in (SOV) Japanese.

4. Former British Prime Minister Anthony Eden is said to have complained to an interpreter who produced an 'information-perfect' rendition of his remarks: 'You massacred my speech'.

5. The elusiveness of *le mot juste* is usually cited to explain why literary and poetic text is unsuited to simultaneous interpretation, but the high frequency of 'incidental' and new qualification (or low redundancy) are probably as great an obstacle at the representational stage as is the retrieval challenge at production.

6. Differences in text genre are extensively discussed in relation to translation by the text linguistic school (e.g. Reiss and Vermeer 1984), and in a Relevance context by Gutt (1991).

7. Especially in the case of English, a stress-timed and accented language. This is arguably a case of a language-specific factor in SI.

8. Prosodic modulation also makes up for the Addressee's lack of a visual dimension: he receives only a disembodied speech stream through a headset. Interpreters rarely try to 'dub' the Speaker (synchronising their speech with his gestures, if not lip movements), but if at all, then usually when interpreting for television or other high-exposure events.

9. Interpretations of 'modularity' which assign 'sub-tasks' in language processing to distinct modules sometimes seem bizarre to linguists. Pinker, for example, questions the whole idea of 'modules' of attention or memory (1994: 421).

10. It would seem difficult to extrapolate to SI from experiments in which interpreters are asked to deliberately concentrate on one stream or the other, as has been attempted recently (Darò, Lambert and Fabbro 1996).

11. We interpret the term 'semantic' as used in 1980 to include pragmatic features.

12. Rhythm 'has a beneficial role on all skilled motor activity'(Schaffer 1982, in Cutler 1987).

13. Lederer (1981) assumes that when an interpreter is expressing an idea 'cognitively acquired in advance', output becomes confident and freewheeling (*'en roue libre'*), and only superficial monitoring is taking place. Our present hypothesis predicts that segments of interpreter output with neither silent pauses nor any marked voice modulation reflect dangerous inattention.

14. Lexically, **Anliegen** is a nominalised verb, which may have either a root 'concrete' meaning: 'rest against; adjoin; lean on'; or a wide abstract meaning straddling 'concern, desire, preoccupation', 'message' and 'request'.

15. The latter hypothesis is more likely, since SI is well established in international life; but this kind of result helps to explain why interpreters are not particularly enthusiastic about SI research.

16. Gile's comment (p.c.) that 'it definitely is an error, since the interpreter acknowledged he did not catch her name' illustrates our contrasting 'information'-based and communicative relevance-based definitions of failure.

17. Fortuitously, *'revenir sur'* and 'go back on' share the same concrete/figurative polysemy; this may be an indirect trigger for her formulation.

Chapter 8   Summary and Conclusions

1. Steven Pearl, a former UN chief interpreter, has recently questioned the need to rethink and reformulate discourse in SI to the extent claimed by IT writers (Pearl 1995).

Glossary

Aboutness
minimal semantic relation just beyond mere co-existence; sometimes equated with intentionality (q.v.) in the philosophical sense. Probably the only relation which can be projected *a priori* between a Topic and Comment (q.v.).

argument
(predicate calculus, semantics, syntax): a proposition is conventionally analysed in terms of a predicate and a number of arguments; the relationship of each argument to the predicate is described in terms of its case, its (theta-) role (q.v.) or its position (Subject, Object, etc.). An argument may itself be a proposition or clause, as in e.g. *John knew that it was Tuesday.*

Aspect
semantic feature of an action proposition: a distinction of the duration or boundedness of the temporal activity, such as between continuous or durative (*he's sleeping in the barn*), habitual (*he sleeps in the barn*), completive, perfective etc., which may be marked on the verb (as in Russian or English) or by particles (as in Chinese). Combinations of Tense and Aspect are marked in different ways by different languages; English only marks completive in the past (*has slept*), whereas Chinese can, for example, mark an 'inchoative' Aspect on the present: *waimian xia yu le*, it's raining outside (but it wasn't just now).

assumption
(RT): cognitive unit: a thought (conceptual representation) treated by the individual as a representation of the actual world, including other people's beliefs, desires, etc.; assumptions may be held with varying degrees of strength (Sperber and Wilson 1986/1995: 2 and *passim*).

assumption schema
(RT): an incomplete logical form may be stored in conceptual memory as an assumption schema, which can be completed into a fully-fledged assumption on the basis of contextual information (Sperber and Wilson 1986/1995:73).

attachment
(parsing theory): decision about which constituent(s) of the sentence shall be taken to combine with, or be modified or qualified by, a particular word or phrase.

Background
the set of non-represented interpretative capacities, deeper than the 'Network' of represented assumptions, beliefs, desires, etc., which make it possible, for example, to interpret a picture of a man on a hill with his feet in a certain position as a man walking up the hill rather than sliding down it backwards (see Searle 1992: 175 ff.).

boggle effects
(sentence processing): hesitation, fluffing or self-correction indicating a disruption of normal speech processing.

bottom-up (processing)
construction of larger units from smaller ones; assembly of meaning from a (complex) stimulus, such as a speech string, on the basis of information contained in it as opposed to expectations or other knowledge.

Bounded(ness)
(semantics): a feature limiting or specifying reference in terms of extension in time (e.g. an action verb marked for Tense or Aspect), place, or identity (e.g. a Noun marked as Definite).

cognitive, cognition
of the mind (or intelligence). As currently used, denotes a device or process, human or machine, which manipulates information (conventionally, what can be formulated in propositional terms) by operations on representations. In a narrower sense, may exclude volition (desires, unformulated intentions), reflex behaviour (action without cognition), or perception (precedes cognitive processing).

cognitive device
Natural or artificial device capable of representation.

cognitive effects (see *contextual effects*)
A contextual effect occurring in a cognitive system; a change in an individual's beliefs (Sperber and Wilson 1995: 265).

cognitive pragmatics
theories which explain the use of language in speech communication in terms of the communicators' assumptions about each other's assumptions and their accessibility (not normally related to cognitive semantics (q.v.)).

cognitive science
'the study of intelligence (reasoning, perception, language, control of movement), embracing parts of several academic disciplines: experimental psychology, linguistics, computer science, philosophy, neuroscience' (Pinker 1994).

cognitive semantics
theories of meaning which see semantic structures as conceptual structures and categories in terms of prototypes; some versions of it (e.g. Fillmore's frame theory) recognise no boundary between linguistic and extralinguistic worlds.

cognitive structure
association of concepts ('epr') in memory, in which the entities, properties or the relations between them may be more or less clearly specified.

coherence
(discourse analysis, rhetorical structure theory): an underlying semantic relationship or connectivity of semantic or pragmatic content (or, for some authors, the mental expectation of such a relationship), which enables a hearer/reader to fill in gaps to achieve comprehension (as contrasted with cohesion (q.v.), a property of text). Relevance Theory views both coherence and cohesion as derivatives of relevance.

cohesion; cohesive links
A relation between elements of a text, created by formal linguistic properties and features (cohesive links), like pronouns, articles or adverbs, which link larger units; the concept of cohesion 'accounts for the essential semantic relations whereby any passage of speech or writing is enabled to function as a text' (Halliday and Hasan 1976: 13).

Comp(lementiser) or C position
(generative grammar): position in clause structure which may be filled (for example) by a complementiser like *that*, *whether*, or other subordinating con-junction. C (for Complementiser), heading the Complementiser Clause (labelled CP), is a zero-level category whose maximal projection also contains positions for moved constituents such as clause-initial *wh*-phrases. (CP may not be the highest unit if one accepts other units like Topic phrase or Focus phrase.)

conative
(as used here): expression used by a speaker to manipulate a hearer's attitude to the utterance or proposition under its scope.

conceptual encoding (see *procedural encoding*)
(RT): linguistic encoding, by a word or phrase, of a concept which forms a part of larger conceptual representations.

conference interpretation
distinguished from other forms, such as community, court and liaison interpreting, by aspects of the interpreter-client relationship, formality, proxemics, etc. (See page 1, Chapter 1).

consecutive interpretation
A mode of interpretation in which the Speaker pauses every few minutes to allow the interpreter to render each successive segment. Notes taken by professionals for consecutive interpretation show some common features (layout, indentation, segmentation, and some symbols), but are otherwise essentially individual and of ephemeral value: they cannot normally be read either by others, or even by the interpreter some time later, when the context of the meeting has faded from memory.

content (of an utterance)
(as used here): the (truth-conditional) propositional material expressed by the utterance (plus, optionally, its higher-level explicatures), as opposed to 'procedural' information directing an addressee to contexts for deriving implicatures.

context
that subset of existing mentally represented assumptions (originating from perception or memory, or decoded and inferred from speech input) which interacts with newly impinging information (whether received via perception or communication) to give rise to contextual effects (q.v.) (adapted from Carston and Uchida 1998).

context-free
of a rule or rule-system: whose application generates the predicted (true, well-formed, or effectively observed) output independently of environmental variables. While a context-free grammar may generate well-formed sentences, it is unlikely that any system of context-free rules could yield relevant meaning from natural utterances.

contextual effects
meaning, understood as the creation, abandonment, strengthening and/or weakening of assumptions in a cognitive device which results from processing information in contexts.

contextual implication
synthetic implication obtained by combining new assumptions P non-trivially with context C.

contextualisation
(as used here): process by which contexts used in any form of understanding become available or are retrieved.

conventional implicature
(Gricean pragmatics): a non-truth-conditional inference not derived from superordinate principles like the cooperative maxims (q.v.), but which is simply attached by convention to certain expressions: *but,* for example, is said to encode the same truth-functional content as *and* with the added conventional implicature that there is some contrast between the conjuncts (Grice 1961, in Levinson 1983: 127). Conventional implicatures are expected to be language-specific, and to have relatively determinate meaning (see also *implicature, conversational implicature*).

conversational implicature
(Gricean pragmatics): a non-truth-conditional inference derived from certain general features of discourse via pragmatic principles, in particular the assumption that speakers may license inferences by exploiting the communicators' shared awareness of tacit 'maxims' of cooperative conversation, which are deemed universal (cf. *conventional implic-ature, cooperative maxims*).

cooperative maxims
(Gricean pragmatics): principles of cooperative behaviour in communicative exchanges, such as 'be informative (clear, brief, orderly, truthful, relevant...)': according to Grice, hearers may infer literal or non-literal meanings when speakers appear to be complying with, or flouting, one or more of these maxims.

décalage (or **lag**)
(simultaneous interpretation): time elapsed between the production of a stimulus by the Speaker and its rendition by the interpreter (not usually distinguished from EVS).

decoding
the first phase in utterance comprehension, comprising phoneme/word recognition and the application to the resulting strings of syntactic and semantic rules for the language concerned, yielding logical forms (q.v.).

defeasible
cancellable: utterances encode and create implicatures or explicatures which are subsequently defeasible with varying degrees of felicity. Presuppositions which are difficult to cancel include those in e.g. *'the late Chairman Fabre...'* or *'she..'* (if for instance, the interpreter has misheard and/or misconstrued the demise of the Chairman, or the female gender of a participant). Assertions may also be cancelled, as in e.g. *He didn't lose a little finger—*, which is cancelled by the continuation ...*they amputated his whole arm!*

deictic (also **indexical**) **expression** (**deixis**)
expression whose interpretation depends on (is 'indexed to') the situation of discourse (time, place, environment, speakers), e.g. *he, you, here, tomorrow, this, that*.

dependent relevance
In a coherent discourse, two utterances may be connected by a relation of dependent relevance either in virtue of the fact that the first contains propositions used in establishing the relevance of the second, or that one is affected by the interpretation of the other. Connectives like *moreover, you see, after all*, for example, express dependent relevance by instructing the hearer to establish an inferential connection between two segments (Blakemore 1987: 122). The concept may be extended to include relations involving concepts or propositions which are not necessarily encoded, but only evoked by the discourse.

dichotic (listening) task
(psycholinguistics): requires a subject to attend simultaneously to competing stimuli (Garman 1990: 80).

directive
(as used here): feature of discourse which directs the hearer to text or context which contributes to deriving an explicature or implicature (as distinct from the use of the term in speech-act theory, to denote a *speech act* which attempts to get the listener to do something).

discourse
(as used here): language in use (Saussure's *parole* as conrasted with *langue*); an extended utterance produced with a communicative intent.

Discourse Representation Theory (DRT)

model-theoretic account of discourse processing (Kamp and Ryle 1993) in which representations of sentences and texts are incrementally constructed by hearers/readers by the application of construction rules to input sentences, taking into account previous sentences and cohesiveness. Truth-conditions are evaluated with respect to a model of the world.

domain ambiguity

ambiguity between epistemic (q.v.), real-world (content) or speech-act use of certain elements like modals (e.g. *must, should*) and connectives (e.g. *then, so*) (Sweetser 1990).

encyclopaedic entry

(RT): non-linguistic information in memory which is accessed on recognising a word (words like *and, if/then* have only logical and lexical entries (q.v), but no encyclopaedic entries).

encyclopaedic knowledge

long-term stored conceptual knowledge about the world which can be evoked automatically by words, or invoked to make sense of an utterance.

entailment

(semantics): relation between a pair of propositions, standardly noted $\rightarrow$, in which $P_1 \rightarrow P_2$ means that in all the situations in which P_1 is true, P_2 is also true; the truth of P_2 follows from the truth of P_1.

entry point

(simultaneous interpretation): point reached in the reception of an unfolding utterance at which a simultaneous interpreter begins to formulate.

epistemic (vs. root or 'real world') use

relates to consequence, probability, necessity, or possibility in the world of reasoning as opposed to the real world e.g. *you must be ill* (epistemic) vs. *you must go home* (root).

epr

sub-propositional unit of conceptual representation comprising either an entity, a property (of an entity or a relation between entities), or a relation (between properties, or between entities with properties, etc.).

evidential(ity)
discourse feature, marking strength of belief in the truth of all or part of an assumption or proposition, indicated in discourse by a word, like *obviously, apparently, probably, manifestly, undoubtedly*, a phrase like *I think, as you can see, we know that, after all*, or a device like stress or word order.

ear-voice span (EVS)
in simultaneous interpretation, time elapsed between the reception of a stimulus by the interpreter and its rendition in the output language.

explicature (see also *higher-level explicature, implicature*)
(RT): An inferential development of the logical form (q.v.) encoded by the utterance, recovered by a combination of decoding and inference: the greater the element of decoding, the more explicit is the explicature. 'In general RT sees the explicit side of communication as much richer and involving a much greater element of pragmatic inference, than Griceans have thought' (Wilson and Sperber 1993: 14).

explicit(ness)
(RT): An assumption communicated by an utterance is explicit if and only if it is a development of a logical form encoded by that utterance (Sperber and Wilson 1986/1995: 182). Explicitness is a matter of degree.

felicity conditions, felicitous
(speech act theory): conditions which must be satisfied, according to pragmatic conventions, for a speech-act to be successful.

focal scale
a scale of implicatures of decreasing strengths which may be communicated (in theory) by placing different parts of an utterance in focus.

focus
special status given to an element in an utterance, usually by a device like word order or intonation (stress) to contrast it with an alternative element (or set of elements) either overt, implicit or expected.

frame
(cognitive semantics): a structured cluster of concepts in memory linked to each other by association and often retrieved together (see Fillmore's definition, Chap. 1 p. 7).

frame theory
(cognitive semantics): suggests that information is stored in memory in structured units or 'frames' (scripts, scenarios, schemas, memory packets etc.), which may be retrieved *en bloc* via any one of their members.

garden path
(parsing theory): a syntactic or other relation which is anticipated or projected onto an incoming utterance but is later rejected, forcing reanalysis at some cost in effort or disruption of processing (see *boggle effects*).

Head-driven licensing parser (HDLP)
(parsing theory): HDLP models assume that structure is built exclusively from Heads of constituents in the input string, so that every attachment must be licensed by an element in the already existing structure. An HDLP requires that no satellites of a verb phrase, like arguments or adverbials, can be attached before its Head verb appears. Critics object that the model is implausible for Head-final languages.

hedge
to produce language in such a way as to leave some options open for interpretation, or avoid allowing only a single interpretation (in SI, usually motivated by temporary uncertainty about the source meaning).

higher-level explicature
complex proposition constructed by embedding a proposition under a propositional attitude or speech-act description, e.g. 'Speaker hopes that *p*' or 'Speaker wants to know if *p*'.

illocution(ary force)
(speech-act theory): the intention of a Speaker in producing an utterance, which may be more or less explicit or encoded in clues to how the propositional content of an utterance is to be taken, realised either grammatically (interrogative, imperative forms etc.), by 'illocutionary force indicating devices' like mood markers, modal adverbs or explicit performative verbs, or by other pragmatic means (exploiting context). Illocution is said to reflect the intentionality which accompanies the propositional contents in discourse (Searle 1983, 1992).

implication
a (logical) conclusion obtained from a set of assumptions by deduction. Logical implications may be trivial, analytic (those necessary and sufficient for grasping the content of an assumption), or synthetic (which further exploit the information

by applying deductive rules to several assumptions together) (Sperber and Wilson 1986/1995: 104-5).

implicature
(Gricean pragmatics): whatever is implied, suggested or meant by an utterance, as distinct from what is said (Grice 1989: 24).
(RT): an assumption (usually one of several ranging in strength) which is licensed, but not explicitly communicated, by an utterance in a communicative context (Sperber and Wilson 1986/1995: 56-7; 182).

implicit
Meaning inferred from co-processing information derived from decoding the utterance with an assumption external to it (from whatever source), rather than simply by development of the logical form of the utterance (see *explicature*, *implicature*).

inference
the act of forming an assumption by processing one or more other assumptions (derived from whatever source).

information
something which justifies change in a [cognitive] construct that represents physical or mental experience (Webster's dictionary, definition e).

informationally encapsulated
property of an analytic process which limits the type or source of information which can contribute to it.

intentional(ity), intentional state
in the most general philosophical sense, a feature of directedness or Aboutness: 'that property of many mental states and events by which they are directed at or about or of objects and states of affairs in the world' (Searle 1983; this sense is distinguished with a capital I). In linguistics/psychology, an individual's (scalar) belief in, or desire for, the truth of assumptions or states of affairs (including the desire to inform and communicate such beliefs and desires), and their composites and derivatives, such as fear (belief that something is true and desire that it be false), hope (desire that it be true with belief that it might be (i.e. under a modality)), etc.

interpretive theory (IT)
(translation studies): also called *théorie du sens*; a theory of translation professed by the 'Paris school' (see Chap. 2).

interpretive resemblance
(RT): relationship by which one representation (e.g. a thought or utterance) represents another (a thought, utterance or a representation of another's thought as derived from his utterance) in virtue of a resemblance between their logical forms, as in e.g. reported speech, quotation, metaphor, or (according to E.-A. Gutt (1991)) translation.

interpretive use
speaker's use of language to express a thought which itself represents another thought or utterance (his own or attributed to someone else) in virtue of a resemblance in content (logical, semantic, conceptual) (Carston and Uchida 1998); contrasted with *descriptive use*, in which a form (proposition) purports to be true of a state of affairs (Sperber and Wilson 1986/1995: 228-229).

lag ·
(simultaneous interpretation): also called EVS (ear-voice span) or *décalage (*q.v): time elapsed between an expression in input and the production of its equivalent.

language of thought (LOT)
a conceptual mental language, richer than any natural language, which mediates language acquisition and translation (after Fodor 1975, 1983, 1987).

lexical entry
entry in memory giving (a) lexical expression(s) corresponding to (a) concept(s).

lexical presupposition
a presupposition encoded or created by a word or phrase by virtue of the frame it evokes (Fillmore 1982, 1985).

logical entry
(RT): entry in memory containing information about the logical or syntactic use of a word corresponding to a concept (see lexical entry, encyclopaedic entry); e.g. the logical entry for 'GIVE' might specify three arguments corresponding to Agent, Theme and Beneficiary roles, and the three corresponding syntactic slots as Subject, Direct Object and Indirect Object. The entry for 'KNOW' would allow the Object slot to be filled either by a proposition or a Noun Phrase, while the entry for 'CONNAITRE' would not.

logical form
(generative grammar): a level of syntactic representation intermediate between surface structures and semantic representations; understood as an interface

between the computational component of mind and the mind's conceptual/ intentional systems.

(RT): a structured arrangement of concepts; the logical properties of a conceptual representation in virtue of which it is involved in logical processes and enters into relations such as contradiction or implication with other conceptual representations (Sperber and Wilson 1986/1995:72).

mental model
a mental structure, usually temporary, associating conceptual representations by analogy with states of affairs as presented to the organism via perceptions, long-term memory or linguistic input. An MM is built from tokens playing a symbolic role and arranged to represent a (physical or conceptual) state of affairs (Johnson-Laird 1983: 397 ff.).

Message
(translation studies): what a translator or interpreter is supposed to convey from a Speaker to his Addressees.

metadiscoursal
general term designating expressions referring to the discourse or wider event itself, including 'discourse deictic' expressions and overt cohesive links (q.v), e.g. *these three points, as was mentioned, let me now address*, etc.

modal, modality
(propositional logic; linguistic semantics): feature or operator assigning some degree of necessity or possibility to a proposition. In linguistic semantics, the 'modality' of an utterance accompanies but is distinct from the proposition expressed, and may include tense, mood, aspect, degrees of evidentiality (the speaker's commitment to the truth of the proposition) from possibility to negation, or degrees of strength of an assertion or suggestion.

modular(ity)
organisational property of a system, like the human mind (Fodor 1983), or language knowledge (generative grammar), dividing it into sub-systems with limits on their interaction.

module
a substantially self-contained process (see modularity).

ostension
(RT): the making manifest of a communicative intention; (as used here, by extension) the use of linguistic and other signs and devices which specify

communicative intentions locally by pointing to contexts (see *procedural encoding*).

ostensive communication
(RT): transmission of meaning via a stimulus that comes with a communicative intention, i.e. makes it mutually manifest that the speaker intends by this stimulus to communicate some relevant assumptions.

paraphrase
one of several potential different arrangements of a sentence or utterance having, or intended to have, the same meaning (or more restrictively, the same semantic representation).

peripheral system
(cognitive modelling): a perceptual or post-perceptual receptor module that autonomously produces fast, provisional representations which are then revised against other knowledge and with the help of conscious reasoning (Fodor 1983).

perlocution
(speech-act theory): the effect of an utterance on its hearers (Austin 1962).

placeholder
(as used here): a linguistic element which stands in for an entity, property, or relation of modality not yet resolved.

polysemy
(semantics): the property (of a lexical item) of having more than one meaning. In contrast, the wider concept of *ambiguity* accounts for indeterminacy by reference to pragmatic (contextual) as well as language-internal (semantic) factors.

pragmatic(s)
the study of the interpretation of utterances (see also Levinson 1983). 'Pragmatic' describes that dimension of linguistic communication which exploits the assumed accessibility of contexts, and inferential abilities in receivers, to communicate implicatures and a wider range of explicatures than would be possible simply by the use of a code.

pragmatic fidelity
(translation studies): degree of success of a translation or interpretation in communicating the same assumptions (via implicatures and explicatures) as its source discourse.

pragmatic indicator (marker)
item (particle, intonation, word-order arrangement etc.) providing a clue to relevant contexts for processing, or to the relations of propositions to each other.

predicate
the operative core of a proposition: a predicate may be one-place, as in 'TALL (x)', two-place, as in 'BUY (x, y)', or more complex, predicating properties of and relations between multiple arguments (q.v.). Existence ('there is (an) x') and definition/equation ('x is (a) y'), which are properties and relations very commonly signified, may also loosely be understood as 'existential' or 'equational' predicates (although the 'existential operator' $\exists$ is strictly speaking independent of predicate-argument structure).

presupposition
what is assumed in an utterance, as contrasted with what is asserted, and cannot therefore be cancelled by simple negation of the proposition (sometimes assimilated to 'old' as opposed to 'new' information) [adapted from Crystal 1997].

Principles and Parameters
(generative grammar): theory of a universal grammar defined by principles which may take different forms specified by parameters set for different languages; a theory used to account for language variation and language acquisition.

procedural encoding (device)
(RT): encodes information on how to process conceptual representations, as contrasted with their content (conceptual encoding).

proposition
an association of entities, properties and relations in which one is predicated (q.v.) of others; in the analysis of linguistic products, each clause or sentence is often loosely assumed to encode a proposition, but a finer definition including elementary presupposed existential and attributive predications (q.v.) usually yields several, e.g. in *The old man lit his awful cigar*, Clark and Clark (1977) recognise at least 6 propositions, viz. *there is a man*; *he is old*; *there is a cigar*; *the cigar belongs to the old man*; *the cigar is awful*; *the old man lit the cigar*.

propositional attitude
utterances usually present propositions under some explicitly or implicitly conveyed attitude to them on the part of the Speaker, such as some degree of belief or desirability.

propositional form
(RT): a logical form (a structured arrangement of concepts) is propositional if it is semantically complete (unambiguous, with reference assigned) and therefore capable of being true or false (Sperber and Wilson 1995: 72).

propositional representation
In Mental Models theory, a propositional representation is contrasted with other types of representations which may enter into mental modelling, such as images (Johnson-Laird 1983).

quantifier
(semantic/logical analysis): a linguistic operator such as *all, some, each* etc. which encodes bounds of quantity over expressions. The scope and distribution of quantifiers differs subtly between languages.

realis/irrealis
a scale of evidentiality which presents propositions under various degrees of reality, from truth through possibility to negation, encoded in particular (but not completely) in verb meanings, tenses and moods (conditional, subjunctive), or modal verbs (like *may* or *should*) or adverbs (like *supposedly, hopefully*).

recursion
said of a rule capable of repeated application (e.g. in English, the placing of an adjective before a Noun, or attaching a relative clause); the definition of a proposition is recursive in that one proposition may contain another. The communicative possibilities of recursive syntactic embedding are limited by comprehenders' processing capacity.

Relevance
(RT): Property of utterances, defined in two principles. The first (cognitive) Principle of Relevance states that human cognition is geared toward the maximisation of relevance (the achievement of maximal contextual effects for minimal processing effort). The second (communicative) Principle states that every act of ostensive communication communicates a presumption of its own optimal relevance; the ostensive stimulus is relevant enough to be worth the addressee's effort to process it, and is the most relevant one compatible with the communicator's abilities and preferences (Sperber and Wilson 1995; Carston and Uchida 1998).

representation
an arrangement of symbols or other forms which carries information (q.v.) about something beyond itself (Carston and Uchida 1998). In connectionist models,

information is not strictly considered to be represented by, but is presumably encoded in, the 'states' of components of a network.

scope
the part of discourse affected by the meaning of a particular form, such as a quantifier, a modal or a marker of attitude or illocutionary force. The scope of a form may vary with its position, as seen from displacing a word like 'only' in a sentence; but scope is often not fully or unambiguously encoded in syntax and semantics (e.g. *I only saw him leave on Tuesday*).

script, scenario
a sequence of events remembered as a unit, and which may be evoked as a whole by a word or phrase (cf. *frame*).

selectional rule, selectional information
(generative grammar): specifies restrictions on permitted combinations of lexical items, excluding certain combinations as anomalous except in special (e.g. metaphorical) uses; for example, inanimate subjects are excluded from the Subject position of a word like *sleep*.

semantic representation
representation of the meaning of a sentence or utterance derived solely from the application of rules of grammar (subcategorisation, lexical selection, case, reference etc.), with no reference to context, expectations or other information.

sens
in the 'interpretivist' theory of translation (IT): the Speaker's Message, comprising semantic substance and his *vouloir-dire* (i.e. content and communicative intent).

sentence modifier
a term, e.g. an adverbial such as *probably*, or *on Tuesday*, with scope over a whole sentence.

sovereign Speaker
a primary communicator, i.e. one whose Message is generated from his own thoughts and communicative intentions, as distinct from a translator or interpreter (a secondary communicator).

speech act
in the strongest sense, an act performed by an utterance (a bet, promise, investiture, curse, etc.); in the wider sense used here, an intentional utterance.

thematic (structure, information)
role or participant structure of a proposition; information about this which enriches its representation, helping a comprehender/interpreter to hypothesise about the logical relations in and between propositions, and their relation to the speaker's intentions.

theta (θ) role
(generative grammar): term used in government-binding theory (GB) for a semantic [or 'thematic'] role such as AGent, PATient, BENeficiary, GOAL etc.

theta(θ)-attachment
(generative grammar): in GB theory, attachment on the basis of the θ-criterion, which requires that every argument is assigned just one θ-role and that each θ-role is assigned just one argument.

top-down (processing, comprehension)
derivation of a smaller unit of information (e.g. sentence or word meaning) from a larger one (e.g. general knowledge, or presumptions about the Speaker's intentions).

Topic-Comment
utterance structure found in languages like Chinese, Korean or Japanese (said to belong to a typological category of 'Topic-prominent' languages) comprising an initial expression (Topic) then, after a pause or particle, a second expression (Comment) which is somehow 'about' it. Topic is 'typically a VP or NP (and/or a time or place phrase)' which 'sets the spatial temporal or individual framework within which the main predication holds'; 'is definite or generic (refers to something the speaker knows about)'; 'always occurs sentence-initially' (except for connectives); and can be separated from its Comment by a 'Topic marker' such as a pause or pause particle (Chinese *a, ya, ne*) (Li and Thompson 1976). This structure appears to constrain the possible semantic relation between the parts far less than, for example, structures marked as Subject-Predicate-Object, or Matrix-Subordinate. The interpretation of the relation therefore depends largely on non-syntactic elements, including pragmatic cues or utterance-external knowledge. In a *Topic Chain*, a Topic may appear once only and remain valid for several Comments.

truth conditions
conditions in which a proposition may be judged true or false of a (model of) a world. Traditional (speech-act) pragmatic theory recognises a non-truth-conditional dimension in utterances (standardly called their *illocution*) in addition to the propositions they contain.

U-semantics (utterance-semantics)
(cognitive semantics): a theory which 'aims to account for the relation between linguistic texts, the contexts in which they are instanced, and the process and products of their interpretation [...]; such a theory [...] does not begin *with* a body of assumptions about aspects of the interpretation process which belong to linguistics proper and whatever might belong to co-operating theories of speaking and reasoning and speakers' belief systems' (Fillmore 1985: 222).

utterance scope
property of an expression or discourse device, such as an evidential adverb or a description of a propositional attitude (*I think, it seems to me*), which attaches its value to a whole utterance (*hopefully we'll be there by ten*) rather than to only one constituent, as in e.g. *Hopefully he strode off...*, where *hopefully* has VP scope. (Cf. *sentence modifiers,* and the generative grammarians' description of 'sentence adverbials' (Jackendoff 1972)).

vagueness
(low) degree of specification or determinacy of any epr. An *ambiguous* expression or sentence has two or more distinct syntactic-semantic readings; a *vague* expression allows a range of interpretations by leaving some aspects of meaning (reference, boundedness, set-membership etc.) unspecified (adapted from Crystal 1997).

weak interaction
ability of a basically 'downstream' process to inhibit, but not excite or trigger, operations in an 'upstream' module.

working memory
(as used here): the extent of representations which are salient and accessible at a given time: in SI, probably usually includes auditory, visual and some phonologically resolved images ('echoic' memory), some conceptual structure (mental model) some linguistic forms (lexicon), and some task instructions (Executive).

References

Abney, Steven. 1989. A computational model of human parsing. *Journal of Psycholinguistic Research*, 18(1), 129-144.

Abney, Steven and Johnson, Mark. 1991. Memory requirements and local ambiguities of parsing strategies. *Journal of Psycholinguistic Research*, 20(3), 233-250.

AIIC (Association Internationale des Interprètes de Conférence/International Association of Conference Interpreters). 1993. *Advice to students wishing to become conference interpreters*. AIIC Training Committee brochure. AIIC: Geneva.

Altmann, Gerry and Steedman, Mark. 1988. Interaction with context in human sentence processing. *Cognition* 30, 191-238.

Anderson, Linda. 1979. *Simultaneous Interpretation: Contextual and Translation Aspects*. M.A. Thesis, Concordia University, Montreal (unpubl.).

Attardo, Salvatore. 1997. Competition and cooperation: beyond Gricean pragmatics. *Pragmatics and Cognition* 5(1), 21-50.

Austin, John. 1962. *How To Do Things With Words*. Oxford: Clarendon Press.

Baddeley, Alan. 1986. *Working Memory*. Oxford: OUP.

Baddeley, Alan and Hitch, Graham. 1974. Working memory. In Gordon Bower (ed.), *The Psychology of Learning and Motivation* Vol. 8, 47-90. New York: Academic Press.

Bader, Markus and Lasser, Ingeborg. 1994. German verb-final clauses and sentence processing: evidence for immediate attachment. In Charles Clifton, Lyn Frazier, Keith Rayner (eds.), *Perspectives on Sentence Processing*, 225-242. Hillsdale, N.J: Lawrence Erlbaum.

Barbizet, Jacques. 1964. Le problème du codage cérébral, son rôle dans les mécanismes de la mémoire. *Annales médico-psychologiques* 1, 1-27. Paris: Masson.

Barik, Henri C. 1973. Simultaneous interpretation: temporal and quantitative data. *Language and Speech* 16, 237-271.

Barik, Henri C. 1975. Simultaneous interpretation: qualitative and linguistic data. *Language and Speech* 18, 272-297.

Biq Yung-O. 1989. *Ye* as manifested on three discourse planes: polysemy or abstraction? In James Tai and Frank Hsueh (eds.), *Functionalism and Chinese Grammar*. South Orange, N.J.: Chinese Language Teachers' Association Monograph Series no. 1, 1-18.

Blakemore, Diane. 1987. *Semantic Constraints on Relevance*. Oxford: Blackwell.

Broadbent, Donald E. 1958. *Perception and Communication*. London: Pergamon Press.

Bros-Brann, Eliane 1976. Critical comments on H.C. Barik's article "Interpreters talk a lot, among other things". *AIIC Bulletin* IV(1), 16-18. Geneva: AIIC (Association Internationale des Interprètes de Conférence).

Brown, Donald. 1991. *Human Universals.* New York: McGraw Hill.

Brown, Gillian and Yule, George. 1983. *Discourse Analysis.* Cambridge: CUP.

Carston, Robyn and Uchida, Seiji (eds.). 1998. *Relevance Theory: Applications and Implications.* Amsterdam and Philadelphia: John Benjamins.

Cenkova, Ivana. 1985. *Teoretické aspekty procesu simultanniho tlumoceni* (Theoretical aspects of simultaneous interpretation). Ph.D Thesis, Department of Literature, Charles University, Prague (unpubl.).

Chafe, Wallace. 1994. *Discourse, Consciousness and Time.* Chicago: University of Chicago Press.

Chao Yuan Ren. 1968. *A Grammar of Spoken Chinese.* Berkeley: University of California Press.

Cheng, Robert L. 1983. Focus devices in Mandarin Chinese. In Charles Tang Ting-chi, Robert L. Cheng and Li Ying-che (eds.), *Universe and Scope: Presupposition and Quantification in Chinese. Studies in Chinese Syntax and Semantics,* 53-102. Taipei: Student Book Co.

Chernov, Ghelly. 1979. Semantic aspects of psycholinguistic research in simultaneous interpretation. *Language and Speech* 22(3), 277-295.

Chernov, Ghelly. 1992. Conference interpreting in the USSR: history, theory, new frontiers. *Meta* 37(1), 149-162.

Chomsky, Noam. 1957. *Syntactic Structures.* The Hague: Mouton.

Chomsky, Noam. 1965. *Aspects of the Theory of Syntax.* Cambridge, Mass.: MIT Press.

Chomsky, Noam. 1981. *Lectures on Government and Binding.* Dordrecht: Foris.

Chomsky, Noam. 1986. *Barriers.* Cambridge, Mass: MIT Press.

Clark, Eve and Clark, Herbert. 1977. *Psychology and Language.* New York: Harcourt Brace Jovanovich.

Coseriu, Eugenio and Geckeler, Horst. 1981. *Trends in Structural Semantics.* Tübingen: Günter Narr.

Craik, Kenneth. 1943. *The Nature of Explanation.* Cambridge: CUP.

Crain, Stephen and Steedman, Mark. 1985. On not being led up the garden path. The use of context by the psychological parser. In David Dowty, Lauri Kartunnen and Arnold Zwicky (eds.), *Natural Language Parsing: Psychological, Computational and Theoretical Perspectives.* Cambridge: CUP.

Crocker, Matt. 1994. On the nature of the principle-based sentence processor. In Charles Clifton, Lyn Frazier, Keith Rayner (eds.), *Perspectives on Sentence Processing,* 245-266. Hillsdale, N.J: Lawrence Erlbaum.

Cutler, Anne. 1987. Speaking for listening. In Alan Allport, D. MacKay, Wolfgang Prinz, E. Scheerer (eds.), *Language Perception and Production,* 23-40. London: Academic Press.

Cutler, Anne and Isard, Stephen. 1980. The production of prosody. In Brian Butterworth (ed.), *Language Production, Vol. 1: Speech and Talk.* London: Academic Press.

Damasio, Antonio. 1994. *Descartes' Error.* New York: Putnam.

Darò, Valeria, Lambert, Sylvie and Fabbro, Franco. 1996. Conscious monitoring of attention during simultaneous interpretation. *Interpreting* 1(1), 101-124.

Darwin, Chris J. 1975. On the dynamic use of prosody in speech perception. In A. Cohen and S. Nooteboom (eds.), *Structure and Process in Speech Perception.* Berlin: Springer.

Davidson, Peter. 1992. Segmentation of Japanese source language discourse in simultaneous interpretation. Special Issue no. 1, *The Interpreter's Newsletter*, 2-11. Trieste: Università degli Studi di Trieste.

Dawrant, Andrew. 1996. *Word-order in Chinese-English Simultaneous Interpretation: An Initial Exploration.* M.A. Thesis, Graduate Institute of Translation and Interpretation Studies, Fujen University, Taipei (unpubl.).

Déjean Le Féal, Karla. 1980. Die Satzsegmentierung beim freien Vortrag bzw. beim Verlesen von Texten und ihr Einfluss auf das Sprachverstehen. In *Sprache und Verstehen*, vol. 1, 161-168. Tübingen: Gunter Narr.

Déjean Le Féal, Karla. 1982. Why impromptu speech is easy to understand. In Nils E. Enkvist (ed.), *Impromptu Speech: a Symposium*, 1982, 221-239. Åbo Research Institute, Åbo Akademi Foundation.

Dillinger, Michael. 1989. *Component Processes of Simultaneous Interpreting.* Ph.D. Thesis, Dept. of Educational Psychology, McGill University, Montreal (unpubl.).

Donovan, Clare. 1990. *La fidélité en interprétation.* Thèse de Doctorat, E.S.I.T., Université de Paris III (unpubl.).

Emmorey, Karen and Fromkin, Victoria. 1988. The mental lexicon. In Frederick Newmeyer (ed.), *Linguistics: The Cambridge Survey (Vol II), Language: Psychological and Biological Aspects*, 124-149. Cambridge: CUP.

Fabbro, Franco, Gran, Laura, Basso G. and Bava A. 1990. Cerebral lateralization in simultaneous interpretation. *Brain and Language* 39, 69-89.

Fabbro, Franco, Gran B. and Gran, Laura. 1991. Hemispheric specialization for semantic and syntactic components of language in simultaneous interpretation. *Brain and Language* 41, 1-42.

Fabbro, Franco and Gran, Laura. 1997. Neurolinguistic research in simultaneous interpretation. In Yves Gambier, Daniel Gile and Christopher Taylor (eds.), *Conference Interpreting: Current Trends in Research*, 9-27. Amsterdam and Philadelphia: John Benjamins.

Fauconnier, Gilles. 1985. *Mental Spaces.* Cambridge, Mass: MIT, Bradford Books.

Fillmore, Charles. 1975. *Santa Cruz Lectures on Deixis.* Bloomington: Indiana University Linguistics Club.

Fillmore, Charles. 1982. Frame semantics. In The Linguistic Society of Korea (ed.), *Linguistics in the Morning Calm*, Vol. 1, 111-137. Seoul: Hanshin Publishing Co.

Fillmore, Charles. 1984. Remarks on contrastive pragmatics. In Jaček Fisiak (ed.), *Contrastive Linguistics: Prospects and Problems*, 119-141. Amsterdam and Philadelphia: John Benjamins.

Fillmore, Charles. 1985. Frames and the semantics of understanding, *Quaderni di Semantica*, VI-2, 222-254.

Fodor, Jerry. 1975. *The Language of Thought.* Cambridge, Mass.: Harvard University Press.

Fodor, Jerry. 1983. *The Modularity of Mind.* Cambridge, Mass.: MIT.

Fodor, Jerry. 1987. *Psychosemantics.* Cambridge, Mass.: MIT.

Frazier, Lyn. 1985. Syntactic complexity. In David Dowty, Lauri Kartunnen and Arnold Zwicky (eds.), *Natural language parsing: psychological, computational and theoretical perspectives.* Cambridge: CUP.

Frazier, Lyn and Clifton, Charles. 1996. *Construal*. Cambridge, Mass.: MIT, Bradford Books.

Frege, Gottlob. 1952 (1892). On sense and reference. In Peter T. Geach and Max Black (eds.), *Translations from the Philosophical Writings of Gottlob Frege*, 56-78. Oxford: Blackwell.

Fukuii, Haruhiro and Asano, Tasuke. 1961. *Eigotsuyaku no jissai* (An English interpreter's manual). Tokyo: Kenkyusha.

Funnell, Elaine. and Allport, Alan. 1987. Non-linguistic cognition and word meanings: neuropsychological exploration of common mechanisms. In A. Allport, D. MacKay, W. Prinz, E. Scheerer (eds.), *Language Perception and Production: Relationships between Listening, Speaking, Reading and Writing*, 367-403. London: Academic Press.

Garman, Michael. 1990. *Psycholinguistics*. Cambridge: CUP.

Garnham, Alan. 1987. *Mental Models as Representations of Discourse and Text*. Chichester: Ellis Horwood.

Gathercole, Susan and Baddeley, Alan. 1993. *Working Memory and Language*. Cambridge: CUP.

Gernsbacher, Morton A. and Shlesinger, Miriam. 1997. The proposed role of suppression in simultaneous interpretation. *Interpreting* 1(2), 119-140.

Gerver, David. 1969. The effects of source language presentation rate on the performance of simultaneous conference interpreters. In E. Foulke (ed.), *Proceedings of the 2nd Louisville Conference on Rate and/or Frequency Controlled Speech*, 162-184. Louisville: University of Louisville.

Gerver, David. 1971. *Simultaneous Interpretation and Human Information Processing*. Ph.D. thesis, University of Oxford (unpubl.).

Gerver, David.1972. *Simultaneous and Consecutive Interpretation and Human Information Processing*. London: Social Science Research Council Report, HR 566(1).

Gerver, David.1974. Simultaneous listening and speaking and retention of prose. *Quarterly Journal of Experimental Psychology* 26, 337-342.

Gerver, David. 1976. Empirical studies of simultaneous interpretation: a review and a model. In Richard W. Brislin (ed.), *Translation*, 165-207. New York: Gardner Press.

Gerver, David and Wallace H. Sinaiko (eds.), 1978. *Language Interpretation and Communication. Proceedings of the NATO Symposium on Language Interpretation and Communication, Venice, 1977*. New York: Plenum Press.

Gibson, Edward. 1991. *A Computational Theory of Human Linguistic Processing: Memory Limitations and Processing Breakdown*. Ph.D. thesis, Dept. of Philosophy, Carnegie Mellon University (unpubl.).

Gile, Daniel. 1985. Le modèle d'efforts et l'équilibre en interprétation simultanée. Special Issue on Conference Interpreting, *Meta* 30(1), 44-48.

Gile, Daniel. 1987. Les exercices d'interprétation et la dégradation du français: une étude de cas. *Meta* 32(4), 420-428.

Gile, Daniel. 1988. La connaissance des langues passives chez le traducteur scientifique et technique. *Traduire* 136, 9-15.

Gile, Daniel. 1989. Les flux d'information dans les réunions interlinguistiques et l'interprétation de conférence: premières observations. *Meta* 34(4), 649-660.

Gile, Daniel. 1990. Scientific research vs. personal theories in the investigation of interpretation. In Laura Gran and Christopher Taylor (eds.), *Aspects of Applied and Experimental Research on Conference Interpretation*, 28-41. Udine: Campanotto.

Gile, Daniel. 1992. Predictable sentence endings in Japanese and conference interpretation. Special Issue no. 1, *The Interpreter's Newsletter*, 12-23. Trieste: Università degli Studi di Trieste.

Gile, Daniel. 1993. Translation/interpretation and knowledge. In Yves Gambier and Jorma Tommola (eds.), *Translation and Knowledge* (SSOTT IV), 67-86. Turku: University of Turku, Centre for Translation and Interpreting.

Gile, Daniel. 1995. *Regards sur la recherche en interprétation de conférence*. Lille: Presses Universitaires de Lille.

Gile, Daniel. 1997. Conference interpreting as a cognitive management problem. In Joseph H. Danks, Gregory M. Shreve, Stephen B. Fountain and Michael K. McBeath (eds.), *Cognitive Processes in Translation and Interpretation*, 196-214. London: Sage.

Givón, Talmy. 1984, 1990. *Syntax: a functional-typological introduction*. Amsterdam and Philadelphia: John Benjamins.

Goldman-Eisler, Frieda. 1972. Segmentation of input in simultaneous translation. *Journal of Psycholinguistic Research* 1(2), 127-140.

Goldman-Eisler, Frieda and Cohen, Michele. 1974. An experimental study of interference between receptive and productive processes relating to simultaneous translation. *Language and Speech* 17, 1-10.

Green, Georgia. 1989. *Pragmatics and Natural Language Understanding*. Hillsdale N.J.: Lawrence Erlbaum.

Grewendorf, Günter and Sternefeld, Wolfgang. 1990. Scrambling theories. In Günter Grewendorf and Wolfgang Sternefeld (eds.), *Scrambling and Barriers*, 3-40. Amsterdam and Philadelphia: John Benjamins.

Grice, Paul. 1967. *Logic and Conversation*. Unpublished MS. of the William James Lectures, Harvard University.

Grice, Paul. 1989. *Studies in the Way of Words*. Harvard University Press.

Gutt, Ernst-August. 1991. *Translation and Relevance: Cognition and Context*. Oxford: Blackwell.

Haegeman, Liliane. 1991. *Introduction to Government and Binding Theory*. London: Blackwell.

Haider, Hubert (ed.), 1991. *Representation and Derivation in the Theory of Grammar (Studies in Natural Language and Linguistic Theory, Vol. 22)*. Dordrecht: Kluwer.

Halliday, Michael. 1985. *An Introduction to Functional Grammar*. London: Edward Arnold.

Halliday, Michael and Hasan, Ruqaiya. 1976. *Cohesion in English*. London and New York: Longman.

Hara, Fujiko. 1988. Understanding the silent culture of the Japanese. Special Issue on Translation and Interpreting in Japan, Guest ed. Daniel Gile, *Meta* 33(1), 70-78.

Haviland, Susan and Clark, Herbert H. 1974. What's new? Acquiring new information as a process in comprehension. *Journal of Verbal Learning and Verbal Behaviour* 13, 512-521.

Hawkins, John. 1983. *A Comparative Typology of English and German: Unifying the Contrasts*. London and Sydney: Croom Helm.

Hawkins, John. 1988. The unity of German-English contrasts: inferring a typological parameter. In C. Duncan-Rose and T. Vennemann (eds.), *On Language: Rhetorica, Philologica, Syntactica; a Festschrift for Robert P. Stockwell*. London: Routledge.

Haviland, S. and Clark, Herbert H. 1974. What's new? Acquiring new information as a process in comprehension. *Journal of Verbal Learning and Verbal Behaviour* 13, 512-521.

Herbert, Jean. 1952. *Manuel de l'interprète*. Geneva: Georg.

Herbulot, Florence. 1990. Le traducteur déchiré. In *Etudes traductologiques: en hommage à Danica Seleskovitch*, 267-280. Paris: Minard Lettres Modernes.

Holz-Mänttäri, Justa. 1984. *Translatorisches Handeln. Theorie und Methode*. Annales Academiae Scientiarum Fennicae B 226. Helsinki: Suomalainen Tiedeakatemia.

Huang, James C-T. 1982. *Logical Relations in Chinese and the Theory of Grammar*. Ph.D. dissertation, University of Southern California (unpubl.).

Huang, James C-T. 1988. *Wo pao de kuai* and Chinese phrase structure, *Language* 64, 274-311.

Huang Shuan Fan. 1975. *A Study of Adverbs*. The Hague: Mouton.

Ilg, Gérard. 1978. De l'allemand vers le français: l'apprentissage de l'interprétation simultanée. *Parallèles* 1, 69-99. Geneva: Université de Genève, Cahiers de l'ETI.

Jackendoff, Ray. 1972. *Semantic Interpretation in Generative Grammar*. Cambridge, Mass.: MIT Press.

Jackendoff, Ray. 1990. *Semantic Structures*. Cambridge, Mass.: MIT Press.

Jackendoff, Ray. 1996. How language helps us think. *Pragmatics and Cognition* 4(1), 1-34.

Jekat, Susanne and Klein, Alexandra. 1996. Machine interpretation. *Interpreting* 1(1), 7-20.

Johnson, Mark. 1989. Parsing as Deduction: The Use of Knowledge of Language. *Journal of Psycholinguistic Research* 18(1), 105-127.

Johnson M., Bransford J. and Solomon S. 1973. Memory for tacit implications of sentences. *Journal of Experimental Psychology* 98, 203-5.

Johnson-Laird, Philip. 1983. *Mental Models*. Cambridge: CUP.

Just, Marcel A. and Carpenter, Patricia. 1992. A capacity theory of comprehension. Individual differences in working memory. *Psychological Review* 99, 122-149.

Kade, Otto. and Cartellieri, Claus. 1971. Some methodological aspects of simultaneous interpreting. *Babel* 17(2), 12-16.

Kalina, Sylvia. 1998. *Strategische Prozesse beim Dolmetschen: theoretische Grundlagen, empirische Fallstudien, didaktische Kosnequenzen*. Tübingen: Günter Narr.

Kamp, Hans and Reyle, Uwe. 1993. *From Discourse to Logic*. Stuttgart: Kluwer.

Katz, Jerrold. 1978. Effability and translation. In F. Guenthner and M. Guenthner-Reutter (eds.), *Meaning and Translation: Philosophical and Linguistic Approaches*, 191-234. London: Duckworth.

Keenan, Edward. 1978a. Some logical problems in translation. In F. Guenthner and M. Guenthner-Reutter (eds.), *Meaning and Translation: Philosophical and Linguistic Approaches*, 157-189. London: Duckworth.

Keenan, Edward. 1978b. Language variation and the logical structure of universal grammar. In Hans-Jakob Seiler (ed.), *Language Universals*. Tübingen: Günter Narr Verlag.

Kempen, G. and Hoenkamp, E. 1982. Incremental sentence generation: implications for the structure of a syntactic processor. In J. Horecky (ed.), *Proceedings of the Ninth International Conference on Computational Linguistics*. Amsterdam: North Holland.

Kimball, John. 1973. Seven principles of surface structure parsing in natural language. *Cognition* 2(1), 15-47.

Kintsch, Walter and Van Dijk, Teun A. 1978. Toward a model of text comprehension and production. *Psychological Review*, 85(5), 363-394.

Kitano, Hiraoki. 1993. *Speech-to-Speech Translation: a Massively Parallel Memory-Based Approach*. Amsterdam: Kluwer.

Kondo, Masaomi. 1988. Japanese interpreters in their socio-cultural context. Special Issue on Translation and Interpreting in Japan, Guest ed. Daniel Gile, *Meta* 33(1), 70-78.

Kratochvil, Paul. 1968. *The Chinese Language Today*. London: Hutchinson.

Krusina, A. 1971. Main factors determining the process and quality of simultaneous interpretation. In *Studies on Language and Theory of Translation* II. Prague: Acta Universitatis 17 Novembris.

Kunihiro, Masao, Nishiyama, Sen and Kanayama, Noburo. 1969. *Tsujaku: Eikawa kara dojitsuyaku made* (Interpreting: from English conversation to simultaneous interpreting). Nihonhososhuppankyokai.

Kurz, Ingrid. 1992. Shadowing exercises in interpreter training. In Cay Dollerup and Annette Lindegaard (eds.), *Teaching Translating and Interpreting I*, 245-250. Amsterdam and Philadelphia: John Benjamins.

Kurz, Ingrid. 1994. Conference interpretation: expectations of different user groups. *The Interpreter's Newsletter* 5, 13-21. Trieste: Università degli Studi di Trieste.

Lambert, Sylvie. 1989. One ear may be better than two. *The Interpreter's Newsletter* 2, 11-16. Trieste: Università degli Studi di Trieste.

Lambert, Sylvie. 1990. Shadowing. *The Interpreter's Newsletter* 4, 15-24. Trieste: Università degli Studi di Trieste.

Laplace, Colette. 1994. *Théorie du langage et théorie de la traduction. Les concepts-clés de trois auteurs: Kade (Leipzig), Coseriu (Tübingen), Seleskovitch (Paris)*. Paris: Didier-Erudition.

Le Ny, Jean-François. 1978. Psychosemantics and simultaneous interpretation. In David Gerver and Wallace H. Sinaiko (eds.), *Language Interpretation and Communication*. New York: Plenum Press, 289-298.

Lederer, Marianne. 1981. *La traduction simultanée*. Paris: Minard Lettres Modernes.

Lederer, Marianne. 1986. L'implicite et l'explicite. In Danica Seleskovitch and Marianne Lederer (eds.), 1986, *Interpréter pour traduire*. Paris: Didier Erudition.

Lederer, Marianne. 1990. Cognitive complements in interpreting. In David Bowen and Margareta Bowen (eds.), *Interpreting, Yesterday, Today and Tomorrow*, American Translators Association Scholarly Monograph Series, Vol. IV, 1990. New York: SUNY, Binghampton.

Leech, Geoffrey. 1983. *Principles of Pragmatics*. London: Longman.

Lenerz, Jürgen. 1977. *Zur Abfolge nominaler Satzglieder im Deutschen*. Studien zur deutschen Grammatik, 5. Tübingen: Narr.

Lenk, Hans. 1978. Handlung als Interpretationskonstrukt. Entwurf einer konstituenten- und beschreibungstheoretischen Handlungsphilosophie, in Hans Lenk (ed.), *Handlungstheorien interdisziplinär II. Erster Halbband,* 279-350. München: Fink.

Levelt, Willem. 1989. *Speaking: from Intention to Articulation*. Cambridge, Mass.: MIT.

Levinson, Stephen. 1983. *Pragmatics*. Cambridge: CUP.

Li, Charles and Thompson, Sandra. 1976. Subject and Topic: a new typology of language. In Charles Li (ed.), *Subject and Topic,* 457 ff. New York: Academic Press.

Li, Charles and Thompson, Sandra. 1981. *Mandarin Chinese. A Functional Reference Grammar*. University of California Press.

Li, Audrey Y. H. 1990. *Order and Constituency in Mandarin Chinese*. Dordrecht: Kluwer.

Lichtheim, L. 1885. On aphasia. *Brain,* 7, 433-484.

Lonsdale, Deryle. 1997. Modeling SI: a cognitive approach. *Interpreting* 1(2), 235-260.

Lonsdale, Deryle. 1998. Modeling cognition in SI: methodological issues. *Interpreting* 2(1/2), 91-117.

Luscher, Jean-Marc. 1994. Les marques de connexion: les guides pour l'interprétation. In Jacques Moeschler, Anne Reboul, Jean-Marc Luscher, and Jacques Jayez, *Langage et pertinence*. Nancy: Presses Universitaires de Nancy.

Lyons, John. 1977. *Semantics*. London and New York: Cambridge: CUP.

McGurk, Harry and Macdonald, John. 1976. Hearing lips and seeing voices. *Nature* 264, 746-8.

Mackintosh, Jennifer. 1985. The Kintsch and van Dijk model of discourse comprehension and production applied to the interpretation process, *Meta* 30(1), 37-43.

Mackintosh, Jennifer. 1994. User expectations survey: interim report. *AIIC Bulletin* XXII(2), June 1994, 13-17. Geneva: AIIC (Association Internationale des Interprètes de Conférence).

Marr, David. 1982. *Vision*. San Francisco: Freeman.

Marslen-Wilson, William and Welsh, Alan. 1978. Processing interactions during word recognition in continuous speech. *Cognitive Psychology* 10: 29-63.

Marslen-Wilson, William. 1987. Functional parallelism in spoken word-recognition. *Cognition,* 25, 71-102.

Massaro, Dominic. 1975. Language and information processing. In Dominic Massaro (ed.), *Understanding Language: An Information Processing Analysis of Speech Perception, Reading and Psycholinguistics,* 3-28. New York: Academic Press.

Massaro, Dominic. 1978. An information-processing model of understanding speech. In David Gerver and Wallace H. Sinaiko (eds.), *Language Interpretation and Communication,* 299-314. New York: Plenum Press.

Massaro, Dominic and Shlesinger, Miriam. 1997. Information processing and a computational approach to simultaneous interpretation. *Interpreting* 1(2), 12-53.

Massaro, Dominic 1978. Mattern, Nanza. 1974. *Anticipation in German-English Simultaneous Interpreting*. M.A. Thesis. University of Saarbrücken (unpubl.) .

Miller, George. 1956. The magical number seven, plus or minus two: some limits on our capacity for processing information. *Psychological Review,* 63(2), 81-97.

Miller, George, Galanter, Eugene, and Pribram Karl. 1960. *Plans and the Structure of Behaviour*. New York: Holt, Rinehart and Winston.

Monsell, Stephen. 1987. On the relation between lexical input and output pathways for speech. In Alan Allport, D. MacKay, Wolfgang Prinz, E. Scheerer (eds.), *Language Perception and Production: Relationships between Listening, Speaking, Reading and Writing*, 273-312. London: Academic Press.

Moser, Barbara. 1976. *Simultaneous Translation: Linguistic, Psycholinguistic and Human Information Processing Aspects*. Ph.D. thesis, University of Innsbruck (unpubl.).

Moser, Barbara. 1978. Simultaneous interpretation: a hypothetical model and its practical application. In David Gerver and Wallace H. Sinaiko (eds.), *Language Interpretation and Communication. Proceedings of the NATO Symposium on Language Interpretation and Communication, Venice, 1977*, 353-368. New York: Plenum Press.

Moser-Mercer, Barbara. 1991. Paradigms gained, or the art of productive disagreement. *AIIC Bulletin* XIX(2), June 1991. Geneva: AIIC (Association Internationale des Interprètes de Conférence).

Moser-Mercer, Barbara. 1997. Beyond curiosity: can interpreting research meet the challenge? In Joseph H. Danks, Gregory M. Shreve, Stephen B. Fountain and Michael K. McBeath (eds.), *Cognitive Processes in Translation and Interpretation*. London: Sage.

Moser-Mercer, Barbara, Lambert S., Darò V. and Williams S. 1997. Skill components in simultaneous interpreting. In Yves Gambier, Daniel Gile and Christopher Taylor (eds.), *Conference Interpreting: Current Trends in Research*. Amsterdam and Philadelphia: John Benjamins.

Nida, Eugene and Taber, Charles. 1969. *The Theory and Practice of Translation*. Leiden: Brill.

Nord, Christiane. 1994. Translation as a process of linguistic and cultural adaptation. In Cay Dollerup and Annette Lindegaard (eds.), *Teaching Translation and Interpreting 2: Insights, Aims, Visions. Papers from the Second Language International Conference, Elsinore, Denmark 4-6 June 1993*, 60-67. Amsterdam and Philadelphia: John Benjamins.

Norman, Donald A. and Shallice, Tim. 1980/1986. Attention to action: willed and automatic control of behaviour. In Richard J. Davidson, Gary E. Schwartz and David Shapiro (eds.), 1986, *Consciousness and Self-regulation*, Vol. 4. New York: Plenum Press.

Oléron, Pierre and Nanpon, Hubert. 1964. Recherches sur la traduction simultanée. *Journal de psychologie normale et pathologique* 62, 73-94.

Olsen, Susan. 1985. On deriving V-1 and V-2 structures in German. In Jindřich Toman (ed.), *Studies in German Grammar*, 133-163. Dordrecht: Foris.

Paneth, Eva. 1957. *An investigation into conference interpreting*. M.A. Thesis, London University (unpubl.).

Paradis, Michel. 1994. Neurolinguistic aspects of implicit and explicit memory: implications for bilingualism. In N. Ellis (ed.), *Implicit and Explicit Language Learning*, 393-419. London: Academic Press.

Pearl, Stephen. 1995. Lacuna, myth and shibboleth in the teaching of simultaneous interpreting. *Perspectives* 3(2), 161-190.

Peirce, Charles. 1955. Abduction and induction. In Justus Buchler (ed.), *The Philosophical Writings of Peirce*. New York: Dover.

Petsche, H. 1993. Hirnelektrische Vorgänge bei verbalem Denken. *Neuropsychiatrie* 7(1), 13-17.

Pinker, Steven. 1994. *The Language Instinct*. London: Penguin Books.

Pinter, Ingrid. 1969. *Der Einfluss der Übung und Konzentration auf simultanes Sprechen und Hören*. Ph.D. Thesis, Philosophische Fakultät, Universität Wien (unpubl.).

Pöchhacker, Franz. 1994. *Simultandolmetschen als komplexes Handeln*. Tübingen: Günter Narr.

Pollard, David. 1994. Empty words: modal adverbs. In Chan Siuwai and David Pollard (eds.), *An Encyclopaedia of Translation*, 216-222. Hong Kong: Chinese University Press.

Prince, Ellen. 1979. On the given/new distinction. Proceedings of the Chicago Linguistics Society 15, 267-278.

Pritchett, Bradley. 1988. Garden path phenomena and the grammatical basis of language processing. *Language* 64, 539-576.

Pritchett, Bradley. 1992. *Grammatical Competence and Parsing Performance*. University of Chicago Press.

Radford, Andrew. 1981. *Transformational Grammar: A First Course*. Cambridge: CUP.

Rambow, Owen and Joshi, Aravid. 1994. A processing model for free word-order languages. In Charles Clifton, Lyn Frazier, Keith Rayner (eds.), *Perspectives on Sentence Processing*, 267-301. Hillsdale, N.J.: Lawrence Erlbaum.

Reboul, Anne and Moeschler, Jacques. 1998. *Pragmatique du discours*. Paris: Armand Colin.

Reddy, M. J. 1979. The conduit metaphor—a case of frame conflict in our language about language. In Andrew Ortony (ed.), *Metaphor and Thought*, 284-324. Cambridge: CUP.

Reinhart, Tanya. 1981. Pragmatics and linguistics: an analysis of sentence-topics. *Philosophica* 27: 53-94. (Repr. Indiana University Linguistics Club 1982.)

Reiss, Katharina and Vermeer, Hans. 1984. *Grundlegung einer allgemeinen Translationstheorie*. Linguistische Arbeiten 147. Tübingen: Niemeyer.

Richard, Jean-François. 1980. *L'attention*. Paris: PUF.

Rozan, Jean-François. (1956) 1959. *La prise de notes en interprétation consécutive*. Geneva: Georg.

Rumelhart, David. 1992. Towards a microstructural account of human reasoning. In Steven Davis (ed.), *Connectionism: Theory and Practice*, 69-83. Oxford: OUP.

Saussure, Frédéric de. 1972 (1916). *Cours de Linguistique Générale*, édition critique Tullio de Mauro (ed.). Paris: Payot.

Schaffer, L. 1982. Rhythm and timing in skill. *Psychological Review* 89, 109-22.

Schank, Roger and Abelson, Robert. 1977. *Scripts, Plans, Goals and Understanding*. Hillsdale N.J.: Lawrence Erlbaum.

Schiffrin, Deborah. 1994. *Approaches to Discourse*. Oxford: Blackwell.

Searle, John. 1969. *Speech Acts*. Cambridge: CUP.

Searle, John. 1983. *Intentionality*. Cambridge: CUP.

Seleskovitch, Danica. 1965. *Colloque sur l'enseignement de l'interprétation.* Geneva: AIIC (Association Internationale des Interprètes de Conférence).

Seleskovitch, Danica. 1968. *L'interprète dans les conférences internationales: problèmes de langue et de communication.* Paris: Minard Lettres Modernes.

Seleskovitch, Danica. 1975. *Langage, langues et mémoire: étude de prise de notes en interprétation consécutive.* Paris: Minard, Lettres Modernes.

Seleskovitch, Danica and Lederer, Marianne. 1986. *Interpréter pour traduire.* Paris: Didier Erudition.

Seleskovitch, Danica and Lederer, Marianne. 1989. *Pédagogie raisonnée de l'interprétation.* Paris: Didier Erudition.

Setton, Robin. 1993. Is non-intra-IE interpretation different? European models and Chinese-English realities. *Meta* 38(2), 238-256.

Setton, Robin. 1994. Experiments in the application of discourse studies to interpreter training. In Cay Dollerup and Annette Lindegaard (eds.), *Teaching Translating and Interpreting 2: Insights, Aims, Visions. Papers from the Second Language International Conference, Elsinore, Denmark, 1994,* 183-198. Amsterdam and Philadelphia: John Benjamins.

Setton, Robin. 1997. *A Pragmatic Model of Simultaneous Interpretation.* Ph.D. thesis, Chinese University of Hong Kong (unpubl.).

Setton, Robin. 1998. Meaning assembly in simultaneous interpretation. *Interpreting* 3(2), 163-200.

Shallice, Tim. 1988. *From Neuropsychology to Mental Structure.* Cambridge: CUP.

Shannon, Claude and Weaver, Warren. 1949. *The Mathematical Theory of Communication.* Urbana: Univ. of Illinois Press.

Shi Dingxu. 1992. *The Nature of Topic Constructions and Topic Chains.* Ph.D. Thesis, Univ. of Southern California (unpubl.).

Shlesinger, Miriam. 1989. *Simultaneous Interpretation as a Factor in Effecting Shifts in the Position of Texts on the Oral-literate Continuum.* M.A. Thesis, Univ. of Tel-Aviv (unpubl.).

Shlesinger, Miriam. 1995. Stranger in paradigms. *Target* 7(1), 7-28.

Smith, Neil and Tsimpli, Ianthi-Maria. 1995. *The Mind of a Savant.* Oxford: Blackwell.

Sperber, Dan and Wilson, Deirdre. 1986/1995. *Relevance: Communication and Cognition.* Oxford: Blackwell.

Sperber, Dan and Wilson, Deirdre. 1998. The mapping between the mental and the public lexicon. In Peter Carruthers and Jill Boucher (eds.), *Language* and *Thought,* 184-200. Cambridge: CUP.

Stenzl, Catherine. 1983. *Simultaneous Interpretation: Groundwork towards a Comprehensive Model.* M.A. Thesis, Birkbeck College, University of London (unpubl.).

Strolz, Birgit. 1992. *Theorie und Praxis des Simultandolmetschen.* Ph.D. Thesis, Geisteswissenschaftliche Fakultät der Universität Wien (unpubl.).

Sweetser, Eve. 1990. *From Etymology to Pragmatics.* Cambridge: CUP.

Takahara, Paul. 1999 (forthcoming). Pragmatic functions of discourse markers in English and Japanese. In Jef Verschueren (ed.), *Pragmatics in 1998: Selected Papers from the 6th International Pragmatics Conference, Vol. 2.* Antwerp: International Pragmatics Association.

Tanenhaus, Michael. 1988. Psycholinguistics: an overview. In Frederick Newmeyer (ed.), *Linguistics: The Cambridge Survey. Vol II. Language: Psychological and Biological Aspects*, 1-37. Cambridge: CUP.

Tanenhaus, Michael, Carlson, Greg, and Trueswell, John C. 1989. The role of thematic structures in interpretation and parsing. *Language and Cognitive Processes* 4, 211-234.

Tang, Charles Ting-chi, Robert L. Cheng and Li Ying-che (eds.), 1983. *Studies in Chinese Syntax and Semantics. Universe and Scope: Presupposition and Quantification in Chinese*. Taipei: Student Book Co.

Taraban, Roman and McLelland, James. 1988. Constituent attachment and thematic role-assignment in sentence processing: influences of content-based expectation. *Journal of Memory and Language* 27, 597-632.

Tommola, Jorma and Niemi, Pekka. 1986. Mental load in simultaneous interpreting: an on-line pilot study. In I. Evensen (ed.), 1986: *Nordic Research in Text Linguistics and Discourse Analysis*.

Tooby, John and Cosmides, Leah. 1992. The psychological foundations of culture. In Jerome H. Barkow, Leah Cosmides and John Tooby (eds.), *The Adapted Mind: Evolutionary Psychology and the Generation of Culture*. New York: OUP.

Tsao Fengfu. 1979. *A Functional Study of Topic in Chinese: the First Step towards Discourse Analysis*. Taipei: Student Book Co.

Tsao Fengfu. 1990. *Sentence and Clause Structure in Chinese: a Functional Perspective*. Taipei: Student Book Co.

Turner, Ken. 1997. On 'Pragmatic considerations in semantic analyses'. In *Pragmatics and Cognition* 51, 163-176.

Tyler, Lorraine and Marslen-Wilson, William. 1982. Speech comprehension processes. In Jacques Mehler, E. Walker and M. Garret (eds.), *Perspectives on Mental Representations*. Hillsdale, N.J.: Lawrence Erlbaum.

Van Dijk, Teun and Kintsch, Walter. 1983. *Strategies of Discourse Comprehension*. New York: Academic Press.

Wilson, Deirdre and Sperber, Dan. 1993. Linguistic form and relevance. Special Issue on *Relevance Theory*, vol. 2, Guest eds. Deirdre Wilson and Neil Smith, *Lingua* 90, 1-24.

Wilss, Wolfram. 1978. Syntactic anticipation in German-English simultaneous interpretation. In David Gerver and Wallace H. Sinaiko (eds.), *Language Interpretation and Communication. Proceedings of the NATO Symposium on Language Interpretation and Communication, Venice, 1977*, 335-43. New York: Plenum Press.

Zhong Shukong. 1984. *Shiyong kouyi shouce* (A Practical Handbook of Interpretation). Beijing: Zhongguo Duiwai Fanyi Chuban Gongsi [China Foreign Language Translation Publishing Co.].

Zhuang Mingliang. 1991. Han-ying tongshen chuanyi de jiqiao (Techniques in Chinese-English simultaneous interpretation). *Zhongguo fanyi* 1991(2), 24-27.

Name index

Subject index